Old and Middle English Literature from the Beginning to 1485

This descriptive history surveys the entire canon of Old and Middle English literature, and provides both general reader and student with the basis for a sympathetic understanding of this impressive body of work. It gives a detailed account of the first Anglo-Saxon creative ventures from *Beowulf* and the Cynewulfian poems to the works of Alfred, Aelfric, and Wulfstan. It discusses the effects of the Norman Conquest, the early Middle English romances, the origins of the Arthurian legends, the medieval dramas, *Piers Plowman*, the Pearl Poet, John Gower, and the monumental works of Geoffrey Chaucer.

Old and Middle English Literature is the first book in the five-volume *A History of English Literature*, under the General Editorship of Hardin Craig, which will encompass the complete body of English writing from its beginnings to the present.

The other books in this Collier Books series, each the work of a specialist in the field, are:

The Literature of the English Renaissance 1485-1660 (AS411)

The Literature of the Restoration and the Eighteenth Century 1660-1798 (AS412)

English Literature of the Nineteenth and the Early Twentieth Century 1798 to the First World War (AS413)

English Literature of the Twentieth Century (to be published)

A History of English Literature

HARDIN CRAIG, *General Editor*

Volume I
 Old and Middle English Literature from the Beginnings to 1485
  George K. Anderson

Volume II
 The Literature of the English Renaissance, 1485-1660
  Hardin Craig

Volume III
 The Literature of the Restoration and the Eighteenth Century, 1660-1798
  Louis I. Bredvold

Volume IV
 English Literature of the Nineteenth and the Early Twentieth Centuries, 1798 to the First World War
  Joseph Warren Beach

Volume V (in preparation)
 English Literature of the Twentieth Century

GEORGE K. ANDERSON

OLD AND MIDDLE ENGLISH LITERATURE FROM THE BEGINNINGS TO 1485

Volume I of *A History of English Literature*

COLLIER BOOKS

NEW YORK, N.Y.

This Collier Books edition is published by arrangement with Oxford University Press, Inc.

Collier Books is a division of The Crowell-Collier Publishing Company

First Collier Books Edition 1962

Preface

THIS VOLUME is a reprint, with additions and corrections, of the first section of a comprehensive *History of English Literature* prepared under the general editorship of Hardin Craig and published by Oxford University Press in 1950. The sections of this general history now being issued separately by Collier Books are: George K. Anderson, *Old and Middle English Literature from the Beginnings to 1485*; Hardin Craig, *The Literature of the English Renaissance, 1485-1660*; Louis I. Bredvold, *The Literature of the Restoration and the Eighteenth Century, 1660-1798*; Joseph Warren Beach *English Literature of the Nineteenth and Early Twentieth Centuries, 1798 to the First World War*.

It was the purpose of the whole project to furnish a readable and useful account of the development of English literature which would be helpful not only to college and university students and teachers but also to the general reader. It aimed, of course, at a presentation of basic facts about books, writers, literary monuments, artistic movements, and historical and critical backgrounds; but it was intended chiefly as a means of showing what was there and how to find the means of learning more about what was there, so that the reader could, if he so wished, go more deeply into those various aspects of English literature which might be of special interest to him.

The preparation of an adequate bibliography was therefore a matter of importance. In the dozen years since the first publication of this work, however, there has been an enormous output of historical and critical studies of English literature. The bibliography for each volume has in consequence been revised and considerably enlarged. The great interest in medieval studies during the past generation is implicit in the fact that since 1925 well over 7000 studies of varying length and nature have treated Old and Middle English literature alone. It is hoped that the present volume will help to explain in some measure the reasons for this interest.

GEORGE K. ANDERSON

Contents

**Old and Middle English Literature
from the Beginnings to 1485**

Chapter 1

The Literature of the Old English Period

1. The Temper of the Middle Ages

WITHIN THE FRAMEWORK of history, all English literature is either medieval or modern. To designate any part of it as medieval is to describe it, explicitly or implicitly, as belonging to the era that formed the great bridge over which the Western world advanced from the confusion following the collapse of Rome to the complex modern world. This era of the Middle Ages, which endured for approximately the millennium between the years 500 and 1500, represents man's efforts to develop a new system of life after the old system had gone down in the ruins of the classical world of Greece and Rome.

To cross a bridge, one must follow a prescribed path and make use of an existing structure. It should be no surprise, therefore, that the Middle Ages achieved a spiritual and intellectual unity that had not been attained before and was not to be attained again. This unity is manifest in the overwhelming power of the two great human institutions of the Middle Ages: the Church in religion and the feudal system in society. While these two predominant institutions were developing and consolidating their power, the Middle Ages throve and prospered; when cracks began to appear in the two great structures, the Middle Ages likewise began to decline.

Both the Church and the feudal system assumed the supremacy of a central authority, that of the Pope and of the royal sovereign respectively. The kingdom of God was Christ's and the Pope was His vicar on earth. The hierarchy of the Church administered the affairs of Christ's kingdom in this world; but glory, honor, worship, and power were the homage due to God for the wonders of His works. This hierarchy was an organization at once compact and complex; it did not grow overnight. Each official of the Church was responsible to the official immediately above him in the hierarchy; but ultimately

11

all were responsible to the Pope, who was both a spiritual and
—in respect to the immense material possessions of the Church
—a temporal sovereign.

So it was also in secular life. The king of a country owned
every square inch of land in that country except that in the
possession of the Church; he embodied that country. The land
was leased by the sovereign to his nobles, who in return owed
him homage and the more tangible tokens of obligation in the
forms of taxes and military service; and again, each lesser
noble owed immediate returns to the noble next above him
in the social scale. Beneath this weighty structure labored the
common man—the Anglo-Saxon churl, the Middle English
serf or villein. As the Middle Ages progressed and men with
special agricultural and mechanical skills made their presence
felt in the feudal society, there appeared the freeman, the
commoner, and the yeoman. But there was no middle class in
the accepted sense of the word until the medieval world
yielded to the modern; and in this remarkable social fact lies
perhaps the chief difference between the Middle Ages and the
modern world.

Between Pope and king there was often strife during the
Middle Ages, but the real outcome of such natural conflicts
could never be in doubt for long. The Pope was the true over-
lord; the power of the Church could always, in the final test,
surpass the power of the State. When the State was able to
stand victorious against the batteries of interdict and excom-
munication that the Pope could wield, then the Middle Ages,
in a political sense, had come to an end.

The Church, which means the great spiritual leaders who
had founded it, had evolved a theological point of view that
took the world for what it was, good as well as bad, and
showed how, by devotion to a belief—its prescribed belief—
and to a code of conduct—its prescribed code of conduct—
this world could be improved against the final day when God's
judgment should come in flame and terror and distribute rewards and punishments according to His grand design. This
belief and this code of conduct were enforced under the strict-
est penalties for disobedience or for lack of faith. The Kingdom of God was ranged meanwhile in perpetual warfare
against the Kingdom of the Devil, and there could be no dis-

charge in that war. On the other hand, there was very little curiosity about the world in which we live and even less speculation about the physically unknown. As to worldly factual knowledge, the era was notably ignorant, although willing to accept the miraculous and the supernatural without serious question. Humanity, it believed, was on its way to Hell or to Heaven, as the case might be for the individual human soul; this earth was therefore a scene of pilgrimage to the appointed destination, or, to alter the metaphor, it was a way station or a watchtower in which God's judgment was to be awaited. Consequently, in all the moral and spiritual literature of the Middle Ages, the other world, in opposition to the world in which we live, was always a supreme consideration. There is very little in the moralistic or religious writings of the period that is not colored by the importance of preparing the reader for the world to come, either the City of God or the City of Satan.

This is not to say that people went through life during the Middle Ages with their eyes constantly fixed on the Celestial City or on the wild infernos pictured by their poets and prophets. The everyday problems of living faced by the average man and woman were then, as always, commonplace; and human nature was the same then as it is now. The churl or villein cultivated the land belonging to a master earl or baron; the artisan and merchant went about their business in the unpaved, unlighted, smoky, unsanitary towns and settlements, infested with livestock by day and with brigands by night; the housewife occupied herself with meals and chores; the nobleman hunted or hawked or made small talk before his ladies, unless he was obliged to take up spear and sword for his liege lord or king. These people were not obsessed continually by the peril in which their immortal souls might be standing. Medieval teaching nevertheless emphasized the future life far more than did either the teachers of classical antiquity or those of the modern world; and this emphasis, because of the universal control of the Church over writing, marked medieval literature in characteristic fashion.

No English writings have come down to us from a period before the Middle Ages. Old English, or Anglo-Saxon, literature is fundamentally medieval literature, except that the years from 600, let us say, until the Norman Conquest do not witness the highest integrated development of either the Church or the feudal system. Old English literature, for reasons that will be clearer in a moment, gives the impression of being, if not more backward, at least less versatile than the Middle English writings. For the Middle English period—an era of some four centuries following the Norman Conquest—clearly produced a civilization and an art that represented an advance over what the Anglo-Saxon had contributed. Middle English culture was both more complicated and more comfortable, with a much wider range of human experience, a broader horizon of humanity, and, in consequence, a greater opportunity for man's endeavor than had characterized Anglo-Saxon culture. Middle English literature reflects unmistakably all this growing spaciousness in living.

2. The Anglo-Saxons

Except for the observation that Christianity made a few feeble beginnings in Britain before the year 500, we can disregard completely the Roman conquest of Britain and the ensuing occupation of the island, which lasted through the first four centuries of the Christian era, because these are the business of the historian and the ethnologist. No literature has survived from England at the time of the Roman occupation, and it was centuries later before there was any trace in English literature of an influence from the Celtic Briton tradition. The great fact in the centuries following the end of the Roman occupation (410) was the arrival in Britain of Germanic invaders, called henceforth Anglo-Saxons, from the northwestern shores of the Continent and the region of the Scandinavian peninsulas, who began to make settlements in the island as early as the middle of the fifth century and had within a century and a half established themselves over most of what is now England. With the advent of Anglo-Saxon literature comes also the beginning of English literature.

This Anglo-Saxon conquest of Britain was a piecemeal affair, undoubtedly savage as a whole and in given localities actually obliterating. The Britons were driven westward into the mountainous country of Wales and the further extremities of Cornwall and Strathclyde. The Anglo-Saxons were thus enabled to set up small kingdoms (at one time seven in number —the so-called Heptarchy), which in the course of a few centuries were merged into four larger political units—the kingdoms of Northumbria and Mercia of the Angles, Wessex of the Saxons, and Kent of the Jutes. Not until the Old English period is nearly over is there any effective conception of a united England. In the meanwhile Northumbria, Mercia, and Wessex each held political leadership at one time or another. In the detailed sequence of events the salient facts remain the hegemony of Northumbria until about 750 and the rise of Wessex in the ninth century. The leadership of Northumbria is of great significance in the early history of the English Church, with consequent repercussions upon English literature; the supremacy of Wessex is of vital importance to Old English literature because it coincided with a renaissance of letters and manuscript writing, which fixed the West Saxon dialect as the classical dialect of Old English.

Otherwise the interest of the reader of Old English literature in Anglo-Saxon political history need be only incidental. The leadership of Wessex was threatened, throughout the second half of the ninth century, by incursions of Viking Danes, who came near to duplicating what their Anglo-Saxon cousins had done two or three centuries before. But at this time the Danes were restrained by the celebrated King Alfred the Great of Wessex (849-901) to approximately the northern half of England. The West Saxon kings following Alfred won back this Danish reservation, known as the Danelagh. In 975 King Edgar died the ruler of a united England. The fact that within the next generation a fresh invasion by Danish forces resulted in the complete conquest of England (1014) is relatively unimportant, because the conquest was largely dynastic and of short duration. The Saxon line returned in 1042, in the person of King Edward the Confessor, and was maintained for a quarter of a century until the Battle of Hastings, which brings us to another chapter in the history of England and English literature. No doubt the most important historical effect of the Danish occupation of England was the Scandinavian impact upon the English language, which has been, after that of the Latin-Romance languages, the most important influence upon English. An oblique consequence of King Alfred's victory over the Danes in the later ninth century was that the Norsemen, turned aside, sought and obtained lands in Normandy (912). Alfred's contribution to English letters, which was of great value, will be treated later.

The conquests of both the Anglo-Saxons and the Danes are to be construed as another chapter in the history of the Germanic migrations of the early Middle Ages and earlier. Their importance in the cultural history of England is clear; and yet the Venerable Bede, of whom more later, did not consider that the history of England began until the Christianization of the island; and in one sense he was right. We have seen that there were Christians in Britain during the Roman occupation. Missionaries from Ireland, following the tradition of their great Saint Patrick, had traveled in the fifth and sixth centuries through southern Scotland and northern England, where they established a few centers. The most important of these within the English sphere was at Lindisfarne, at that time an island off the Northumbrian coast. But the first official mission to Britain, the object of which was to accomplish the conversion of the island, was sponsored by Pope Gregory the Great and entrusted to one Augustine; it landed in Kent in 597 and was moderately successful. In the next generation a similar mission under Paulinus was carried into the north country and was remarkably effective. These Roman missions came into collision with the Irish missionaries in Northumbria, and the resulting conflict was ultimately resolved by the Synod of Whitby (664), from which we may date the beginning of the English Church, with two archbishoprics, of which that at Canterbury (the site of Augustine's first church) has always held priority. It is of great significance that the date of the council at Whitby, roughly the middle of the seventh century, coincides approximately with the date of our first surviving examples of English literature.

These facts are all manifest when we come to examine the literature of the Old English period. But what of the social history of the Anglo-Saxons before the Norman Conquest? The picture available is necessarily incomplete, because we must naturally depend upon the accessible literature to give us details; and this literature, derived in overwhelming proportion from the aristocratic and churchly levels of this society, cannot be anything but one-sided. When the Anglo-Saxon was still on the Continent, before he had invaded Britain, he had made some contact with the Romans, had picked up some Roman words, some military technique, the knowledge of the vine, and possibly some details of legal procedure. He was then living in a tribal state, and probably he retained this way of life for some time after he arrived in Britain. Those members of the tribe who could claim descent from the founder of the tribe constituted the aristocracy—the *earls*. (It is clear that the Anglo-Saxon tribe was built upon a clan structure that was originally extremely tightly knit.) Those who could not claim such descent, including captives from other tribes and their progeny, were the common *churls,* whose status was that of a bonded laborer and servant. This society was uncomplicated enough, except for the somewhat uncertain position of the so-called *freemen,* who apparently had achieved this status as a reward for some special service rendered to those above them. At the head of the tribe was the king, who held the position of ruler through heredity (as a descendant of Woden, king of the gods) and through the consent of the earls. When the tribe was at peace, the king depended much upon the counsel of his *witan,* or elders; when the tribe was at war, he had absolute powers of an almost mystical nature.

This social structure, though somewhat modified in later years toward an absolute monarchy, was essentially the same throughout the Old English period. The growth of feudal power all over Europe during the ninth, tenth, and eleventh centuries, the higher degree of concentration of that power in the hands of the sovereign, was undoubtedly manifest in England also, though again the details are often obscure. Yet even during the generation that saw the Norman Conquest, the *witenagemot,* or assembly of counselors, had considerable political strength. The great influence wielded at this same time by the chief earls, or "king's thanes"—men like Earl Godwin, for example—was, as so often happens in a feudal society, the result of weak ruling by ineffective kings. There were obviously democratic potentialities in the Anglo-Saxon state, but we need be under no illusion that their society was democratic. From a study of their criminal codes, we see that different members of this society were assessed at different values, and a male of whatever class was always worth more *wergild*, or blood money, than the corresponding female. And over all hung the inescapable aroma of the authoritarian in both Church and State.[1]

Indeed, the relative insignificance of women in the social scene marks the Old English period as different even from the Middle English. Women had a hard enough time of it at best in the Middle Ages, partly because they had no opportunity to do much of anything except in the domestic sphere and partly because Christian tradition traced the fall of man to a woman. The Anglo-Saxon woman had legal rights; a high moral standard was exacted of her; she was accorded a certain respect that is intrinsic in the Germanic temperament; but she was supposed to be seen and not heard. If we were to judge by Old English literature alone, we would conclude that only queens, princesses, abbesses, a few wives, and a scattering of mistresses comprised the female population of England at that time. The element of sex, as we shall see, is virtually absent from this literature.

For all that, however, we may assume that women were the usual house- and home-keepers that they have always been; it was merely that the fashions of Anglo-Saxon culture, then as now, have shunned a feminized society. Therefore, in spite of their comparative obscurity, we may assume further that women added their inevitable personality to the life of those rather crepuscular times. From the literature we get occasional glimpses of the occupations of the average man and woman—we know something of their hunting, fishing, farming, and weaving; of their seafaring and methods of fighting; of their eating and drinking and doctoring. We see much less, however, of their intimate domestic life and of their loves and hopes, although we see almost too much of their hating and violence. It is all sinewy and gristly, coarse to the touch, ignorant, intolerant, and gloriously unwashed. What intellectual life these

---

[1] The rights and responsibilities of the individual remained a permanent basis for all subsequent English law; but the penalties and procedures were modified to some extent by the Norman and Angevin kings, who introduced the jury system and more equable dispositions of civil cases. The Englishman has remained to this day a litigious person.

people possessed seems to have come entirely from the Church which continually struggled to keep civilization alive in an age but little removed from a benighted era. But at least we can no longer rightfully call these centuries the Dark Ages. Besides, such generalizations only go to show the fatal fallacy of attempting to read and interpret life from the imperfect written records of an era. Even the apparently clod-like Anglo-Saxon of this period might have uttered indignantly the simple

speech of the murderer in *Macbeth:* "We are men, my liege!"

3. Some Fundamental Facts Relating to Old English Literature

It is permissible to refer to the period under discussion and the literature it produced as either "Old English" or "Anglo-Saxon," although the academic preference at present is for "Old English," since it bespeaks a continuity of the English language and literature from the beginning to the present time. As to the language, the uninitiated can scarcely expect to cope with Old English literature save in translation, for although it was a Low German language and the direct ancestor of Modern English, it nevertheless possessed an inflectional system, which has been sloughed off almost entirely by the time we get to Modern English; and its vocabulary had not yet been enriched by the borrowing of foreign words, which have added so much versatility to the resources of Modern English.

As to the literature, it was the fashion for a long time in the nineteenth century and even in the preceding generation of the twentieth to take a condescending attitude and say that Anglo-Saxon literature represented English literature in its most backward and elementary form. In actual fact, Old English literature is impressively effective if it is read with sympathy and understanding—even its harshest critics have conceded its mass and power—although it is, when compared to the literature of other eras of English history, somewhat restricted in scope. And there are certain facts that should be borne in mind by the reader who approaches Old English literature for the first time. In the first place, it is predominantly the product of the medieval Christian Church, whether its subject matter be pagan or Christian. The non-Christian warriors had their stories and their songs, but it was the

Christian cleric who wrote them down. The submerged churls also had their folklore, and this too was salvaged from oblivion by the Christian. It is no doubt a tribute to the vitality of these pagan elements that they outlived in some measure the fortunes of a losing war against the churchman. For many a cleric evidently retained a secret liking for these non-Christian relics and so perpetuated them for later generations. When he was not engaged in professional religious writing, he was acting as editor and censor of the work of older pagan bards. Moreover, since these non-Christian remains were sometimes strong enough to batter down Christian prejudices, we may look for a blend, however incongruous at times, of the Christian and pagan anywhere in Old English literature.

In the second place, it must be remembered that this Christian domination of Anglo-Saxon writings, while it rendered a great service to non-Christian antiquity, was also a handicap. As it did not encourage intellectual originality, there is a curiously static quality in Old English literature. We need not, therefore, concern ourselves overmuch with mere chronology as we trace the course of Anglo-Saxon writings; it will be sufficient to note the types of literature produced. The same thing, incidentally, is true of Middle English literature, at least until the fourteenth century.

In Old English literature we can recognize both the heroic epic of non-Christian origins and the Christian epic of Biblical narrative; also a particular kind of reflective verse known as the elegiac lay and a little handful of personal lyrics, both of which types are to be referred to the aristocratic tradition of earls and churchmen. Next we may consider a scattered residuum of popular literature, found in riddles, charms, proverbial, sententious, or "gnomic" verse. Finally there is a large body of miscellaneous prose writing—following for the greater part the classical models of patristic and Ciceronian rhetoricians, Roman and Greek philosophers, grammarians, and scientists—and the inevitable out-pouring of sermons, homilies, preceptual discourses, saints' lives, and doctrinal admonition. Any one of these various types of literature can mingle with another. Some works of the time were written in Latin rather than the vernacular.

A special reminder concerning Old English poetic form and

style is necessary. English literature has had its periods of strictness of poetic form—as we shall see, the neoclassical requirements of the seventeenth and eighteenth centuries were especially rigorous. Yet it is doubtful whether English verse has ever had such formalistic standards as obtained during the Anglo-Saxon period. The metrical form practiced by Germanic bards is the best indication of the importance as well as the firmly established conservatism of the traditional technique of the *scop*.[2] The Old English poet, like his Germanic colleagues, used an irregular line, divisible into two half-lines, or hemistichs, and customarily given four main stresses to the line—two to the half-line. Sometimes we may encounter a line with more than four main stresses, but such hypermetric lines are rare. So long as four main stresses are recorded, it makes little apparent difference how many unaccented syllables are in in the line, but there is a habit of making the final foot in each half-line compact.

As for style and manner, the *scop* was expected to make generous use of formulas and appositional phrases for the sake of emphasis, inasmuch as he was originally composing to be heard rather than read—or so we believe; and to stimulate the imagination of his listeners in accepted poetic style, he resorted to compound words or phrases, particularly those that in their combination and suggestive force had some special metaphorical value—in other words, the *kenning*[3] (such as "battle-light" for sword; "peace-weaver" for woman; "helmet of night" for darkness).

One further note about Old English prosody: it has long been recognized that the metrical pattern of each half-line usually belongs in one of five categories.[4] This may be true of

[2] The Old Norse *skop* and Old High German *scoph* signify a jest, even a mocking (cf. Modern English *scoff*); no doubt the idea of entertainment is uppermost in the Old English word.

[3] Based on Old English *cennan*—to cause to know, to acquaint; hence "a teaching" or "an illustration" or something related to that idea.

[4] Type A: / x | / x ; Type B: x / | x / ; Type C: x / | / x ; Type D: / | / x x ; Type E: / x x | / Extra unaccented syllables are permitted, especially in the first foot of Types A, B, and C. See S. O. Andrew, *The Old English Alliterative Measure*, Croydon, 1931; M. Kaluza, *A Short History of English Versification from the Earliest Times to the Present Day*, London, 1911; J. Schipper,

the vast majority of half-lines in Anglo-Saxon verse, but it is not at all likely that the poet ever had any deliberate metrical design in mind in his handling of these categories. The careful scansion of the first thousand lines of *Beowulf*, for example, leaves one little the wiser on this point. Unquestionably the important thing was to get the four main stresses into the line; the matter of the resulting metrical feet always suggests to the reader accident rather than plan. So also does the alliteration, or initial-rhyme, as some call it.

This alliteration is found under the main stresses. In any given line the third of the four stressed syllables—that is, the first stressed syllable in the second half-line—establishes the alliterative design. The third stressed syllable alliterates with the first; sometimes also with the second; rarely, if ever, with the fourth. The alliteration is usually represented by identical initial consonants; at times, however, what is known as vowel alliteration appears, wherein a vowel can alliterate with any other vowel. It is probable that this vowel alliteration is actually an alliteration of consonants, in the sense that the physical effort of beginning a word with a vowel produces a consonantal sound, the so-called glottal stop. At any rate, the stresses will fall upon the important words in the line—upon nouns, verbs, adjectives, and pronouns; and since these important words in the line alliterate, it is clear that the alliteration is not only a metrical but also a syntactical device. End-rhyme, a feature of Modern English poetry, is virtually unknown in Old English; when it does occur, it is normally between two half-lines in the same metrical line—in other words, it is a definite internal rhyme. The combined effect of the medieval Latin hymns and of French lyric forms is yet to be felt in English literature. On the other hand, assonance, as a deliberate device, is fairly common.

It is only to be expected that in verse of such formalistic tendencies the devices may frequently hamper poetic flights, and technique often triumphs over essential poetry; but one who remembers the despondent interjections in *The Wanderer,*

History of English Versification, Oxford, 1910, and particularly John C. Pope, *The Rhythm of "Beowulf,"* New Haven, 1942; A. J. Bliss, *The Metre of "Beowulf,"* Oxford, 1958.

the lonely human cry in *Wulf and Eadwacer,* the fervent yet proud sorrow of *The Dream of the Rood,* and the restless yearning for the ocean in *The Seafarer* will hardly be prepared to complain that there is no such thing as an Anglo-Saxon lyric.

4. The Heroic and Christian Epics

The Heroic Age of a people is a kind of childhood through which all peoples seem to pass, when heroes and their deeds are all-important. These heroes may be historical figures; they may be semi-divinities. Probably they all had some sort of historical basis. The point is, however, that they typify the ideals of the people who made them heroes; these ideals are what the people considered essential to existence itself. All epic heroes, for example, are physically remarkable and superhumanly courageous, because strength and courage are necessary for the survival of all who must fight the hardships of nature in a rude environment. Most epic heroes have the same general attributes, except that here and there particular racial traits may distinguish them: there is the steady, sober, confident, and rather unimaginative Beowulf, characteristically Germanic; the brilliant, erratic, unpredictable Irishman Cuchulain; the romantic, fiery, beauty-loving, adventurous Greek Odysseus— all strong, brave, inspiring, and at the same time comforting to those who created them.

It is clear that heroes followed ethnical rather than national boundaries. A Burgundian hero, for instance, would not long remain the private property of the Burgundians; his fame would travel from tribe to tribe until he became the pride of the whole Germanic world. Here the itinerant *scop* seems to have been particularly useful in assisting the epic process. The feats of the hero were celebrated in short epic lays, which later served as the basis for longer heroic epics.[5] The various stories about the heroes were transmitted through oral tradition, and

---

[5] Possibly these longer heroic epics were formed by the actual linking together of more than one of these earlier short epic lays. It is more likely, however, that they were composed by individual authors who were merely familiar with the older lays and used them as the foundation for their own original compositions. The matter is obscure and has not been definitely settled.

the *scop* gave them the poetic form sanctioned by his profession, a form that has already been described.

There are four surviving poems that can be called heroic epics in Old English literature—*Widsith, Beowulf, The Fight at Finnsburg,* and *Waldere.*

Widsith presents in its 143 lines one of the supreme problems for the Old English literary antiquarian. A certain Widsith speaks, telling of his career as a wandering *scop,* mentioning names of kings who ruled when he lived and listing those whom he visited; and he narrates in some detail a battle in the career of Offa, ruler of the Angles. In spite of the opinions of some scholars, the piece cannot be wholly autobiographical. No man could have visited kings two or three centuries apart. Obviously the poem is a composite. The first catalogue of kings—a primitive type of genealogical verse, by the way—is of great antiquity, written possibly before the coming of the Anglo-Saxons to Britain, certainly at some time early in the sixth century. The rest of the poem comes later; the "autobiographical" lines last of all. The entire composition, put into its present form by the *Widsith* poet, dates from the late seventh or early eighth century; but the oldest parts of *Widsith* are the earliest bits of English verse surviving. The manuscript we have, however—that in the Exeter Book[6]—is

[6] There are four important manuscripts in which most Old English poetry has survived, namely:

The Exeter Book, copied about 975, given by Bishop Leofric of Devonshire to Exeter Cathedral. Leofric died in 1072. The collection is of poetry only.

The Beowulf Manuscript (MS. Cotton Vitellius A xv), written about 1000, now in the British Museum, contains prose as well as verse.

The Junius Manuscript (MS. Bodleian Junius 11), from about 1000; this manuscript takes its name from the fact that it was printed by one of its owners, the Huguenot scholar François Dujon ("Junius") (1589-1677) in 1655. It is now in the Bodleian Library at Oxford.

The Vercelli Book, which also contains a large number of prose compositions. It was probably copied in the eleventh century or later and in some way reached Vercelli, in northern Italy, where it is preserved in the library of the Cathedral. No good reason has been advanced for its presence thus far from its native land, beyond the obvious fact that Anglo-Saxon scholars traveled extensively from England to Rome and other parts of western Europe.

from the latter half of the tenth century. The gap of two or three centuries between the date of composition and the date of manuscript holds true for most Old English poetry.

Widsith, then, remains a piece of antiquity valuable as an index to Germanic heroes and their legends. Its authentically ancient tone seems to assume that the listener will have full knowledge of all these buried kings and heroes. Quite possibly each of the kings mentioned in the poem was the subject of a heroic epic or even an epic cycle. Infinitesimally few such epic pieces have been recovered, however, and we shall probably have to be content with speculation, because another *Beowulf* is scarcely likely to turn up in either the near or the distant future.

Out of the mass of critical and scholarly literature devoted to *Beowulf* since its first edition in 1815, a few facts are well-nigh indisputable: (1) the poem is a succesful attempt to reproduce a picture of the Heroic Age of the Germanic peoples;[7] (2) the Beowulf Poet wrote the poem in its present

---

The founder of the Church of Saint Andrew at Vercelli was Cardinal Guala, papal legate in England from 1216 to 1218; perhaps the connecting link lies here.

It should be noted that the date of composition of pieces found in these four repositories has no necessary relation to the date of the manuscript itself. Most surviving Old English poems were written between 750 and 950; but the manuscripts are nearly always dated after 950.

Other Old English poems, of course, are scattered about through many manuscripts. Most of these have been gathered into either the British Museum or the university libraries, but a few are still to be found in various church or cathedral libraries and in some few instances in the private possession of individual families. A great deal of Old English prose is also scattered in this way.

[7] The theory that *Beowulf* is a true *Kulturepos,* an epic of ancient Germanic civilization, has received its most convincing statement from Klaeber, the latest and in many ways the most brilliant editor of the poem. "As an eloquent exponent of Old Germanic life it stands wholly in a class by itself. As an exemplar of Anglo-Saxon poetic endeavor it reveals an ambitious purpose and a degree of success in its accomplishment which are worthy of unstinted praise. In noble and powerful language, and with a technical skill unequaled in the history of our ancient poetry, it portrays stirring heroic exploits and, through these, brings before us the manly ideals which appealed to the enlightened nobles of the age. It

form, on the basis of older material current among the Germanic peoples, some time between 675 and 850; and (3) the manuscript in which *Beowulf* is found, the famous Manuscript Cotton Vitellius A xv, dates from around 1000.

Beowulf falls logically into three parts, each dealing with the major feats in the hero's career. Beowulf mortally wounds the anthropoid monster Grendel, who has been terrorizing for twelve horrible winters the mead-hall of Hrothgar, king of the Danes. The hero then dives down into a submarine cave to kill Grendel's mother, who has tried to avenge her son. He returns to his home in Geatland,[8] where, in his old age, he fights a successful but to him fatal battle with a fire-dragon that has been guarding an ancient curse-laden treasure, a *motif* recognizable to all who are familiar with the Wagner Ring Cycle. In addition, the poem presents in a flashback a feat of Beowulf's youth—his swimming contest with Breca of the Brondings. Scattered about are allusions to his marvelous aquatic achievement following the death of his king, Hygelac, and to the protracted wars between the Swedes and Geats. There is also a tendency on the part of the Beowulf Poet to digress upon legendary figures—digressions that seem at first confusing but which are always useful for purposes of comparison or contrast with characters presented in *Beowulf*. In fact, one long digression, the difficult Finnsburg Episode, has an obvious relation to a poem soon to be mentioned, *The Fight at Finnsburg*. *Beowulf* as a whole is introduced by an eloquent Prologue giving the account of the Viking burial of a half-mythical King Scyld of the Danes and is concluded by an impressive description of Beowulf's own funeral, following his death in the fight with the fire-drake. Among the felicitous passages in the poem are the many lyrical lines of elegiac nature.

---

combines the best elements of the old culture with the aspirations of the new." (F. Klaeber, *Beowulf,* New York, 1922, 1936, cxxii.) As an expression of the attitude that places *Beowulf* at the top of Old English literature, these lines speak for themselves.

[8] No altogether satisfactory explanation has yet been offered of the locale of Geatland. It may be assumed, however, that the Geats were a Scandinavian people. The most reasonable theory identifies them with the Götar, who inhabited the southern tip of what is now Sweden.

The Beowulf Poet, as a good Christian, tried to soften the savagery of the story by introducing occasional pious references to the Lord and by including many didactic lines, often strongly homiletic in tone. It can be shown that he knew the Vulgate Bible and was not unfamiliar with Virgil. The elemental, however, still reigns supreme in *Beowulf*. The rough boasts of the hero, the feasting and ceremonial talk, the elaborate courtesy and ritual—these belong to epic tradition. But the grim ferociousness of the "mighty merewife," Grendel's dam; the muscular, voracious devouring of the Danes by Grendel; the agonized yells of "God's adversary" when he feels Beowulf pulling out his arm from the shoulder; the flames spouting from the monstrous head of the fire-dragon— these form the stuff of the horrible, which has an appeal to the romantically simple and the sophisticated intellectual alike. The pagan acceptance of Wyrd, goddess of Destiny, vies in incongruous fashion with the orthodox installing of God as supreme ruler of the world. And the raw drama of strong men fighting against inexorable foes and conquering though dying is not to be viewed lightly. But it is all very masculine; few women care for *Beowulf*.

Lack of space forbids the quoting here of extensive passages from the poem, but certain lines are especially recommended. There are the final measures of the Prologue, the stern commentary on the passing of Scyld; the grim stage-entrance of Grendel; the horrifying account of the destruction of Grendel's prey; the picturesque contest with Breca in the storms of the winter sea. There are the lines describing the behavior of the Danes on the morning after Beowulf's fight with Grendel, how they went to visit the scene and then came home rejoicing—and here we are told something of the real genesis of a heroic epic, for the Danes spoke of Beowulf's deed, and one, who knew the form and pressure of bardic tradition, told the tale "with apt skill" according to that tradition. In this same passage come characteristic allusions to other Germanic heroes: to Sigemund of the Volsungs, who killed a dragon (this is the earliest surviving reference to the great Norse Saga of the Volsungs), and to the wicked King Heremod, who serves as the moral antithesis to the character of Beowulf. Then there are the banqueting scenes, vivid in their barbaric splendor. A most noteworthy passage, sometimes called the first bit of landscape in English literature, although this honor would be a difficult one to bestow justly, is the description of the approach to Grendel's lair.

Furthermore, the Beowulf Poet had a strong lyrical impulse, which shows itself in the lament of the last guardian of the treasure over which the fire-dragon later came to keep watch; in the brief glimpse of an old man who has lost his son; and in the various moralizing lines spoken by old King Hrothgar. The misgivings uttered by young Wiglaf after the death of his friend Beowulf, his youthful voice prophesying war and desolation and carnage now that his war leader has "laid aside laughter," are at once melancholy and grim and in complete accord with the elegiac tradition.

The Beowulf Poet, however, remains only a name. Possibly he was a Dane, or of Danish extraction, who composed in England an epic poem on Scandinavian traditions, gave it a suitable Christian flavor, and achieved so successfully a common Germanic appeal that it was accepted by Englishmen as belonging to their own spiritual heritage. Perhaps the poem was modified slightly by subsequent scribes; but there is no good reason for doubting that the work in its present form represents substantially the achievement of the Beowulf Poet himself. Its somewhat mixed dialect—basically West Saxon with occasional Mercian and even Northumbrian admixtures—is not remarkable; but in view of the probable date of composition, it was most likely composed in either Northumbria or Mercia and written down later by scribes using a West Saxon dialect.

All in all, *Beowulf* deserves a place at the head of Old English heroic epic poetry. From the profusion of moral precept sprinkled through it, the poem has been considered by some as an early instance of the "handbook for princes" literature that was common in the Middle Ages and early Renaissance. The same, however, could be said for almost any heroic epic, especially one written by a cleric. It is enough to think of *Beowulf* as reflecting the glory of departed kings and of a departed Old Germanic civilization, exemplified by one who was a model of virtue as that civilization saw it.

The Fight at Finnsburg, a fragment of some 40 lines written at about the same time as *Beowulf*, affords us a momentary view of a battle in the hall of King Finn of the Frisians; The antagonists are the Danes on the one hand and the Frisians and their allies on the other. It confirms the hint given in the cognate Finnsburg Episode in *Beowulf* (which is a sequel to the events in *The Fight at Finnsburg*) that the war was internecine, precipitated by treachery and probably carried out in the same spirit.

A similar ruin is *Waldere,* which consists of two short epic fragments discovered in Copenhagen in 1860. There is reason to suppose that these are but parts of an extensive poem on the story of Walther of Aquitaine (or Walter of Spain), a narrative subsidiary to the great Volsung-Nibelungen sagas of Germany and Scandinavia. There is no telling how closely the Old English version follows this story, told best by Ekkehard of St. Gall (d.973). The first Anglo-Saxon fragment is part of a speech by the maiden Hildegund, urging on her lover, Walter, to fight the pursuing Frankish warrior Hagen; the second fragment opens with some lines apparently spoken by King Gunther of the Franks and continues with Walter's truculent reply. Except for the relation of these fragments to their cognates in continental legend, there is nothing notable about *Waldere.*

There were probably many other heroic epics in Old English literature, now irretrievably lost; it is not likely that *Beowulf* stood alone. We can be sure, at any rate, that the tradition of the heroic epic persisted for a long time after the composition of *Beowulf.* As late as the tenth century there are two unusual representatives: *The Battle of Brunanburh* and *The Battle of Maldon. The Battle of Brunanburh* is the entry in most of the manuscripts of *The Anglo-Saxon Chronicle* (to be described later) for the year 937. It is a terse, vivid account in characteristic Anglo-Saxon bardic verse of the defeat of a combination of Norsemen and Scots by the English under Athelstan, one of the most able successors of King Alfred. It describes the slaughter and makes use of the favorite scene of the wolf and raven, hungry for carrion, possessing the battlefield after the fighting. But it exults, with almost laureate devotion, in a national victory. *The Battle of Maldon,* on the other hand, is a tale of defeat, the destruction of a band of Englishmen under Byrhtnoth by a force of invading Danes in the year 991. The piece is fragmentary, although it is not likely that much is missing. The usual ugly matter of battle is spread before us, but an especially strong call to unflagging courage against odds rings out above all. The two poems show that, whatever the outcome of a battle, the relation of war lord to his *comitatus* was still to the Anglo-Saxon of the tenth century a sacred thing; and in spite of the supposedly softening presence of Christianity, the spirit of this relationship was as vital a few decades before the Battle of Hastings as it was in the days of the Beowulf Poet.

The man of action, the leader, is needed in all the emergencies that a hardy, active, practical people face. Is it little wonder that the glory of the hero never departed entirely from the scene during the Old English era? Has it ever, indeed, departed from the Germanic nations? If the epic tradition is an aristocratic tradition, so too is the military.

Christianity is, of course, the theoretical antithesis of the military; and sad indeed have been the results when the two opposing philosophies have been harnessed together. The priest brought to Anglo-Saxon England a culture far beyond what the pagan world of the Germanic peoples had known. But after the conversion of Britain it was not long before the priest was himself Germanic; and his instincts were evidently sympathetic to the older tradition. And so there appeared, under the auspices of the Church, another tradition of Anglo-Saxon epic literature that attempted to maintain a blend of the warrior's outlook and Christian thought, institutions, and spirituality.

As we have seen, the double source of Christianity in Anglo-Saxon England—a Celtic current originating in the north of the island under the influence of missionary followers of St. Patrick (fifth century) and a Roman mission that reached Kent under Augustine in 597—resolved itself into the establishment of the English Church at the Synod of Whitby in 664. The literature produced by this conversion will be mentioned later. For the moment, the main fact is that of the Christianization. The Anglo-Saxon, while he grasped eagerly the promise of Christianity, was at heart in love with his own traditions. It is difficult to imagine Grendel as appearing before a consistory of seventh-century churchmen; indeed, it is grotesque. But one must not be surprised to find the Christian Beowulf Poet telling of fire-drakes or buried treasures or contests under water with strange female monsters, for these belonged to his folklore and he liked to recall them.

The Venerable Bede, of whom more later, tells the charming story of Caedmon, a humble cowherd in the employ of Hild, abbess of Whitby (d.680). It is the old legend of an untutored peasant inspired by the divine gift of song. When Caedmon retired from the banquet while the festive harp was passed and went to his bed, an angel came to him and commanded him to sing; in spite of his confessed incompetence, he sang a short lyric in praise of Creation, a lyric quoted by Bede and known now as *Caedmon's Hymn*. The next morning he astonished the wise men by his ability to improvise song in praise of divinity and divine story. According to Bede, Caedmon composed much thereafter on the narratives of Genesis and Exodus, on Christ's incarnation and passion, on the teachings of the apostles and the day of doom, and on the heavenly kingdom and its sweetness. If Bede's account is to be accepted literally, then Caedmon is the first extensive poet, identified by name, in English literature.

In a single manuscript, the so-called Junius Manuscript, there survive some epic poems that tally in part with the list given by Bede: there are the two *Genesis* poems (known as *Genesis A* and *Genesis B*), *Exodus, Daniel,* and *Christ and Satan,*[9] the last of which includes the Fall of the Angels, the Harrowing of Hell, the Resurrection, the Ascension, the Pentecost, the Last Judgment, and the Temptation. In the Exeter Book another poem, *Azarias,* is closely associated with *Daniel.* Since all these poems cannot possibly be by the same individual, we speak of them as belonging to the Caedmonian cycle, for there are far too many differences among them of language, style, dialect, and spirit (within the same tight prosodic framework of the *scop*) for one man to have done them. As an illustration of what appears to be the composite nature of some of these Caedmonian poems, consider the

[9] The name *Christ and Satan* is inappropriate, since only the last poem of the group under this title (which, incidentally, can be referred to successive points in the services of the liturgical year at Easter and Pentecost) has anything much to do with Satan.

classic case of *Genesis*. For a long time this work was believed
to constitute a whole; but one passage of some 600 lines
came to be recognized as altogether different in language and
manner from the remainder of the poem. This passage, now
designated as *Genesis B,* was thought by the German scholar
Sievers (1850-1932)[10] to be the translation of an Old Saxon
(Old Low German) poem; and this poem, or rather portions
of it, actually came to light later. *Genesis A* has always been
dated from the early eighth century; *Genesis B,* on the other
hand, can hardly have been translated before the ninth century. No particularly good explanation of how the Old English poem came to have such a translation included in it has
ever been advanced; but the fact is that there was much
traveling by English clerics on the Continent and therefore
much internationalism, so to speak, in European literary
scholarship of the time. An Anglo-Saxon poet probably picked
up the German poem and brought it back to incorporate it
in the English poem, either his own or someone else's.

These Caedmonian poems can obviously be described as
heroic epics with characters taken from Biblical story. Instead of being delivered before a king and his guests, however,
they were more probably delivered before a religious gathering, although the aristocracy may also have been among those
present. They were hardly intended to be read at the period
of their composition, but they undoubtedly came to be read
in manuscript before the Norman Conquest. They include all
the characteristics of the *scop's* tradition: the set formulas and
the *kennings,* the alliterative verse, the repetitiousness as well
as the resonance. Christ or Moses or Daniel assume the place
of the hero Beowulf, and the qualities of all are strikingly
similar. The apostles of Christ remind one, at least super-
ficially, of the thanes who accompanied Beowulf on his sea
journey to Hrothgar's land. The Caedmonian poems, however, show a notable command of landscape; perhaps in this
reflection of the northern English moorlands and mountains
there is evidence of their Northumbrian origins.

No doubt it is too much to expect that in these Caedmonian

[10] Eduard Sievers, *Der Heliand und die angelsächsische Genesis,*
Halle, 1875. Part of the German original was discovered in 1894
in the Library of the Vatican.

poems there should be a realization of high tragedy and *katharsis;* but, for example, there is at least sympathy in the treatment of Satan, the archfiend, who is very much an individualist in *Genesis B*—a worthy precursor of Milton's Satan in *Paradise Lost.*[11] Yet we must not allow ourselves to overestimate these poems or those of the Cynewulfian cycle. They represent neither puerile garrulity, on the one hand, nor sublime literary art, on the other. But, as is so often the case in all Old English poetry, the Caedmonian poems have massive, unpolished vigor, handicapped by the demands of the bardic style. The obvious unfavorable criticism of the Caedmonian poems is that they are extremely uneven, for the moralizing tendency of the early churchman cannot be avoided, and deserts of doctrine follow hard upon occasional meadows of true poetry.

The Cynewulfian poems, however, which are the true followers of the Caedmonian poems both in time and in literary development, are much more self-conscious in their artistic efforts and exhibit to a much greater degree the influence of the monastic churchman; indeed, by comparison the Caedmonian poems impress one as perhaps archaic and even at times primitive in their imagery and expression. The Cynewulfian poems possess a further interest: they are the first signed poems in English literature. Four of them—*Juliana, Elene, Christ,* and *The Fates of the Apostles*—have, scattered through certain lines in each, the signature *"Cyn(e)wulf,"* written in isolated runic letters.[12] Although much investigation

[11] There is some evidence that Milton knew *Genesis B.* He was acquainted with the German-born Huguenot scholar Franciscus Junius (François Dujon) (1589-1677), after whom the Junius Ms. was named, while the latter was librarian to the Earl of Arundel. Although Milton was already blind at this time (1652-3), it is still possible that he learned Anglo-Saxon from Junius or at least became aware of material in the Junius Ms. In reference to this, see J. W. Lever, *"Paradise Lost* and the Anglo-Saxon Tradition," *Review of English Studies,* XXIII, 97-106.

[12] *Runes,* or runic letters, constitute the written alphabet of the early Germanic peoples. The letters are partly Roman, partly Greek, and partly from an obscure alphabet of probably Middle Eastern origin. See Bruce Dickins, *Runic and Heroic Poems,* Cambridge, 1915. Below, under the comment on the *Runic Poem,* we see two of the runic letters surviving in the ordinary Anglo-Saxon alphabet used in England in historical Old English times.

has tried to reveal the identity of this Cynewulf, little is known about him—in fact, nothing definite except that he was assuredly a cleric, possibly of high rank, who lived about 800. The passage in *Elene* containing his signature has been considered autobiographical by some; it proclaims the poet to have been formerly sinful, though no details are given. We may suspect that the poet's moral condemnation of himself was as exaggerated as was John Bunyan's. At any rate, now that he is no longer young, God's ministers have taught him to write poetry, and he has therefore found true happiness. There is here a reminiscence of the Caedmon story, and for this reason alone the autobiographical value of the passage deteriorates. It matters little, after all, because Cynewulf, whether a man or a tradition—and there is no good reason to doubt his existence either as a writer or as the founder of a poetic school—was a poet of much talent. Most of the four signed poems, as well as other pieces referred to the Cynewulfian cycle—*Andreas*, the two *Guthlac* poems, the impressive *Dream of the Rood*, *The Phoenix*, *The Harrowing of Hell*, and *The Bestiary* (or *Physiologus*), all of which will be commented upon presently[13]—have the descriptive ability and a delicate feeling for external nature combined with an ascetic tone that is both curious and arresting. All of them have a certain literary finish found elsewhere in the poetry of the period only in *Beowulf* and some of the elegiac poems. It is as if the Caedmonian poems were pioneers in the Christian epic; Cynewulf has contributed both mysticism and conscious art beyond the average—we are justified in calling it literary sophistication. Worth noting, too, is the presence of women as the leading characters in two of the signed poems; Christian female martyrs have overcome the limitations of sex and have assumed a heroic role.

All of the remaining important narrative and religious didactic poems in Old English literature remind the reader of either the Caedmonian or the Cynewulfian cycles. There has

[13] *Elene, The Fates of the Apostles, Andreas,* and *The Dream of the Rood* are in the Vercelli Book; the rest are in the Exeter Book. There are two poems on Saint Guthlac, a Mercian saint who died in 714. The first, *Guthlac A*, is based on the traditional life of the saint; the second, *Guthlac B*, is an adaptation in verse of a Latin life of Guthlac by one Felix of Croyland.

been no complete agreement among scholars about which of these cycles a given poem may represent. In addition to the unsigned poems that have a particularly deep impress of Cynewulfian influence, there are a few others, all from at least 800 and probably later. Only *Judith,* in the Beowulf Manuscript, a stirring fragment recounting the deeds of a vigorous Hebrew heroine of the Apocrypha—not a saint, be it noted—is more Caedmonian than Cynewulfian. The others seem very much mixed; but such characteristics as one finds in them are found especially in the signed poems of Cynewulf. Still, it is not possible to demonstrate that Cynewulf himself was the author of any one of them; it is more likely that they were written by individual unnamed poets belonging to his school of poetry, who lived in the generations following Cynewulf. These compositions are inclined to rhetoric rather than to narrative action. Conspicuous among them are the pervading presence of the church militant in *Andreas,* the notable sea passages in the same poem, the mystical death scenes in *Guthlac B,* and the ecstatic vision of *The Dream of the Rood,* into which pity and tears have been infused in rare degree. In *The Phoenix* we are dealing with a poem of Alexandrian origin, for it is adapted in part from the fourth-century poet Lactantius's *De Ave Phoenice.* There is in consequence a tropical lushness about this poem that sounds bizarre in terse Anglo-Saxon language; yet, in spite of such incongruity, there is an intense emphasis upon the symbolism of the phoenix as a token of immortality. The *Bestiary,* or *Physiologus,* can be more appropriately treated in its relation to the much more striking Middle English *Bestiary.*

5. Other Old English Poetry

The Christian epic shows that the cleric, while he was aware of the grimness of nature and the mighty adversaries of the soul, was able to soften them through the essential hopefulness of his religion. The paganism that lies in the hearts of men, however, was often permitted to break through. Frequently the Anglo-Saxon, like other Germanic peoples, viewed life as bitter struggle against inevitable defeat by time, the great destroyer; he felt the brutality of the northern winter, the immensity of the sea around him, the transiency of human strength, and all of these must have given him moments of melancholy that no amount of Christian persuasion could altogether allay. This is evident in an attractive series of Old English poems dedicated to the timeless and ageless themes, *ubi sunt?* and *sic transit.* Where are the fleeting glories of this life, which time has obscured and effaced? To the poems thus dedicated we have given the name elegiac.

Most of the individual surviving elegiac poems belong to the ninth century or later, but they derive from a tradition at least as old as that of the heroic epic—witness the many fine elegiac lines in *Beowulf*—and should be called bardic rather than clerical. Indeed, the first poem to be considered here is not so much a pure elegiac poem as a kind of epic song, although its lyric nature is clear both in mood and in form, and its healthy pessimism is entirely typical of elegiac verse. *Deor's Lament,* or *The Song of Deor,* in the Exeter Book, may be a piece of great antiquity and certainly is one of obscurity. It is the utterance of a rejected *scop*—possibly of one in search of a new patron—who consoles himself by comparing his misfortunes with those of heroes and heroines of legendry and by reflecting that, as their troubles passed, so can his. The author was probably a poet of the eighth century who placed himself imaginatively in the position of a cast-off bard, but he may belong to the seventh century. In any event, he is dealing with a situation that would be understood and sympathized with by any aristocratic audience of the period. Supplanted in the favor of a generous king (and we know from *Beowulf* how desirable to the Heroic Age a generous king could be) by another *scop,* Deor recalls the smith Wayland, imprisoned and bound by his foes; the princess Beadohild, ravished by Wayland in revenge for his treatment; a nameless, lovesick Geat; and the tyrannous Eormanric of "wolfish thought"—and then he remembers further that their misfortunes somehow ended: "and this too shall pass away." *The Song of Deor* has an unusual stanzaic structure as well as a refrain—a form of epic lay not uncommon, however, among the Norse. This poem, with its many references to often very mysterious personages and events, has been a subject of intensive scholarly research.

The eternal verity that time flies, and human sorrows and

joys with it, is developed more fully in *The Wanderer,* an eloquent poem of a brooding sadness altogether typical of the Germanic mind, which, when it is not hilarious, is subject to moments of intense melancholy. This poem is altogether pagan, although a few pious Christian lines have been tacked on by some earnest cleric. Some, however, have seen the poem as Christian throughout. The structure of the work is not simple: a narrator begins by commenting upon the situation and circumstances of an exile who has lost friends and king; then the introspective wanderer himself speaks. Glimpses of the sea and its desolation are followed by scenes in a mead-hall, in a ruined building, and in the waste of falling hail and snow. The reverie is triumphant in its pagan denial—pride, pomp, and circumstance have vanished as completely as if they had never been. For this wanderer possessions, friends, men, and women are all transitory; the very foundations of this earth are empty and valueless.

A fitting partner for *The Wanderer* is another poem in the Exeter Book—*The Seafarer*—which magnificently represents maritime England in those dim and shadowy generations. The first and better half of the poem is a vivid account of the life an Anglo-Saxon sailor lived in his frail little nut-shell of a boat; the speaker recognizes that in spring and summer the earth is fair and happy, in spite of the boding song of the cuckoo, and many live in idle comfort. But as for him, the sea calls him to drive forth over its wastes, and he cannot resist the call. Another companion is *The Ruin,* also in the Exeter Book, a beautiful example of Old English elegiac verse. Unfortunately it is a badly mutilated fragment; but its tone of eloquent regret arising from the contemplation of a ruined city sounds forth above the often obscure words and phrases. It remains a fitting capstone to the sort of poetry it represents, this description of epic ruin and decay, shot through with a *Welt-schmerz* that nothing can assuage.

But the emotion in these pieces is generalized; the sorrows of domestic life or of the relations of one individual to another are not commonly treated. And yet a few personal lyrics have survived; perhaps there were many more. Perhaps the everyday nature of personal relationships was considered beneath the dignity of the bardic tradition, but there remain nevertheless a trio of interesting poems. These three, *The Wife's Lament*, *The Husband's Message*, and *Wulf and Eadwacer*—all in the Exeter Book—are suggestive of the dramatic as well as the lyric. In *The Wife's Lament* a woman has been separated by captivity from her husband and breathes bitterness, homesickness, and hatred. *The Husband's Message*, more placid in tone, is the utterance of a husband who hopes that he can rejoin his wife over the sea with the return of summer and the cuckoo. We have here more than an echo of *The Seafarer*. Among these three poems, the greatest scholarly attention has been devoted to *Wulf and Eadwacer*. It has a strophic structure and a refrain, like *The Song of Deor*. The speaker, a woman, desires her lover, Wulf, and expresses disgust for her husband, Eadwacer. This brief poem is intense and passionate, one of the very few pieces in Old English literature with high sexual content. For sex is something the Anglo-Saxon of this period took pretty much as a matter of course. Some have seen in *Wulf and Eadwacer* the fragment of a dramatic sketch, or at least of a dramatic monologue. Something of the same point, however, could be made of *Widsith*, *The Song of Deor*, and *The Wife's Lament*. Another theory would link *Wulf and Eadwacer* with the Odoacer Saga of Germany, but the evidence for this is generally too flimsy to make the theory acceptable; it may well be related, however, to the Wayland Saga.

Although there is in Old English literature plenty of religious poetry, there is little of the true religious lyric, hymn, or ode. *The Dream of the Rood*, in isolated passages, is a kind of hymn; *Caedmon's Hymn*, already mentioned, is another. Whether Caedmon actually composed the latter, as Bede attributes it to him, can be neither established nor disproved. It is a brief verse in praise of God the Creator, who first made the heavens and the earth and the sun to shine upon man. The *scop* in *Beowulf* echoed these ideas; perhaps both passages owe a debt to some earlier work now lost. *Doomsday*, from the Exeter Book, is based upon a Latin poem, *De Die Judicii*, ascribed by some to Bede and by others to Alcuin. The speaker in this poem is a solitary individual harassed by the dread of Judgment Day. It is full of heart-searchings and soul-questionings, the lament of the wicked flesh, for the flame and ice of Hell will engulf the sinful. Yet it ends on a powerful note of hope in the prospect of Heaven, where all sorrows will cease.

As would be expected of any Germanic literature, we find in Anglo-Saxon writings a remarkable predilection for moralizing. English literature as a whole has been thoroughly impregnated with teaching and aphorism; indeed, English literary criticism has been prone to base judgments more on the sense of a literary work than on its aesthetics. Even our oldest pieces contain didactic elements mixed with the epic or the lyric, as the case may be. *Beowulf* has many lines of preachment, as do *The Wanderer* and *The Seafarer*. One ancient little poem, known as *Bede's Death-Song*, although it probably had nothing to do with Bede, is outright admonition. This is obviously the point also in *The Address of the Soul to the Body*, which must be referred to the literature of the Soul and Body, a topic represented best by the Middle English poem.

One need not go very far into medieval literature to encounter warnings about the imminence of Hell, some of them couched in most horrifying language. Yet there are some less terrifying comments upon life and living even in this spiritually timid period. Some 300 lines of surviving Old English poetry give observations upon the nature of things. These so-called *Gnomic Verses,* or *Maxims,* will be found in the Exeter Book; associated with them in the same book are other poetic pieces, which need not be named here. All of these verses belong to that type of literature best known to the Western world through the Biblical Book of Proverbs; they are ageless and anonymous. What is significant about them is not their achievement as *belles lettres,* for they are bald prosaic statements in general, but the fact that they yield us half-opened vistas of the life of the common people of the time, their occupations and fortunes, their arts and recreations, as well as a prospect of the perennial aspects of external nature, from the stars in the sky to the birds of the field.

Much the most effective poetry of popular or semi-popular origin, however, is the collection of *Riddles* in the vernacular. There are almost a hundred of these in the Exeter Book. In addition, there are collections of riddles in Latin by churchmen like Aldhelm, Bishop of Sherborne; Tatwine, Archbishop of Canterbury; and Eusebius, Abbot of Wearmouth. The Anglo-Saxon riddles in the Exeter Book are much the same as their Latin cousins; and back of them all is the ancient and honorable liking of simple people for the riddle, the conundrum, and the puzzle. At one time Cynewulf was considered to be their author, but it is obvious that no one man could have been responsible for the collection as we have it. They were probably written by many kinds of people, mostly clerics, of course; but a few earthy ones are obviously secular and base-born. They present in a moderate number of lines— some, indeed, are very brief—a general picture of an individual, an object, or a natural phenomenon. The reader or listener is left to identify the subject; and it may be remarked that many a modern scholar has racked his brains to get the possible answer. These riddles are ingeniously worded; and from the necessity of combining vagueness with suggestiveness it follows that they are often highly poetical. In subject matter they range from the satirical and the ribald to the romantic and the eloquent. Some are not much more than elaborate *kennings;* in fact, the type of mind that can develop a *kenning* and a riddle can soon make the transition to allegory, subtle philosophy, and the occult digging into astrology and alchemy that characterizes the mind of many a medieval writer.

Although they may be insignificant in artistic achievement, miscellaneous minor poems are always worth considering in any study of a given period. The Exeter Book contains many of these. For example, there is *The Harrowing of Hell,* recounting the favorite medieval story of Christ's three days in Hell; it is eclipsed by a long but powerful account in prose. It is hardly necessary to descant upon the many minor poems in the Exeter Book and the Vercelli Book treating the topics of man's failings—his presumption, his greed, his worldliness, and his sinfulness—and the necessity to reform himself, to resign himself to the design of God, and to lead a Christian life. A rather peculiar piece, however, is *The Riming Poem.* Here a rich man, enduring post-mortal punishment and wishing for the good old times he had on earth, is lamenting his sorry lot. This time the chief interest of the work is that, in addition to the customary alliterative measure, there is end-rhyme. Since these rhymes are often detrimental to the sense of the text, and since this metrical device is almost unknown elsewhere in Anglo-Saxon poetry, it has been thought that this poem is something of an experiment with a new form. As is generally believed, this experiment may have been suggested by the Latin hymns of this period, which used rhyme.[14]

We may pass over scattered didactic poems in the Exeter Book with the comment that they deal with such subjects as the advice of a father to his son, the wonders of Creation, the desirability of alms, the fate that befell Pharaoh's army in the Red Sea,[15] and the perennial question of Judgment Day. Similarly negligible are the few poems of epic nature scattered through *The Anglo-Saxon Chronicle*, because they are not only uninspired but purely local in their original appeal.

Here and there in various manuscripts appear *Charms*, to be said aloud, with due ritualistic observance, against such perplexing problems as bewitched land, a sudden stitch in the side, swarms of bees, and manifold ills of the body; this is the kind of thing an ignorant churl would remember from his grandmother and employ in emergencies not precisely covered by Holy Writ. One poem of 29 short stanzas describes in each stanza a letter of the runic alphabet, the alphabet used by the ancient Germanic peoples. In kindergarten fashion we learn from this *Runic Poem* the names of the runes in Old English.[16] Two of these letters, the *thorn*, þ (TH), and the *wen*, Þ (W), particularly the former, were in general use

---

[14] Some Norse poems, of later date than the Anglo-Saxon *Riming Poem*, made use of the device. In any case, the Old English poem, which was once attributed to Cynewulf, is of late date, possibly around the year 1000.

[15] Occasionally the minor bard is moved to epic utterance. Mention has been made of *The Battle of Brunanburh*, which is found in *The Anglo-Saxon Chronicle*. Other poems dealing with historical occasions appear in the *Chronicle*. Still other pieces celebrate a town (an *encomium urbis*); probably the best of these is the *Durham Poem* of the twelfth century.

[16] It should be remembered that the runic alphabet in Old English has a few more letters and consequently a few more symbols than the Norse runic alphabet. The *Runic Poem* in Old English is therefore a trifle longer and more elaborate than the corresponding *Runic Poem* in Old Norse, which is an interesting cognate poem.

throughout the Anglo-Saxon period. Similar in their antiquarian interest are relics like the Franks Casket, the Newcastle Column, the Falstone Ring, and the Brussels Brooch,
which have inscriptions of great value to both the archaelogist
and the linguist; one of these, the Ruthwell Cross, contains
lines found in *The Dream of the Rood,* and the relation of
the two has vexed scholars for a long time. Since one is a
blurred fragment and the other is a truly finished poem, and
since the blurred fragment is rather old, the most likely theory
is that both are derived from some common source of considerable antiquity.

6. Anglo-Latin Literature of the Old English Period

It should by this time be obvious that the priest dominated
the literature of the Old English period. But however sympathetic he might be to the traditions of the pagan past and
however willing to perpetuate the old or to create new works
in the same traditions, the priest remained the educator and
spiritual guide, and as such he would use prose for his professional purposes.

We may assume that all the surviving prose before the time
of King Alfred the Great (849-901) was written in Latin by
clerics. We find that the earliest piece of Anglo-Latin prose to
have any particular importance is *De Excidio et Conquestu
Britanniae,* by Gildas (*c.*500-579), a Welsh churchman. It is
a dreary chronicle whose importance is chiefly negative, in
that it says nothing concerning King Arthur,[17] although it
treats Britain in the fifth century. Another work of this
kind, the value of which is also mainly historical, is the *Historia Britonum* from the early ninth century. This is probably
a composite of historiographical material put together and
fitted with a preface by Nennius, disciple of Bishop Elbotus of
Bangor, Wales. The original author of the chronicle may have
been a Briton of the late seventh century. The *Historia Britonum* travels from Adam through a succession of Roman emperors to the early settlement of Britain and the invasions of

---

[17] It is possible that Arthur, a Celtic hero, has been partly identified in later story with Ambrosius. But, apart from a passing reference to Arthur in connection with the *Historia Britonum* of
Nennius, discussed below, all Arthurian material will be considered as part of Middle English literature.

the Anglo-Saxons. Here King Arthur makes his celebrated first entrance upon the stage of literature as a *dux bellorum* who fought against the Saxons in twelve great battles. He soon gives way, however, to Saint Patrick, and nothing more is heard of him in this work.

It would seem that Theodore of Tarsus, who was made Archbishop of Canterbury in 668, and his assistant Abbot Hadrian were chiefly responsible for the stimulation of Anglo-Latin writings at this time. Both men were natural teachers, and their intellectual equipment was varied in a gratifying degree. Some beautiful specimens of book-making and illumination originate at this early date, such as the late seventh-century *Gregorian Gospels;* the *Graeco-Latin Acts of the Apostles,* an outstanding example; and the magnificent *Lindisfarne Gospels* of Northumbria, with their interlinear glosses in the vernacular, invaluable to the student of the early Northumbrian dialect. In the next century come the *Rushworth Gospels,* equally valuable, but this time chiefly Mercian.

Although the Venerable Bede was undoubtedly the greatest of the Anglo-Latin writers of the age (Saint Anselm is to be considered a Middle English figure), Aldhelm, Bishop of Sherborne (d.709), was nevertheless one of the most important. Yet the individual works from Aldhelm's pen are not necessarily significant except to the special student of the period. He had a great reputation in his generation as a song writer, but unfortunately none of these songs can now be discovered. Of his surviving works there is first of all a series of letters exhibiting a rather turgid, helter-skelter Latin style. Aldhelm was not the first, nor was he the last, to indulge in garish rhetoric and pedantic learning. These letters discuss current matters of education and religion, with some autobiographical details. Then there are his homilies on virginity, which are not noteworthy in substance for an early churchman, although one of them is in a metrical Latin version with the device of a double acrostic—the initial letters of the opening lines form a hexameter verse; the final letters of the same line give this same hexameter verse backwards. Such metrical gewgaws, added to the almost wanton versatility of his rhetorical and oratorical effects, paint Aldhelm as a Celt rather than as a Saxon in temperament and very likely in ethnical origin.

The most valuable work by Aldhelm, however, is a prose miscellany: a treatise on many subjects—the esoteric quality of the number seven; metrics and prosody, with illustrations from a remarkable number of classical and post-classical Latin writers; and a set of riddles in verse. These riddles are to the Anglo-Latin writings of the period what the *Riddles* of the Exeter Book are to the vernacular. Again the author indulges in acrostics and learning for the sake of learning, and truly the scope of the subjects of these riddles is surprising in its variety and in its extravagant mixture of the sublime and the ridiculous. The last riddle, a long poem in praise of Nature, exhibits in its closing lines Aldhelm's devotion and sensitivity to the beauties of landscape.

To be sure, the bookishness of Aldhelm's Latin verse is not a fair basis for a proper appraisal of his poetry. There is no doubt that he headed a little school of writers, none of whom is of sufficient importance to warrant much discussion. The members of this Aldhelmian school were, with the exception of Eusebius, Abbot of Wearmouth (*fl* 725), from the south and west of England. In the Northumbria of this late seventh century there was a fine flowering of scholarship at Lindisfarne, Jarrow, Wearmouth, and Durham; and it was in this fertile soil that the greatest of Anglo-Latin writers of the Old English period flourished.

The Venerable Bede was born near Durham in 673 and died in the abbey at Jarrow in 735. He was brought up by Benedict, a Northumbrian cleric of aristocratic family, a patron of architecture, a scholar in Latin and probably in Greek, and the possessor of a good library. Under the influence of Benedict, the gentle, rather sentimental, and extremely pious Bede blossomed in words and works. He adopted the life of a cloistered scholar, amassed for himself what learning was available to him, and earned for his endeavors the homage of posterity, for Dante recognized him among the greatest scholars of Christendom who had immortal abodes in the Region of the Sun.[18] Bede's humanism had breadth and range; he mastered the Latin classics, possibly certain aspects of the Greek language, prosody, mathematics, medicine, history, and physical science; he also had the liberal sympathies

[18] As told in Dante's *Paradiso*, Canto x, 131.

and willingness to adapt this culture to his way of life, which mark the true lover of the humanities. All in all, he gives the impression that his was a mild but keen, somewhat romantic mind, which never deviated from the general orthodoxy of true religious belief, although it was tolerant of the opinions of others.

Bede's writings are many. They are mostly religious works, such as his voluminous commentaries on the Bible, often worked out with great elaborateness. There are also, however, works on scientific subjects and natural phenomena, lives of martyrs and saints, and his masterpiece, *The Ecclesiastical History of the English People (Historia Ecclesiastica Gentis Anglorum)* (731), which is still a fountainhead for historiographers of the Middle Ages. Even though his works are important in themselves, his influence does not stop there, for through the young men whom he taught further glory accrued to his name. The most famous of these students was Ecgbert, who assisted in the establishment of York as a seat of learning in the eighth century; Alcuin studied at York before he went to France to help the cause of learning under Charlemagne; and from Charlemagne's Palace School the direct highway to the Renaissance in Western Europe is not difficult to follow.

It is impractical to discuss Bede's works in detail. As a measure of the learning of his time, his *On Metrics, On Orthography*, and *On the Tropes of the Scriptures* serve to illustrate his clerical didacticism; *De Temporibus, De Ratione Temporum*, and *De Natura Rerum* exemplify his encyclopedic knowledge of "the divine operation, which created and governs the universe—astronomy, meteorology, geography, and medicine";[19] his various saints' lives and *Lives of the Holy Abbots* represent his contributions to ecclesiastical biography. However, his *Ecclesiastical History*, when placed beside the

[19] To be sure, the subjects of these smaller works represent the conventional material of medieval school learning: the Seven Liberal Arts comprising the *trivium*—grammar, logic, and rhetoric—and the *quadrivium*—geometry, astronomy, arithmetic, and music. The meteorology and medicine, however, Bede pushes a little farther than the usual requirements of the *quadrivium;* yet these particular topics were included under geometry and astronomy, respectively.

chronicles of Gildas and Nennius, for example, stands un-matched. None of the Middle English chroniclers shows a more careful consideration of authority, a greater desire to get to the truth of things, or a better grasp of the fundamental situations about which he writes. After a brief description of the British Isles and an account of the conquest of Britain by the Romans, Bede warms to his theme. For him, the true history of the English people begins with the appearance of Christianity in Britain; therefore, from St. Alban to Theodore of Tarsus, Bede never loses sight of his objective. And al-though the pages of this history contain not a few legends and stories of miracles, which Bede, as any devout church-man of his time, accepted, still there are very few essential facts in the work that have been refuted by present-day historians.

The *Ecclesiastical History* is often moving without resort-ing to sheer rhetoric. The salient passages in it are those recounting the story of the Anglo-Saxon conquest; the bio-graphical sketches of prominent churchmen or of humble Christians; and two unusual sections that call for special at-tention. The first of these two is not history but legend; it is a description of the heavenly vision seen by Drihthelm of Cunningham—the only Old English account, exclusive of that in the legend of *The Harrowing of Hell,* of the classical visit to the other world. Here are described the fire and storms of Hell, the sufferings of the pitiable wretches cast therein, and the terror-inspired will to do good that comes upon the quak-ing spectator. We shall comment on some spectacular Middle English representatives of this tradition in a later chapter, for the punishment of sinners is dear to the heart of the monitory writer in the Middle Ages. It may be said that Bede avoids the purely lurid, which is not necessarily true of his Middle Eng-lish colleagues. The second of these passages is most impres-sive to any reader of Anglo-Saxon literature, no matter how casual his contact. It comes in the story of the Christianiza-tion of Northumbria by the missionary Paulinus. The fair words of the holy man have made such an impression upon the pagan thanes and wise men of King Edwin that an old counselor is moved to liken man's life to the momentary flight of a bird in wintertime through the warmed banquet-hall, in which there is light, life, and joy; but what came before or what comes after is utter darkness. So, indeed, the Beowulf Poet tersely observed in the last lines of the Prologue to *Beowulf*, in speaking of the Viking burial of King Scyld: "Men cannot tell in truth, hall-counselors or heroes under heaven, who received that burden." Or, as Tennyson's Merlin sang more than a thousand years later of the infant Arthur: "From the great deep to the great deep he goes."

As for Alcuin (735-804), it has already been observed that he played an important part in the conduct of Charlemagne's Palace School. His works themselves, however, contribute little to English literature; Alcuin is not the equal of Bede either in literary skill or in intellectual versatility. It takes a courageous and confirmed scholar to wade through Alcuin's tracts on the Bible; the academic comments on doctrine, discipline, and morality; the historical pieces and pedagogical dialogues. The most readable of Alcuin's surviving writings are some letters and a few poems. He is an eclectic sort of writer who does not hesitate to follow closely the work of earlier Biblical authorities. He is also a controversialist and a sincere but inelastic dogmatist. If there is any one of his works that stands above its fellows, it is his homily *On the Belief in the Holy Trinity*. He did much, in his capacity as teacher, to aid the art of writing in his time, although his own attempts are stodgy and pedestrian. It is evident that his unquestioned personality must have been expressed more effectively in speech than in writing.

A realization of Alcuin's position and achievement adds greatly, nevertheless, to an understanding of the work of Alfred the Great. European scholarship was at a low level during the sixth and seventh centuries; but with the accession of Charlemagne, who was resolved that his kingdom should take the lead in everything, matters took a turn for the better. Charlemagne had had little education, but he desired learning and went to great lengths to bring into France the best scholars available. Alcuin was, in his opinion, the ideal man for his work; and Alcuin justified his selection by putting vigor into the Palace School and by developing, through his personality and scholarship, a new group of enlightened young clerics. The new impulse, thus stimulated, freshened the culture of Western Europe for centuries to come.

We may as well pass over the remaining miscellanea of Anglo-Latin writings from the years after Alcuin, although the Welshman Asser, who died in 910, left behind an invaluable biography of King Alfred. The fact is that these miscellaneous writings as a whole are unimportant; they merely show how far England was lagging behind the Continent in respect to significant medieval ecclesiastical literature. With the exception of Bede and Aldhelm, the Anglo-Latin writers in the Old English period perpetrated dreary and insignificant stuff. It is noteworthy that the better writers of this category came from the north rather than from the south of England. Northumbria and Mercia between them, it will be recalled, held the political and cultural leadership until about the year 800; and by the time Wessex was dominant, Alfred the Great had begun the tradition of English prose writing in the vernacular.

7. Alfred the Great

King Alfred of Wessex fully deserves the epithet "Great" because of his achievements in the struggles both of war and of peace. He was born in the midst of conflict and spent his early manhood in wars against the Viking Danes. A great invasion of these ruthless warriors had taken place in 865; and when Alfred came to the throne in 871, affairs were in a critical state. During the next half-dozen years the West Saxons were often brought to the verge of subjection. Considering the hit-and-run nature of the fighting, it is remarkable that Alfred was able to force King Gudrun of the Danes to the Treaty of Wedmore as early as 878. The military skill and personal leadership of one who could accomplish this are obvious enough; and if Alfred had not won this military victory, he would never have had the opportunity to put into effect his plans for the betterment of his people. Asser's biography, already referred to, tells us that even in his most perilous days Alfred was trying to read and learn and was bemoaning the fact that there were no good teachers in England. We discover from the same authority, incidentally, that the king was a rather sickly man and very far from the physical ideal of a Beowulf or a Roland.

The realization of the poverty of Wessex was the spur to prick Alfred on to his grand literary and educational program, which was to translate into English "some of those books most necessary for all men to know" [20] and then to get all Englishmen who could to read and study them—a program that Alfred, in spite of manifold discouragements, was able to carry out for the more enlightened of his people.

There are definite literary achievements that belong to Alfred's reign and are associated with his name, but an important problem relating to the canon of his works lies in the uncertain extent to which he himself was the author of these so-called Alfredian writings. Was he actually the translator of all of them? In most instances it has been accepted that Alfred himself was the man responsible, for there is a certain style in most of these works—simple, didactic, unpretentious, almost popular, and unquestionably charming—which can be termed Alfredian. In the preface to the translation of Pope Gregory the Great's *Pastoral Care* he is explicit; he speaks in the first person and states categorically that he translated "sometimes word by word, sometimes sense by sense," as he learned the Latin language from his teachers, who are named by name.

Thus in five important works, translations of what Alfred believed to be the most authoritative works of his time, covering all the knowledge of his age, there is reason to accept Alfred's immediate participation. These are Boethius's *Consolation of Philosophy (De Consolatione Philosophiae)*, a philosophical work of the early sixth century derived chiefly from Platonic thought; Bede's *Ecclesiastical History,* already described; Orosius's *Compendious History of the World;* *Blostman,* based on the *Soliloquies* of Saint Augustine; and Gregory the Great's *Pastoral Care,* on the functions and duties of prelates. Here is a clear indication of the fundamentally liberal interests of the gentle and intelligent Alfred—the choice, for his people, of the most comprehensive history of his nation; and inclusive geography and encyclopedia of the

---

[20] Quoted from the preface to the Alfredian version of Gregory the Great's *Pastoral Care (Cura Pastoralis).*

age; a work defining the ideals of religious administration; an idealistic philosophy, which is always a refuge in times of trouble; and the incarnation of the patristic and ascetic attitude toward life. Besides these, Alfred is responsible for the codification of the laws of his kingdom, based in part upon the shorter codes of one or two kings of earlier Anglo-Saxon times and in even greater part upon the Mosaic Law.

Furthermore, Alfred encouraged and systematized the writing of *The Anglo-Saxon Chronicle*. This important national history is in different hands and from different parts of England; it extends through the Old English period well into the twelfth century; and the tradition of chronicle writing, as we shall see, continued for much longer. There are entries in the *Chronicle* for years as far back as the time of Christ, but these are merely items added to give some fullness to the story. The most complete and authentic entries begin with the reign of Alfred. *The Anglo-Saxon Chronicle* is a casual, often a spirited narrative, containing allusions not only to battles long since fought but also to the contemporary scene. One other Alfredian piece, *The Proverbs of Alfred*, is a late tribute to Alfred's reputation as a wise man. Some of the sayings in this work may actually have been written down in Alfred's lost *Handbook;* but the collection as a whole is undoubtedly later than Alfred and is probably nothing more than another of those bundles of worldly wisdom found in all ages and attached to the names of great men. The example of the Biblical Book of Proverbs, associated with King Solomon, is a natural parallel. We have noticed the same kind of writing in the *Gnomic Verses.* Alfred's *Handbook* (*Enchiridion*) just cited was known to Asser and to the twelfth-century chroniclers; unfortunately it has disappeared. It seems to have been a mélange of history, aphorisms, Biblical story and commentary, and perhaps some scientific information; it may also have contained some songs by Alfred's favorite lyric poet, Aldhelm.

There is no certain chronology of the Alfredian translations, and in this fact lies another important problem bearing upon the Alfredian canon. A reasonably satisfactory list would follow the order: Gregory, Boethius, Orosius, Bede, and Augustine; but good arguments could be advanced in favor of other sequences. Essentially it matters very little. We may leave the *Pastoral Care* with the remark that, aside from its revealing preface, it is, after all, a technical work of value only to the church historian. Bede's *Ecclesiastical History* has already been discussed; it is well, however, to remember that the Alfredian version is in the vernacular. Its medium is simpler, more unsophisticated, less cultivated than Bede's dignified Latin. The rustic story of Caedmon, for example, is told more appropriately in the Alfredian translation than in Bede's original; the pathetic majesty of Caedmon's death requires no orotund Latinity. The *Compendious History* remains interesting because Alfred inserted in it an account of the great Northland given him by two voyagers—the Norwegian Ohthere, who told what he knew of the northernmost extremities of Europe, and the Danish (or possibly English) Wulfstan, whose adventures were confined to the Baltic Sea.

Boethius's *Consolation of Philosophy* is one of the most important works in early European literature and, next to the body of Catholic doctrine and dogma, the most important philosophical influence felt in the Middle Ages. Its author was a member of an aristocratic Roman family and was consul in 510. His fortunes, however, suffered disaster; he was charged with being politically inimical to the Emperor Theodoric, was imprisoned, and was finally put to death in 525. His plans for modernizing and translating all the works of Plato and Aristotle therefore never came to fruition; but he died a philosopher and an authority on metrics and music. It is not known for certain whether or not he was a Christian, although he joined in a controversy among Christian churchmen in which his position was orthodox enough.

The *Consolation of Philosophy* remains Boethius's masterpiece. It is in five books and is written in alternating sections of prose and of verse—the prose mainly exegetical, the verse mainly lyrical. In the first book Boethius tells of his misfortunes and describes the appearance before him in prison of a woman of grave mien, his guardian Philosophy (Wisdom). She enters into conversation with him and discovers that he does not know what he himself is; this absence of self-knowledge is the cause of his misery. In the second book, Philosophy brings Fortune into the picture. Fortune shows Boethius the kind of happiness she can bestow and then demonstrates that such happiness is exceedingly fickle. In the third book, Philosophy promises to show Boethius true happiness. This, by syllogism, she shows to be in God alone, for since God is admittedly the highest good, and since the highest good is obviously true happiness, then God must Himself be that true happiness. Evil must therefore be non-existent, for God is all-powerful and, being good, cannot allow evil. The fourth book brings Boethius to the question why evil exists; and why it seems so often to triumph. Philosophy replies that the victory of evil is apparent only; vice is never unpunished. She next considers Providence and Fate and shows that every fortune is for the best. The last book treats of man's free will and God's foreknowledge; it attempts to show that these ideas are not mutually contradictory; the conclusion is finally reached that God is a foreknowing spectator of all happenings, and the omnipresent eternity of His vision coincides with our future actions.

Strictly speaking, the Alfredian Boethius is not so much a translation as an adaptation. The five books of the original are flattened out into forty-two chapters. Boethius's logical design is therefore dislocated, and Alfred has seized the opportunity to add and subtract, in characteristic fashion, as he sees fit. The result is that Boethius is more fairly represented in Chaucer's than in Alfred's version, although, curious as it may be, Chaucer's translation is both dull and unimaginative when it is compared to Alfred's. Yet some of the essential poetry of the original penetrates into the Anglo-Saxon vernacular, particularly the idyllic description of the Golden Age, the hymns of praise to the Creator, and the passages distrustful of Fortune. As it happens, there is also in Old English a verse-translation of the Boethian lyrics (*metra*), which some have attributed to Alfred. The author is particularly happy in his amusingly quaint accounts of Orpheus and Eurydice and of Ulysses and Circe. In the first of these the Christian Anglo-Saxon king is suspicious of the beauties of Greek mythology and such "lying tales"; in the second he is nonplussed by the tale of sexual attraction. In the main, however, the reader must discover for himself the strength as well as the weakness of this hitherto underestimated piece of Old English literature.

The *Soliloquies* of Saint Augustine are joined to a rework-ing of that Church Father's *De Videndo Dei* to form the Al-fredian version. Of this work, the middle portion is the best instance in Old English literature of the anthology of sayings, the *florilegia* or "blossoms" of a classical piece or of its writer. The entire work has the ambitious double task of explaining the nature of God and the nature of the human soul. Today it is likely that Alfred's preface would have greatest appeal, and it is indeed a gracious passage, symbolic, in the long-sustained metaphor of the laborious building of a house, of everything Alfred was and of everything he tried to do.

Enough has been said already about *The Anglo-Saxon Chronicle* to make clear its general nature; its many versions have been preserved in seven surviving manuscripts.[21] Who-ever wrote the entry for 755 told a stirring story of personal strife between Cyneheard and Cynewulf. The Danes and the West Saxons move about constantly through admirably terse military narrative; revealing indeed is the story of the coming of the Danes in 1004, when they were bribed away instead of fought off. The analysis of William the Conqueror in the entry for 1087 is a classic; so is the dismal tale of King Stephen's reign in the last portion of the *Peterborough Chronicle,* which extends to 1154, the latest date of the seven manuscripts.

8. Aelfric, Wulfstan, and the Homilies

At first glance the tenth century, following Alfred's death, seems a story of material gains only. Actually, however, Eng-lish literature owes a great debt to the Church in the tenth century. Early in the century there had been a kind of renais-sance of religion in France, a reform and revivifying of the Benedictine Rule, which meant for the churchman a sterner insistence on spiritual living and a more rigid execution of monastic duties, as well as an inspiration to ecclesiastical and educational writing. In England the most important fosterers

---

[21] These seven are: (1) the Winchester (or Parker), extending to 1070; (2) the Aethelflaed, to 977; (3) the Abingdon, to 1066; (4) the Worcester, to 1079; (5) the Peterborough, to 1154; (6) the Canterbury (MS. Cotton Domitian A VIII), to 1058; and (7) another Canterbury manuscript (Cotton Otho B XI), to 1001.

of the movement were Dunstan, Archbishop of Canterbury, who introduced the reformed Benedictine Rule; Oswald, Bishop of Worcester, who encouraged the clergy of his bishopric to exposition of the Rule; and Aethelwold, Bishop of Winchester, who made the Winchester school of theologians famous and who is further celebrated because in his *Concordia Regularis* he describes the method by which the Easter liturgical play *Quem Quaeritis?* was to be performed. Aethelwold also translated the reformed Benedictine Rule into English about the year 960.

The most important individual in English literature between the death of Alfred and the Norman Conquest, however, was Aelfric. He was born about 955, lived in the monastery at Winchester until 987, where he received instruction in the Benedictine Rule, and then traveled to Cernel, Dorsetshire, to teach the Rule there. He devoted himself to his career as a religious writer and rose to the position of Abbot of Eynsham, Oxfordshire, where he died about 1025. Scholars have exploded the possibility that either of two other churchmen named Aelfric—one of them Archbishop of Canterbury from 995 to 1006 and the other Archbishop of York from 1023 to 1051—had any part in the writing of the pieces commonly ascribed to "Aelfric."

Forty homilies,[22] the first set of *Catholic Homilies*, composed about 990, are his first writings of importance. Another set of 40 was written a few years later (990-94). To many these 80 homilies are the most significant of Aelfric's works. But he also was responsible for a Latin grammar (995), based upon that of the Latin grammarian Priscian. He compiled some scientific works, but whether these were original with him or the work of others is not clear. The ambitious *Lives of*

---

[22] The homilies of the Anglo-Saxon period, whether by Aelfric, by Wulfstan, or anonymous, are formal pieces, either for direct instruction in the schools or for use in the celebration of the services of the liturgical year. They were not considered as pieces to be delivered from the pulpit, as a modern preacher might deliver his sermons, though doubtless some were thus employed. The subjects and occasions of these Old English homilies were traditional, and the sentiments expressed in them were altogether conventional. In most respects these statements apply also to Middle English homilies.

the Saints (996) rivals the *Catholic Homilies* as typical examples of Aelfric's prose; indeed, the individual biographies are often not much more than homilies. In addition, Aelfric wrote many tracts on ecclesiastical matters and commentaries on books of the Bible, and translated a few parts of the Old Testament.

Aelfric admits that the *Catholic Homilies* are derived from various Church Fathers, from Bede, and from Pope Gregory the Great, but disclaims any influence of Anglo-Saxon poetry upon his works, except for that of an anonymous and altogether obscure *Passion of Saint Thomas*. He obviously is familiar, however, with the technique of this poetry, for there are in his works many echoes of the language of the heroic and Christian epics, and his tendency toward alliteration and the repetition of synonymous words and phrases in many of his prose works is unmistakable. In this way Aelfric becomes the poet of Old English prose; if Alfred wrote the simple prose of the vernacular, Aelfric inaugurated the tradition of rhetoric in English prose. It is unnecessary to linger over the *Homilies* either individually or as a collection. They are expositions of orthodoxy, sincere in purpose, intended primarily for the churchman rather than the congregation, but somewhat inflated in style and condescending in tone toward their audience.

We shall pass over Aelfric's *Grammar*, but his *Colloquy on the Occupations*, much less ambitious, is more vital. Here a teacher asks his pupils about their occupations, and they reply in some detail. The work is far from a piece of proletarian literature—the complacent tone of the academic churchman is too strong for that—but it is remarkable for the little glimpses afforded of the life of the laborer and the tradesman, who are generally ignored by other writers of the age; and it further demonstrates the disturbing fact that social problems tend to remain the same, regardless of age or environment.

So strong is Aelfric's homiletic tendency that the *Lives of the Saints*, some 40 in number, constitute in actuality only another series of *Catholic Homilies*, this time with saints for topics. Not only do prominent English saints appear—Ethelred, Alban, and Swithin—but also Roman and Greek Christian martyrs, Old Testament, New Testament, and even

Apocryphal heroes and heroines. Many lines are eloquent, particularly in the lives of Saint Oswald of Northumbria and Saint Swithin. Nowhere is there a better illustration of Aelfric's poetic prose style than in the best of the *Lives of the Saints;* some of them have actually been published as metrical compositions.[23] But the biographical element in nearly all is overcome by the didactic; the naïve, honest teacher is often reluctant to discuss some delicate matters in the vernacular, "for it is not fitting . . . lest the pearls of Christ be held in contempt." This artless solicitude for his audience characterizes more than one of Aelfric's works, and it is significant of his approach as a teacher. In some ways the best exemplification of this trait is the *Interrogationes Sigewulfi,* or *Queries of Sigewulf,* a slightly abbreviated translation of Alcuin's *Handbook on Genesis.* This work reflects upon the troubles of the Creator in establishing a moral order, upon the beauties of Creation, and upon such knotty problems as the reasons for evil, the beginnings of man, and his God-like possibilities as such. But these reflections are too vague to satisfy. Mystery, reticence, a reluctance to reveal too much lest the whole truth be known to those who can ill use it—these have always been the stock-in-trade of the teacher and the defender of tradition.

Although he appears at times to have been rather unenthusiastic toward those whom he was endeavoring to teach, Aelfric was diligent in the work of popularizing history and authority. His *Hexameron* deals with the six days of creation; his *Heptateuch* is a translation, with extensive commentary, of selected portions of the Pentateuch, the Book of Joshua and the Book of Judges. The commentaries on Job and Esther need no discussion. The *Canones,* or *Pastoral Letters*—one written during the 990's and another dated 1014—are significant as the most complete statement of their time on the duties and functions of a priest. Aelfric, it is obvious, was primarily the teaching churchman and traveled a path narrower than that traveled by Bede; but although his intellectual and spiritual ranges were more limited than Bede's, he never

[23] These are an important milestone in the history of English biography in the vernacular; the biographical material in Bede's *Ecclesiastical History* and *Lives of the Abbots,* together with other saints' lives, are of course in Latin.

theless went his way with assurance and contributed notably to the vast body of English prose.

It must not be supposed that the homilies of the Old English period were all arid stretches of theological exposition, stripped of all humanity and all sense of reality. The poetic nature of Aelfric's style has already been touched upon, and his occasional insight into the life of the times is only too easily overlooked. His successor as a writer of notable prose is more emotional—at times a kind of rhapsodist in passionate prose. Wulfstan rose in the Church to be Bishop of London in 1001, Bishop of Worcester in 1002, and Archbishop of York from 1002 until his death in 1023. His was clearly a remarkable personality, but unfortunately very little is known about him except what can be learned from the chronicle of his professional career and the few manuscripts containing homilies and epistles assignable with some degree of certainty to Wulfstan himself. Yet he stands as an impressive though shadowy prophet of evil in the grim latter days of the reign of Ethelred the Unready, a true Jeremiah of the Danish Conquest.

Some of the sermons once attributed to Wulfstan are now ascribed to Aelfric; indeed, the whole matter of the authorship of the many homilies composed in England during the early years of the eleventh century is an extremely complex problem. Modern scholarship has granted Wulfstan fifteen surviving homilies, with the possibility that at least nine others are conceivably his. The most impressive of these is undoubtedly the fiery *Sermo Lupi ad Anglos*,[24] composed early in 1014, after King Ethelred had fled to Normandy and while Swein of Denmark was ravaging England. In many ways this homily is the most distinguished piece of impassioned prose produced by an Englishman before the Norman Conquest. Times are bad; Englishmen have been chiefly to blame, and now they must turn back to God, who has been punishing them for their decline of faith, the slackness of their churchmen, the treachery of their rulers, and their own cowardice and sloth. By treachery families have been split, subjects have been sundered from their lords; violence sits gloating in high

[24] Wulfstan often called himself Lupus, the Latin equivalent of the "wolf" in the first part of his name.

places, and the longer it goes on, the more evil the day. The only answer is to turn to God and the right way of life, to follow God's law in our external and in our inmost thoughts, and to live in fear of the dread Day of Judgment that must come upon us, earning thereby whatever good rewards the Almighty may see fit to bestow upon us. The harangue is punctuated by rhythmic phrases of similar device: "let him believe who will!" "let him understand who will!" "let him do more if he can!" which add to the emotional and dramatic tone of the whole. From all this it is clear that Wulfstan, high in the hierarchy of the English Church, was much more of a rabble-rouser than the reasonable and persuasive teacher Aelfric; but then, from the very eminence of his bishopric, Wulfstan was called upon to keep vigil in very bad days and to sound the tocsin of alarm. In any event, no account of the early days of English prose can possible ignore either Wulstan or Aelfric.

There were probably a multitude of other writers of homilies and sermons in this active era between 950 and the Norman Conquest. At the very beginning of this span of years, for instance, a number of homilies were collected into one manuscript, which, according to the mysterious vicissitudes that beset all Anglo-Saxon manuscripts, ended up eventually in the keeping of the Marquis of Lothian at Blickling Hall in Norfolk and were therefore known as the *Blickling Homilies*. It is now conceded that these 19 homilies were compiled from different sources at different times; but they represent clearly the product of the spiritual and educational reforms set in motion by Dunstan, Aethelwold, and others. As would be expected of any group of homilies originating at a date near 1000, the *Blickling Homilies* have much to say about Judgment Day, which was believed likely to arrive at the turn of the millennium. Indeed, the most powerful of these homilies bears the warning title, "The End of the World Is Near." The immediate subject of most of them, however, is a church festival or some aspect of the Christian mysteries. They are less elaborate than either Aelfric's or Wulfstan's homilies; they are given more to legend and to the careless mixture of scriptural material and subjective pious reflection. As a whole they are vigorous and sometimes poetic, although the poetry is likely to be of a didactic nature, approaching in spirit and frequently in phraseology the gnomic passages in the general poetry of the period or the moralizing passages in *Beowulf*. Some parallels in style and phrase between one of the homilies and *Beowulf* have led to the intriguing speculation that the author of the homily was actually quoting *Beowulf*. Perhaps the most significant trait of the best of the *Blickling Homilies* is the emphasis upon death, the disfiguration of the grave, the terror of the Latter Day, and the necessity for a moderate kind of life to avoid the disaster that would otherwise overwhelm the unfortunate individual. In other words, the *Blickling Homilies* constitute an important contribution to the eschatological chapter of the great book of medieval didacticism.

Similar in nature though somewhat later in date are the *Vercelli Homilies*, so called from their presence in the Vercelli Book. These, however, bear more definitely upon the subject of redemption through the Passion of Christ. They are stern and monitory, of course; they boom out in heavy clerical language the theme of *sic transit*. All 23 of these homilies agree that it is thus the world wags; let us try to do better.

Some scattered saints' lives not attributed to Aelfric, but possibly influenced by him, need not detain us. There was also some translation from the Bible. Such translation was either in a more or less free vernacular style, or else it was interlinear—that is, it was inserted between the lines of a Latin version and tended to follow the Latin word order and syntax slavishly. Both types of translation were from the Latin Vulgate Bible; this fact, added to the combined prestiges of scriptural authority and the Latin language, meant that even the freer English texts were not good specimens of Old English prose. At most, only portions of the Bible were translated.

Three beautiful examples—beautiful, at least, from the standpoint of medieval book-making and manuscript illumination—are the *Lindisfarne Gospels*, the *Rushworth Gospels*, and the *Vespasian Psalter*. The *Lindisfarne Gospels* is an interlinear translation of a Latin Vulgate Bible text written down by Bishop Eadfrith of Lindisfarne, Northumbria, about 700. This interlinear English text was done in the late tenth century by Aldred of Durham. The *Rushworth Gospels*, also with an interlinear English text, has a Latin original somewhat younger than that of the *Lindisfarne Gospels;* the first part of this English text, comprising all of Matthew and a little more than a chapter of Mark, was written by the Mercian Farman of Harewood, and the second part by Owun, who uses a more northerly Mercian dialect. Both men worked late in the tenth century. These two Gospels are invaluable to the linguist, as is the *Durham Ritual-Book,* a contemporary Latin prayer book with another English interlinear translation, containing also a number of the Psalms. The *Vespasian Psalter,* on the other hand, is a free paraphrase in Latin of the original Biblical text, in the form of thirteen Latin hymns, with a ninth-century English interlinear text. Beside the *Vespasian Psalter* could be placed half a dozen and more other psalters, many of which have translations in verse or prose. As for the independent translations, the most complete is the *West Saxon Gospels,* from some time between 1000 and 1025; it has been attributed to Aelfric, probably incorrectly, since Aelfric himself does not acknowledge it.

To the general reader of English literature, the works of Aelfric, Wulfstan, and the authors of the long catalogue of miscellaneous didactic pieces just mentional do not offer a very inviting prospect. They are admittedly for the professional medievalist. They are sincere to the core, but their prevailing gravity of thought and warning attitude are oppressive; and their one-sided unwillingness to recognize what the modern age considers worthwhile in life is nothing less than appalling. Yet even to the unsympathetic reader there will appear occasional sights and sounds of the way the Anglo-Saxons lived; and it would be a blind person indeed who failed to see in them the *modus vivendi* of the devoted churchman, his ideals, and the manner with which he performed in obscurity functions as important as those of the unappreciated coral insect. For if the Church held civilization together during the early Middle Ages, as is unquestionably the fact, it was through such men as Dunstan, Aelfric, Wulfstan, and countless others that it did so.

9. Secular Didactic Writing and Prose Fiction

To judge by surviving literature, it was seldom indeed that the Anglo-Saxon teacher ever thought to instruct his pupil in anything that did not have a religious cast, although one can assuredly be moral without being doctrinaire. But enough remains from this period to indicate that, in his liking for moral ideas, the Anglo-Saxon was as typically English as any later Englishman. The gnomic element in his poetry, already considered, is important; and if all these gnomic passages were to be taken from their matrix and assembled in one place, the result would be an impressively large volume of moral precepts. The same thing can be said of the prose.

Disregarding perennial types of instructive pieces like *The Dialogues between Solomon and Saturn* or *Hadrian and Ritheus,* we discover that the most notable example of this literature of secular precept is the collection of Latin maxims known as the *Distichs of Dionysius Cato.* This collection, one of the most celebrated moral "authorities" of the Middle Ages, was composed by an unkown author in the third century. The English translation renders the compilation only in part. It is not impossible that Aelfric was responsible; the English version has been attributed to him by some scholars. But the fact remains that the *Distichs* were known to scholars everywhere in the tenth century; they had already been used literally as a schoolbook for centuries, and it is more than doubtful that any free literary taste was at work in translating them. As a matter of record, only about half of the 144 distichs of the original have been given in the Old English translation. They do not form any logical sequence; they belong to the collected aphorisms that are a part of all early literature anywhere. They cover almost every conceivable human situation—they warn against flattery, against indulgent parents, against impractical religions, against vainglory, against ill-health, and against countless other dangers. In other words, they represent a fount of practical worldly wisdom, strongly colored by an earthy pagan quality; but neither the Anglo-Saxon nor the Middle English churchman saw any objection to using them for didactic purposes. As it happens, the habit of combining the mundane example with the spiritual lesson grew upon churchmen as the Middle Ages progressed.

Mere entertainment, moreover, can sometimes be turned to edifying purpose. We have seen this illustrated by the heroic and Christian epics. On the other hand, there are stories whose primary and sole purpose is to divert. Toward the very end of the Old English period there are some indications at least that the art of fiction was already turning into new and broader channels. The heroic and Christian epic traditions, in spite of a few sporadic examples, had become outmoded. Beside *The Battle of Brunanburh* and *The Battle of Maldon* in the old style, for instance, we can place a small group of compositions in the new style. These pieces do not have a native English flavor; they contain the spices of strange lands from across the sea. We have, in effect, reached a point of transition from the older form of fiction, the epic, to the beginnings of the medieval romance, which will be treated in the next chapter.

One of these newer pieces is *Apollonius of Tyre*. This story, originally an old Greek romance, got into the collection of legends known later in Western Europe as the *Gesta Romanorum,* of which more later. An Anglo-Saxon writer translated it into English near the middle of the eleventh century —a few years, perhaps, before the Battle of Hastings. Although the Old English version is fragmentary, it shows clearly the lines of difference between the old heroic epic and the new medieval romance. Both have high adventure, to be sure—the familiar matter of generations of bards and minstrels. There was actually no invention of incident on the part of the translator of *Apollonius of Tyre;* he was merely introducing to England the fictional building blocks of the Greek author. Nevertheless, one must realize that in a romance like *Appolonius of Tyre* the incidents have been piled up into a greater complexity of detail than in the straightforward heroic epic. But most striking of all is the fact that *Apollonius of Tyre* is a love story with a happy ending attained only after various trials, separations, and apparent disaster. The difficulty of imagining Beowulf as a blushing lover is enough in itself to distinguish the Anglo-Saxon heroic epic from this later fiction. Besides, Apollonius, whatever his position at Tyre or Antioch, knows no real national or local boundaries. His story is one of countless examples in the later medieval literature of a young man in love, striving to win his goal over tyrannical parents or villainous rivals or hostile elements. "Forever wilt thou love, and she be fair!"

Similarly the *Letters of Alexander to Aristotle* inaugurates in England the important medieval romance cycle of Alexander, which will be treated later at its appropriate place in Middle English literature. Here it is enough to remark that the Alexander legend became known to Western Europe as early as the fourth century. In the ninth century there appeared a series of fictitious letters between Alexander and his teacher Aristotle. These were translated by an Anglo-Saxon cleric; this translation was included in the Beowulf Manuscript. Alexander, in the course of his conquests, has arrived in India. He wants Aristotle to know the wonders of this far-off land, with its amazing giants, elephants, fleece-bearing and jewel-laden trees, horned serpents, mice in the likeness of foxes, snowstorms and volcanoes in close proximity, and countless other prodigies. Alexander is boastful, arrogant, and childish. He is astounded by the hardships of his adventures and puffed up by his successes, but he wishes he could see his mother and sisters back in Macedonia. He has the swaggering ingenuousness of an epic hero. The tropical lushness of the details of his story, however, is something different from the Nordic atmosphere of *Beowulf* or the Scandinavian sagas; it bespeaks an enlarged geographical horizon, a greater experience with things remote and foreign, however fantastically they may be presented. A careful reading of the *Letter of Alexander to Aristotle* makes unnecessary any special attention to *The Wonders of the East,* in the same manuscript and of approximately the same date, which concentrates with obvious relish upon the unnatural natural history of the legendary East, with animal and human monstrosities too numerous to relate. Yet obviously when Othello was regaling Desdemona with his remarkable adventures among remarkable people, or when Lyly was decorating *Euphues* with some of his surprising similes, they were only giving expression to an ancient and venerable tradition.

10. Informational Writing before the Norman Conquest

From what material has weathered the buffetings of centuries, it is apparent that the learning of the Anglo-Saxon period was not always directed toward the propagation of theological teachings or of general Christian morals. There was evidently a considerable amount of interest in matters that may be termed practical science. But there was no spirit of investigation or willingness to submit to experimentation in the hope of building a new world. The science of the period was for the most part a body of residual knowledge; it represented the hard experience of bygone ages heaped up until it had become an authoritarian resort of last appeal. A great deal of it was folklore pure and undefiled; some of it can be traced to the classical world of Hippocrates, Galen, and Pythagoras; but even more of it stemmed back to a dateless age when people first observed that the moon rose and set at definite intervals and that, when a certain plant was ingested, certain specific physiological functions were affected. In brief, this science may be said to represent the sum total of the knowledge of natural phenomena current in contemporary Europe.

There were always leaders of this science at any given period, and the age before the Norman Conquest in England was no exception. It has been seen that the Venerable Bede, for example, was versed in mathematics and the rudiments of both astronomy and cosmography. In this respect he was a true medieval academician. Alfred's translation of Orosius's *Compendious History* attempted to pass along what was known of geography. Alcuin's efforts at the Palace School of Charlemagne must have included mathematics and the ninth-century equivalent of physics. There were doubtless many others. A striking example of the occasional emergence of an unobstrusive scholar into the light of history is the late tenth-century cleric Byrhtferth, or Bridferth. He wrote a life of Saint Dunstan and a *Commentary* on Bede's scientific works, but his most important performance was his *Enchiridion,* or *Handbook*. It is difficult to see how one could learn much arithmetic from this incoherent jumble, but the work contains enough general information to give an indication of the range of interest possible for an active mind in the Anglo-Saxon age.

We can give considerably more credit to the *Herbarium Apuleii*. The original is in Latin and is popularly attributed to the second-century storyteller Apuleius, author of *The Golden Ass*. Actually, however, it is a superb example of the accumulation of the lore of ages. Composite as it is, it remained one of the great authorities for physicians of the Middle Ages. Its content is extremely interesting, especially when we realize that some of the oldest and homeliest remedies may be retrieved there at any time for the benefit of mankind. The *Herbarium* is at once a handbook of plant life and a *materia medica;* it describes a plant and then shows to what practical purposes it can be put. The factual matter, however, is cluttered up in typical fashion with information about the astrological properties of the plants, and the resulting hodgepodge is often fantastic. The English translator of the *Herbarium,* who wrote during the eleventh century, is always hopeful: the plants will cure any and all diseases. Similar to the *Herbarium* is the *Medicina de Quadrupedibus,* a conglomeration of recipes or prescriptions that specialize in the use of animals' organs. It is remarkable, for instance, how useful a fox or a scorpion can be to a sick person.

The grand resultant of all the component forces—pagan folklore, classical learning, superstition, pseudo-science, and crude experimental findings—is the *Anglo-Saxon Leechbook.*[25] This astonishing mélange was apparently gathered together in England in the tenth century. Having indicated its composite sources, we must perforce emphasize that the degree of originality it exhibits is virtually zero. It consists of a treatise on medicine and then a large assemblage of prescriptions. In so far as it is organized at all, the medical section is arranged from the standpoint of the disease to be treated. The *Leechbook* is, indeed, on a higher scientific level than either the *Herbarium* or the *Medicina de Quadrupedibus.* For one thing, it is relatively free from the prayers, charms, and exorcisms that mar the other compilations. The long and elaborate prescriptions are a revelation; one wonders how many of even those strong-stomached Anglo-Saxons could hope to survive such assaults upon the human system. But the *Leechbook,* quite apart from any intrinsic scientific value

[25] *Leech* is from the Old English *laece,* "a physician." The blood-sucking worm called a leech evidently derives its name from the medicinal use of the worm in blood-letting or phlebotomy.

it may possess—and such value is really very little—shines as a brilliant sidelight on the life of the times. It is instructive to realize that people in every age have suffered from colds and toothaches and indigestion; it is helpful to know that King Alfred suffered from what appear to have been stomach ulcers. For some reason it has been particularly difficult to convince readers that the writers of Anglo-Saxon literature were not all ghostly unrealities. The *Leechbook* shows that they were at least human.

A similar smaller collection of prescriptions, the *Saxon Leechdoms*, merely echoes the larger work just described. Another interesting addition to the medical library of the age is the *Peri Didaxeon*, the special importance of which lies in its opening section, in which the reader is given, in rather esoteric language, the philosophical concepts of medieval medicine. As a final supplement to all this medical writing there are several scattered pieces that in themselves are sufficient commentary on the scope of Anglo-Saxon biological science. They cover such matters as the growth of the foetus, the determination of foetal sex, lunar influences on disease, and the interpretation of dreams. Still others walk the borderline between fact and fancy. Here, as always, the most exasperating quality of these works is not their ignorance or their scientific unsophistication or their lack of perspective, for which there is excuse enough—it is their complete lack of a coherent organization, which alone damns their whole scientific structure. The Middle Ages never grasped the significance of inductive reasoning—if indeed they dared to use it—and so never approached a true scientific attitude.

Linguistic science among the Anglo-Saxons was purely derivative. We have seen how Aelfric's *Grammar* and *Glossary* were based on Priscian and Donatus. No further development of this point is called for, but a word should be said about the various glosses that have survived. These are embryonic dictionaries; in effect, however, they are only word lists that give a Latin word of some difficulty with its English equivalent beside it. There are several of these glosses scattered about over Western Europe—ample testimony of the travels of Anglo-Saxon scholars during the centuries before the Norman Conquest. Glosses found thus at different places have usually been named simply after the town or city in which they were discovered; we have, therefore, the *Epinal, Erfurt, Brussels, Boulogne,* and *Leiden Glosses,* as well as some native English manuscripts. In date they range between 700 and 1000. There is no attempt in them at definition, etymology, or illustration, but they are nevertheless indispensable in determining the denotation of many Old English words.

The Old English period and the Middle English period both belong to the Middle Ages. Although the Norman Conquest, which underlies the entire Middle English era, wrought many important changes in English life and introduced many particular innovations into its art and literature, one is justified in assuming that all the important types of literaure composed in Anglo-Saxon England continued to be written in the Middle English period, subject, of course, to the inevitable alterations that attend any great social and political upheaval.

So overpowering was the prestige of French civilization in England for some three centuries after 1066, however, that many of the Anglo-Saxon traditions in English literature seemed to suffer total eclipse. Such an eclipse was more apparent than real. English literature in the Middle English period proved to be more varied, more sophisticated, more experienced in the potentialities of life and the problems of humanity, but was still endowed with the same vitality, massiveness, power of observation, and ability to express itself vividly that it had possessed before the Norman Conquest. Unfortunately, the reputation of individual writers of the Anglo-Saxon period was allowed to lapse. Bede and Alfred, perhaps, continued to live as names and influences, but the great majority of authors—many of them, as we have seen, gifted beyond the average—sank into anonymity. With the changes in language imposed by the influx of the French came an inability to read and to understand the older works; and as both literature and literacy in the Middle English period remained the particular property of a highly conservative and intellectually static clergy, the significant works of Anglo-Saxon times lay buried in cathedral or monastery libraries, where they became generally forgotten. It was not until the Renaissance, with its humanism, that the antiquities of English literature came once more to light. Nor should we cavil at the fact that much of this resurrection of interred Anglo-Saxon literature took place because rebels in Church and State were looking for ancient authorities to support their Protestantism and republicanism. If it had not been for these self-seekers, a great deal less would be known today about Anglo-Saxon speech and literature than is actually the case.

A great deal is still not known, however, and will very likely never be discovered. The same statement applies in slightly less degree to Middle English literature. It seems fair to assume, if we take Old and Middle English literature together, that at least as much has been lost as has been brought back to life. In other words, generalizations about this body of literature will probably apply to no more than half of what was actually written during this period. What we have, of course, is distinctive enough. If we confine ourselves for the moment to Old English literature, we discover that it is naïve and rudimentary, sometimes clumsy and awkward, sometimes inadequate, sometimes strikingly effective, but always endowed with personality and never ignoble. We could do with far less of the priest in it and far more of women and artists. But with all its faults it nevertheless affords an admirable base on which to rear the splendid edifice of English literature; and whatever else it may be, it is always one with the whole English literary tradition.

Chapter 2

The Literature of the Middle English Period to "Piers Plowman": The Romances

1. England, 1066-1485

THE NORMAN CONQUEST, when viewed against the mighty background of medieval European history, seems little more than a dynastic conflict, in which an older, somewhat decadent order—Anglo-Saxon England—yielded to a newer, more vigorous, more capable force. But, in the smaller panorama of English history, the Norman Conquest is a truly great upheaval, the full consequences of which are not easy to describe briefly. It was the triumph of a new aristocracy, for the Duke of Normandy supplanted the Saxon thanes and earls with his Norman knights. It brought Norman blood to the courts of the king as well as to the offices of the Church. It meant the establishment of a Norman system of law. Especially it meant the imposition on the Old English language of Norman French, which came to have the peculiar prestige of the conqueror; the vernacular, while it was not suppressed, was nevertheless pushed down into the ordinary walks of life. For a time it was no longer the language of literature in England, except where here and there a cloistered Saxon chronicler saw fit to write it; and a good two hundred years were to elapse before it achieved even a moderate return to social graces and artistic prestige. In 1265, an English king, Henry III, in political difficulties, condescended to issue a proclamation in English; in 1362 English came to be used in the courts of law; in 1385 it was possible for a thoughtful citizen to view with perturbation the prospect that English children might not learn French in the schools. The effect of this difficult up-hill struggle of the English language to become the universal medium of its own people cannot fail to show itself in Middle English literature.

The early Middle English period, from the Norman Conquest to about 1300, represents the culmination of the Middle

Ages in England. The rule of the Church during these years was absolute; its power over the lives of every human being was for the time unbreakable. A strong evangelical movement in the late eleventh century had produced two such dissimilar indications of religious zeal as the cult of the Virgin and the First Crusade—the most emotional and lyrically mystical of the many aspects of the medieval Church, as well as the most militant. That the later Crusades, which continued intermittently throughout the early Middle English period, degenerated for the greater part into opportunistic junkets led by self-seeking Christian potentates, does not of itself bring reproach to the sincere, self-sacrificing, visionary adventurousness of the First Crusade, which achieved in 1099 the rather short-lived Kingdom of Jerusalem and brought the Holy Sepulchre into the possession of Christians. The cult of the Virgin, on the other hand, became an imperishable treasure of Catholic Christianity, and its influence upon the society of the time in general and upon the attitude of this society toward women in particular cannot be overemphasized. For the first time, apparently, this race and age recognized that, although Christ was divine, His mother had been a woman; therefore all women were worthy of a greater respect than had hitherto been accorded them; and chivalry became not only a word but a tradition.

In the meantime, learning had begun to flourish at Oxford. To be sure, Paris was still the great center of academic training in medieval Europe, as it had been since the days of Charlemagne's Palace School. In 1167, however, a quarrel between King Henry II of England and King Louis VII of France had resulted in forbidding English scholars access to learning in France; they had perforce to get their training in England. Oxford was the logical place for this training, since schools had been conducted there for an indeterminate time during the twelfth century. In the early thirteenth century similar study was inaugurated at Cambridge. The coming of the Friars—the Dominicans reached England in 1221, and the Franciscans in 1224—helped immeasurably in the creation of a real scholastic tradition in the English schools. The gap between learning in England and the tradition of Alcuin had once more been closed; and the focusing of learning at the centers of Oxford and Cambridge had been accomplished. In terms of the literature of the period, this meant the spread into England of scholasticism and the scholastic point of view. More will be said later about the Scholastics' contribution to Middle English writings; it need only be pointed out here that, although the Scholastics represent a distinctively medieval type of philosophical outlook and theological statement, their influence upon Middle English literature was never overwhelming.

Politically speaking, the history of the medieval state in England is a checkered story. The Norman Conquest meant that England was to be bound up in French affairs for a long time; at first she was considered secondary to France. Neither of the younger sons of William the Conqueror—his eldest had preferred to remain Duke of Normandy—was in any way the equal of his father. The reigns of these mediocre Norman kings, William Rufus (d.1100) and Henry I (d.1135), were followed by the terrible anarchic days of the futile Stephen, whose barons rode roughshod over the land.

Henry II, grandson of Henry I and son of Matilda, daughter of Henry I and the Countess of Anjou, brought more French lands to the Crown with his accession in 1153, and still more—Poitou, Guienne, and Gascony—with his marriage to Eleanor of Aquitaine in 1154. The English sovereign could now claim territories as far south as the Pyrenees. The advent of the Angevin kings, better known as the Plantagenets, coincides with the gradual leveling of distinction between Norman and Anglo-Saxon and the general recognition of the fact that these two together now constituted the Englishman. Such evidence of the passing or eclipse of Anglo-Saxon prestige is multiplied after King John of England lost Normandy to the French in 1204.

Henry II was a strong ruler and made notable contributions to the English constitution by his preference for the jury system in legal procedure and by his opening of Ireland and Wales to English exploitation. His successors were mediocre or worse. John, who reigned from 1199 to 1216, was a political incompetent who alienated the Church, as well as his own subjects, lost Normandy, and was obliged to relinquish much of the absolutism of feudalism to his barons in the famous Magna Charta granted on Runnymede Island in 1215.

But Edward I (d.1307) was a born administrator and a fitting embodiment of the best in early Middle English history. He controlled the sale of baronial land, gave greater opportunity to the villein, incorporated Wales into the Crown, and in particular summoned the Great Parliament of 1295—an action that expressed in deeds what Magna Charta had expressed chiefly in words. Edward's relations with Scotland, however, were not happy. The Scots were technically vassals of the English kings, but by this time they had developed a spirit of independence. Edward tried to suppress this spirit by disposing of the patriot William Wallace (1305), but without success. Edward's death left the matter unsettled, and his pathetically futile son, Edward II (d.1327) was decisively defeated at Bannockburn in 1314. The upshot of this first important instance in the long line of border wars was the Treaty of Northampton, signed in 1328, which acknowledged Robert Bruce as King of Scotland and abolished the feudal ties between England and Scotland.

The major conflict of the late Middle English period was the long, disastrous war between England and France, in which the Scots often served as allies of the French. This Hundred Years War and its consequences spelled the ruin of the Middle Ages in Western Europe. It meant the arresting of social advance in both moral and economic progress. It held back the movement of the people toward their acceptable natural rights; it began the tradition in Europe of the mercenary soldier, who was to plague the continent for centuries. The war began in 1338 and continued intermittently until 1453; at first the English, in such battles as those of Crécy (1346) and Poitiers (1356), were victorious and concluded a conqueror's peace in the Treaty of Bretigny (1360), which gave to England almost half of southern and southwestern France. The second phase of the war, which began in 1369, was somewhat indecisive, although it marked a distinct waning of English power. Yet under Henry V a third and, from the standpoint of the English, most triumphant phase began in 1415. Henry's objective was nothing less than the throne of France itself; and after the battle of Agincourt (1415) he entered Paris, reconquered Normandy (1417), and in

1420, by the Treaty of Troyes, had himself named "heir of France." But he never became King of France. Moreover, his sudden death in 1422 coincided with a resurgence of French power and prestige, at first slight, then suddenly kindled by the amazing phenomenon of Jeanne d'Arc (1412-31). The psychological stimulus given by this uneducated, mystical peasant girl is one of the miracles of history and is too familiar to need review here. For a score or more years after Jeanne was burned at the stake the war dragged on; but French nationalism had been thoroughly aroused, and French victory was inevitable. By 1453, all that was left of the English conquests in France was the port of Calais; a century later this too dropped back into French hands.

There was little doubt, however, that England in the late thirteenth and fourteenth centuries was slowly developing into a nation of world importance. The Hundred Years War, of course, retarded this development; but trade and commerce grew apace, and the town-dweller was a new and unabashed arrival upon the social scene. Of special importance was the formation of trade groups, or guilds, which were partly recreational, partly social, partly religious, and altogether political.

Yet the Hundred Years War was not the only calamity to befall the nation in the fourteenth century. That was man-made, and, in a sense, its effects could be in part foreseen. But the terrible pandemic of bubonic plague, the Black Death, which swept Europe two or three times in the fourteenth century, first reached England in 1348 and in the next year or two killed off from one third to one half of the population. It was an impartial scourge, treating knight, yeoman, priest, and burgess alike; but its effects were felt particularly among the upper classes, who were much fewer in numbers than the commoners. The immediate impact of this disaster was apparent in the realization by the laboring classes that they were needed, that they were actually important in the social scheme. As a result, the peasants demanded more and more, although they did not get what they asked for. Legislation was unable to cope with the problem. A generation later, in 1381, came a savage rebellion, the so-called Peasants' Revolt, which was a premature attempt to assert the equality of the rights of man.

This fourteenth-century trend toward socialism was killed in the bud, yet it was not wholly without result. It frightened both the nobility and the landowners and ultimately led to a great decrease in the number of villeins; in this way it widened still further the serious cracks that were appearing in the feudal edifice.

The story of England's vicissitudes during the Middle English period is still not complete. Edward III, who had begun the Hundred Years War as a vigorous young man, died in 1377, an embittered old man. His grandson Richard II, a mere boy, was the royal pawn moved about by his uncles. He had the manhood, however, to assert himself in the Peasants' Revolt, when he did much to quiet the mob that had broken into London, and in 1389 he dismissed his regents, to rule for several years ably, even brilliantly. Then defects of character, unfortunately, led him slowly but steadily into tyranny. He became embroiled with his cousin Henry of Lancaster. Henry managed to defeat him and to bring about his rejection by the nobility. Once deposed, he was soon murdered. Henry, ruling as Henry IV, had trouble with the Scots, who had been engaging in border forays throughout the reign of Richard II, and with the Welsh. He weathered these storms, however, and his son was able to reign as Henry V, a power in the conduct of the Hundred Years War. But the long reign of Henry VI, from 1422 to 1461, was a chronicle of ill-starred incapacity, complicated by the chronic bankruptcy of the Lancaster government. Henry's cousin, the Duke of York, was strong, ambitious, and blessed with the support of many thousands of Englishmen who were dismayed by the disasters of the Hundred Years War in its later stages. When Henry VI went insane in 1453, it seemed likely that the Duke of York would be chosen to succeed him; but the Duke's hopes were dashed when, in that same year, Henry's queen gave birth to a son. The Duke of York, dismissed by Henry, who heeded closely his wife's warning that the Duke might be able to bar their son from the succession, regarded this dismissal as a personal as well as a national affront. Early in 1455, he gathered his supporters and marched on London. So began the Wars of the Roses, between the houses of York and Lancaster.

The Wars of the Roses were small civil conflicts in which the people as a whole had very little part. There were marches and counter-marches, bloody battles, depositions and usurpations. The unsettled domestic conditions naturally engendered by the wars were not brought to a state of stability until young Henry Tudor, Earl of Richmond, defeated and killed Richard III at Bosworth Field, Leicestershire (1485), thenceforth to reign as Henry VII, first of the Tudors. Ten years before, the first book had been printed in English; seven years later, Columbus, on the *Santa Maria,* reached Watling Island in the Bahamas.

2. Some Observations on Middle English Literature

The long and difficult struggle of the English language to recapture social and artistic prestige after the Norman Conquest has its parallel in Middle English literature. In the circumstances, it could scarcely have been otherwise. Since the language of the court was basically French until the beginning of the fifteenth century and the language of the Church was Latin throughout the period, and particularly since court and Church were the only important influences bearing upon the literature that has survived from the age, the literature in the vernacular necessarily occupied a secondary position during most of the Middle English period. Nevertheless, one must never overlook the essential originality of the Englishman at every stage of his history.

Yet it is no exaggeration to insist that, until the Age of Chaucer, when the Middle English period had clearly passed the halfway mark, there was no important piece of English literature written in the vernacular that was not a shadowing, an imitation, perhaps an outright translation of a French or a Latin original. It is therefore impossible to consider Middle English literature apart from its French and Latin sources; it was bilingual, even trilingual, until about 1400. Indeed, not until the Renaissance did the French influence yield temporarily to that of other foreign literatures—the Italian and the Spanish. Moreover, the somewhat static nature of both the monastic and the courtly points of view in the literature of the time makes it convenient to study Middle English writings according to the types of literature produced rather than as a grand chronological sequence.

Until the fourteenth century was well under way, however, Middle English writings were for the most part anonymous; the number of known individual authors of important works could easily be counted on the fingers of one's two hands. It was in a way an expression of the importance of the mass over the individual. After 1300, however, the individual author frequently asserted himself; we may know comparatively little about Richard Rolle, John Wycliffe, John Gower, Geoffrey Chaucer, the Pearl Poet, or the Piers Plowman Poet, but their writings have a distinctiveness and a true personality that stamp them as writers of something far more individualistic than the outpourings of a cloud of witnesses.

As to Middle English literary form and style, a few general facts should be remembered. After the Norman Conquest, Old English alliterative verse declined rapidly. Only in the pages of *The Anglo-Saxon Chronicle* and in a few isolated pieces, such as *The Grave,* an elegiac piece in the traditional Old English manner (which may, however, be of a date as late as the early twelfth century), or in Layamon's excellent chronicle romance, *The Brut,* do we find a perpetuation of the technique of the Anglo-Saxon *scop.* With the Anglo-Norman period came the universal introduction of end-rhyme; under the prevailing French influence, felt throughout the Middle English era, rhyme was the customary poetic device. Nor, indeed, has English literature, except for sporadic fads and with the special exception of blank verse, ever lost this reliance on rhyme. A revival in the fourteenth century of Old English alliterative verse, practiced by writers from the West Midland section of England, was not particularly strong and died out during the fifteenth century.

The strophic forms in Middle English verse were, in the lyrics, free and varied, often extremely ingenious. The most common verse forms were the short French octosyllabic couplet; the longer, rather lumbering "fourteener" (*septenarius*), or poulter's measure; occasional Alexandrines; and, later in the period, the iambic pentameter couplet. At no time, however, were there the rigid requirements of Anglo-Saxon verse. All in all, a study of Middle English poetry will give the impression that the Middle English poets had fully as much liberty of technique as the poets of today and were fully as willing to experiment.

Inasmuch as the prose of the period was still under the overwhelming influence of Latin—for prose, the medium of the intellect, was still the proud possession of the cleric—it is not surprising that Middle English prose in the vernacular seems awkward, cumbersome, and involved. Yet the best of this vernacular prose had at least some of the virtues of its Latin models. Its total effect is often one of clarity, even though some passages may be obscure. The fact remains that the best prose in Middle English literature is in either French or Latin.

The Middle English language retained the continental value of vowels; and although a few aspects of the great vowel shift that differentiates Old and Middle English from Modern English had manifested themselves by the fourteenth century, it is fair to say that Chaucer would probably have made himself more intelligible to Alfred the Great than to Tennyson, even if, chronologically, he stands about midway between them. As to grammar, Middle English had begun to lose many of the inflectional distinctions found in Old English; the earlier morphological endings were either dropped outright or weakened to a colorless vowel, recognized in orthography by an unaccented *e*.[1] The constant acquisition of French words

---

[1] The greatest problem confronting anyone who reads Middle English literature aloud is how to dispose of the final *e*. This final *e* was in the process of disappearing during the late Middle English period, and it was presumably dropped in pronunciation before it was dropped in orthography. In Middle English prose after 1300 it is virtually impossible to tell whether a given *e* was or was not pronounced. In verse, the *e* was retained for a longer time than in prose (much as a final *e* in Modern French is preserved phonetically in verse or in musical settings). Yet even in Middle English verse one can see irregularities. Of course the date of a particular poem may suggest how the *e*'s should be handled; a piece before 1300 in London or Midland English would undoubtedly be more respectful of the final vowel than a piece from the same dialect in Chaucer's time. The problem is further complicated by dialectal peculiarities: the Northern English, for example, dropped inflectional endings much sooner than the more southerly dialects. By Chaucer's time, however, it is probable that the final *e* was pronounced regularly at the end of lines of verse (giving nearly

throughout the period created, however, a different tonality in Middle English from that which had existed in Old English. The French introduced not only some new sounds, such as *j* and *oi*, but also a different accentuation. Although the tendency was for all words in English gradually to assume a primary accent on the first syllable, in conformity with the usual habit of a Germanic language, a French loan-word often kept its original French accentuation, especially if it had been but recently borrowed. The net result was a greater variety of accent, along with a warmer and more exotic tone. The fact that the final *e* was often pronounced meant a greater number of polysyllables than there are in corresponding Modern English forms; this gave a slower, more languorous tempo to Middle English poetry and possibly also to the prose.

The effect upon the Anglo-Saxon vocabulary of large borrowings of both French and Scandinavian words (the latter from the period of Danish occupation in England) calls for no special comment. The least that can be said is that these borrowings enriched the language enormously, with all the benefits that can accrue from such an enrichment. It is easy, however, to overestimate the immediate effect of the Norman Conquest. If surviving literature is any true sign, English did not receive many French words before the thirteenth century—after the loss of Normandy by the Crown. The Scandinavian importation is more difficult to appraise, largely because of the comparative similarity of the two Germanic stocks; but again, it is noteworthy that the majority of Norse words found in Middle English literature did not appear until the late thirteenth and early fourteenth centuries.

At no time during the Middle English period—even as late as the fifteenth century—was there a true standard literary dialect. Instead, Middle English literature appears in all four

---

all verses a quasi-feminine rhyme effect) and commonly before the chief caesura; probably, also, wherever else it might be needed to sustain the meter. But elision was practiced wherever possible. As to Middle English prose, it is a hardy scholar who would dare to pontificate on how Chaucer read his *Parson's Tale* or how anyone read aloud *The Ancrene Riwle*. A convenient handbook on Middle English dialects and the language of Chaucer is Samuel Moore's *Historical Outlines of English Phonology and Morphology*, Ann Arbor, 1925.

major dialects—the Northern, corresponding to Old English Northumbrian; the Midland, corresponding to Old English Mercian; the Southern, corresponding to Old English West Saxon; and the Kentish. Often these dialects are much mixed in a given work. Yet in spite of these inconsistencies, Middle English is a language of sensuous appeal, expressiveness, and humor. The literature, for all the general naïveté of its intellectual attainment and the frequent spells of dullness in its often pedestrian moralizing, possesses freshness and sinew. It is a serious mistake to consider it mere pioneer's work.

3. Anglo-French Writings

The years immediately following the Norman Conquest witnessed as a matter of course the triumph of French and Latin literature over vernacular literature. The Anglo-French literature—by which comprehensive term one must describe all writing in England by French writers or writers in French —was a powerful, ever-present influence upon English literature throughout the Middle English period. In the chronological sequence of events it is necessary to consider first the Anglo-Norman phase, running to about 1250, and then the more general Anglo-French (Parisian) phase, which is especially important in the fourteenth and fifteenth centuries. To take another dimension, one must deal also with the monastic, courtly, scholastic, and popular aspects of the literature, which, as has already been pointed out, reached their respective peaks in a vague kind of chronological order —the monastic prevailing before 1300, the courtly rising to a high level in the fourteenth century, the scholastic universal in the period from 1200, and the popular discernible in the fourteenth century. The predominance of any one of these aspects, however, did not necessarily exclude the others; it is always possible to find any one of them at any given time in the later Middle Ages.

Nearly all types of the literature of the age were written in England by Frenchmen or by writers in French; one particular type, the Breton *lai*, received pre-eminent treatment. Yet, with the exception of the writings of Wace, Marie de France, and Bishop Grosseteste, it is not necessary to discuss in detail the bulk of Anglo-French literature, for while it is copious, it is also dull. At the same time, a short enumeration of the types of literature produced by Anglo-French authors and of the more important works and writers is certainly in order. First, and probably the most distinguished type represented, would be the romance in its various forms. Here the important names are those of Marie de France; the half-legendary Anglo-Norman Thomas, author of the *Tristan* to be mentioned later; and Robert de Boron, active and eloquent in the spread of the legend of the Holy Grail. All of these belong to the twelfth century or the early years of the thirteenth. There is also a large number of anonymous French writers of romance in the late Middle English era. Some of these, and all of those just mentioned, enter into the picture of the medieval romance to be presented in a later chapter.

The anonymity of most medieval romances is paralleled in the medieval tale, many of which are found throughout the different stages of Anglo-French literature. One form of the tale, the *fabliau,* bespeaks by its very name the French popularity of these short, realistic, anecdotal stories of vulgar origin—the nameless, dateless barrack-room sagas.

It is obvious that most medieval chronicle writing wandered between fact and fiction; almost all the Anglo-French writers of such chronicles were given to invention, probably because French, in contrast to Latin, had less scholarly prestige. Among the authors of this type, the best are Gaimar (*fl.*1150), Wace, Pers de Langtoft (*fl.*1325), and Nicholas Trivet (*fl.*1300). There are also political poems, mostly from post-Norman times. There are a few secular lyrics, although most Anglo-French lyrics are religious. There is the usual glut of religious composition, with special emphasis on Biblical paraphrase and commentaries on the Psalter. The Anglo-French saints' lives often deal with Celtic saints. As would be expected, there is the characteristic moralizing literature of the age, as well as a flow of miscellaneous didactic writings —the saints' legendary, the bestiary, the lapidary, proverbial wisdom as represented by an Anglo-French translation of the *Distichs of Cato,* treatises on chess, on medicine, on falconry and the chase, and allegorical visions best illustrated by Bishop Grosseteste's *Chasteau d'Amour.* There is even some drama; in fact, if we accept the twelfth-century *Adam* as Anglo-

French, it is the earliest mystery play composed in England. All of these Anglo-French compositions will be considered, at least inferentially, when the time comes to examine the basic types of Middle English literature in the vernacular.

Wace (*c.*1100-*c.*1174) was a true Norman, born in Jersey and living for at least part of his life in Caen and Bayeux; but it appears likely that he spent much time in England. It must be admitted that it is stretching a point to include him among strictly Anglo-French writers. As the most famous of several Anglo-French authors of *Bruts,* however, he deserves special mention. The *Brut* was often not much more than a catalogue of the kings of Britain, with some attention to the deeds of the more notable of them. It was clearly the product of political pressure—the Norman was anxious to substantiate the claim of his Duke to the throne of England by attaching him to a glorious past. Wace elaborated this type of metrical composition by making an Anglo-Norman verse paraphrase of some of Geoffrey of Monmouth's famous *Historia Regum Britanniae.* The Wace *Roman de Brut* (*c.*1155) lies back of the important *Brut* of Layamon, to be treated later. Wace does not hesitate to enliven the material of Geoffrey of Monmouth through judicious omissions and the addition of animated, often realistic details. The other composition of Wace that will repay some study is his *Roman de Rou,* a history in the same octosyllabic verse of the Dukes of Normandy, beginning with Rollo (Rou), who acquired Normandy (Neustria) from Charles the Simple in 911-12. It seems that Wace, like the bard Deor of Old English times, was supplanted by a historical chronicler, one Benoit, and so did not carry the *Roman de Rou* beyond the early years of the twelfth century.

These ingenuous legends are of the essense of romance; and no teller of romances in the Anglo-French domain was more gifted than Marie de France. Almost nothing is known about her identity, to say nothing of her life. The dates of her birth and death are alike unknown, although she flourished about 1175. Even her nationality is in doubt, but there is every likelihood that she was of Norman birth, of royal blood, and of English residence. These details, the subject of much controversy, will probably never be established; but Marie's works remain. Two of them, the *Esope* (*c.*1180), a collection

of moral beast-fables thought to have been written for the
edification of William Longsword, natural son of Henry II,
and the *Espurgatoire* (*c*.1185), a translation of a vision poem,
St. Patrick's Purgatory, by Henry, a monk of Saltrey, are so
inferior to the *lais* both in originality and in general achievement that they may be passed over as average medieval religious and didactic literature. Indeed, there are many more
significant examples of their types to be found elsewhere in
Middle English literature. But the *lais* (*c*.1167) are a different
matter.

The word *lai* is used throughout the period in such a
general way that it is very confusing. Perhaps the classic
definition of this literary type is the statement in the Prologue
to Chaucer's *Franklin's Tale:*

> Thise olde gentil Britouns in hir dayes
> Of diverse aventures maden layes,
> Rymeyed in hir firste Briton tonge;
> Whiche layes with hir instrumentz they songe,
> Or elles redden hem for hir plesaunce . . .

to which might be added the lines at the opening of the
Middle English "Breton *lai*," *Sir Orfeo:*

> We redyn often and fynde ywryte,
> As clerkes don us to wyte,
> The layes that ben of harpyng
> Ben yfounde of frely [wondrous] thing.
> Sum ben of wele and sum of wo,
> And sum of ioy and merthe also,
> Sum of trechery and sum of gyle,
> And sum of happes that fallen by whyle,
> Sum of bourdys [jests] and sum of rybaudry,
> And sum ther ben of the fayre [faery]
> Off alle thing that men may se,
> Moost to lowe [praise] forsothe they be.
> In Brytayn [Brittany] thise layes arne ywryte,
> Furst yfounde and forthe ygete—
> Of aventures that fillen by dayes,
> Wherof Brytouns made her layes;

When they myght owher heryn
Of aventures that ther weryn,
They toke her harpes with game,
Maden layes and yaf it name.

Of course this composite definition limits the *lai* to the Breton
lai. Unfortunately, the etymology of the word *lai*, in spite
of earlier romantic attempts to associate it with Germanic
and Celtic words for *song*, remains altogether obscure. It is
probably, however, a fair supposition to relate it to a poetic composition to be delivered in song or chant with musical accompaniment. It would seem that *lais* could originally have been
either lyric or narrative and possibly were both. To take only
one example, we have seen how close was the relation between epic and lyric in such a piece as the Old English *Song
of Deor*, which might well be called an Old English *lai*. Moreover, although none of them survives, many short *lais* of
strictly English (Germanic) origin were composed in Anglo-
Saxon during the eleventh century. Some of these were taken
up by the Normans and translated into Anglo-French, such
as the *lai* about Havelok, possibly attributable to Gaimar; the
lai about Horn; and several others.

As for the Breton *lai*, it appears to have been the same
sort of poem as other early *lais*, except that it was Celtic
Breton in origin and made use of Celtic story materials and
setting and possibly Celtic metrical and musical forms. It is
certain that all such *lais* fell into one of three categories.
There were the very early *lais*, the true *lais* bretons—short
songs of indefinite nature sung in the original Breton tongue
with musical accompaniment. It is a pity that none of this
category has survived. Then there were the *lais narratifs*—
short romance-narratives based upon earlier folk materials,
with more or less Celtic characters and locales, written in
French octosyllabic couplets. These were the most sophisticated and withal the most courtly forms the *lai* could assume.
Finally, there were the *lais lyriques*, the nature of which is
self-evident from their designation. Some thirty of these survive in French. The relation of such poems to the *lais narratifs*
is undoubted but obscure; very likely they represent lyric
elaborations or embellishments of episodes found in the *lais*

narratifs[2]; and again the parallel of the relation between a strophe of the *Song of Deor* or some early Germanic heroic epic and these *lais* will occur to the observant reader.

The *lais* of Marie de France are to be construed as *lais narratifs*. Yet in every case Marie has undoubtedly made use of independent romance and epic material, has fused it with a marked amount of folklore, and has achieved an integrated narrative of delicacy, sparkle, poetic insight, and an artlessness that is as deceptive in its simplicity as it is effective in its execution.

There are a dozen *lais* ascribed to Marie de France and almost as many anonymous *lais* that, although probably not hers, came from the same soil at about the same time and may have been the product of a Marie de France cycle; some later Middle English vernacular romances have also been classified as Breton *lais*. What is most important about Marie's *lais*, aside from their artistic skill and essential poetry, is that, once granted their complete femininity of outlook, they exhibit a surprising range. They are, furthermore, capable of being interpreted in a variety of ways. They are not solely reflections of the psychology of courtly love, nor are they merely embodiments of lax amorosity. They are not necessarily symbolic in virtually every detail, nor are they only the chants of idle singers. And yet they have all been studied and successfully interpreted in each of these lights and have gained the approval of the critic accordingly.

A careful reading of the *lais* is an excellent introduction to the whole subject of the medieval romance. Not only are these narratives crammed with many of the commonplaces of incident and motif characteristic of the longer and later romances, but also the prevailing note of *courtoisie*, the essential chivalric spirit, is here inescapable. It is only fitting that a woman should have written the *lais*, for, as will be seen, the romance is a markedly feminized form of the older heroic epic. These *lais* and the romances to follow are escapist liter-

---

[2] A reasonable example would probably be Marie de France's *Lai de Chievrefueil*, or *Honeysuckle Lay*, which is a mere fragment of the story of Tristan and Isoude. It contains some descriptive details and a strong lyrical tone; nevertheless, the emphasis is still on the narrative.

ature; they face away from the dogmatic theology of monastic literature and from the harsh practical marriages necessitated by the feudal system. For example, the element of illicit love, which runs like a bright thread through most of these *lais,* is but a compensation in the mind of the medieval lady for the fact that her marriage was most likely to be loveless and political rather than romantic.

To her admirable story material, Marie has given just the right leaven of humanity: the regret of the lady for her dead lovers in *Chaitivel;* the idyllic glamour of the love scenes in *Lanval* (*Guingamor*); the pathetic attempt of the girl in *Les Dous Amanz* to reduce in order to make the burden lighter for her lover; the account of approaching daybreak in *Le Freine;* the naïveté of the breath-taking revelation in *Guingamor* that what has seemed to the happy knight three days in the company of his beloved is actually three centuries of mortal time—all this told with economy of detail, simplicity of direction, and, most important of all, a genius for poetic suggestiveness.

Although it may be an anticlimax, we must give attention to didactic and allegorical pieces in Anglo-French literature. Most of these works are in verse. Like the romance, the medieval allegory transcends frontiers of language. Of the many available representatives of this class, one or two call for more than casual attention. William of Waddington's *Manuel des Péchiez* is better known from the treatment given it in Robert Mannyng of Brunne's *Handlyng Synne* than for its original composition. As for Bishop Grosseteste (d.1253), he is more important as an Anglo-Latin than as an Anglo-French writer; but his *Le Chasteau d'Amour,* a mystical allegory of homiletic nature, is typical.

It is a fair castle, the castle of Love. Its rocky foundation is impressively colored in green, blue, and red; the castle itself is radiant white within. It is the body of the sweet maid Mary. [It is scarcely necessary to observe that all these colors have symbolic value. So do the towers, the turrets, the bailies, and the barbicans.] Its constable is Charity. It is a shelter against the raging foes triune—the world, the flesh, and the devil.

But then, as is all too often the case, the elaborately built allegory is sidetracked into argumentative discourse—this time on the reasons for the coming of Christ.

> God converses with the Son and the four Daughters of God—Mercy, Truth, Peace, and Right. Mercy hopes that imprisoned Man will be released from incarceration and servitude; Truth and Right object; Peace suggests the payment of a ransom. Christ offers to sacrifice Himself for the release of Man.

The poem, not the best of Grosseteste's works, is rescued from mediocrity by its lyrical tone, its sincerely devout mood, and its pleasant avoidance of the prolix.

Into this category falls one major work to be mentioned again, John Gower's *Mirour de l'Omme* (*Speculum Meditantis*). It is enough to insist here that there is a great deal of this literature of edification in the writings of the period, whether allegorical, homiletic, or prophetic, in verse or in prose, in English, French, or Latin, or perhaps in all three. It soon becomes apparent that the Anglo-French literature, taken by and large, although it is in a sense a bypath of Middle English literature, remains an important and underestimated factor in the expression of the medieval mind in England.

4. The Anglo-Latin Writers

As the chief medium of the medieval literature of knowledge, Latin held sway well through the Renaissance. Even today, in shreds of academic ritual and in the preponderant Latinity of our learned vocabulary, we see the remains of this influence. In Middle English literature, Latin was the only language used in serious writing emanating from the Church and the universities; it was also the language of state and judiciary until the Middle Ages in England had nearly passed away; it was the accepted tongue of the physician, the philosopher, and the man of science in all their official utterances. This is to say that, as compared with both the vernacular and the Anglo-French, Anglo-Latin writings had academic prestige; but, while they made important contributions, they were restricted in scope.

At first the Middle English Anglo-Latin literature smelled of the lamp of the cloistered scholar. With the coming of the Friars and the founding of the universities, it took on the somewhat fresher atmosphere of the forum and study hall. Thanks to the efforts of priests and clerics, it even reached at times into the courts of nobility and royalty. Henry I of England was known as Beauclerc; but his descendant Richard I gave his intellectual interest to the troubadours, and the later Angevin kings do not impress posterity with their academic attainments. In effect, whereas Anglo-French literature and Middle English vernacular writings often had the feudal aristocracy for patrons, Anglo-Latin literature in this period was sponsored almost entirely by the Church and her spiritual and intellectual progeny.

The medieval academic mind is inextricably bound up with the theological and scholastic, usually found in combination. As early as the twelfth century there are, for example, the works of Anselm of Aosta (1033-1109), who may be regarded as the first of the great English Scholastics. He is a beautifully balanced representative of the devoted and orthodox theologian, with a keen, logical, cool mind. His tract on the Atonement, *Cur Deus Homo,* and his discourse on the Trinity, *De Fide Trinitatis,* both take the position that rational proofs must always be tested by the Scriptures; in brief, he becomes at once the complete medieval authoritarian—God is absolute Truth itself.

This identification of God with the sole Truth is the primary aim of the medieval scholastic mind. We shall have occasion to use the term "scholastic" more than once in the following pages. It is in reality a technical term that needs some definition. Scholasticism, based upon certain models of Greek philosophy, had its inception in the Palace School of Charlemagne. It laid emphasis first of all on the intellectual procedure of logical reasoning, or dialectics. It resulted in an elaborate system of Christian rationalism. Its grand purpose was to relate to God both man and nature, which constitute the world in which we live. As a secondary objective, it aimed at the reconciliation of philosophy (or human knowledge) and theology (the word of God). The cornerstone on which this magnificent structure of reconciliation was reared was the thesis that philosophy rests upon reason, while theology rests upon truth derived from divine revelation. But because God is the author of all truth, it is impossible to think that He could teach in the natural order anything that contradicts what He teaches in the supernatural order.

Gradually fields of knowledge other than that of abstract philosophy were worked into this rational system—problems of psychology, metaphysics, cosmology and natural science, and ethics. Individual Scholastics might differ on the extent to which reason was to be employed—Abélard, for example, believed that reason could actually explain matters of faith; Anselm, more mystical, denied that reason could penetrate such intangible mysteries. Yet all agreed on the underlying theory of knowledge, which taught that outside the mind there were things fundamentally universal that correspond to our universal ideas; moreover, they differentiated between sense knowledge (from which human wisdom was derived) and purely intellectual knowledge. Their general outlook on the world of nature was Aristotelian, but they insisted that the grand design of nature, its purpose and significance, was due immediately to the intelligence and provident author of nature, who is God.

It is nevertheless true that most works in Middle English literature are touched only remotely by scholasticism. The majority of the important writers evaded the problems that teased the Scholastics; consequently, it is much less satisfactory to attempt a study of Middle English writings by a "history of ideas" method than to study the literature of, let us say, the neo-classical period in this way. Men like Anselm, Duns Scotus, John of Salisbury, and William of Ockham are less important to a study of English literature than Chaucer, the Piers Plowman Poet, or the Pearl Poet. Anselm, Duns Scotus, and their colleagues belong primarily to a history of philosophy or theology; they are specialists, and there is little excuse for squeezing out Chaucer to make room for Albertus Magnus. No account of medieval Anglo-Latin writing, however, can ignore the Scholastics, even if their influence is, outside the domain of the clerical, vague and unimpressive.

Let us return for the moment, then, to Anselm. Although he was Italian born, he stands almost alone as an exemplar of early Norman clerical traditions, towering far above his immediate contemporaries. These contemporaries in England were for the most part Anglo-Latin chroniclers,[3] almost all of them falling strictly in the Anglo-Norman period. That the catalogue of these writers is so long is owing in part to the fact that the Normans wanted to justify themselves to the people of the country whose government they had seized. Besides, they were naturally acquisitive and intellectually eager; now that the land was theirs, they wanted to know its history, or what they imagined to be its history. Some of these chroniclers, therefore, went to *The Anglo-Saxon Chronicle* or Bede or Asser; some went to Germanic and Celtic legend; some drew upon their own fertile imaginations. The result is, of course, no better history as a whole than was served up by either the English vernacular or the Anglo-French chroniclers, although where there were so many there would always be an intelligent, conscientious exception.

It is no particular discredit to these earnest historiographers that we dismiss them here rather abruptly. There are too many more important figures, and even to the specialist in the Middle Ages, these men are but chroniclers who wrote in indifferent Latin about the events of their own time, men who had the special advantage of being contemporaries of many of the events about which they wrote, but who were for the most part devoid of a true sense of history, of the ability to evaluate their material and to bring it into perspective. The eleventh- and twelfth-century chronicles of Florence of Worcester, Ordericus Vitalis, Henry of Huntingdon, Ailred of Rievaulx, Roger of Hovedon, Ralph of Diceto, Richard of Devizes, and Gervase of Tilbury are negligible today for anything but scholarly perusal. Jocelyn of Brakelond inspired

[3] Such men were the straw from which the bricks were made. The fact remains that the term "Anglo-Latin," as applied to the writers of the twelfth and thirteenth centuries, is rather misleading. It is not possible to segregrate the Englishman writing in Latin from the Frenchman or the Italian or the German using the same linguistic medium, since they all belong to the clerical tradition. The standard histories of the Middle Ages inevitably emphasize this fact. Fortunately, these important so-called "minor" men and their "minor" works have been zealously sought out and carefully treated; see the bibliography to this chapter.

Carlyle to the writing of *Past and Present;* beyond that fact, he too can be ignored. William of Newburgh had perhaps the best historical sense of the time and applied this sense to some criticism of his contemporary colleagues. William of Malmesbury (1095?-1142), however, wrote with the most zest and the best feeling for the significance of his material; his *Gesta Regum Anglorum,* or *Chronicle of the Kings of England,* completed about 1140, is the most graphic account written in the century of the Norman Conquest. So far as schools of chronicle writing are concerned, the monastery of St. Albans produced two men, Roger of Wendover and Matthew Paris (d.1259), who stand out above the mass; their efforts established a historiographic tradition at St. Albans, which reached a terminus in the person of Thomas of Walsingham, who flourished in the first quarter of the fifteenth century. As for Matthew Paris, he is a biographer of note as well as a general chronicler. To him is attributed a life of Edward the Confessor and some lives of the abbots of St. Albans. His two important works, the *Chronica Majora* and the *Historia Minor,* extend to the middle of the thirteenth century and exhibit an independent grasp of details on the part of their author.

The entire business of medieval Anglo-Latin chronicling can be summed up in the work of three men, who contribute in turn the fanciful, the critical, and the compendious. If William of Malmesbury, Matthew Paris, and others among those just mentioned were sober historians in the main, Geoffrey of Monmouth certainly was not. Yet Geoffrey will live on when most of his contemporaries have been forgotten. He was born about 1100, probably of Welsh ancestry, became a Benedictine monk and ultimately Bishop of St. Asaph's, dying in 1154. Before 1135 he had written a book about Merlin, now presumed lost. He later associated this Welsh seer and magician with King Arthur in the *Historia Regum Britanniae.* This, Geoffrey's masterpiece, remains one of the most important works of medieval England. It was written between 1135 and 1147. Its ultimate source was Nennius's *Historia Britonum,* described earlier; but Geoffrey embellished this work with all manner of additions. It is at times impossible to decide when he was drawing upon British and Germanic legendry, general folklore, or his own highly romantic imagination. Suffice it to say that, on the evidence of surviving literature, Goeffrey virtually created Arthur as a hero of romance and set in motion the enormously complicated Arthurian romance cycles. Whatever the origins of Arthur and his company and whatever Geoffrey's motives in creating this legend, the fact remains that the more scholars penetrate into the saga of the great king who became the champion of all Christianity, the more directly the path leads to Geoffrey. Needless to say, Geoffrey did not initiate the whole legend; he had folk tales and ancient stories ready at hand, but he had the will and the ability to synthesize these into something new and remarkable.

To concentrate upon the Arthurian material in the *Historia Regum Britanniae,* it is evident that Geoffrey gave not less than 41 sections to the story of Arthur (Book 8, Chapter 19 to Book 11, Chapter 2 inclusive). From Uther's unchaste love for Ygerna, Duchess of Cornwall, comes the begetting of Arthur through the magic aid of Merlin. Ygerna's husband dies; she and Uther are married; Uther, after several successful wars, dies and is succeeded by Arthur. There is a splendid coronation. Immediately, however, Arthur must fight pagans and rebel subjects who do not accept the story of his magic birth. He conquers the Scots and the Picts, the Irish, Icelanders, Norse, as well as the inhabitants of southern Europe. He is meanwhile married to Guanhumara. The climax of his career comes with his war against the Romans, who claim tribute. He entrusts his kingdom to his nephew Modred, and eventually defeats the Romans under Lucius Tiberius. In the interim Arthur disposes of the notorious giant of Michael's Mount. But he dreams bad dreams; and his disturbed thoughts are justified. Modred usurps his throne in Britain, seduces Guanhumara, and foments rebellion against Arthur. Then comes the final great battle in Cornwall, with Modred's defeat and death, Arthur's mortal wounds, and his departure to Avalon to be healed. Gawain and Modred are the only important knights to be mentioned. Arthur is, it will be noted, fundamentally an epic hero.

If many others following Geoffrey saw fit to elaborate these already glamorous beginnings, it is but a tribute to the hardy elements of the first stock. And not only is Arthur to be traced in Geoffrey's chronicle; had it not existed, King Lear, Cymbeline, Sabrina, and Gorboduc would have been unknown to future writers, as would Old King Cole. So far as being a historian is concerned, however, Geoffrey was an impostor and a hypocrite, although a good publicity agent for the Norman and Angevin kings; his most discerning contemporaries recognized this, particularly Giraldus Cambrensis.

Gerald de Barri, or Giraldus Cambrensis (1146?-1220?), another Welshman, is a chronicler because of his works dealing with the conquest of Ireland by Henry II (1170). He was a chaplain of Henry, but he appears to us today primarily as a courtier, whose social ambitions were but poorly recognized. He touched elbows with many of the most prominent churchmen of his day; his life must have been rich if not unduly remunerative. For Giraldus was a flamboyant kind of individual —boastful, amusing, almost a Mercutio—but energetic and inquisitive. Indeed, he is no less interesting as a traveler than as a chronicler. His *Topographia Hibernica*, or *Topography of Ireland* (1187), together with his *Description of Wales* will testify to his own experiences; the first was the result of his travels in Ireland shortly after the conquest of that country, while the second was written after he had accompanied the jurist, Ranulph de Glanville, on a tour to preach the Third Crusade to the Welsh. In addition, Giraldus was a copious correspondent, orator, commentator, and poet, although some of the work ascribed to him is probably spurious. He was sufficiently devoted to his sacred profession to write *Gemma Ecclesiastica*, a book of instruction to Welsh priests. He remains a palpable personality at a time when such personalities are difficult to apprehend.

The trio of notable Anglo-Latin chroniclers is rounded out by Ranulph, or Ralph, Higden (d.1364), a Benedectine monk of Chester, whose *Polychronicon* was a universal encyclopedia of history, one of the most popular works of its kind written in medieval Europe, and the subject of a sprightly translation into the vernacular by John de Trevisa (1387).

Of course there were many other such writers who have

melted away into virtual oblivion. There were also some individuals who cannot be called chroniclers so much as commentators. If the age had been more aware of satire, they would be called satirists. In effect, they serve as a sort of bridge from the monastic and theological to the scholastic, yet their outlook is best described as generally humanistic.

The earliest of these is John of Salisbury (d.1180), a friend of Thomas à Becket and a pupil of the great scholar Abélard of Paris, a teacher and a Bishop of Chartres, author of a tract on statesmanship, the *Policraticus,* and a treatise on logic, the *Metalogicus.* The first of these has been called an encyclopedia of miscellanies; in its method it illustrates admirably the eclectic taste of the Middle Ages and the tendency among even its greatest writers toward the impressive yet superficial conception of learning and culture. Besides these works, John composed a history of the Popes, a life of Anselm, and a Latin lament for the saintly Becket. There is no doubt that John was the finest English humanist of his generation, and a list of the Latin authors with whom he was more or less familiar—Virgil, Horace, Ovid, Persius, Juvenal, Martial, Statius, Lucan, Cicero, Seneca, the older and the younger Pliny, Livy, Sallust, Suetonius, Valerius Maximus, and Quintilian—reads like a roll call of all the authors of Roman antiquity whom the most learned of the medieval scholars could be expected to know. Moreover, he knew some Greek. Chaucer, who was anything but a poorly read man, could do no better, and Chaucer came two centuries later. In the main, however, John's work was miscellaneous and his life was a versatile exercise of well-differentiated talents.

There are a few other men over whom one is sorely tempted to linger—Peter of Blois (d.1190), a learned pedant; Nigel Wireker, author of the *Speculum Stultorum,* an authentic satirist; Jean de Hauteville and his *Architrenius* ("Chief Weeper"), almost as mordant an observer as Wireker; Alanus de Insulis, or Alain de Lille (1114-1203), a portrayer of the academic life as well as of the wonders of nature; Geoffrey de Vinsauf, most celebrated prosodist and expert on rhetoric of his day; and Walter Map, or Mapes (fl.1200), one of those indispensable wits and gossipers who enliven any age. Fortunately, every age seems to produce one. He himself claimed

Welsh descent, but this claim is not universally accepted. He was Archdeacon of Oxford and something of a scholar to boot; his reputation was such, however, that he came to be saddled with the authorship of works ribald, gay, reckless, irreligious, and whimsical. He is scarcely to be considered the originator of Goliardic verse, of which more later. He is perhaps responsible for some miscellaneous Latin poems of no importance. But he certainly is the author of *De Nugis Curialium,* or *Courtiers' Trifles* (1180-93), which deserves to last as long as any single work from the last quarter of the twelfth century. It is not sufficient to call it merely the first and best of medieval bedside books. Walter is out to tell us what is going on in the courts of Henry II and of Richard I, and when we hear too much about the romantic aspects of Richard the Lion Heart, it is salubrious to read *De Nugis.* It is all unsystematic and untidy; the author is interested first and last in talking of important people he has met and of stories he has heard, some worthwhile, some inconsequential. He tells Welsh legends of demons, fairies, vampires, and condemned ghosts laid by the sprinkling of holy water. He tells the inhuman story of the necrophilic prince, from whose relations with his dead mistress there was born a Medusa head. He touches upon the theme of *Guingamor* in the legend of King Herla, where centuries pass in the twinkling of an eye. He relates tales with most realistic dialogue, such as the tale of Sceva and Ollo. He gossips prodigiously about the great Earl Godwin of Anglo-Saxon England, about the able Louis the Fat of France, about the worthless William Rufus of England. He tells of the origins of the Hospitallers, the Templars, the Cistercians, and other orders. To judge by his outspoken comments, he is bitterly censorious of the friars, except for the Carthusians. He is cynical about the venality of Rome, but he believes in ecclesiastical law and in the power of the clerks. In his social outlook he is obviously aristocratic to the point of snobbishness.

Of the individual pieces in *De Nugis,* however, none is more famous than the *Dissuasio Valerii,* or *Advice of Valerius to Ruffinus not to Marry,* which opens the fourth Division of the work. This piece is a direct source of some of the immortal sentiments expressed by Chaucer's Wife of Bath in her famous Prologue. The *Dissuasio* does not lend itself readily to outline; its structure is that of a series of wise saws attributed at one time or another to great men and scholars of antiquity, to whom women were anathema. Some of it is merely the age-old misogynistic jesting of the disillusioned man; some of it is wrapped up in the theological prejudice against women that poor Eve brought upon her sex. So it had been with the older cognate works on which Walter drew: the *Golden Book* (*Liber Aureolus*) of Theophrastus and St. Jerome's *Epistle against Jovinian*. The concluding paragraph of *De Nugis* is so typical of its author's saline, astringent manner that it is worth quoting in part:

Wishing, therefore, to save this witless pamphlet from being thrown into the mud from the mantel, I shall bid it hide in my company. I know what will happen after I am gone. When I shall be decaying, then for the first time it will be salted; and every defect in it will be remedied by my death, and in the most remote future its antiquity will cause the authorship to be credited to me, because, then as now, old copper will be preferred to new gold. It will be as now a time of apes, not of men; because they will deride the things of their present, having no patience with good men. In every century its own present hath been unpopular, and each age from the beginning hath preferred the past to itself; hence my times have despised me, because they could not despise my epistle. My merit saveth me from being moved thereby.

It is impossible to discuss here the various works in which Walter Map is supposed to have taken a hand; it is especially difficult to decide about his part in the development of the Arthurian legend. As the minor romancier and contemporary of Walter, Hugh of Rutland, observed sardonically, many men could lie as well as Map. It is therefore safer to disbelieve rather than to believe in his manifold products.

To go from Walter Map, courtier and wit, to Alexander Neckam is to return to the combination of monastic and scholastic, which is characteristic of the late twelfth century. Legend has it that Neckam's mother was wet nurse to Richard

the Lion Heart; and this legend is symbolically if not historically sound, in that the same supposedly naïve age produced
two men of ability thus widely dissimilar in tastes and achievements. Neckam was a professor at Paris and a miscellaneous
scholar. Although he was given to social treatises and didactic
reflections, as in his *Vita Monachorum* and his version of
Aesop's *Fables,* he was more effective as a perpetuator of the
old traditions of natural science. His masterpiece, *De Naturis
Rerum,* reminds one of a similar work by Bede; but Neckam
is more inclined than Bede to blend fact and fiction or to
garnish some accurate observation with the usual credulous
superstition. It was still too early for Neckam to have profited
by the efforts of the scholastic scientists of the thirteenth
century.

In regard to Anglo-Latin poetry of the period, the situation
is generally unsatisfactory, at least in the matter of authorship, putative or otherwise. So far as narrative poems in the
epic manner are concerned, there is a *Vita Merlini* (possibly
Geoffrey of Monmouth's missing *Book of Merlin*), which
shows the desire common to a few Anglo-Latin writers of the
time to wander in fresh meadows. So do the authentic *St.
Patrick's Purgatory* by Henry of Saltrey and the *Visio Philiberti.* The first of these, we have seen, was the source of
Marie de France's last known work; it has, moreover, a rous-
ing Middle English vernacular version, to be mentioned later.
The *Visio Philiberti* is a part of the common literature of the
Body versus the Soul, which is given its most effective treatment in a thirteenth-century vernacular poem of striking personality. In 1187 a certain Joseph of Exeter composed in six
books a very competent account in verse of the fall of Troy
and thereby contributed to the swelling medieval interest in
one of the great narrative cycles of all literature.

The best of the Latin lyric poetry in the Middle Ages was
international in scope and, of course, religious in substance.
These poems, as well as their often impressive secular companions, belong to a general discussion of the medieval lyric.
There is reason to suppose that secular love poetry of the
troubadour's variety sprang up in England after the advent of
Eleanor of Aquitaine as queen of Henry II. No satisfactory
survivals, however, have turned up. The Provençal influence

is seen in the more intellectual poetry of the debate: in the discourses between water and wine, between the heart and the eye, and particularly in *De Phillida et Flora,* where two young women argue the question whether their respective lovers, a soldier and a clerk, are either of them important in the scheme of things. To round out the poetic picture, it is on record that Latin miracle plays were performed at the royal court during the reigns of the Norman kings. The performances were not frequent, however, and no clear picture of their staging or production emerges.

The center of medieval scholasticism was Paris; England shone academically in the reflected light of the University of Paris and of the Sorbonne until the Middle English period was more than half gone. In England there was no Thomas Aquinas (*c.*1225-74), greatest of medieval theologians; or no Albertus Magnus (1193-1280), the Universal Doctor, although Alexander of Hales (d.1245) made an effort to reduce medieval learning into a vast Novum Organum with his *Summa Theologiae.*

One of the followers of Alexander of Hales, and a far greater man, was Robert Grosseteste (1175-1253).[4] He was a native of Suffolk, but will always be associated with Oxford and Lincoln. At Oxford he was an omnivorous reader and a tireless student, preparing commentaries on the treatises of Aristotle, a translation of the *Ethics,* not completed until 1244, and several discussions and translations of the works of the Church Fathers. He was obviously acquainted with Greek and Hebrew and was as well an unusual Latin scholar. He was also versed in natural science and in medicine. While at Oxford he held an office that corresponded to that of Chancellor at the University of Paris. Later he became Bishop of Lincoln. Undoubtedly one of the most prolific of the scholastic writers, he had a most uncommon range of interests; to the type of work already mentioned one must add treatises on mathematics, theological polity, and agriculture, as well as practical Church politics. He seems to have been a lover of music, if not actually a musician. His influence upon subse-

---

[4] Grosseteste must obviously be considered among the Anglo-French as well as the Anglo-Latin writers; reference has already been made to his *Chasteau d'Amour.*

quent English learning was profound. Not only was this influence felt in the normal channels of the Church; he gained the respect of such a comparatively hard-headed man of science as Roger Bacon. Matthew Paris's noted tribute to Grosseteste is well worth repeating:

> He had been the rebuker of Pope and king, the corrector of bishops, the reformer of monks, the director of priests, the instructor of clerks, the patron of scholars, the preacher of the people.

The many-sided aspects of Grosseteste's talents, which make even carefully selected quotations sound somehow unfair to those talents, can be illustrated to a certain extent by comparing his *Compendium Scientiarum* and his *Hymn to the Virgin and Son*. The *Compendium* was the great compilation of knowledge in Grosseteste's day; in fact, it is an encyclopedic classification of the wisdom of the thirteenth century. Except for Roger Bacon's various *opera*, it is the most important English contribution to medieval science. The *Hymn to the Virgin and Son*, on the other hand, is lyrical and impassioned. We have already noted the mystical qualities of his *Chasteau d'Amour*. Still another side of Grosseteste is revealed in his *Letters*, addressed to friends, princes, and potentates. At times he sounds like a premature Martin Luther, as when he protests to Pope Innocent IV against the appointment of the Pope's nephew to a prebend of Lincoln: "Filially and obediently, I decline to obey, I oppose, I rebel." He was a lifelong foe of the legal and illegal plundering that both Church and State carried on among the lesser nobility and among the commoners; It is no mere coincidence that he was a personal friend of the rebellious Baron Simon de Montfort and that he could speak with affirmation of the "community of the whole kingdom." Such seemingly nationalistic sentiments sound strange against the feudal background of the thirteenth century, even if that feudalism was becoming decadent. For it must be remembered that Grosseteste lived in the time of the signing of Magna Charta but did not live to see the Great Parliament of 1295. Hence he becomes a prophet of English unity, of the rise of the commoners, of the decline of the Church and of the feudal state.

Of Grosseteste's great contemporary, Roger Bacon (1214?-1294?),[5] there is only this to be said: from the point of view of the modern scientist, he was the greatest of all medieval scientists; indeed, the only one with a prevailingly modern, inductive method. Yet he was plagued by the medieval passion for synthesis, with which his *Opus Majus,* his lesser *Opus Minus* and *Opus Tertium,* and his individual tracts, *De Vitiis Contractis, Questiones de Plantis,* and *De Coloribus,* are chiefly concerned.

But the works of Roger Bacon and even of the greatest of English theologians, Duns Scotus (1265?-1308?), had an almost neglible influence upon English letters in the Middle Ages. For that matter, it is doubtful whether either of them is as valuable in a study of English literature as the obscure bibliophile Richard de Bury (1287-1345), bishop of Durham and tutor to Edward III. De Bury's *Philobiblon* may be only a liberal dillettante's praise of books for themselves; but it was the most eloquent of such encomia until the appearance of Milton's *Areopagitica.*

> In books I find the dead as if they were alive; in books I foresee things to come; in books warlike affairs are set forth; from books come forth the laws of peace. . . Books delight us when prosperity smiles upon us; they comfort us inseparably when stormy Fortune frowns on us. . . What pleasantness of teaching there is in books, how easy, how secret! How safely we lay bare the poverty of human ignorance to books without feeling any shame! They are masters who instruct us without rod or ferule, without angry words, without clothes or money. If you come to

[5] To appreciate the true position of Roger Bacon, it is necessary to know something of the knowledge possessed by the Middle Ages concerning the world of natural phenomena; see particularly R. Steele, "Roger Bacon and the State of Science in the Thirteenth Century," Ch. 3, Vol. II of *Studies in the History and Method of Science,* edited by Charles Singer, Oxford, 1921. A fuller list of appropriate reference works bearing upon medieval science will be found in the bibliography to this chapter.

them, they are not asleep; if you ask and inquire of them, they do not withdraw themselves; they do not chide you if you make mistakes; they do not laugh at you if you are ignorant. O books, who alone are liberal and free, who give to all who ask of you and enfranchise all who serve you faithfully!

Seldom, indeed, do we meet with such a romantic expression of the joys of human knowledge. The enthusiasm of *Philobiblon* is worthy of the Renaissance. It is not typical of the Middle Ages to commit itself thus to the enjoyment of reading for its own sake. Certainly to the Scholastic a book was a repository of knowledge; and knowledge, as we have seen, was ultimately from God. The book should therefore be written and read wisely, as a means of communication between Heaven and Earth. Yet Chaucer gives us a delightful picture of his own love of reading—obviously for its own sake; and we can rest assured that many others besides the great narrator in medieval literature derived the same pleasure from the written word.

By the middle of the fourteenth century, the monastic heyday had spent its force; scholasticism had gone into a slow decline, not to be revivified until the humanism of the Renaissance had given the necessary blood transfusion. William of Ockham (1270-1349), Walter Burleigh (1275-1345), and Thomas Bradwardine (1290-1349) showed a spreading rebelliousness not only against the teachings of their master Duns Scotus but also against the institutions of the Church itself—a rebelliousness that came to full flower in Wycliffe. In retrospect, we see that the Anglo-Latin literature of the Middle Ages was dedicated primarily to the quest for the sojourner Truth. It was an attempt to reach a New Jerusalem through a study of mankind in terms of God and the Devil; by an examination of the world as it exists, a manifestation of God and His adversary; by vision, homily, precept, and the appeal to authority. By using a language common to the intellectuals of all Christendom, Anglo-Latin writers achieved a cosmopolitanism that English literature was not to know again until the twentieth century. In fact, the whole medieval world was but further evidence that all—Pope and baron, soldier and yeoman, commoner and king, Walter Map and Duns Scotus—were *filii Dei,* sons of God.

5. The Middle English Romances

In the ninth and tenth centuries, and for some two hundred years thereafter, were composed the French epic poems known generically as *chansons de geste.* These were rather polite examples of fairly short heroic epics; and one of them, the famous *Chanson de Roland,* is customarily recognized as the French national epic. Most of these *chansons de geste* dealt with the great Carolingian epic cycle, although subsidiary legends like *The Four Sonnes of Aymon* and *Huon of Bordeaux,* which developed late, could almost be called independent. These pieces were primarily martial and masculine (although Roland is given a fiancée, she appears in the text of the poem only long enough to drop dead when she hears of Roland's passing). It is most probable that poems analogous to the French *chansons de geste* originated in England during the eleventh century, if not earlier. Perhaps *The Battle of Brunanburh* and *The Battle of Maldon* may be considered representative of the genre. Such poems would naturally have dealt with Saxon or other Germanic heroes. Unfortunately, these have not survived in any number sufficient to justify generalizations on the matter. Very likely, however, in the occasional allusions to Hereward the Wake or to Wade and his magic boat we may be seeing their ghosts; and almost certainly some of the chivalric romances of later date and of an origin apparently humbler than that of the romances from the royal entertainment hall owe their beginnings to these hypothetical Anglo-Saxon *chansons de geste.* At about the same time—that is, from the ninth to the twelfth centuries—similar pieces were composed in Irish, Breton, and Welsh.

The French *chansons de geste* were for the most part from Normandy, Picardy, and the Ile de France. Analogous stories from the south of France—from Aquitania, Anjou, and especially from Provence—took on a somewhat different cast. Probably the comparative proximity to Rome and the close influence of classical story are partial reasons for this difference; on the other hand, certain individuals who admired tales from Rome, such as William, Count of Poitiers (*c.*1100), and his poet followers, may have shaped the Provençal form of epic to their own desires. At any rate, the debt of these southern French writers to the storytellers of Greece and Rome (whom they would know, of course, through Latin sources only) is very real and accounts in part for the name of the type of story they evolved—the Roman story, or the romance. (The word *romance* was applied at first to the vernacular itself, then to a composition written in the vernacular, as distinct from Latin works, then to the type of composition under discussion.)

Thus it came about that the early medieval romances grafted upon the heroic deeds of arms of the *chansons de geste* the no less exciting deeds of love as typified in southern story, across which fell the shadow of the Roman poet, Ovid, prince of storytellers and an authority on the techniques, remedies, and significance of love. The warrior-knight serves his king and sovereign; but he serves also his ladylove, who is a symbolic sovereign, and owes to her the feudal duties of homage and service, in return for which she may grant him her love. As for the service, it may be a matter of rescuing the lady from peril; it may be a greater matter of fighting for some ideal in the name of the lady. The mutual love of knight and lady is always a sacred thing that must never be defamed.

Here the presence of women in the medieval scene asserts itself most powerfully. It is no accident that the two greatest patrons of the chivalric fashion during its literary adolescence should be two great ladies, one of them, Eleanor of Aquitaine, a queen of England. Women in general prefer the story of love to the story of battle; they have always preferred a knightly hero to an honest but socially remote epic champion like Beowulf. Besides, the courtly lady of the Middle Ages had very little in the way of romance to console her; she was a marriageable commodity with political value. Very likely her best opportunity for emotional experience lay in illicit affairs. Whatever the cause, the chivalric romance contains a large element of the illicit; the heroine is either married or spoken for by someone other than the knightly hero, at least in most instances. Consequently we are confronted by the diverting paradox of a story which glorifies and idealizes sexual love, which concedes without moral comment the presence of the technically illicit, but which is obliged to resort to the clandestine in order to protect the lady's name, although she is being ennobled by her experience. So in the two most famous love affairs of medieval romance—those between Lancelot and Guenevere and between Tristan and Isoude—the husband is always inconveniently lurking at hand, nearly always, it must be added, in blissful ignorance of the true situation. One is reminded of the obscure observation of the unknown critic who said that there were only three story plots in the world, and the eternal triangle made two of them.

No doubt the enthusiastic praise of the Virgin noted in many writers of the tenth and eleventh centuries and the obvious increase in importance of the Mother of God in medieval ritual had much to do with the growth of the social importance of women in the later Middle Ages. At the same time, it must not be supposed that the Church, the custodian of public morals and even of public thought at this time, could sympathize whole-heartedly with the chivalric movement, which was essentially secular. In effect, the Church was opposed to what it considered the adulterous story of Tristan and Isoude and what these lovers represented. It was too canny, however, to forbid the audiences at the courts of Marie de Champagne or Eleanor of Aquitaine to read or listen to such stories, if indeed it would have been able so to prevent them. Instead, the Church inspired the writing of romances similar to the chivalric romances but more moralistic and didactic. Some of the best medieval romances, in fact, are of the category of the moral romance (or anti-romance). Occasionally their didacticism is masked; at other times it is undisguised, and then the favorite device is that of allegory. It therefore becomes necessary to counterbalance the chivalric romance with the moral and allegorical romance, and to pose Lancelot, Tristan, or Parthenope of Blois against Perceval, Galahad, or the Gawain of *Sir Gawain and the Green Knight*.

So much for the skeletal outline of the genesis of the medieval romance. It is a complex organism, exhibiting almost everywhere—in the audience as well as in the story—the presence of women and looking always to the French for

models. The earlier romances up to the year 1300 or there-
abouts were probably intended to be delivered orally. They
were in verse, usually in the typical French octosyllabic
couplet (although there is a good deal of elaborate experimentation in the later stages), and they were recited or
chanted by a professional entertainer, the minstrel or troubadour. Some romances of the early period had a strophic
structure, and a musical setting of some kind seems occasionally to be presumed. Others adopted a mixture of lyric and
informal, almost conversational, prose narrative—the so-
called *chante-fable,* represented by that gem of French romance, *Aucassin et Nicolete.* In the West Midland of the
fourteenth century, the romances, along with other types of
literature, assumed in verse the alliterative long line, which
marked the "alliterative revival." Eventually—it is most uncertain when—romances were circulated in manuscript and
were read in the private hall or bedchamber. This was certainly true by the fourteenth century. Indeed, we should like
very much to know in what manner the effective poems of
Chrétien de Troyes (*fl.*1175) or of Marie de France were
actually meant to be enjoyed. With the introduction of the
romance written to be read, it was not long before it appeared
in prose form, and, as will be seen, all romances were basically prose in form by the end of the Middle Ages.

It is hardly practicable to attempt here any complete list of
even the Middle English vernacular romances. Enough can be
said, however, to make clear the essential commonplaces of
story and situation that enabled this form of fiction to hold
its ground for a good four hundred years, and something can
be said about the origins of the important cycles of medieval
romance. The classic comment by a contemporary is that
made by the late-twelfth-century French cleric Jean Bodel:

> Ne sont que trois matières a nul home entendant,
> De France, et de Bretagne, et de Rome la grant . . .

which suffices even yet as a rough classification. We are to
understand from this statement that even in the Middle Ages
it was recognized that there was a French, a British, and a

classical background to medieval story. The chief objection to Bodel's classification is that he makes no distinction between the Celtic and Germanic in his term "de Bretagne"; and while the Celtic elements, through the complicated tapestry of the Arthurian romances, are far more glamorous and influential upon the fiction of posterity, the ruder Germanic elements cannot be disregarded.

What we call the "matter of England," for example—the romances of presumably Germanic source—is especially distinctive. Half a dozen leading Middle English romances fall into this category, and each one has some sort of progeny in the form of later romances, often in prose. They also appear in some cases as ballads, which are but shorter, more popular treatments of individual episodes from the romances. All of these Middle English romances of Germanic setting have, of course, French counterparts that are probably in every instance the original romance, although this point is debatable. Furthermore, most of the romances of this group are slightly older than many others.

It is not unlikely that the Middle English romances *King Horn, Havelock the Dane, Guy of Warwick, Bevis of Hampton, Athelston, William of Palerne,* and probably *Eger and Grime,* all go back to Anglo-Saxon *chansons de geste* of the tenth, eleventh, and twelfth centuries; *William of Palerne,* which has a foreign setting, survives in a poem of much later date, and *Eger and Grime* belongs to the time of the Renaissance. These Anglo-Saxon *chansons de geste* would probably have been shorter, rougher, more military and "epic" and less amoristic than the extant romances. This, however, is mere conjecture, since the romances in question had already assumed the general contours of the chivalric romance, although the craftsmanship of the authors was less sure of itself. This implies that the writers of these romances were not polished entertainers, and although they may have exhibited their wares in the courtly hall, they more likely turned to the courtly staircase and perhaps descended to the courtly kitchen, there to delight the squires and serving-wenches. A general air of simplicity hangs over most of these romances. The heroines, for example, are more forthright here than in the Celtic and

Continental romances: Rimenhild, Felice, and Josian bear little resemblance to Isoude or, for that matter, to charming little Nicolete. They tend to show their love most obviously:

> She loved so this Horne Child
> That almost she wexed wild.

At the same time, there are the usual courtly vows, the conventional fights and adventures, the same happy reunions and reconciliations at the end.

King Horn (*c.*1225-50) tells in typical octosyllabic couplets the story of young Horn, dispossessed of his heritage by Saracens, winning fame and reputation in foreign lands, loved through thick and thin by the princess Rimenhild, eventually winning back his kingdom—the characteristic "male Cinderella." This romance is, furthermore, a kind of classic example of the development of a romance cycle. Thus, the somewhat younger *Horn Childe and Maiden Rimnild* keeps the main outlines of *King Horn,* but all the straightforward crudeness and vigor of the original have begun to evaporate. Not only is this romance poorly written, verbose, and trivial, so as to deserve richly the dubious honor of being included in Chaucer's satirical *Sir Thopas,* but it is also swamped with incidental and descriptive minutiae, such as accounts of food and drink, of clothing and armor; in other words, it illustrates the typical late romancier's weakness for the specific. Again, *Hind Horn,* a popular ballad found in the great collection of English and Scottish popular ballads edited by Francis J. Child,[6] shows how incidents from a well-circulated romance could seep down into the lower crust of society, there to be celebrated by some humble Walter Scott. This aspect of medieval narrative must be touched upon later. Finally, it should be noted that a fifteenth-century prose romance, *King Ponthus and the Fair Sidone,* is a reworking of the Horn story, apparently drawn from the French romance. *King*

---

[6] *The English and Scottish Popular Ballads,* 5 vols., Boston, 1882-98. The general reader, however, will find a one-volume edition (Boston, 1904) containing the well-known essay by George L. Kittredge a convenient reference. *Hind Horn* is No. 17 of the collection.

Ponthus as a romance is immaterial, but it is elaborately developed as a handbook for gentlemen. In other words, the *King Horn* cycle exhibits admirably the two-headed nature of the medieval romance as entertainment and as instruction, and also the fact that the stories, while intended basically for aristocratic audiences, were not necessarily unknown to the people as a whole.

The Lay of Havelok (*c.*1300) is another romance of the "male Cinderella." It is a kind of municipal epic, in that it established a heroic legend concerning the founding of the town of Grimsby. It is a tale of a young prince, Havelok, cast out by a wicked usurping uncle, and of Goldborough, a young princess tyrannized over by an equally wicked foster father. Havelok is befriended by Grim the fisherman (possibly the same figure that appears in the late *Eger and Grime*), and rises from a lowly station to marry Goldborough, who, ironically, has been handed over in marriage in order that she may be socially degraded. Ultimately Havelok and his bride regain the throne of Denmark, and the villains are punished. His return to royal prestige is rapid. It is possible that he has an origin in history—the two most frequently suggested prototypes in real life are Olaf Trygvasson, the noted Danish Viking of the tenth century, and the more shadowy figure of Olaf (Anlaf) Cuaran; but it was even more likely Reginwald, uncle of Anlaf Cuaran, who flourished in the ninth century.

The same kind of historical genesis is possible in the case of *Guy of Warwick,* a medieval romance that had the widest currency in the Middle Ages, although to a modern reader it is insufferably wordy and dull. The Middle English version, written later than the French, dates from about 1300. Guy may be Wigod of Wallingford, a courtier in the time of Edward the Confessor. As he appears in this romance, however, he is a thoroughly conventional romance hero. In the first part of the story he is socially inferior to the heroine Felice, but by feats of arms he wins her hand. In the second part Guy turns to religion in an approved medieval manner: he becomes a pilgrim and journeys to the East, fighting Saracens on the way, eventually returning to England as a hermit and dying in the odor of sanctity. Perhaps the most striking passage in the poem is that dealing with Guy's fight against the

African giant Colbrand, who is a champion for the Danes under Anlaf (Trygvasson). The romance, however, is a hodgepodge. Its popularity is shown, nevertheless, by the fact that the story had various reincarnations in subsequent generations. There is a medieval sequel, *Reinbrun, Gy Sone of Warwike,* for Guy is one of the two or three romance heroes to have a warrior son. There are short, balladlike pieces from the Renaissance or later—*Guy and Phillis, Guy and Colebrande, Guy and Amarant*—two or three long versions from as late as 1630; and the account may be closed with mention of the *Speculum Guy,* which takes the religious, ascetic side of Guy and makes it into a manual of ethical and spiritual conduct.

Another very popular romance, *Bevis of Hampton,* also from about 1300, a piece of undoubted French or Anglo-French source, is fully as incoherent as *Guy of Warwick,* although it is much more sprightly. The feature of this story is the formidable lady Josian, who has about her some aspects of the Unapproachable Female like Atalanta or Brunnhilde, even if her aloofness toward men lies chiefly in her uncompromisingly monogamous nature. Having given her love to Bevis, and having been forced into a loveless marriage with another man, she thinks nothing of hanging her new husband on their wedding night. Both *Bevis of Hampton* and *Guy of Warwick* are pilloried in Chaucer's *Sir Thopas,* not without reason.

It is unfortunate that more attention cannot be given here to *Athelston* (*c.*1350). The central theme of this terse, melodramatic, and uncourtly romance is the conflict between King Athelston of Wessex and his Archbishop of Canterbury over the intrigue of a treacherous courtier, a conflict that reminds one inevitably of the collision between Thomas à Becket and Henry II, or the less known quarrel between Stephen Langton and King John.

As for *The Tale of Gamelyn,* it had the most distinguished history of any of the English medieval romances in the present category. It is a vigorous yarn, dating from about 1350, concerning the career of Gamelyn, who is abused by his elder brother and the sycophantic clergy who have attached themselves to the latter. Gamelyn is finally able to assert himself,

attacking the brother and the hostile clergy, cracking many
of their crowns, and then taking refuge in the woods, where
he becomes another Robin Hood. He is eventually reconciled
with the king and is exalted above his brother. As a final
reward, it is said that he got himself a fair wife; but courtship
does not enter into the story. Instead, we have a lusty tale of
the people, not refined in any sense. The kinship with Robin
Hood is implicit in the fact that Gamelyn appears in the cycle
of Robin Hood ballads as Gamelyn, Gandelyn, or Gamwell—
later as Scarlet. *The Tale of Gamelyn* is, in other words, an
excellent example of a romance in name only, which originated among the poorer popular minstrels who made full use
of the material of folk tales, notably in their presentation of
the hero as a "male Cinderella," a wrestler of talent, a be-
friender of the common man. As such, it is linked with *King
Horn* and with *Havelok,* although it is even less aristocratic
than either. One interesting point is that it survives in the
manuscripts of Chaucer's *Canterbury Tales;* but it is clearly
not Chaucer's work. Perhaps Chaucer had planned to write
a version and assign it among the Canterbury pilgrims to the
Cook, for the manuscripts sometimes refer to it as "The
Cook's Tale of Gamelyn." It would have been an appropriate
choice for the earthy Cook, too, because the piece is unsophisticated but lively and forthright, with plenty of horseplay
and scrimmaging, animal spirits and crudeness. Its vitality
is apparent in the fact that it survived through ballad lore to
reappear in Thomas Lodge's *Rosalynd* in the Elizabethan Age,
and to furnish the background for at least the first part of
Shakespeare's *As You Like It.*

William of Palerne is a clear example of the alliterative
revival of the fourteenth century; it is, in fact, one of the
earliest of these alliterative poems. In its story of the lovers
who elope into a series of trials and tribulations, in which they
are aided by a magnanimous werewolf, the romance comes
closer to the old Greek romances than do any of the pieces in
this so-called Germanic group. It has a few distinctive points
and is reasonably well told; but much of its narrative is of the
run-of-the-mill variety. As for *Eger and Grime,* it is as much
Celtic as Germanic, with its giants, its other world, its rather
grotesque fancy. The active Horn, the athletic Havelok, the

champion Guy, the rough Athelston, the boisterous Gamelyn —they are the ones who make up the real criterion of the "matter of England."

From the morass of speculation and investigation in which scholars have for generations been struggling, there can be collected only a few facts about King Arthur that cannot be hotly disputed by certain factions, and even those few facts may conceivably be discounted in the future: first, although the historical authenticity of Arthur is still elusive, there is no denying the probability that some such person actually lived and boasted at least a local following; second, there is obviously an Arthurian epic tradition; third, the Arthurian legend had a Celtic origin and was first circulated in Celtic lands. The entrance of Arthur into the pages of literature coincides with the brief account of the deeds of Arthurus, *dux bellorum*, in the *Historia Britonum* attributed to Nennius (*c*.800). It has been seen, however, that the *Historia Britonum* is a compilation of the traditions of several generations. Thus the passage mentioning Arthur may possibly have originated as early as 660 or 675. Gildas, writing his *Book of Gildas* in the early sixth century, would be nearest in point of time to the alleged Arthur; yet he says nothing of the hero. But Gildas is at best more of a Jeremiah than a Josephus, and he tacitly confirms the statement later found in Nennius that the Britons waged a bitter and temporarily successful fight against the invading Saxons. The *Historia Britonum* names twelve battles, culminating with the Battle of Mount Badon (*c*.500), whereby Arthur achieved epic fame, inflicting upon the Saxons a defeat so severe that there was ever afterward peace in his time.

Arthur, therefore, bears every sign of being authentic—an actual savior of his people in a time of emergency, a fit subject for epic treatment, which came about in the inscrutable way that epics originate. It is clear that legends about him and his followers sprang up on Welsh soil. The most accessible account is that in the Welsh medieval legend *Kilhwch and Olwen*, in *The Mabinogion*. Arthur's followers here were a rude and fantastic lot. There is no doubt, however, about the genuineness of the Welsh Arthurian epic tradition or about the logical development of Arthur as a national champion.

Presumably this Arthurian saga flourished on Celtic terrain between the sixth and the twelfth centuries. It was probably carried over to Brittany by Welshmen who emigrated in the ninth century, and having been implanted on the Continent, it grew and prospered.

The great determining figure who shaped the destiny of this Arthurian material, however, was Geoffrey of Monmouth, whose *Historia Regum Britanniae* has already been mentioned. It would seem at first glance that it was an open-and-shut case of a single author's devising a story and casting his influence over all later treatment of that story. However, it is actually not so simple as that. Geoffrey undoubtedly adapted his material with imagination and effective narrative display, and it is true that he gave the Arthurian legend its strongest impetus toward the world of feudal chivalry. Still, there was a good deal of vital epic stuff already in existence on which he could draw—indeed, some of the details, such as the Round Table itself, an old Welsh folk motif, he actually saw fit to ignore. To assign to him, therefore, full credit for having invented the story of Arthur is to obscure the true situation. The fact is that the Arthurian legend attained its great success through a variety of factors—a popular hero and an attractive story, an able literary sponsor, and successive generations of sympathetic audiences.

It is easy to follow the career of Arthur. Nearly everything in medieval romance dedicated to the portrayal of the king in his epic state stems from Geoffrey of Monmouth. The Middle Ages, in fact, seemed content to draw Arthur as a sovereign of mysterious, illegitimate birth, who wins his throne and maintains it, extending his power and prestige by a series of military achievements. He is married to Guenevere (Guanhamara) and loses her to Modred or to Lancelot. He defeats and kills Modred but is wounded and passes to Avalon, whence, according to many, he will return when there is need of him. The grandiose conception of Arthur as a perfect knight and king, the embodiment of virtue, is never more than implied in the medieval legend. Indeed, the king is soon subordinated in popular interest to his knights; he remains a figurehead to be taken for granted. At times he is ineffective and childish; there is no doubt that he, like Charlemagne and

Robin Hood, suffers a typical weakening, an "epic degeneration," as time goes on. The deeds of his great knights—
Gawain, Lancelot, Tristan, and the questors for the Grail—
are too much for him.

Geoffrey's account was translated into French in Gaimar's
Estorie des Engles (*c.*1150), now lost. A few years later, the
Anglo-French poet Wace, in his *Roman de Brut,* developed
the story into a chivalric phase—he elaborated details, infused
the spirit of chivalric lore, made the Round Table known to
subsequent writers, and introduced the idea of the return of
Arthur. The true breadth of Arthur as a British hero, however,
is best delineated by Layamon in his *Brut* (*c.*1200), an important poetic chronicle and legendary history, to be discussed
later. This vigorous narrative is more readable than Geoffrey's
Historia; it makes much of the Round Table and of the latter
days of Arthur; moreover, it deepens the atmosphere of magic
that surrounds both Arthur's coming and his passing. The
Brut has not succumbed to the French passion for Lancelot.
Gawain appears, as do Bedivere and Kay, but the story is
still that of Arthur, the generous champion, a true epic hero
smoothed at the edges, no braggart, but chivalrous and sensitive. The sources of the *Brut* have never been fully revealed.
Much was derived from Wace; but Layamon's scope is broad,
and the inference arises that he invented a good deal of his
material and was, in fact, a much better creative artist than
is commonly associated with the year 1200 in English literature.

Aside from Layamon's contribution, only one other Middle
English account of Arthur is effective. We shall disregard the
chronicles of Robert of Gloucester, Robert Mannyng, and
Thomas Bek; a longish late ballad, *The Legend of King
Arthur;* and, for the moment, Malory's *Morte Darthur.* A
long romance, *Morte Arthure,*[7] is graphic; better still is the
fact that it concentrates upon the latter days of the king, for
the symbolic breaking up of this great system of chivalry has
always appealed most strongly to writers of saga and has

[7] This romance must be distinguished from Malory's *Morte Darthur* and from the romance of the Lancelot cycle, *Le Morte
Arthure,* mentioned on page 115.

generally brought out the best poetry of which they are capable.[8]

The early years of Arthur's life, on the other hand, are bound up with the legend of Merlin. This famous practitioner of magic at Arthur's court is of pure Welsh ancestry. An account in the *Historia Britonum* of Nennius tells how Vortigern, that luckless British king who was swallowed up by Hengest and Horsa, attempted to establish an impregnable citadel. His magicians advised him that only the blood of a boy born without a father could sufficiently hallow the site of such a citadel as to make it invincible. The boy, Ambrosius, discredits the magicians by revealing two subterranean dragons, one red and one white, who are fighting a mortal combat. The red dragon puts the white one to flight; this Ambrosius interprets as an omen of British victory. Ambrosius, the wonder-boy, who may or may not be the result of a confusion in legend with the historical Ambrosius Aurelianus, the last important figure in Roman Britain, is taken by Geoffrey of Monmouth and combined with the figure of Myrddin, a prophet and magician of the Welsh—thus creating the Merlin legend. Unfortunately, Geoffrey's *Book of Merlin*, as we have seen, has not survived; but the nature of its contribution is clear from references to Merlin in Geoffrey's *Historia*. A Latin *Vita Merlini*, of doubtful authorship, amplifies the character somewhat.

The full literary development of Merlin, however, comes from the Anglo-French poem *Merlin* by Robert de Boron (*c.*1200). While it is true that Geoffrey had associated Merlin with Arthur, it is de Boron's treatment of the story that gives us our present-day conception of Merlin. Robert de Boron's

[8] It is this theme of tragic disintegration that lends such effectiveness to Malory's final book that it is the most impressive section of *Morte Darthur*. Tennyson's *Idylls of the King*, a work of uneven merits but of consistent craftsmanship and often great beauty, is probably the most eloquent when it treats of the defeat of the ideals and objectives of the Round Table. In part the disintegration results from the disillusionment that attacks the whole Arthurian court after the scandal of Lancelot and Guenevere; in part it comes about from the inevitable wearing out of any order of society, no matter how high-minded its purpose.

work was turned into French prose and continued, in the thirteenth and fourteenth centuries, through the so-called "Vulgate" *Merlin* and the important *Livre du Roi Artus*. Some idea of the nature of the Merlin legend can be gleaned from the Middle English *Arthour and Merlin*, in two separate versions from the thirteenth and fourteenth centuries respectively. This is a complicated account of the immediate predecessors of Vortigern, proceeding to the reign of Vortigern himself; next we hear of the prococious boy of devilish origins, who is christened Merlin by a hermit. Merlin distinguishes himself in the presence of Vortigern by revealing the two dragons, but this time the white dragon, representing the Saxons, destroys the red dragon, representing the British; and so Merlin is a better prophet of history than the boy Ambrosius. Unfortunately Vortigern is slain, and Uther Pendragon succeeds him; it is he who founds the Round Table and secretly begets Arthur on Ygerne. Merlin, who has counseled Uther in all the latter's activities, reveals the true parentage of Arthur when this mysterious lad is able to pull the magic sword Excalibur out of the stone. Merlin is a master of ceremonies at Arthur's coronation; thenceforth he is at the right hand of the king. The English version does not carry us to the downfall of Merlin at the hands of the seductive Nimue (Vivian); this is the work of the French romanciers and does not appear in English literature until Malory's *Morte Darthur*.

Lancelot, the most famous of Arthurian knights, is of doubtful origins, but he owes his development to the French. He is first mentioned by Chrétien de Troyes, and the greatest influence in the perpetuation of his legend was the thirteenth-century French prose *Lancelot*, on which is based the only notable treatment of Lancelot in English, that in Malory's *Morte Darthur*. For Lancelot was never so popular in English literature as Gawain or as Arthur himself. Even if we assume that he was the immediate creation of Chrétien de Troyes, which is highly uncertain, he was nevertheless endowed with certain mythical attributes, probably to bring him into symmetry with other famous Arthurian heroes, such as Gawain and Tristan. He is of fairy birth, a foundling on the shores of a lake, whence the name "Lancelot of the Lake," sometimes applied to him. His propensity for wearing black, white, and red in tournaments has attracted the attention of folk-lorists.[9] It is enough to say, however, that the French authors reared Lancelot into a magnificent structure. On the Continent he surpasses Gawain, Perceval, and Tristan in prestige. There are ten Middle English romances about Gawain to two about Lancelot, until Malory tipped the scales in favor of Lancelot by using a French source. Yet eventually Lancelot's victory is won even in England, for in the later stages of medieval romance the English treat Gawain badly. Then when the legends of the Holy Grail have circulated to the point of the Quest of the Grail, it is Lancelot who, in spite of his sinful love for Guenevere, achieves the Grail, if only vicariously. It is actually won by Galahad, Lancelot's son.

So Lancelot, for all his fame, is celebrated in only two Middle English romances before the time of Malory. One of these, *Lancelot of the Laik*, is late and unusually inept. The other, bearing the rather confusing title *Le Morte Arthure*, is quite another matter. It tells vividly and even eloquently the case of the maid of Ascolot; the ultimate discovery of the love of Lancelot and Guenevere; the sad battle between Lancelot and Arthur, who, although he is the wronged husband, has to be urged on to combat with Lancelot through the angry proddings of the aggressive and boasting Gawain, whose brothers Lancelot had inadvertently killed. The conclusion of this romance narrates the passing of Arthur, who dies and is received in Heaven. Guenevere is buried with Arthur, and on that spot is founded the Abbey of Glastonbury. Here for the first time is an effective rendering of a story which has caught the poetic imagination of posterity and which has for that reason become one of the most famous acts in the Arthurian drama.

In the case of Gawain, the true hero of Middle English romance, we have a character who was originally a sun divin-

[9] Black is associated with death or the other world; white, with purity; red, with courage. The combination of these three colors is further associated with certain orders of knighthood, notably with the famous Teutonic Knights. A relic of the tradition is seen in the choice of these colors for the flag of modern Germany. The linking of Lancelot with a lake is symbolic of a supernatural origin for the hero. Fountains, wells, springs, and lakes are often related in folklore to the entrance to the other world.

ity: his particular epic attributes were that he possessed a magnificent sword—the original Excalibur—which gave off dazzling rays; he rode a splendid white steed, Gringolet; and his strength grew during the morning and declined after noon. Geoffrey of Monmouth made Gawain (Walwain) the chief support of Arthur. It is possible that some early French *lais* made him the lover of Guenevere before Lancelot; but Gawain is never so much a lover as an epic hero in the English pieces, although he has the perfect manners and courtesy demanded of a chivalric knight. Whether the unamorous nature of Gawain, as opposed to the fiery ardor of Lancelot, is in any way significant of the relative tastes of British and French is a difficult question. Once Lancelot had been exalted, of course, the decline of Gawain even in Britain could not be avoided. There can never be two champions in the same field.

Fortunately the Middle English writers were able to transmit a picture of Gawain before he was thus debased. Perhaps the finest of Middle English romances, *Sir Gawain and the Green Knight,* is an admirable memorial to the great Gawain, "gay, good, and generous, jolly and gentle and full chivalrous." Since this paragon of romance is probably the work of the so-called Pearl Poet, it will be discussed later. Let it suffice to remark here that the poem is a beautiful and serious double *exemplum* of the two great ideals of knighthood—physical valor and moral courage—handled with a touch of nature that lifts it above its contemporaries. That the story has both Celtic and French analogues will be scarcely surprising. The fact that the Pearl Poet was a West Midlander, and the additional fact that *Sir Gawain and the Green Knight,* along with some other pieces in the Middle English Gawain cycle, has a setting in the west of England—all the way from the Severn Valley to Carlisle in the far northwest—combine to suggest that the Gawain tradition lingered longest in that section of the country, just as the legend of Arthur seems to be centered in the southwest.

To pass over the two variants of *Sir Gawain and the Green Knight,* which are the early fifteenth-century *The Grene Knight* and *The Turke and Gowin,* is a simple business; perhaps it is a matter of momentary interest that in the grotesque and incomplete *The Turke and Gowin* are represented the legends of still another Celtic region, the Isle of Man. More important in glorifying Gawain is *Golagrus and Gawain,* a Scottish romance of about 1475. This poem recounts the successful siege of the castle of Golagrus by an expedition of Arthurian knights including Gawain, Kay, Lancelot, and the seldom seen Ywain. It is Gawain, however, who conquers the foe and brings him to submission before Arthur; but not before Gawain, to soothe the feelings of his defeated enemy, pretends that he himself has been vanquished by Golagrus. Of such is the kingdom of meek but valiant heroes. *The Awntyrs of Arthure at the Terne Wathelyne* presents Gawain in a long and inconclusive fight with one Sir Galleroune; but the main interest of the story is the apparition of Guenevere's mother, who comes from Hell to warn her daughter against lecherous living.

The best of Chrétien de Troyes's romances is probably *Yvain.* There is a fairly close Middle English translation and paraphrase of this work in *Ywain and Gawain* (c.1325). Although the art of the English poet is not the equal of his predecessor's, the romance is worth reading. It is full of incident, yet it is well integrated; and in some ways the narrative situations are uncommon. The profusion of incidents, in fact, may give the impression of an incoherence that is actually not there, although many a Middle English romance sins in that respect. To be noted especially is the magic fountain, a well-established symbol for the entrance to the other world; the romance is in effect a singularly poetic representation of the classical voyage to the lower world. Furthermore, the figure of Lunet is that of the "damsel errant," the messenger, the confidante, the generally helpful personage to be recognized in later fiction. The devoted lion is, of course, the hero of the old legend of Androcles. The combat of the two friendly champions, fighting in ignorance of each other's identity, is another commonplace. The madness of Ywain and his wanderings in the woods are stock motifs. This is not to say that Chrétien's original poem was merely derivative, but it illustrates strikingly the dependence that any writer of romance, however fresh his treatment, necessarily had upon the materials of traditional story.

Because it appears in two other distinct versions and in an effective popular ballad as well, *The Weddynge of Sir Gawen and Dame Ragnell* deserves brief notice. It is a late romance of the fifteenth century, based upon some older tale, perhaps a Breton *lai*. Underlying the whole is the folk motif of the Loathly Lady, a mortal woman laid under a spell and cursed with a hideous body until some mortal man redeems her by doing her will regardless of the effect upon himself. Since Chaucer's *Wife of Bath's Tale* is the best version of the story in Middle English, we shall meet this theme again. Gawain is here the real hero, who finds himself involved with a repulsive hag in order to save Arthur's life and who marries the beldame as a part of his knightly bargain, only to win in actuality a fair wife. It is to be observed that Arthur is placed in a difficult and embarrassing situation and seems incapable of breaking out of it by himself; all the vitality of action has passed to his knight. As for Gower's *Tale of Florent* in the *Confessio Amantis*, it is merely another version. The ballad, *The Marriage of Sir Gawain*, seems to be based upon *The Weddynge*. The union of Gawain and Ragnall was blessed by a son—according to *The Weddynge*, the boy is legitimate; according to the *fabliau*-like *The Jeaste of Syr Gawaine*, he is not. But this son has his own romance, *Libeaus Desconus*, or *The Fair Unknown*, which is an attractive but uneven and overlong romance, containing nearly every kind of narrative commonplace imaginable.

While Gawain had hitherto played a heroic and always moral role, he also appeared both in popular as well as comic forms. *The Jeaste of Syr Gawaine* has just been mentioned. *The Avowynge of King Arthur, Sir Gawan, Sir Kaye, and Sir Bawdewyn of Breaton* is a dull example of the tale of boasting, not at all comparable to the brilliant vaunts of the knights of Charlemagne in the analogous French *Pèlerinage de Charlemagne*. *Syre Gawene and the Carle of Carelyle*, however, has more to commend it.

The quartette of Arthur, Kay, Gawain, and Baldwin are obliged to spend the night at a churl's house. This churl is monstrous and incredibly boorish; he keeps a boar, a bull, a lion, and a bear as household pets. He takes a fancy to

Gawain and bestows his daughter upon the not unwilling hero for the night. It turns out in the morning that the churl has taken a vow that whoever spends the night at his house must do the churl's will or die; it has required twenty years to find guests who would be thus compliant. Now the churl will repent. He impresses Arthur, who finally makes him a knight of the Round Table, Sir Ironside. Gawain, as a concession to *la belle* Grundy, marries the daughter. The churl in contrition founds the abbey of Carlisle.

The story is told also in ballad.

Whereas Gawain had at least a semi-divine beginning and a long, varied history, Perceval had a meteoric career and, it must be admitted, a confusing one. Perceval represents the type of folk character best described as the Perfect Fool, or the innocent, completely naïve boy whose mind can be written upon as a slate. He has an obscure and uneventful boyhood, in which his native genius may flower undisturbed to burst upon an astonished world in a sudden frenzy of achievement. He is, in fact, a spectacular "male Cinderella." This was the early conception of Perceval; later he came to be regarded as the ideal type of knight to compete in the Quest of the Holy Grail, and it is in the legend of the Grail that he plays a major part. This, however, is not the case in either the Middle English *Sir Percyvelle of Galles* (*c.*1375) or the Welsh *Peredur,* from *The Mabinogion.* The French authors, beginning with Chrétien de Troye's *Perceval,* or *Le Conte de Graal,* and continuing through the prose romances of the thirteenth century, the *Perlesvaus* and *Perceval,* have been mainly responsible for the tradition of Perceval as a Grail hero.

Perceval, in fact, never struck much response from Middle English audiences; *Sir Percyvelle of Galles* is the only romance about him in the vernacular. It describes the fatherless hero, reared in the woods by his mother, one day meeting Ywain, Gawain, and Kay. They take him to Arthur's court, where he avenges the insult offered to the king by an intruding Red Knight—a bully who has brought about the death of Perceval's father. Perceval then embarks upon a series of knightly adventures, rescuing in particular the Lady Lufamour and achieving true knighthood, which he has ardently craved since his childhood. The noteworthy point is that the Perceval of the English romance is simple, generous, devoted, and unconquerable, but not sublime. One would never see in him the character of Wagner's Parsifal. Not so in the French romances, however; here he attains the Grail itself. Yet when Lancelot becomes the supreme Arthurian knight, even Perceval must yield to him. Although Lancelot is at first only the godfather of the marvelous boy Galahad, he is later made the actual father through a singularly ingenuous deception practiced on him by the daughter of the Grail-King Pelles. Indeed, if it had not been for the inconvenient fact of the affair with Guenevere, Lancelot would himself have attained the Grail.

The origins of the Grail legend are fully as obscure as those of the Arthurian saga itself, and its development is far more involved. It is impossible to reduce to brief dimensions the total ramifications of the problem. Out of a mass of narrative motifs—some pagan, some Christian—there was woven together, probably in Britain, the amazing legend that in the popular mind is associated as much as any one concept with the Middle Ages. From memories of heathen rites in the spring festivals of regeneration, such as the ancient festivals of Adonis and Thammuz—and with particular attention to details of similar Celtic observances—mingled with Christian symbolism and secular fantasy, there grew the idea of the magic vessel that could produce food, heal wounds and bodily illness, and purify the human soul. The synthesis of these various elements, to repeat, was probably accomplished in Celtic Britain. Was there some Geoffrey of Monmouth to act as the genius of this synthesis? He has not survived in history, if indeed he ever existed; but his patron, we suspect, would have been Henry II of England, who believed firmly in the power of the troubadour to stimulate, in religious as well as political ways, the prestige of the House of Anjou.

It is necessary to divide all Grail romances into two kinds—those dealing with the early history of the Grail (the Joseph of Arimathea sub-cycle) and those dealing with the Quest of the Grail (the Galahad-Lancelot-Perceval sub-cycle). An important fact is that although Britain was probably the cradle of the Grail legend, she seems to have been interested only in the beginnings of the saga, not the development. Before Malory in his *Morte Darthur* boiled down the massive French romances into something approaching a coherent narrative, there was only one important Middle English romance on the subject. We can overlook the pedestrian efforts of the fifteenth-century London skinner, Henry Lovelich, author of *The History of the Holy Grail* (*c.*1450), since he pales into insignificance beside Malory. The Middle English romance in question is the mediocre *Joseph of Arimathea* (*c.*1400), which explains how Joseph, who "begged the body of Jesus" after the Crucifixion, was imprisoned but was consoled in prison by Christ, who brought him the dish containing His blood shed on the Cross. Joseph became a missionary extraordinary, as did other members of his family. After several conversions in the East, attended by militant doings, they all came to England, bringing with them the holy vessel; here Joseph founded the Abbey of Glastonbury. This is, by 1400, an old story, and yet it is infrequently told by the continental romanciers. Perhaps the particular interest that the geography of Joseph's peregrinations must have held for Englishmen would account for the emphasis placed on Joseph of Arimathea in England.

Although the mercurial Walter Map was once given credit for the long French *Queste del Saint Graal,* which forms only a part of the enormous *Conte du Saint Graal,* it is unlikely that he had anything to do with it. The *Conte* is the first attempt to collect into a comprehensive whole the complex contributions to the legend made in the thirteenth century. When the Grail was lost through the neglect and sinfulness of its custodian, it behooved all the knights of the greatest king of Christendom to recover it if they could. One by one they fail, until only Galahad, Lancelot, Perceval, and Bors are left. The outcome, with Galahad in the running, could scarcely be in doubt. Lancelot comes into a room next to that in which the Grail is reposing and is struck senseless. Perceval, tempted by the Devil, is delayed in his quest, but is able to view the Grail and even to partake of it. The plodding Bors also is able to get into its presence. It is Galahad the peerless, however, who actually attains it, and he is forthwith translated to Heaven. If it did nothing else, the Grail legend, which came to be sponsored by the Church above all other legends in medieval romance, established the most powerful and famous tradition of moral story in the Middle Ages. But it accomplished more. There is pathos and nobility in the relations of Lancelot and Galahad, and a glowing, mystical effulgence bathes the Grail and all who come into communion with it.

Originally independent of the Arthurian saga, the legend of Tristan (Tristam, Tristram) has become one of the most celebrated cycles of Arthurian romance. The love of Tristan and Isoude is older than that of Lancelot and Guenevere. Tristan, in fact, is at least semi-mythical among Celtic heroes —he is the great hunter, the great musician, the great dragon killer, to which must be added the more modern accomplishments of skill at chess playing and at deceiving husbands. No doubt much of his saga was first told in short *lais,* of which Marie de France's *Lai de Chievrefueil,* or *Honeysuckle Lay,* would be one. In the twelfth century these *lais* were incorporated into longer poems, the most famous of which was by an Anglo-Norman writer named Thomas. Although Thomas's poem has been lost, there have been many redactions and paraphrases of it, the most notable being Gottfried of Strasburg's, which serves as a model for later continental versions of the story, although the credit for establishing the full-length narrative must remain Thomas's. Another version, based on Thomas, is the Middle English romance *Sir Tristrem,* written not long before 1300. Its author, allegedly Thomas of Erceldoune or Thomas of Chester, remains a vague and unsatisfactory identity, about whom a certain amount of legend has sprung up.[10] The continental versions

10 The existence of Thomas Chester (Chestre) or Thomas of Erceldoune, also known simply as Thomas the Rhymer, is attested by a few chroniclers; in the French *Scalacronica* (*c.*1360) he is named with soothsayers and prophets. His reputation as a seer was high in Scotland until the beginning of the present era. His legend, which parallels curiously the later continental career of Merlin, is celebrated by a popular ballad. (No. 37 in the Child collection), which has several variants, and in a longer poem, approaching in form a short romance. Child's own comment on the legend, given

were at least partially amalgamated in Sir Thomas Malory's *Morte Darthur,* and a few others grew up still later on the Continent, at least one of which, with a romantic ending, is fixed by Wagner in his great music-drama, *Tristan und Isolde.*

Tristan, a nephew of King Mark of England, is orphaned young and is befriended by the obscure Rouhand. While still a boy, he is kidnapped, but manages to get back to England, where his parentage is revealed to Mark, who knights him. We have here, of course, the traditional uncle-nephew relationship. It seems that Mark must pay the Irish a tribute of one hundred striplings a year. Tristan fights King Moraunt (Marhaus) of Ireland, and by killing him settles the question of the tribute. But Tristan is dangerously wounded; in his head is left a piece of Moraunt's sword. After wandering for three years, he is taken care of by Ysoude, sister of Moraunt, who does not know who

---

in the headnote to his printings of the ballad versions, is worth quoting:

"Thomas of Erceldoune's prophetic power was a gift of the queen of the elves; the modern elves, equally those of northern Europe and of Greece, resembling in respect to this attribute the nymphs of the ancient Hellenic mythology. How Thomas attained this grace is set forth in the first three fits of a poem which bears his name. This poem has come down to us in four somewhat defective copies: the earliest written a little before the middle of the fifteenth century, two others about 1450, the fourth later. There is a still later manuscript copy of the second and third fits. All the manuscripts are English, but it is manifest from the nature of the topics that the original poem was the work of a Scotsman. All four of the complete versions speak of an older story. This was undoubtedly a romance which narrated the adventure of Thomas with the elf-queen *simply,* without specification of his prophecies. In all probability it concluded with Thomas's return to fairy-land after a certain time passed in this world. The story of Thomas and the elf-queen is but another version of what is related of Ogier le Danois and Morgan the Fay."

To this it might be added that the various stories about Thomas the Rhymer make it clear that his is a case of a mortal seduced by a supernatural lover, who spends some time in the other world and returns a marked man or woman. The most famous version of this theme is the legend of Tannhäuser; another and a more courtly specimen is the legend of Launfal.

Tristan is. Naturally Tristan sings the praises of Ysoude to King Mark, who forthwith sends the youth back to Ireland to claim her for his uncle's bride. Although Ysoude now recognizes Tristan by the nicked sword and would kill him to avenge her brother, she decides instead to become queen of England. On their way to England, Tristan and Ysoude, through the hand of the maid Brangwen, drink a love potion intended for Ysoude and Mark; thenceforth they love recklessly and passionately. The remainder of the romance details their love as well as their successful stratagems in outwitting Mark. There is a crafty, wicked, tattling courtier Meriadok, who keeps the lovers in constant turmoil. Finally they are caught, but even then Ysoude is able to avoid conviction at her trial by ordeal. None the less, the lovers are ultimately banished and spend a year happily in the forest. Here Mark one day finds them asleep with a naked sword between them. This symbol of chastity, however, had been placed in position a few minutes before by Tristan, who had seen the king coming. Eventually the king forgives Ysoude, and Tristan marries Ysoude of the Fair Hands, daughter of the Duke of Brittany. This marriage is not happy, for Tristan is constantly trying to return to his fated love, Ysoude of Ireland. And in company with his new brother-in-law he is wounded in his old wound.

Here the Middle English romance breaks off. But we know that Tristan died shortly thereafter as a result of his wound. According to one version, Ysoude of Brittany became aware of the true situation. Tristan, seriously ill, sends for Ysoude of Ireland. He gives orders that if the ship is actually bringing her, it must hoist a white sail; if she is not aboard, it must carry a black sail. Ysoude of Ireland is aboard; but Ysoude of Brittany has learned of the arrangement, and in spite she tells Tristan that the ship shows a black sail. Tristan turns to the wall and dies, and Ysoude of Ireland, arriving too late, dies of a broken heart; the lovers are united in death. According to other versions, however, Tristan and Ysoude enjoyed their love for years, until one day Mark, the most benumbed of cuckolds, killed Tristan while the latter was playing the harp before Ysoude.

The one fact that is incontrovertible in this legend is that Tristan and Isoude loved through thick and thin and did not scruple; and Tristan at least came to an unhappy end. Moreover, the lovers derived from their love a spiritual as well as a physical satisfaction. In other words, they fulfilled perfectly the chivalric pattern. Their sheer dishonesty, however, surprises even the cynical twentieth-century purveyor of fiction; it is no wonder that the moralists of the medieval period, particularly in the Church, viewed the story with grave misgivings or worse. Nor is it any wonder that the love of Tristan and Isoude should serve as a symbol of the moral lassitude that overcame the Round Table, the rift within the lute that widened and made the music mute. This symbol Tennyson and other poets of the nineteenth century emphasized. The Middle Ages, however, preferred to use Lancelot and Guenevere as the guilty examples; Malory, indeed, allows the story of Tristan to trickle out without comment. It seems appropriate, nevertheless, to forget about the prosaic and rather inept version that Thomas of Chester, or whoever it was, has given us in the lone surviving Middle English romance, and the tediously detailed chronicle with which Malory cluttered up the middle sections of his *Morte Darthur,* and instead to end our survey of the Arthurian saga with a contemplation of the two star-crossed lovers, who for better or worse transcended the conventions of society. From Uther and Ygerne through the Holy Grail to Tristan and Isoude, the wheel has come full circle.

The best romances of the "matter of France" group lie in the realm of French literature, although some of them may have been written in England and therefore may be considered Anglo-French. There is nothing in English literature on the story of Roland comparable in excellence to the effective *Chanson de Roland.* All the "matter of France" romances in English, however, are based upon the great edifice of the cycles of Charlemagne. The situation is altogether analogous to the one that confronts the student of Arthurian romances. Charlemagne has replaced Arthur as the center of the circle; Charlemagne's knights, instead of the fraternity of the Round Table, are the radii. As Arthur proves himself mortal and degenerates in prestige, so does Charlemagne. As the chief interest of the saga soon shifts from Arthur himself to his knights, so do the followers of Charlemagne take the glory away from their sovereign. In place of Lancelot and Gawain stride Roland and Oliver, as well as characters only a little less important, such as the fighting Archbishop Turpin, Guy of Burgundy, and the villain, Ganelon. Subsidiary heroes, representing older saga material as well as later legends of dynastic or family importance—including the four sons of Aymoun, Ogier the Dane, Renaud de Montaudon, and Huon of Bordeaux—attach themselves to the cycle as feudal retainers of the first Holy Roman Emperor. Even Saracens of heroic stature, such as Ferumbras and Otuel, are converted to Christianity in order to partake of the benefits and prestige of the Carolingian empire.

Derivative as they may be, the English romances of Charlemagne exhibit the characteristics of their French antecedents. They are martial, rugged, and intensely patriotic in their regard for *la douce France*. They are less chivalrous than their French prototypes and are much closer to the old *chansons de geste* than to the type of romance illustrated by the *Queste del Saint Graal* on the one hand or the *Tristan* on the other. They are belligerently Christian and savor much of propaganda—precisely what should be expected of a product of crusading faith, especially when one remembers that the Crusades originated largely in French territory. As might be anticipated, these romances often come close to the grotesque or the fantastic or the incredibly naïve. All will be forgiven a wayward character, even a pagan Saracen, if he will consent to be baptized a Christian. This is not to imply that the French Carolingian romances were deficient in *courtoisie*. On the contrary, later romances of this cycle, such as *Renaud de Montaudon* or *Huon of Bordeaux,* are polished and romanticized to an almost silken gloss. It does suggest, however, that the English writers of this type of romance were more interested in the saga for its story than for its courtly elements; and these authors were probably of less than courtly background and outlook.

It is therefore unnecessary to give these romances more than passing notice. A cycle concerning the Saracen hero,

Ferumbras, is represented in English by *The Sowdone of Babylone* (*c*.1400), animated and artless, with a heroine, Floripas, who thinks nothing of killing her nurse and betraying the Sultan, her father, into the hands of the Christians because she is in love with Guy of Burgundy. The complex adventitious material dealing with Charlemagne's wars against the Saracens, which leads to the hypothesis of the existence of a long cyclic poem, *Charlemagne and Roland*, now lost, is given rather inept handling by English authors. *Roland and Vernagu* (*c*.1350) is so bathetic as to deserve special mention.

> The Saracen giant, Vernagu, is fighting against the dauntless Christian champion, Roland. Their combat is frequently interrupted by long debates on the merits of Christianity. Vernagu listens willingly enough to Roland's missionary efforts. They fight all day, and at night Vernagu, being fatigued, is graciously permitted to sleep. In fact, Roland places a stone under his head to lessen his snoring. Vernagu is impressed by this act of kindness, but after due deliberation he decides that, having heard and digested Christian dogma, he will continue to fight. The battle thereupon terminates with the slaying of Vernagu.

A few lines at the end of the poem link it with the cycle of the mighty Saracen Otuel (Otinel). In *The Sege of Melayne* (Milan), a romance a little younger than *Roland and Vernagu*, the Christians are in dire starits: Rome is captured and sacked by the exulting Saracens, and the fighting Archbishop Turpin reproaches the Virgin most roundly for allowing matters to come to such a pass. The piece is incomplete, but the French story indicates that the situation was later saved for the Christians. It is significant, however, that Charlemagne has now become a nonentity; Roland is inept; the Archbishop has become the hero. As in the case of *Athelston*, perhaps this romance signifies the struggle between Church and State in the Middle Ages.

The Otuel cycle is represented also by the Middle English *Otuel* (*c*.1350), in which the doughty hero of that name confronts Roland in a drawn battle, is converted, and then becomes so great a power on the Christian side that he is able to save Roland, Oliver, and Ogier from an entire Saracen army. The piece, however, it tedious and uninspired, as are other versions of the story.

In lesser degree the same reproach of dullness could be leveled against the remaining miscellaneous romances of the "matter of France" group. Lord Berners' fifteenth-century translation of *Huon of Bordeaux,* not printed until the de Worde edition of 1534, is smooth and undistinguished; Caxton's edition (1489) of *The Right Pleasant and Goodly Historie of the Foure Sonnes of Aymon* is a little more exciting. If one wants *The Song of Roland* in its true excellence, one should read the French original, not the Middle English *Song of Roland* (c.1450), which is a feeble paraphrase. Probably the best of these later romances is *The Taill of Rauf Coilyear* (Ralph Collier), written in Scotland between 1475 and 1500. This seems to have originated in Britain, but it is, after all, the old legend of peasant confronting king, of which, between ballads and romances, there are a dozen surviving examples in Middle English literature alone. Charlemagne, beset by a storm, is forced to seek shelter in the collier's hut. The peasant, not recognizing his royal guest, gives the king some lessons in courtesy. The story is thenceforth not unlike *The Carl of Carlisle,* with Charlemagne replacing Gawain and the other knights, and Ralph replacing the Churl. The king takes his lesson in good spirit, and promotes Ralph to be marshal of France, after some striking demonstrations of the collier's prowess at knightly arms. The poem gives realistic details of contemporary Scottish life, and it is amusingly independent in tone. Though some have seen in it a satire on chivalric literature. it is more likely that it was intended to express the self-assertiveness of the lower classes and should therefore be regarded as an example of the literature of revolt rather than of sheer burlesque.

As for the other great French Worthy of the World, Godfrey de Bouillon, leader of the First Crusade, he is the subject of continental legendary and romance treatment. The only Middle English piece to represent him is *Chevelere Assigne,* or *The Knight of the Swan,* which is an effective mixture of various folk themes—the belief in the adultery of a woman who gives birth to more than one child at a time, the wicked mother-in-law, the calumniated wife, the false servant, the kindly peasant, the "male Cinderella," to say nothing of ordeal by combat and the transformation of human beings into animals or birds. The attaching of the motif of the Swan Knight to the story of the Holy Grail, as typified by Lohengrin, is the business of late continental legendry.

The final group indicated by Jean Bodel, the "matter of Rome," is represented by two cycles of wide currency—the Alexander and the Troy legends—and by a third, the story of Thebes, which is in the nature of literary caviar.

The legend of Alexander the Great, as we have seen in our survey of Old English literature, was circulating in Europe before the year 1000. The genesis of this legend is characteristic. The great reputation of a historical or semi-historical figure leads some enterprising individual to collect the traditional stories concerning this figure and give them to the world, no doubt embellished by some new details. In this case, the enterprising individual is the author of the Greek *Pseudo-Kallisthenes,* of indeterminate date. From the *Pseudo-Kallisthenes* comes a Latin version by Julius Valerius, preserved only in a summary from the ninth century. In this same century came *The Letters of Alexander to Aristotle* already noted. The Italian Archpresbyter Leo (*c.*950) produced a popular *Historia Alexandri Magni, Regis Macedoniae, de Prœliis,* which set a fashion for most of the later romanciers.

Evidently the French noticed the legend at an early date; the masterpiece of their literature about Alexander is the 20,000-line *Roman d'Alexandre,* the work of several writers in the last quarter of the twelfth century, which has at least left its mark upon modern prosody, for the iambic hexameter it used has been known ever since as the Alexandrine. Two special qualities distinguish the English treatment of the cycle. In the first place, the Middle English pieces are for the greater part epics rather than romances; in fact, they come close at times to the metrical chronicle. There is almost no love-making in them and but little attention to the etiquette of society in which women are present. In the second place, it has often been noted that they are didactic and even somewhat academic, as if the author were bent primarily upon portraying a heroic type of warrior and setting up the standards of conduct required of a noble king. Clearly the importance of Alexander as one of the Nine Worthies of the World and the sheer brilliance of his military achievements transcend any supposed popularity he might possess as a chivalric lover; and unlike his associates, Arthur and Charlemagne, he preserves his epic prowess and integrity to the end.

The best and probably the most comprehensive Middle English romance of the cycle is *The Lyfe of Alisaunder* (*c.*1325), which follows in the main the romance of the thirteenth-century Eustache of Kent (*Roman de toute Chevalerie*). All the essential outlines of the cycle are included here except the marriage of the hero to Roxana. The mysterious begetting of Alexander parallels the story of the birth of Arthur; then comes an account of the youth of the prince, of his succession, of the conquest of Carthage and other rival kingdoms, of the wars with Darius. In the second half we are told of the travels of Alexander to India, with the fabulous geography of the region familiar to us from the Old English accounts, and finally of the betrayal of the king by Candace and of his poisoning. In spite of the occasional admixture of magic elements and the rare little touches of humanitarian feeling on the part of the hero, *The Lyfe of Alisaunder* remains a straightforward epic with most of the literary fashions of the classical epic. There are, however, a few rather gracious lyrical passages, used chiefly as decorative details which keep the poem from being a mere epic chronicle. All in all, this work is at least a faint approximation of the French *Roman d'Alexandre*.

The alliterative *Alexander* fragments, based presumably upon some earlier poem of considerable length, deal in part with the career of Alexander's putative father Philip, with his education, and with the military career of the "marvelous stripling"; but the pieces as a whole are moralizing and monotonous. In the fifteenth century a prose translation of Leo's Latin work, known as the "prose" *Alexander*, served to pull together the many stories in a manner comparable to that of Malory's *Morte Darthur*. The tendency is strong, in this fifteenth century, to epitomize in prose. Yet even as late as 1580 the verse *Alexander Buik* was published in Scotland, although the poem was composed in 1438. In other words, although the cycle of Alexander may never have had the glamour and high romance of the legend of Troy, it manifestly possessed a long and genuine appeal and served its purpose as a type of literature acceptable as a handbook for princes. The spectacular career of the Macedonian youth may have contributed little to human progress, but it could hardly be waved aside.

For the legend of Troy the medieval poets naturally turned to classical sources. Yet their firsthand knowledge of these sources was derived almost entirely from the Latin, since familiarity with the Greek language (to say nothing of the literature) was rare except in the eastern Mediterranean. Virgil was therefore the great ultimate authority on the story of Troy; Homer was not much more than a name in Western Europe before the middle of the fourteenth century. Besides, Homer was a Greek and therefore prejudiced against the Trojan cause, which was unfortunate for him, because the Trojans were the ancestors of the Romans, who in turn were the alleged ancestors of the Christian world. Indeed, if medieval tradition was to be believed, the hero Aeneas had a descendant, Brutus, who founded Brutlond, or Britain. This theory, plus the probable garbling of the saying of Aristotle that Homer told of fictitious events according to artistic rules, let to the feeling, put bluntly by Chaucer, that Homer "made lyes."

None the less, the account of the Trojan War in the *Aeneid* did not suffice, and so the medieval world came to rely on Homer for its Troy legend, if only through some second-hand versions. In tracing this legend from its beginnings, we may list the following sources: (1) Virgil's *Aeneid;* (2) two basic supplements in the Latin chronicles—by one Dictys of Crete (*Dictys Cretensis Ephemeris de Historia Belli Trojani*) in the fourth century and one Dares of Phrygia (*Daretis Phrygii de Excidio Trojae Historia*) about a century later; (3) a prose epitome of the story of Troy by Thebanus, otherwise unknown; and (4) the competent medieval French romance, the *Roman de Troie,* by the cleric Benoi(s)t de St. Maure (1184). A few years after the composition of the *Roman de Troie,* a certain Joseph of Exeter wrote an Anglo-Latin version based on Benoit's account. A full century later, that is, about 1285, Guido delle Colonne produced his *Historia Destructionis Troiae,* which had much direct influence upon subsequent writers. The major credit for founding the medieval tradition of the Troy legend, however, should go by all rights to Benoit de St. Maure. And with the *Roman de Troie,* from which, as has been said, Joseph of Exeter and Guido delle Colonne got their material, one comes to a fork in the road. The work of Benoit comprises both phases of the legend as we find it later in the Middle Ages: (a) the phase that treats of the Trojan war as a whole, with its origins and consequences; and (b) the phase that treats of the particular romance of Troilus and Cressida. Subsequent writers take either of these phases for their subject, but not both together.

The genesis of the Troy legend as a whole was, then, the usual matter of successive increments added to the original classical epic base; but Troilus and Cressida had curious beginnings. In the classical epics Troilus is mentioned briefly as among the many sons of Priam fighting in the war. Dictys and Dares do not speak of him at all. Nor is the notorious Pandarus, the go-between, allowed more than a reference or two in Homer; and even then he appears merely as a wealthy nobleman. The magnification of Troilus into a hero of rank second only to that of the great Worthy, Hector, seems to have been the achievement of Benoit. Cressida, similarly exalted, is the cross-product of two other females of Homeric tradition—the two slave girls, Briseis and Chryseis. The accusative case of *Briseis* ("daughter of Briseus") is *Briseida;* it was this name that Benoit conferred upon the heroine. Not until Boccaccio's *Filostrato* of the mid-fourteenth century does the name appear as Criseida, presumably suggested by Chryseis, or rather a fusion of Briseis and Chryseis in the accusative case. The reasons for such a fusion, however, and some of the other details of the origin of the lady's name are trivial.

The best Middle English account of the Troy legend as a whole is *The Gest Historiale of the Destruccion of Troy,* a northern English poem of about 1450; of the others, only *The Seege of Troye* (c.1425) and Lydgate's contemporary *Troy Book* need be named. The *Gest,* based on Guido, covers everything from the beginnings of the feud between Greeks and Trojans attendant upon the Quest of the Golden Fleece (when the first Troy was destroyed by Jason and Hercules) through the founding of the second Troy, the abduction of Helen and the outbreak of the Ten Years' War, the details of the siege and the eventual sack of the city, the escape of Aeneas, and the return of the Greeks, down to the final episodes of Ulysses and his wanderings, which culminate in his death at the hands of his son. Perhaps we might observe that the prose *Recuyell of the Historyes of Troye* has a particular historical importance because it was the first book to be printed in English (1474). It is a translation by Caxton himself of Raoul de Fevre's *Le Receuil de Troyennes Ystoires* and was evidently a popular epitome.

In spite of the elaborate romance Chaucer put into the mouth of his Knight, there is no evidence that the English ever cared much for the Thebes legend. Indeed, until Lydgate's *Story of Thebes* of about 1420 there was no English companion-piece to Chaucer's *Knight's Tale*. Lydgate's effort is a mediocre one, and his obvious imitation of Chaucer is uninspired. Nevertheless, for anyone who could not read the *Thebaid* of Statius or the French *Roman de Thèbes*, it was the only available account of the building of Thebes and the war of the Seven against the city, about Creon and the unhappy Oedipus. Even to the general English courtly audience, the story was a rarity.

The Germanic romances, the Arthurian romances, the romances of Charlemagne, and the romances of classical origin —these comprise the major cycles of Middle English romance. There remain more than thirty surviving English romances of miscellaneous nature, without taking into account their French sources and analogues, many of which were doubtless written in Anglo-French territory. These can crowd their way only briefly into the next few pages. Some of them are manifestly moralistic, didactic stories; some of them are mainly historical; a few thread a devious path between the romance and the *fabliau* on the one hand and the saint's life on the other. Most of them, in fact, are the product of the romance tradition in its later stages, when its storehouse of incident and situation had been exhausted. They give the impression of being unoriginal composites of all kinds of older romance material.

Seven Middle English romances, the so-called Eustace-Constance-Florence-Griselda (ECFG) cycle, illustrate the particular virtue of Christian fortitude in the face of endless crises; these can be supplemented by five other works more conveniently assigned to another category. The seven romances comprise *Sir Isumbras, Octovian, The King of Tars, Sir Eglamour, Torrent of Portyngale, Sir Triamour,* and *Le Bon Florence of Rome;* to these must be added Chaucer's *Clerk's Tale,* as well as his *Man of Law's Tale; Emare* and *Lai le Freine* two Breton *lais,* the latter of which is derived from Marie de France's *lai* of the same name; and the saint's life of Placidas. "Male Cinderellas," giant champions, Saracens, false recognition, sieges, alarms and excursions are some of the commonplaces that parade through the lines of these poems; but in all it is inflexible Christian courage that wins the day against adversity compounded. On the other hand, the romances of friendship (*Amis and Amiloun* and *Sir Amadace*) are more memorable. *Amis and Amiloun,* of the thirteenth century, is the tale of two sworn brothers who stick to each other through all kinds of ordeals. On the whole, these romances are well told, in spite of their arrant melodrama. *Sir Amadace,* a much later romance than *Amis and Amiloun,* tells of a knight who gives almost his last penny to help bury a knight; as a reward, the spirit of this knight (representing the old folk motif of the Grateful Dead) spares Amadace from the necessity of killing his wife and child.

The most attractive of these miscellaneous romances, however, is *Roberd of Cisyle* (c.1400). It is an earnest, sincere, and eloquent account of the haughty King Robert, who falls asleep with the words of the Magnificat ringing in his ears and who then awakes to find that he is only a fool; an angel has taken his form and is ruling in his place. After a humiliating experience in the gutter as a mere court jester, Robert learns the meaning of the verse that proclaims that He has brought down the mighty from their seats. His lesson learned, Robert humbly resumes his rank as King of Sicily. This story, incidentally, is one of the most effective of Longfellow's *Tales of a Wayside Inn;* it is as effective in the nineteenth century as it was in the fifteenth.

Two historical romances, *Titus and Vespasian (The Destruction of Jerusalem),* from the fourteenth century, and *Richard Coer de Lyon (c.*1400), are of no special importance; their subject matter speaks for itself. Neither are *The Knight of Curtesy (c.*1450) or *Melusine (c.*1500), both of which are related in a vague way to the traditions of a historical noble family.[11]

The longer romances of composite nature are the most definite evidence that this literary type fell into decadence. They are extremely long, with interminable successions of incident. Often the narrative is clogged with excessive attention to details; but more frequently the fault is that there is no shading of the incidents themselves, and therefore no plot, no proper beginning, middle, or end. It is a remarkable individual who can keep in mind the course of events in *Sir Degrevant, Generydes, Parthenope of Blois,* or *Ipomadon,* though none of these is bad reading if taken in small doses. *Ipomadon,* which has as cognates *The Lyfe of Ipomydon* and a prose *Ipomedon,* stems from an Anglo-French romance by Hugh of Rutland; but it is much less effective than the original. *Parthenope* has an impressive beginning—the hero enters a magic boat that conveys him to an unearthly city, where he finds his fay love Melior. It is a fair repast of supernatural love: Melior enjoins Parthenope never to look upon her, as Cupid enjoined Psyche. The romance then disintegrates, however, into tedious incident. All four of the romances named above belong to the period from 1375 to 1430. *The Squyr of Low Degre (c.*1450) is insignificant; its nature can be gauged accurately from its title. There is a Middle English version of *Apollonius of Tyre,* found in Gower's

[11] *The Knight of Curtesy* may be related to the De Coucy family tradition; a member of this family had a celebrated affair with Gabrielle de Vergy in the twelfth century. *Melusine,* which has a later treatment known as *Partenay,* is based upon legends associated with the distinguished Lusignan family of France. This legend has been extremely popular on the Continent, where it is still more or less the ultimate expression of the "loathly lady" motif represented by the Greek heroine Lamia, the snake-woman.

Confessio Amantis. Floris and Blancheflour is a pleasant romance of two inseparable young lovers, which reminds one of the beautiful *Aucassin et Nicolete*. Where *Aucassin et Nicolete*, however, is a gem of sophisticated narrative deceptive in its simplicity, *Floris and Blancheflour* is merely naïve and quaint, although not without its amusing and titillating lines.

If any of these miscellaneous romances deserve to be read more often, it would be the group referred to as Breton *lais*. The nature of these pieces was discussed in relation to the *lais* of Marie de France. There are nine Middle English romances thus designated, including Chaucer's *Franklin's Tale*. They either are avowedly from Breton sources or else partake of the same general characteristics as those of the known Breton *lais*. All of them are comparatively short and of considerable poetic potentialities (although *Sir Degare* and *The Earl of Toulouse* are commonplace enough to fall behind the others), in addition to which their recognizably Celtic qualities—setting, nomenclature, humor, and feeling for nature and the supernatural—are obvious. Three of them, *Lai le Freine* (c.1335), *Sir Launfal*, and *Sir Landeval*, are so close in substance to the corresponding *lais* by Marie de France that they would seem to be no more than later versions in English. *Lai le Freine* is, in fact, direct from Marie. *Sir Launfal* comes, most likely, through an earlier English translation of Marie; *Sir Landeval*, with two variants (*Sir Lambewell* and *Sir Lamwell*), is in a subsequent literary generation, since it was written near 1475. The author of *Sir Launfal* is by tradition the same shadowy Thomas Chestre to whom was attributed the Middle English *Tristan*. *Sir Orfeo*, believed by some to be also the work of Chestre, is a beautiful and sensitive telling of the pathetic story of Orpheus and Eurydice; *Emare* is a sterling representative of the Constance legend, best known through Chaucer's *Man of Law's Tale*; *Sir Gowther* is a spectacular version of the popular continental legend of Robert the Devil, the boy who was born of fiendish paternity because his mother wanted him regardless of source.

It is a temptation to linger over other fiction, such as *Sir Cleges*, for instance, which hovers uncertainly amid the boundaries of the *fabliau*, the pious tale, and the romance.

Perhaps it is only fitting to leave the romance with the thought that it had now reached the stage where it was no longer confined by narrow limits but ranged freely among other forms of fiction. With a little admixture of other types, such as the *fabliau* and the *exemplum,* it was ready to become the source of the modern novel. It was now able to draw not only upon the folklore of Western Europe but upon the story materials of the Mediterranean and the Orient. What it needed, to become modern fiction, was to develop a sense of interrelation in its incidents—in other words, a sense of plot—and to portray human characters instead of types. Only a Chaucer or a Pearl Poet could as yet do this consistently; and one reason Chaucer could accomplish his excellent characterization was that he did not hesitate to make use of the other more realistic forms of fiction available in his age. This the courtly romancer could not seem to do, probably because he felt that realism was beneath the dignity of his epic art. It is therefore time now for us to turn to the less aristocratic forms of medieval fiction.

6. The Medieval Tale

It becomes increasingly apparent that fiction is the type of Middle English literature likely to live longest. Storytelling has been called a universal art, and this truism is never so obvious as when an attempt is made to discuss medieval popular narrative. Stories with similar incidents and situations spring up before the reader in bewildering number from all parts of the Western world, so that the important question of the transmission of these stories is impossible to settle. If any single answer is likely, it is that the instinct for story is so strong in human hearts and minds as to be spontaneous; and, since human experience is necessarily finite and circumscribed, the story must follow one or another of a limited number of patterns.

At the same time, it is true that ordinary stories for ordinary people were not considered of much value during the Middle Ages unless they could be used for teaching; and yet their number was legion, and it was always possible to affix some kind of moral to any one of them, as indeed was done in a surprising number of instances. One noteworthy fact is that the popular tale in Western Europe had a marked affinity for the Orient. To some this may mean only that the Middle English, for example, became aware of these stories through the Crusades and the contacts with the Near East resulting therefrom; but this is a very short view of the situation. The East, with its ancient civilizations, would be a vast treasure house of fiction at any time; and every folklorist knows how often stories told throughout Europe can be traced with a certain inevitability to some Oriental source or analogue. The trouble, as usual, lies in the difficulty of distinguishing between source and analogue. Does a given story come from some Oriental story, or do the given story and the Oriental story go back to some other story, which antedates all the surviving stories? Whatever the situation, there is no gainsaying the very ponderable "matter of the Orient" to be found in the medieval tale. This question applies not only to the narrative motif or character type but also to such a device as the familiar framework technique for collecting tales; in fact, the assembling of tales seems to have been something of a special occupation of the storytellers of the East.

The same conditions apply to the Middle English tale as to the Middle English romance. The great majority of these tales, like the romances, are in verse; only late in the period do they appear in prose. Both types must be studied in relation to continental versions of the story. A French tale is likely to lie behind an English one; sometimes it is a Flemish or Dutch or even a German source than can be discerned. Occasionally, when the English tale is of obvious didactic nature, a Latin source can be detected. It is never safe, therefore, to ignore a foreign counterpart when investigating a given English tale.

Keeping before us the convenient categories of the religious tale and the secular tale, we may subdivide the religious tale into (a) tales concerning the Virgin, (b) tales of miracles relating to doctrine and sacrament, and (c) *exempla.* The secular tale will include (a) *fabliaux,* or humorous tales, and (b) the particular province of the beast tale, fable, or animal epic, which may include allegories in which animals are the chief figures. Over against both of these categories should be placed the popular ballad, which is preponderantly secular in theme.

Tales of the Virgin appear in large numbers as soon as there is an appreciable cult of the Virgin in Western Europe —in other words, in the eleventh century, if not earlier. Most of the original tales were in Latin and were then translated into French and later into English. Half a dozen large collections were made before 1300, of which *The Vernon Miracles* will suffice as an example. This is the best-known English collection and dates from approximately 1300. The pattern in nearly all these tales is the same: some mortal, either saint or sinner, is in difficulty and prays to the Virgin, who grants him deliverance as a reward for either his sanctity or his repentance, as the case may be.

As for the *exemplum,* it is useless to attempt any enumeration of the hundreds of representatives of the type. It may be defined simply as a short tale to illustrate or give point to a moral teaching. Any homiletic piece is likely to show one or more *exempla;* churchmen, in fact, were often criticized in their own day because they frequently allowed the *exemplum* to run away with the discourse and prostituted their storytelling talents to the popular approbation of their undoubtedly simple-minded flock. Any moral idea could be supported by an *exemplum,* and the *significatio* of the tale was usually driven home by what seems to us an expository sledge hammer, no matter how much a point had to be strained to admit of a moral application. Often, indeed, the moral invoked had but a faint relation to the story; but no matter.

Worth noting also is the fact that the basic substance of the *exemplum* was often the same as that of the *fabliau.* The true *fabliau,* however, would naturally be frowned upon by the clergy, since it was earthy, trivial, and bawdy, a tale that hinged upon a trick, a practical joke, a salacious situation. Therefore the type led a furtive if none the less hardy existence. It had all the currency in the world—by word of mouth; but it seldom got into manuscripts. The best examples surviving in writing are in Chaucer's *Canterbury Tales* (in the stories of the Miller, Reeve, Merchant, Shipman, Friar, Summoner, and Manciple) where they give their gifted author the opportunity for some of his finest narrative achievements. Leaving aside the animal tale for the moment, we find only a handful of Middle English *fabliaux* in the vernacular. The reasons for this are obvious. Chaucer, as we shall see, was something of a law unto himself, although he saw fit to apologize for the stories. But the clergy could not approve—in fact, a *caveat* against secular tales was issued by the authorities at Oxford in 1292. Conservative people would shun the *fabliau;* then, as now, they would be regarded by such people as unfit for the young. Yet though they might bring the blush to the sophisticated lady of the fourteenth century, as they did in the *Decameron,* still they apparently passed muster, if not in the written literature then at least in oral tradition. At all events, the *fabliau* remained tough and satirical, snapping at women and at the clergy. The women were portrayed as untrustworthy, skittish, opportunistic, and lustful; the clergy were venal, grasping, hypocritical, equally opportunistic and lustful; husbands were made to be duped; a man of education was a fool or worse.

The French collections of *fabliaux* are of no concern to us here; it remains only to say a word about the isolated English *fabliaux* since Chaucer's brilliant contributions occupy a place all their own. The most interesting of these independent tales is *Dame Sirith* (*c.*1275).

A certain young wife is importuned by a clerk, but she will have none of him. He goes to an old panderess, Dame Sirith, who promises to help him. She rubs condiments into the eyes of her dog and takes her around where the wife can see the weeping animal, explaining that the dog is her daughter, who once refused a clerk and was transformed by magic into the crying bitch she sees before her. Terrified, the young wife accepts the clerk with alacrity, lest a similar disaster befall her.

The theme of the Weeping Bitch, with its hint of the transmigration of souls, is a striking example of the pervasive Oriental story material already mentioned. As usual, the tale is told with dash and vigor and a lusty bawdiness, which stands the test of time better than much pious reflection.

Dame Sirith relies a good deal upon conversation, which imparts to it the realism to be expected in a *fabliau.* Actually, the piece is dramatic in effect; and thereby hangs a curious detail. There is a short fragment, in set dramatic form, from the early fourteenth century, known as *Interludium de Clerico et Puella*, which parallels in situation the first part of *Dame Sirith*. More than that, some of the lines in the two pieces are the same. The author of the *Interludium* probably knew *Dame Sirith*, but the latter piece is hardly the source; rather we have the common situation of two works coming from a lost common source. The historical importance of the *Interludium*, however—a dramatic composition, obviously secular, and fulfilling the definition of an interlude two centuries and more before the heyday of the interlude—is sufficiently obvious.

The animal story or beast epic in its several forms is distinctive. At the outset, it must be emphasized that all primitive peoples have given much attention to tales about animals, and many races have held on to them even after they have progressed beyond the near-primitive state. For one thing, the animal story gives an admirable opportunity to discuss men in the guise of animals. The earthy habits of beasts may easily represent the earthy habits of men; furthermore, he who tells a beast fable can always shift the responsibility upon the animals:

> I wol nat han to do of swich mateere,
> My tale is of a cok, as ye may heere . . .

Animals have served their purpose both as helpers of mankind and as their pets; they are amusing, and in their pathetic bestiality completely comprehensible to the dullest clod of a man.

The Oriental animal tales of Bidpai and the *Panchatantra*, as well as the famous collection of Aesop, which is a convenient label for the famous fables of many other classical writers, will bear witness to the antiquity of the type. There is fairly good reason to think, however, that Britain was the earliest home of the medieval fable. In the century and a half following the Norman Conquest no less than three collections of fables appeared in England. There is the collection attributed to Alfred, which was given the name of that great king merely for purposes of prestige. Marie de France, as we have seen, was responsible for an Ysopet ("little Aesop"). There are, incidentally, several French Ysopets from 1200 or shortly thereafter; some of them may be Anglo-French. Finally, there is Walter of England's *Anonymus Neveleti*, the last of the twelfth-century collections in point of time. In the next century or so, many of the fables circulated in the three works just mentioned began to appear in sermons and *exempla*. Alexander Neckam, Walter Map, and John of Salisbury all used them; it is clear that the fable tradition in England had become safely established.

The beast epic was a collection of animal tales in verse, semi-didactic, semi-satirical, which originated in the Low Countries during the twelfth century. It is likely that the original versions were in Latin, but a basic work was later composed in French. On this same French work was built the early thirteenth-century *Roman de Renart*, which may be considered the most important of the medieval beast epics. Here the fox Reynard (from the German *Reinhardt*, "strong in counsel") is the hero and central figure. He has various companions with whom he is usually at odds—Chantecler the cock, Isengrim (or Segrim) the wolf, Bruin the bear, Bayard the horse, and others. The different animals typify as a whole the bourgeoisie of the Middle Ages—shrewd, hard-headed, good-natured but self-seeking, bumbling, and fumbling. The escapades in which they find themselves are of the barnyard and countryside; but they are symbolic of human experience in general. Their treatment is often mock-heroic, often heartless, often raucous, but hardly ever cynical; there is in them too much vitality for that corrosive quality.

There is only one important representative of the beast epic in medieval England surviving in the written literature, exclusive of Chaucer's *Nun's Priest's Tale*. That is *The Fox and the Wolf* (*c*.1260), which is, after all, but a single episode from the epic of Reynard.

The fox is not here named Reynard, but is referred to simply as the Fox. He plunders the barnyard of a friary and tries in vain to entice the cock from his perch. Baffled, he goes out into the courtyard, and in attempting to quench his thirst at the well, he falls in. Fortunately for him, the stupid wolf happens along. The fox inveigles the wolf into the upper bucket of the well—by regaling him with the joys of Paradise that are to be found at the bottom—whereupon the greater weight of the wolf lifts the fox out of the well and enables him to escape. The poor wolf, however, must await a severe drubbing from the friars when he is found.

The most diverting part of this poem is the exchange between the fox and the wolf, when the fox insists that the wolf must shrive himself before he gets into the bucket for his ride to Paradise. We are given some melancholy insight into the morals of the wolf and of the fox's wife. There is much to suggest the *fabliau* in this work, which the sturdy staves of the friars at the end of the tale do nothing to dispel; and the whole piece is executed in sprightly and unabashed narrative verse, with little worry about hopes of Heaven or fears of Hell. Whatever moral lesson may be available from the tale, it is up to the individual reader to get it for himself.

The Middle English *Bestiary* (*c*.1225) applies the material of either natural or unnatural history to the didactic. The pattern in all the thirteen sections is the same—a *narratio* describes some of the habits of a particular animal; then these habits are made symbolic of various aspects of Christian doctrine or ethics in a *significatio*. As the lion sleeps with his eyelids open, so our Lord slumbers not nor sleeps; as the whale has a breath of overpowering sweetness, wherewith he draws to him all the little fishes, so are the seductions of the Devil sweet and fatal; as the eagle, dazzled by his flight into the sun, falls to the ground and is revived at a well, so fallen man is revived at the baptismal font; as the turtledove, bereft of her mate, mourns faithfully for him, so the true Christian, deprived of the Saviour, laments His death. One need but look ahead to *Euphues* and the euphuistic style of the English Renaissance to realize how firmly the metaphor came to be entrenched in animal and plant lore.

Before the introduction of printing, it was often the practice of scribes to assemble several pieces of literature into a collection. It will be remembered that the collections of Old English poetry are responsible for most of our present knowledge of that poetry. The lyric, the saint's life, the homily—in fact, most types of medieval literature—were similarly gathered together. It is not important to enumerate here any of the compilations of *fabliaux, exempla,* anecdotes, or beast stories, except to call attention to two particularly famous collections —the *Gesta Romanorum* and *The Seven Sages of Rome.* This, of course, is to ignore for the moment such collections by known authors as Chaucer's *Canterbury Tales,* Gower's *Confessio Amantis,* or Mannyng's *Handlyng Synne.*

The *Gesta Romanorum* is an example of the miscellaneous collection, without framework and without any apparent order in the tales. The title indicates that the stories are about Romans, and this is true to the extent that the characters may have Roman names, or the story may be laid in the time of a Roman emperor. The purpose of the compilation is to teach, to supply the clergy with suitable *exempla.* Many of the tales are furnished with a *significatio* as ingenious—and ingenuous —as those in the *Bestiary.* They are from a variety of sources, some fantastic, some jocose, some pathetic, some absurd. Originally written in Latin, presumably on the Continent, they were translated into French and into English; the English version was done about the year 1450. *The Seven Sages of Rome,* on the other hand, had a definite framework; the compilation, of Oriental origins, was first made in the thirteenth century, and there were nearly a dozen versions by the year 1500. The stories all bear in allegorical fashion upon the central situation in the framework; they are in fact *exempla* on one side or the other of the main question: which can be more loyal, a son or a wife? The tales are far from dull, and it is not difficult to understand why the collection was so evidently popular.

Placed against the background of the medieval popular tale, the popular ballad becomes much more easily comprehensible than it is when treated in a vacuum. A great deal has been written about the type since Bishop Percy's preface to his famous *Reliques of Ancient English Poetry* (1765). The nineteenth century, in fact, gave itself over to romantic theorizing about the antiquity of these ballads and spoke cryptically about their origins as vaguely communal, as taking place when an illiterate, untutored community met together on special occasions and entertained itself by telling stories on subjects of popular interest. The most sane and the most widely held theory about these ballads, from the point of view of the nineteenth century, was that formulated by Kittredge on the basis of the composite ideas of the two greatest collectors of these ballads in the century, Child and Grundtvig. Kittredge described "the characteristic method of ballad authorship" as "improvisation in the presence of a sympathetic company which may even, at times, participate in the process"; but he went on to observe: "It makes no difference whether a given ballad was in fact composed in the manner described, or whether it was composed (or even written) in solitude, provided the author belonged to the folk, derived his material from popular sources, made his ballad under the inherited influence of the method described, and gave it to the folk as soon as he had made it—and provided, moreover, the folk accepted the gift and subjected it to that course of oral tradition which, as we have seen, is essential to the production of a genuine ballad.[12]

But what is genuine ballad? It would seem that only certain requirements need be met to make a popular ballad. There should be a narrative in verse, in a simple form of versification—usually a quatrain, sometimes a couplet—which tells its story with a slight degree of detached impersonality or objectivity. In certain ballads the story is told in a jerky fashion, helped along by a slight change in the element of a refrain, let us say—the characteristic so-called incremental repetition. Some of the ballad experts have made much of the presence of dialogue in the narrative technique; it is true that some of the ballads are given entirely in dialogue, though not all by any means are dramatic. All of the experts agree that a musical setting has always been an integral part of the ballad, and in many of the modern versions the tunes have been preserved. Yet many of the 305 examples in the magnificent collection by Child of the English and Scottish traditional ballads are deficient in one or more of these required characteristics. Not a few are lyrical rather than narrative, though a story is

[12] See the Preface to the Cambridge Edition of Child's *English and Scottish Ballads,* Boston, 1904, particularly p. xxvii. The champion of the present-day point of view about the genesis of the ballads is Louise Pound; see the bibliography covering the present chapter.

implied in all. Therefore it seems safe to agree upon the importance of narrative and musical potentialities as the prime constituents of a ballad; beyond that there is so much allowable scope as to invalidate much of the classic definition of the popular ballad.

For one thing, the older scholars have probably put too much emphasis upon the humble origins of the ballad and upon its antiquity. Many of the ballads are basically dateless folk tales, it is true. But so are many of the romances. While only a few of the ballads deal *per se* with romance material, and probably were never directed at the same kind of audience as the romances, still they hardly come from the soil only, at least not the ballads that have survived. They come from the bourgeoisie and even the lesser nobility—perhaps only the hangers-on at court; they come from townfolk and they come from countryfolk. Of the antiquity of some of them there can be no doubt; the material in these cases is virtually *sans époque,* just as it is in the case of the *fabliau.* In the form in which we possess them today, however, the ballads do not go back farther than the thirteenth century, and only a few of them date before 1500. The Percy manuscript, in which a great many of the traditional ballads of Child's collection were first represented, was written in the middle of the seventeenth century.

In effect, this is to say that the popular ballads were only a special kind of popular tale, romance, *fabliau,* or what you will, for the delectation of the commoner, the hardy yeoman, the guildsman, the more receptive of the burgesses. No doubt they were appreciated by some of the peasants. These people were mostly illiterate during the thirteenth and fourteenth centuries, a fact that helps to explain the persistence of the oral tradition. They had not so much leisure as the lord or lady or cleric, and they were incomparably less sophisticated, for they were ignorant, superstitious, and credulous. They would be content with a scrap of a romance instead of the complete work; they would be interested in hearing about a local scandal or murder or a snappy story or anything else that satisfied the human instinct for the sensational. Such facts would explain the brevity and relative simplicity of the ballads. Unfortunately, we know very little about the opportunities of the people of the thirteenth and fourteenth centuries to gratify their normally urgent instincts for drama. There were miracle plays being played in this period; probably there were folk plays as well. Whether any of these ballads were actually represented dramatically, which would account for the dialogue, the incremental repetition, and even the choral elements in the refrains, is not demonstrable. It is neither impossible nor improbable. No single theory thus far advanced, however, has explained all these elements in convincing fashion. As for the musical setting, it has already been pointed out that the earlier romances and even the epic may have had some kind of musical and rhythmical delivery. It is a pity that we do not have more facts to go by; but in any case the ballad, like the epic, eventually came to be written down, as the various Renaissance and early Modern English broadside ballads attest.

In regard to origins, the only sensible explanation is that every one of the surviving popular ballads had its minstrel author—a village Milton or borough Virgil, perhaps, but still an author—who remembered older versions of most of these stories, just as the Beowulf Poet recalled his antecedents, and who relied upon his occasionally uncertain memory to reproduce his tale. His medium was simpler than the Beowulf Poet's because his talents and his audience were simpler. At the same time, one should have no more illusions about the literary worth of these ballads than about the literary worth of a folk epic, to which these ballads seem exactly comparable. One comes from the aristocracy; the other has a humbler social position. In their purest states, the two types have similar ideals. In considering the English popular ballad, one always thinks of Robin Hood; and who is Robin Hood? As Child observes, he is the product of the ballad muse;[13] he is as true an epic hero as Beowulf, except that he is the projection not of the ideals of earls and thanes but of the yeomen and commoners of Middle English times, who were shoved hither and thither during the reigns of King Stephen or of Richard the Lion Heart, or during the desolate years of the War of the Barons or of the corruption of Edward II. Efforts to attach

[13] See the headnote to *A Gest of Robyn Hode* (No. 117 in Child's collection).

Robin Hood to the tradition of the Huntington family or of the family of Ralph of Chester, as well as efforts to give him a purely mythological kinship with Woden, come to nothing. Robin Hood is, in his prime, a fine archer and woodsman; he is something of a socialist, even a communist; he attacks the worldly riches of nobleman and prelate and shares their wealth with his band; he is an outlaw, but a beloved outlaw who represents the commoner's itch for opportunity at the expense of his feudal masters. He is decent, self-respecting, and chivalrous (though not chivalric); he is God-fearing, devout, but carefree; he has, in short, all the middle-class virtues. Like his cousins in the epic and romance, he suffers a weakening and degeneration later; when Maid Marian enters his life, he becomes colorless, and the center of interest shifts from him to his followers, such as Little John, Scarlet, and even the hedonistic Friar Tuck, as well as countless yeomen and tanners, bakers, pinners, butchers, and the like. He comes to an untimely end, and, like Roland, through the treachery of someone he trusted.

Some of the traditional ballads, it may be conceded, treat of matter more appropriate to the romances, for they are virtually sections of existing romances. In such cases, as in *Hind Horn*, it is safe to assume that the ballad poet is reproducing as best he can some part of the romance of *King Horn*. *The Boy and the Mantle*, wherein a precocious little boy brings a mantle of chastity and puts to shame all the ladies of Arthur's court except Craddock's wife, would seem to be an epitomized version of some lost romance of a satiric type, similar, for instance, to *The Carl of Carlisle*. Other ballads are nothing more than *fabliaux;* there are in them seductions, tricks on husband or wife, meetings of peasants and noblemen, farmers' wives too hot for the Devil himself to handle. A few religious ballads, such as *St. Stephen and King Herod* or *The Carnal and the Crane*, come so close to the religious lyric of dramatic texture that it is a question whether they are properly to be called ballads. This criticism can be made also in reference to the moving "coronach," or ballad of lament, such as *Bonnie George Campbell*.

In addition to the outlaw group, of which the Robin Hood cycle is by all odds the most important, there are two other special groups worth noting. A great many of the traditional ballads are historical; they constitute a cycle of so-called "border ballads," since they treat almost exclusively of the protracted border warfare, from the fourteenth century to the eighteenth, between England and Scotland. More important is the great cycle of ballads, based primarily on folk motifs, which may be called simply the ballads of domestic relations. They comprise more than a third of the whole Child collection. A few are pure folklore, such as the "riddle" ballad, in which a devil asks a mortal riddles and is confounded when the mortal answers them correctly. Ballads like *Lord Randal* and *Edward* tell of the murder of a lover by his sweetheart, or that of a father by his son; *The Twa Sisters,* of the killing of one sister by another. *Lady Isabel and the Elf-Knight* is a variant on the theme of Bluebeard. *Kemp Owyne* tells of the loathly lady who is transformed from a monster into a beautiful girl through the brave and persistent wooing of a knight. There are also darker tales of supernatural love (*Thomas Rymer*), of death wrought by spells (*Clerk Colvin*), of cruel stepmothers (*Fair Annie*), of illicit love in the forest (*Tam Lin*), resulting in what a prudish critic termed "a disgusting amount of childbirth." There are devoted maidens who follow their lovers as faithfully as Nicolete followed Aucassin (*Clerk Saunders*); there are fatal elopements (*Earl Brand*), as well as romantic gypsies (*The Gypsy-Laddie*), rescues of the innocent from hanging (*The Fair Maid Saved from the Gallows*), tyrannical executions of likely young men (*Young Waters*), wicked servants (*Lamkin*), and treacherous pages (*Little Musgrave and Lady Barnard*). The wee penknife lurks in the sleeve to do its deadly work. Barbara Allen condemns her noble lover to death from love-sickness. From the graves of the lovers grow roses and briars to intertwine. It is obviously hopeless to give more than a brief indication of the variety of incident in these ballads—and the wealth of folklore both Celtic and Germanic to reward the antiquarian. The whole cycle of ballads on the restless dead (*The Wife of Usher's Well*), for example, is worth a monograph in itself.[14]

The ballad spirit is still alive today; many of the traditional

[14] See the bibliography covering the present chapter.

ballads can be rooted up in communities in America as well as in Britain, the text sometimes almost intact, though perhaps the musical setting has been modified. Of that last point one can never be sure. But even more impressive than the survival of these traditional ballads, as well as of many a broadside ballad of the seventeenth, eighteenth, nineteenth, and twentieth centuries, is the vitality of the ballad-making instinct. It would seem, however, that the rude talent for versifying and singing that could make up a ballad from known historical events, such as the death of Casey Jones on the Illinois Central, the wreck of Old 97 on the Norfolk and Western, the immuring of Floyd Collins in a Kentucky cave, the collapse of the dirigible *Shenandoah* over Ohio, even the sinking of the *Titanic* in mid-Atlantic—such a talent is the best living argument for the theory that all ballads come eventually from one man, call him minstrel, bard, or poet as you will. A courtly poet made the epic of *Beowulf;* a barroom poet made up the ballad of Frankie and Johnny; a barrack-room poet rendered imperishable the eagles of Mobile and Mademoiselle from Armentières. The audiences did the rest.

7. Chronicles in the Vernacular

With a few exceptions, the total contribution of Middle English historiographers is negligible. Of course, there are many praiseworthy survivals; but it is fair to surmise that the verse chronicles of Robert of Gloucester, Robert Mannyng, or Thomas Bek can have no particular interest save to the specialist, whereas Layamon's *Brut,* Barbour's *The Bruce*, the prose *Chronicle* by Andrew Wyntoun, and the racy translation by Trevisa of Higden's *Polychronicon* (which has already been noted among Anglo-Latin works) will still yield entertainment to the casual reader.

Robert of Gloucester's *Chronicle* is evidently the work of three different men, all from Gloucester Abbey, writing during the last decades of the thirteenth and the early years of the fourteenth century. It is an interesting piece in regard to language, since it was written in the not too common Southwest Midland dialect. As might be expected, it relies upon the work of the Anglo-Latin chroniclers of the twelfth century; yet it is at its best when it tells of some of the events in the reign of Henry III (1216-72), with which monarch it rounds out its story. Robert Mannyng of Brunne, far better known as the author of *Handlyng Synne,* covers much the same ground but continues to the close of the reign of Edward I (1307). John Capgrave's *Chronicle of England,* apparently concluded in 1417, and Hector Boece's *Chroniklis of Scotland* (1527) have self-evident value in the fact that they carry their material into the fifteenth and sixteenth centuries, respectively; they are, however, extremely pedestrian. Thomas Bek of Castelford is still duller; and the substance he gives, which ends with the accession of Edward III (1327), is treated far better elsewhere.

To return, then, to the more interesting chronicles. It has already been said that *The Anglo-Saxon Chronicle* was continued, in the Peterborough Manuscript, to 1154; and this, at least, is apparently satisfactory history told with occasional vividness and good effect. No more damning picture of the years of King Stephen's reign (1135-53) and of the maltreatment of the English people by ruthless feudal lords has ever been painted, not even by the contemporary Anglo-Latin and Anglo-French chroniclers. Perhaps *The Anglo-Saxon Chronicle* may be artless and not very discriminating, but in its lack of pretentiousness it achieves a reliability that is often missing elsewhere.

The value of Layamon's *Brut* has already come to our attention; while the work is always classed as a verse chronicle, it is better interpreted as an epic of the legendary kings of Britain. Its author explains that his name is Layamon (Lawman) and that he is a priest at Ernleye (Arley Regis, Worcestershire). Specifically, the *Brut* (*c.*1205-10) is a narrative poem of more than 30,000 lines (which are generally printed in half as many lines of double hemistichs) recounting the story of the Britons from their founding by a mythical Brutus, descendant of Aeneas, to the year 689. The first half of the poem covers the events from the sack of Troy to the birth of Arthur; the second treats of Arthur, among others, and discusses the decline of British power under the pressure of the Anglo-Saxons. There is no need to summarize this material, since nearly all of it is outlined in Geoffrey of Monmouth's *Historia Regum Britanniae.* Instead, it should be emphasized that

Layamon is a storyteller of great talent, and a simple but skillful handler of an interesting transitional form of Old English
alliterative verse combined with French rhymed verse, who
in addition has a deep sense of patriotism and a poetic instinct
for the dramatic. His lines devoted to the story of Arthur are
particularly good. The king is here depicted as an epic hero,
a Christian champion whose defense of the Faith and whose
personal achievements are thrown into high relief. It is probably the best of the poetic treatments of Arthur as a true epic
hero rather than as the figurehead of an Arthurian romance.
Very little attention is paid to individual knights, but the conception of a knightly sodality, typified by the Table Round,
appealed strongly to the author. We may judge from Layamon's name that he was of Saxon descent; but the Celtic
Arthur is none the less the great British hero in his estimation.
The fusion of Celt and Saxon in Layamon's conception, a
century and a half after the Conquest, is remarkable. Nor is
Arthur the only famous figure to be remembered from the
lines of the *Brut;* the story of Lear is another well-told tale,
far superior to the version given by Geoffrey of Monmouth.

The Bruce is the work of John Barbour (1316?-95), who
may well be considered the first Scottish author of renown.
More is actually known about Barbour's life than is known
about Chaucer's. It is sufficient to note, however, that he was
a student and a teacher at Oxford and Paris, an archdeacon
at Aberdeen, and a royal auditor. There is reason to suppose
that he wrote a poem similar to Layamon's *Brut,* as well as a
work on the genealogy of the Royal Stewarts. *The Bruce,* his
most impressive composition, is much better than the general
run of narrative literature in the period. Comprising more
than 13,000 lines in octosyllabic couplets, it is in twenty
"books," detailing the career of Robert Bruce, patriot of Scotland, hero of Bannockburn, and king of Scotland. It is indeed
a worthy ancestor of Sir Walter Scott's tales, containing as it
does some humor, some fancy, some blood and thunder, and
a complete awareness of the authenticity of the story and its
significance as history.

For much of the information available concerning Barbour
we are indebted to Andrew of Wyntoun's *Oryginall Cronycle*
(*c.*1410), the work of an Augustinian Canon of St. Andrew's

who was later prior at a monastery on Lochleven, Scotland—a careful, serious writer, although the captious might argue that the chief justification for the epithet "original" as applied to his chronicle is that it begins at the beginning. Of an altogether contrasting type is John Trevisa, a rather robust Cornishman expelled from Oxford for the indeterminate crime of "unworthiness," who settled in Gloucestershire and did much translation of Latin works into English. The two most noted of these were the translations of Ralph Higden's *Polychronicon*, which was done in 1387, and of Bartholomew de Glanville's scientific compilation, *De Proprietatibus Rerum* (1398). Leaving aside the latter work, we may observe that the translation of Higden's chronicle is simple and accurate, though scarcely a work of strict scholarship. The most famous passage in it is a section on the state of the language in England during the lifetime of Trevisa, with special reference to the new method (1385) of using English instead of French for teaching purposes—a pungent comment upon a landmark in the uphill struggle waged by the vernacular to reassert itself after the Norman Conquest, and upon the confusion still resulting from the multiplicity of dialects in England and the lack of a standard literary language.

The early Renaissance continued to get history in the same manner as the Middle Ages; the beginnings of modern historiography are not evident before the late seventeenth century. The medieval historians worked generally on a two-dimensional plan; we find but little of the true life of the times in the pages of their chronicles, although we may learn plenty of facts and much about the sequence of events. As has been said before, we are inclined to read these medieval chroniclers, when we read them at all, for that which is not good history.

Chapter 3

Middle English Literature: The Central Period: Medieval Drama

1. The Literature of Contemporary Conditions

IF THE CHRONICLES of the Middle English period, however, do not yield a satisfactory picture of the life of the times, it is always possible to piece out a reasonably good mosaic of medieval social conditions from the occasional references made here and there in Middle English literature. It is nevertheless true that nothing in the period presents so vividly the panorama of medieval society in England as *The Canterbury Tales* and *Piers Plowman*. Chaucer's great masterpiece is a work of infinite variety, and its social observations are generally incidental to the sheer love of storytelling in the heart and mind of our finest narrative poet. *Piers Plowman,* on the other hand, is something of a monolith amid the rocky desert of earnest commentary on the times. Yet it is too often considered as an isolated phenomenon, the mysterious work of one or more obscure authors; and since it is perhaps the favorite plaything for modern experts on the English Middle Ages, other works have been neglected. The fact is that there was a substantial layer of literature critical of the times on which the foundations of *Piers Plowman* were built; and this layer was probably even more firmly established than the surviving pieces indicate.

One may find occasional scraps of verse in the early chronicles offering comment on this or that king or exalted personage, but the satiric intent—the desire to show the discrepancy between what a person or thing pretends to be and what that person or thing really is—this intent does not manifest itself much before the thirteenth century had begun to wane, or, in other words, until the feudal and monastic regimes had begun to lose their holds on the minds of men. We hear, in the political songs of this time (and of the fourteenth century to follow), the strains of exultation at the victory of Simon de Montfort over Henry III, at the defeat of this French foray or that Scottish raid, of lamentation at the death of Edward I and the evil days of his inglorious successor, Edward II. Such pieces are virtually laureate poems; but of the various authors of these only Laurence Minot (*fl.*1350), with his rude, salty, sprightly, and thoroughly hoarse vocal English patriotism, has a tangible identity.

As the fourteenth century progressed, however, with all its significant political, social, and economic developments, the literature of comment became deeper, more incisive, often bitter and cynical—times are bad; principalities and powers are corrupt and tottering; the poor man has no chance; friars are grasping and worldly; women are frivolous and untrustworthy; lawyers and bailiffs are treacherous and venal. What can a man do? Leaving aside most of the individual items in this long but rather inviting bill of complaint, let us consider especially two. One is *The Evil Times of Edward II.* Here is a clear foreshadowing of the whole literature of revolt, with sturdy proletarian backbone, which we can see throughout *Piers Plowman,* written at least half a century later. *The Evil Times of Edward II* (*c.*1320) begins by offering to tell why the times are bad, why the land is full of crime and hunger. The reason is that all the clergy are evil: greed, simony, pride, and lechery possess them all, from the Pope to the most insignificant officer of a chapter. So, too, are the nobility evil, from earl to squire. The arms of the law—judges, mayors, bailiffs, reeves—are corruption incarnate. Merchants cannot be trusted; craftsmen are all rogues. Therefore God is purging the land of its wickedness, and His blight has descended upon all men. The piece is ardent, even passionate, in its denunciation; its author is a man prompted by patriotism and a love of right. The most important fact about it, however, is that it contains in a small compass most of the message of *Piers Plowman,* with this difference, that it is direct and subjective in its attack, while *Piers Plowman* uses the device of medieval allegory. The aggressiveness of both poems, however, is unmistakable.

A companion piece, *A Song on the Times of Edward II,* is more in the nature of a political lyric. The *Song* is one of a few poems associated with the name of Michael of Kildare, an obscure friar at the Abbey of Kildare, Ireland. If Michael was actually the first Irishman to protest against English rule, as is possible, then he holds at least a historical significance. The *Song* makes use of some elements of the fable. The world is evil; hatred is supreme; the law is greedy; pride rules all men; and neither Church nor State is interested in maintaining justice. The writer is reminded of an old fable: the lion was once sitting in justice when the fox and the wolf were brought before him. The innocent ass was added to the group of culprits. The fox and the wolf bribed the lion to condone their offenses; but because the ass was poor and honest, he gave nothing, and so was condemned.

Occasionally the satirical literature is in lighter vein; an excellent example is the amusing *Land of Cockaygne* (c.1275), which embodies the popular continental folk tale of a land where everything is made of things to eat, where rivers literally flow with milk and honey and houses are made of pastry, and where even the birds fly through the air duly cooked and prepared for the table. More savage in tone are the many diatribes found in other poems against the pride of women, particularly in respect to their gaudy clothing and hairdressing, as well as their love of ease, comfort, and luxury. Did not the great Chaucer himself inveigh against those women who, in their fatuous tricking out and adorning of their anatomies, "shewen the boce of hir shap, and the horrible swollen membres, that semeth like the maladie of hirnia, in the wrappynge of hir hoses; and eek the buttokes of hem faren as it were the hyndre part of a she-ape in the fulle of the moone"? [1]

The same objections, with or without the peculiar misogynism of the Middle Ages, for which poor Eve was largely responsible, are obvious in the many poetic flings at the pomp and circumstance of the lives of noblemen. In all cases it is Pride that is responsible—Pride, the most deadly of the Seven Deadly Sins. Nor is the Church guiltless; it is often "under foot," that is, earthy and brought down from its spiritual station. Here is the prevailing tone—Church and State are in a perilous condition; the Church is divided and corrupt; the State is in the hands of unworthy, self-seeking ministers. The poor man—the laborer and the yeoman—is being ground down. There is no hope unless the world can be made better,

[1] From Chaucer's *Parson's Tale,* 422-4.

and little enough hope of that, unless—it is this *unless* that Piers Plowman seeks.

This huge, sprawling poem is one of the chief monuments of the Middle Ages in England. As a human document it is impressive; as a realistic picture of the life of the times it contains memorable passages; but as a work of literary art it falls flat. There was very likely an archetype of the work that has been lost; on the other hand, it is obvious that the poem as a whole represents a popular tradition. There are three versions, known respectively as Text A, Text B, and Text C; and there are no less than 47 surviving manuscripts. Skeat, the first authoritative editor, proposed the date of 1362 for Text A, about 1377 for Text B, and 1393-8 for Text C. Various attempts, possibly successful, have been made to bring Text A and Text B together at about the same date. The three versions differ in many respects and lead to the general impression that Texts B and C are expansions and adaptations of Text A.

Text A, which is the shortest of the three, comprises a Prologue and twelve sections, called passus, divided as follows: four passus of the Vision Concerning the Field of Folk, Holy Church, and Lady Meed; four passus of the Vision Concerning Piers Plowman; and four passus of the Vision of Dowel, Dobet, and Dobest. Text B, which is probably the first extension and adaptation of Text A, consists of the same Prologue, seven passus of the Vision Concerning Piers Plowman, and three Prologues and ten passus of the Vision Concerning Dowel, Dobet, and Dobest. Text C, supposedly a revision of Text B, is the longest of the three; it contains the usual Prologue and divides many of the passus of Text B, to make 23 passus in all.

Until a complete collection and collation of all the manuscripts of all three versions of *Piers Plowman* have been accomplished—and it is expected that such a task will be completed in the not too distant future[2]—nothing definite can

---

[2] Even such a collation, however, will not clear up the uncertainty caused by the fact that *Piers Plowman* represents rather than initiates a tradition. It might clarify the status of Langland as the author of at least part of the poem. It is doubtful whether it would either confirm or disprove the celebrated "lost leaf" theory first

be reported concerning authors and originals. The texts keep referring to the author as Will, which is taken to be the Christian name William and not an allegorical reference to the human attribute. Is this William Langland (Langley) of the West Country, born about 1330, a lay member of the clergy, with a wife Kit and a daughter Calote, a man who led a wandering existence throughout the southern Midlands and who had his marvelous vision, as he says, in the Malvern Hills? Or is it some other Will? Or is it John But, who wrote until "death dealt him a dint and drove him under ground"? That Will (Langland or whoever else) wrote the archetype and John But (or others) developed the other versions is not only possible but even probable. It is the same old problem of multiple authorship that plagued the scholars of *Beowulf*, and the answer is likely to be the same in both instances. If—and it is a rather large "if"—Text A represents the earliest version of the Middle English poem known as *Piers Plowman*, then it was written by a poet of undoubted talents, whom we shall designate simply as the Piers Plowman Poet. Then the work of the Piers Plowman Poet was altered, modified, and revised by other writers whom it is not possible to trace. To be sure, the Piers Plowman Poet himself could have adapted his Text A version to Text B and even to Text C. There would have been years enough—and yet not too many—for the Piers Plowman Poet to have done all the work. On the other hand, in view of the many striking differences between the later Text C and the earlier Texts A and B, the chances are greatly in favor of more than one man's having had a finger in the process.

Be that as it may, the fact remains that the poem is far more important than its author or authors. Written in broad, majestic, alliterative long lines—the most distinguished ex-

stated by John Manly in 1906. This ingenious and provocative theory, which was never able to get beyond the stage of a theory, had it that an obvious incoherence in one section of *Piers Plowman* was due to the loss of a page from the archetype of the poem. Since the archetype is probably no longer in existence, or, if so, is hardly to be recognized among the 47 manuscripts extant, hopes in a definitive result from a thorough collation need not be set too high.

ample of the alliterative revival of the fourteenth century[3]—
it stands forth in bold relief as the greatest vision poem in
Middle English literature; only the transcendent power and
consummate art of Dante's *Divine Comedy* surpass it in
medieval vision literature as a whole. To make any kind of
summary of the poem is at best, however, a difficult business.

Piers Plowman is, in fact, a sequence of vision poems.
The poet tells what he sees in a series of dreams, always
with the inference that he sees more than he tells. He begins
on a summer's day in the Malvern Hills. His first slumber
brings him sight of the fair field full of folk (the World), situ-
ated between the tower of Truth (God) and the dungeon
of evil spirits (Hell). An impressive cross-section of medieval society moves in procession over the scene of the Prologue: plowmen, churchmen, merchants, beggars, hermits,
pardoners, priests, lawyers, drabs from the ditch. A king
appears; and in Text B a whole company of rats and mice,
who introduce—as far as we can tell, for the first time in
literature—the fable of the Belling of the Cat. Yet who the
cat is, whether king or royal personage, or who the leader
of the rats may be, does not immediately appear.

The poet sees a beautiful lady, who informs him that the
tower he sees is the abode of God. The dungeon is the
Castle of Care, in which dwells the father of False. She

---

[3] See the remark on page 76 about this so-called alliterative revival. It should be emphasized that French and Latin forms pre-
dominated in English verse after the Norman Conquest. The
tradition of the long alliterative line, familiar to the reader of
Old English literature, never died out completely. Shortly after
1340, West Midland writers in particular began to use the alliterative long line in a fashion that persisted into the fifteenth century.
One feature of this alliterative revival was that the alliteration
itself was more frequent in the line—instead of the two or three
alliterating words found in Old English poetry, four or even five
alliterating words were not uncommon in the West Midland Middle English poetry. Many of the better known romances are written in this measure, including *Joseph of Arimathea, William of
Palerne, Morte Arthure, Chevalere Assigne, Sir Gawain and the
Green Knight,* as well as a great many poems on contemporary
conditions, of which *Piers Plowman,* is, of course, the most
celebrated.

reveals herself as Holy Church. The poet asks how he is to know False. Holy Church bids him turn around, and he then sees another beautiful woman in rich apparel; she is Lady Meed (Reward or Bribery), who is to be married to False. The wedding is arranged, with Simony and Civil explaining the property involved in the dowry. Theology objects to the marriage, and so it is decided to travel to London to settle the matter. False loses courage and runs away; Lady Meed is apprehended and taken before the king. The king tries her; she pretends to be contrite and offers to glaze a church window but immediately thereafter advises mayors and judges to accept bribes. The king politically attempts to marry her off to Conscience; but Conscience will have none of her and takes occasion to expose *con amore* Lady Meed's vices. Reason is therefore summoned and advises stern justice on the part of the king. These proceedings go to make up in general the first portion of the poem.

The poet rouses briefly from his dream but soon has a second vision, in which the new royal favorite, Reason, is preaching. Through the intervention of Repentance, the Seven Deadly Sins each confess, in passages that for sheer realism cannot be surpassed anywhere in medieval literature. After all the confessions have been heard, Repentance makes supplication for the penitents. They all start forth blindly to seek Truth, but no one can tell the way. Now for the first time appears the Plowman, Piers, who says that he knows the way. After he has described it, the pilgrims accept him as their guide; first, however, he insists that he must plow his half-acre; and he enjoins all who wish to follow him to labor likewise. Another conspicuous passage ensues, discussing the matter of strikes, the unsatisfactory nature of transient employment, and the regimen of the poor. Then it happens that Truth (God) sends Piers a pardon intended for royalty, aristocrats, bishops, laborers, and even a few lawyers and merchants. By inference the lesser clergy and the friars are excluded from the pardon. A doubting priest questions the validity of the divine bull, and in the following dispute the poet awakens from his dream, to reflect upon the comparative insignificance of pardon from the Pope or, indeed, from any part of the ecclesiastical organization, when placed beside the spiritual satisfaction that comes from leading a good life and not trusting to indulgences.

This completes the Vision Concerning Piers the Plowman, but in Text B and Text C there is still the Vision of Dowel, Dobet, and Dobest to be considered. This is a puzzling but historically valuable section, for it prophesies a definite reform in the Church, which is to come from some courageous king, and thus anticipates by almost two centuries the revolution wrought by Henry VIII. The chief purpose of the whole Vision of Dowel, Dobet, and Dobest is missionary, even proselytizing; it urges the conversion of Saracens and other non-Christians and insists that Jesus is the only true Saviour. Faith and Hope may pass one by; but Love is still the Good Samaritan. In eloquent words it paints the Passion, the struggle between Light and Darkness, the victory over Satan, and the glory of Easter. Yet the end is still far off. Antichrist is still to come. As Skeat puts it beautifully:

The Church is assailed by many foes, and can scarcely hold her own; diseases assail all mankind; death "pashes" to the dust kings and knights, emperors and popes, and many a lovely lady; old age can scarcely bear up against despair; Envy hates Conscience, and hires flattering friars to salve Conscience with soothing but deadly remedies, till Conscience, hard beset by Pride and Sloth, cries out to Contrition to help him; but Contrition still slumbers, benumbed by the deadly potions he has drunk. With a last effort Conscience arouses himself, and seizes his pilgrim's staff, determined to wander wide over the world till he shall find Piers the Plowman. And the dreamer awakes in tears.[4]

This moral lesson, however, told as it is with passion and the utmost sincerity, has been taught so often since *Piers Plowman,* and more according to modern ideas, that we do not rank the poem so high on the strength of the moral alone.

---

[4] Quoted from W. W. Skeat, *The Vision of William concerning Piers the Plowman,* 10th ed., Oxford, 1928, xxxv.

The unforgettable pictures of Lechery and Gluttony, in the Shriving of the Deadly Sins, would in themselves establish the Piers Plowman Poet as an unusual painter of satirical powers. The noise and color of the Prologue, in its peculiar style, compares favorably in total effect with any other medieval panorama that might be mentioned. Formless and inchoate *Piers Plowman* may be, sadly deficient in architectonics, lacking in the joy of life; for even the most amusing passages in it—and there are many—represent unconscious humor. The strictures of the alliterative verse are a deterrent to accurate and poetic expression. The power and mass of the work, however, can hardly fail to impress the thoughtful reader. If it is not a work of art, it is none the less a great social document. Summing up as it does both medieval vision and allegorical literature in one great monument, its presence in English literature is invaluable.

The realism in the pages of *Piers Plowman* is not necessarily overdrawn—we can well believe in the louse on Avarice's hat, in the slobbering jowls of the man Avarice, in the tavern scene where Gluttony and his motley companions are bibbing and vomiting, in the blear-eyed countenance of Sloth, in the disorderly squabbles where Wrath is, in the hermits and tramps along the roads of the Malvern Hills, "great lubbers all, with their wenches following them," in the cries of the street vendors of London. But this realism, as so often in medieval literature, is harsh, acid, and directed toward the instinct of disgust; its purpose is primarily didactic, and didactic in the manner of the medieval teacher who desires to emphasize the *contemptus mundi*. Still, it is so vivid in *Piers Plowman* that the remaining pieces in the category of social commentary seem drab in comparison. *Pierce the Ploughmans Crede* (c.1400) is derivative. It sustains the complaints against the orders of friars already expressed in *Piers Plowman* and in many another piece; it also introduces us to Piers himself and to his ragged family. Possibly by the same author is *The Ploughman's Tale* (1395), at one time ascribed to Chaucer, which contains a dialogue between a griffin, who represents the prelates and the general clergy, and a pelican, who represents the author. Both pieces are well worth reading. They seem to be the work of an author of Wycliffite persuasion, who protests specifically against the corruption of the Church and enjoins poverty instead of gaudy worldliness for a worthy priest. *Piers Plowman* itself, however, only implied this protest; and it is not possible to show that the Piers Plowman Poet was a follower of Wycliffe. Instead, he seems to have been a sincere critic of the Church who was nevertheless orthodox in his beliefs.

Of only moderate significance are two poems entitled *The Parlement of the Thre Ages* and *Wynnere and Wastoure*. They are both from the generation following *Piers Plowman*. The first is a lugubrious allegory on the ages of man—vanity of vanities! The second is a political allegory, incomplete, but dealing obviously with the figure of the Black Prince, eldest son of Edward III, and with his relation to the Hundred Years War. No brief account can do more than mention the fact that numerous satirical and social comments are sprinkled throughout these pieces.

There are many other pieces, too, such as the *Dreams of Adam Davy*, a collection of visions telling, childishly and sycophantically, of the dubious glories of Edward II; *Richard the Redeless;* and *Mum and the Sothsegger*. The last two are complaints directed specifically against the turmoil of the reign of Richard II. For these and others there is no space here. We return always to *Piers Plowman*. Is the latter half of the fourteenth century the Age of Chaucer or the Age of Piers Plowman? To some extent, of course, it is both; but Chaucer is too forward-looking to be completely of the age. On the other hand, *Piers Plowman,* for all its broken eloquence and occasional social hopefulness, is very much of the Middle Ages: conservative, as every satire is likely to be, but deeply sympathetic toward the problems of the time. Indeed, from a Marxist point of view, the Piers Plowman Poet is greater than Chaucer; but if based on purely literary standards, such an opinion would not be tenable. It is certainly true, however, that the Piers Plowman Poet is the most distinguished spokesman of the commoner of the Middle English era in his vague yearnings for a better world, which is sometimes called "fourteenth-century socialism." But more effective, and withal more significant of the times, are such lines as:

"By the Rood!" said Repentance, "thou art facing toward Heaven, provided it be in thy heart as I have heard on thy tongue. Trust in His great mercy, and thou mayst yet be saved. For all the wretchedness of this world and its wicked deeds pass like a spark of fire that falls in the Thames and perishes in a drop of water; so do all the sins of all kinds of men who with good will confess them and cry for mercy; they shall never come to Hell."

2. Homily and Legend

Of Middle English literature, as indeed of all medieval literatures, it can truly be said: "The Lord gave the word; great was the company of preachers." But for one Piers Plowman Poet there were a hundred less inspired though equally earnest workers in the employ of the Lord, clerics who labored in homily and precept to make prosperous the state of His kingdom. Most of these homilies and legends were composed in the Middle English period before 1300—in the great age of monasticism. However, there has never been at any time in the history of Christianity in England any notable scarcity of such writings; it is simply that, as the Middle Ages progressed toward the Renaissance, other forms of literature took the center of interest. Moreover, while most of the Middle English sermons originated before 1300, many of the legends go back to the beginnings of the Christian Church.

The starting point for literature of this category was not the sermon but the *Lectio* in the early Mass. This was the reading of an appropriate scriptural text from the Gospels, the Epistles, or the Prophecies. The Benedictines extended the practice to services other than the Mass, and, largely through their influence, the readings came to include some portions of the Scriptures besides the Gospels, the Epistles, or the Prophecies. Commentaries by the Church Fathers appeared next in the readings, as well as biographical material from the *Acta Sanctorum,* the official lives of the saints. The purpose of these changes was to heighten the entertainment value of the services and to give them dramatic effect; in reality it is the same motive as that which produced the Church drama.

It is unnecessary to trace all the steps by which this modification of the original *Lectio* developed, other than to say that the glorifying of saints became popular, and it soon was the customary procedure to devote a large part of the service on a given saint's day to the exaltation of that saint. The number of saints was, of course, constantly increasing, so that there was no difficulty in finding one for every day in the calendar. Another trait of human nature besides the desire for entertainment came to manifest itself, and that was the instinctive preference for a legend over a factual account. In time the legendary matter accruing to the personality of a saint crowded out the mere biographical elements and even the homiletic passages that the saint's life might inspire. Biography, homily, legend, and commentary were soon inextricably tangled; and a new type of literature evolved which was neither fish, flesh, nor fowl, only primarily religious and didactic.

The term *homily* should be distinguished from the term *sermon,* as the Middle English used them. There are the original discourses, or *sermons,* to be delivered to a congregation; other pieces, to be read to the congregation or to be perused in private by the churchman who needed material or inspiration for his services, are called *homilies.* Perhaps such a distinction is only confusing. It is, in any case, enough to say a few words about the composite type. The medieval homilies, with a few notable exceptions, are inferior in interest to those of the Old English period. The legends, however, show a great deal of imagination and are often vivid narratives. In fact, the great virtue of these Middle English legends is their story quality. Moreover, it is often possible to get brief glimpses of the life of the times, incidental though these details of everyday existence may be. Too often, however, the pieces are choked with dialectics; or as sermons they appear wordy, dull, and prosaic in achievement. It frequently happens that allegory is used, often of an elaborate nature, which does not make for clarity.

There are many Anglo-Latin and Anglo-French examples of this kind of literature. Most of the really effective pieces, however, are in the vernacular and bear witness to the vitality of the English hagiographic tradition. Almost a hundred new saints were introduced to the English Church after the Norman Conquest; but the Norman clergy did not succeed in making many of them popular in England. One strikingly new theme is nevertheless obvious in even the early Middle English writings—the theme of the Virgin Mary, which, as we have seen, bore influence upon the fiction of the time as well. Indeed, the homilies dealing with the Virgin are so numerous and continued for so long that the type fell into a certain decadence, as is obvious when one looks at the many rather grotesque tales of the Virgin in later Middle English literature. The earlier pieces, however, are endowed with tenderness and dignity in their treatment of the Mother of God.

These very qualities of tenderness and dignity, with the undoubted sincerity that attends all these works, are their chief points of effectiveness. The average saint led a dull life; he or she was a creature of blind zeal and emotional one-sidedness. The failure of medieval doctrine to adopt anything but an absolute perspective, so that everything is either white or black, is painfully evident in the tendency of these saints to throw tact, reason, and common sense to the four winds while they defend their faith. It is manifestly unfair and certainly impractical to generalize from even a moderate number of instances. But the majority of these medieval saints are martyrs to their faith; they accomplish miracles; they are persecuted; many are killed by infidels. Some, like Eustace, are models of patience on a spiritual plane; others, like Juliana or Cecilia, are exposed to physical torments or to a lingering death, although these ordeals are made painless because of the victim's religious convictions; still others, such as Andrew or George, come very close to being epic or romance heroes. Indeed, the career of George, who was once a humble martyred saint in Cappadocia, later became confused with that of Perseus, the warrior of Greek legend; like Perseus, George rescued a damsel in distress. He finally ended as the patron saint of England—truly an end worthy of a male Cinderella. The truth is that most of these saints derived so much benefit from the operation of the epic process that they are heroes and heroines of legend rather than of biography. No particular attention is any longer given to the mere facts of their lives. St. George becomes a kind of Gawain, and St. John may never have died at all. Occasionally a St. Francis, a true Christian in the finest sense of the word, may come along to charm us; but most of the saints impress one as shadowy figments of an emotional state, created in a hierarchical splendor altogether in keeping with the habits of thought of the medieval mind. They remain abstractions rather than real people of virtuous life.

The sermon itself may be a characteristic plea for a special virtue; it may turn fiercely against the corruptions of society; it may inveigh against women; it may take wing into the allegorical, where it achieves varying success with the modern reader, although not a few are impressive. Many of them, as might be expected, were gathered in collections. These may have been intended for use in individual churches; but possibly they were for the edification of the clergyman himself instead of for the public instruction of his flock. All the important collections of sermons unadulterated with legends are from the thirteenth century. These include the *Bodley Homilies* in prose, and the *Lambeth Homilies,* the *Trinity College Homilies,* the *Kentish Sermons,* and the *Ormulum,* all in verse. The structure of these sermons is almost uniform: first, a statement of the text, theme, or gospel story on which the sermon is to be based; second, an exposition of the same, with or without allegory; and finally, an exhortation and conclusion, with or without summation. The subject matter is, of course, unlimited. Most of the themes have already been mentioned at one time or another, and in general it is sufficient to say that they cover the same range of topics as do orthodox sermons today.

About the *Ormulum* there should be a special note. It is a long verse-collection, comprising nearly 20,000 limping four-teeners (*septenaria*) of sermons on a text of gospel for each of thirty-two days of the year. The original plan had evidently envisaged a sermon for each day of the year, but the design was mercifully not completed. The author, Orm, is a cleric of probably Scandinavian blood, writing in Northeast Midland of about the year 1200. The work, taken as a whole, is almost the dullest piece in English literature, if a superlative must be found. It would be negligible if Orm had not adopted his own system of spelling. Each short vowel followed by a consonant in the same word is marked by the simple yet bizarre device of doubling the consonant, and this device is carried out with apparent consistency. There are also some other scribal peculiarities. Obviously, then, this method is invaluable to the student of the vernacular of about 1200. There is so little in English from that date that when it comes to us in a crude but none the less effective form of editing, it is a godsend.

Most of the so-called saints' lives, on the other hand, should be regarded as so much fiction, appropriate enough for its purpose, but still fiction. It goes without saying that they were popular and numerous. Some of them were derived from older versions, such as Aelfric's *Lives of the Saints,* but a great many were translations and adaptations of the pieces in the huge *Legenda Aurea,* compiled about 1265 by Jacobus a Voragine. The *Legenda Aurea* was continued through the fourteenth century and, after further additions, was printed by Caxton in 1483. There was also, of course, the official *Acta Sanctorum,* which served as chief source for the more important saints' lives.[5]

Homily and legend mixed are found in the large collections known as the *South-East Legendary* and the *North English Legendary,* both from the last quarter of the thirteenth century; between them they account for 150 pieces, arranged according to the calendar. Little need be said about these collections; the type has been described, and the general literary level of the individual pieces is not high. Their significance is obvious. Perhaps an exception might be made for the attractive little group of homilies on female saints, 13 in number, by Osbern Bokenham (1443). They are written in rhyme royal and, for certain touches of characterization alone, deserve to be recognized above the mass. Basically, however, the limitations of the whole type assert themselves in all these pieces, including the uninspired efforts of Chaucer himself, such as *The Second Nun's Tale, The Parson's Tale,* and *The Tale of Melibeus.*

Miscellaneous Biblical and Christian legends are more interesting. We have several treatments of the legend of the

[5] For definitions and discussion of the origin and propagation of these legends, see particularly H. Delahaye, *Les Légendes hagiographiques,* Paris, 1905; see also the bibliography to the present chapter.

Cross, which, it will be recalled, was the subject of one of the most beautiful of Old English poems. Perhaps the best of these is the combination known as the *Southern Legendary Rood Poems,* a late compilation. There is also a variety of treatments of the story of Adam and Eve. Much attention has naturally been given at all times to the Creation and to the Life of Christ. Sometimes a local legend may appear, such as *The Holy Blood of Hayles* (c.1400), which explains at some length the origin of the famous shrine of Hayles in Gloucestershire. This particular legend brings to mind the antecedent story that deals with the Holy Grail, especially the romance *Joseph of Arimathea. The Harrowing of Hell* and its pseudo-scriptural source, *The Gospel of Nicodemus,* have their Middle English incarnations. *The Gospel of Nicodemus,* in fact, seems to have been of wide currency and fairly influential, especially upon certain aspects of the English miracle plays; it appears several times in Middle English versions from the twelfth to the sixteenth centuries. Somewhere in this category comes the lively *Fifteen Signs before Judgment.* A poem by that name was written independently about 1320. It tells in brief but vivid enumeration the horrifying portents to come on each of the fifteen days before Doomsday. And just as the end of the world is foretold in this fashion, so too are the mysteries of the beginnings of Christian life. The origins of the festivals of the Conception of Mary and of the Assumption of the Blessed Virgin are both explained frequently and in detail.

Undoubtedly the most spectacular literature of the legendary group, however, is that dealing with the visions of and visits to the lower world. The significance of this theme as a classical as well as a medieval favorite has already been noted. The combination of Homer, Virgil, and Dante is extremely influential. In Old English there was the notable case of the Vision of Drihthelm, told in Bede's *Ecclesiastical History.* The importance of a vision poem such as *Piers Plowman* is obvious. Mention should be made also of two Latin vision poems, *The Vision of the Monk of Evesham,* by Adam of Evesham (c.1225), and *The Vision of Turcill* (c.1210). In both of these the protagonist visits Hell in person. The Middle English vernacular representatives of the type are *The Vision of St. Paul, St. Patrick's Purgatory,* and *The Vision of Tundale.*

The material in *The Vision of St. Paul* (*c.*1375) is ancient —it has a Greek original and more than a score of Latin versions. Hell, as St. Paul saw it on his visit, is a place of dire torments—burning trees on which hang damned souls who did not go to church; heated cauldrons in which are mixed miraculously snow, ice, dried blood, serpents' venom, lightning, thunder, hail, whirlwinds, and stench; burning wheels, lakes full of poisonous reptiles. But the work pales beside *St. Patrick's Purgatory,* which, like the saint's life of Brandan, introduces Celtic fantasy into a subject that scarcely needed it. The fantasy is nevertheless welcome. The original seems to be the Latin account by Henry of Saltrey, an Anglo-Latin writer of the twelfth century. The story, however, is told by many other writers; it will be recalled that Marie de France was responsible for one version. The Middle English poem was composed about 1325, and there are several later manuscripts. Sir Owayn, or Owayn Miles, a sinful knight, avails himself of the opportunity afforded by St. Patrick to purge himself of his guilt while he is still alive. He descends into a vast pit, where he sees yawning, grinning devils making merry with lost souls. Most of the tortures described in *The Vision of St. Paul* are duplicated; but there is in addition an imaginative refinement of the tortures which is indeed unusual, and some details of the Celtic other world are particularly conspicuous—the desert wastes, the bitter wind, and the high, narrow bridge over a fiery chasm. The piece is believed to have some topographical basis in an actual spot in Donegal, Ireland.

Still, the most elaborate of these three vigorous poems of the underworld is *The Vision of Tundale,* of which the Middle English version was composed near 1400. The story, however, is known all over Europe, from Scandinavia to Italy.

Tundale, a confirmed Irish sinner, on his way to collect some money due him, stopped to dine with one of his debtors. He was stricken and lay as dead for four days. Demons conducted him to the underworld, with only his guardian angel to protect him. Here he saw conventional tortures; but the idea of the eternal nature of all this punishment was conveyed to him most forcefully. When a soul was consumed, its ashes were recovered, and it was forged anew into its original shape, to suffer once again and thus continually its appointed punishment. Great gluttonous beasts devoured it and spewed it up to devour it again. Tundale had to lead a cow which he had stolen over a bridge a hand's-breadth in width, studded with spikes, over a lake full of stinking monstrosities; he saw Satan crushing souls as one would crush grapes. But he also saw the abode of the virtuous, the nine orders of angels, the Trinity, and even God. Awaking from his trance, he was converted and, after spending the remainder of his days in penance and benevolence of works, he went to Heaven.

It is obvious that Dante knew some if not all of this material before he set pen to his great poem of the other world. The modern reader is bound to admire the prodigal imagination, while he remains overcome by the gratuitous cruelty that impregnates almost every page of the three poems. Whenever one begins to have qualms about the parlous state of twentieth-century civilization and begins to admire the idealism and beautifully integrated thought of the Middle Ages a perusal of *The Vision of St. Paul, The Vision of Tundale,* and *St. Patrick's Purgatory* is a most salutary experience.

3. Religious Instruction and Allegory

Where the preacher ceased to be the preacher and became the religious and moral teacher is a matter difficult to decide and perhaps unnecessary to define. For the purposes of the teacher, it would sooner or later become important to have a body of literature that would make easy the dissemination of religious information, the understanding of Christian conduct and ethics, and the general edification of the Christian believer. The devices used for these purposes in the Middle Ages were many, and all of them are now familiar. There was the gathering of information into an ambitious work, and there was also the discussion, in shorter, somewhat technical treatises, of special points of Christian ritual and dogma. In a few instances there were specific handbooks or manuals for the use of a particular servant of the Church. Finally there was the special device of allegory to clothe general works of instruction.

By far the most important of the comprehensive works of this sort is the *Cursor Mundi,* a long, encyclopedic poem of almost 30,000 short couplets, composed in the north of England about 1325 and so called because it purported to be a "Cursor o' werld" ("almost it over-runs all"). No summarizing account can do justice to *Cursor Mundi,* for it manages, in spite of its prodigious length and enormous coverage— from the Creation to the Day of Doom—to maintain interest very well; and although its structure may appear at times to be ramshackle, it is by no means so incoherent a poem as a work of its nature might easily become. Aside from whatever literary value it may possess, which is not great, the poem holds a good deal of interest because its sequence of events bears a similarity to that found in some of the cycles of miracle plays. It may well have been of influence on the budding playwrights of the Middle Ages. Further to be noted is the fact that the author virtually dedicates the work to the Virgin: she is the best of all lovers and the most satisfying of all topics of discourse. There is something in this of a direct slap at the chivalric romances; hence the prologue of *Cursor Mundi* is a clear statement of the psychology that created the anti-romance.

Robert Mannyng of Brunne, who wrote a *Chronicle,* as we have seen, is the author also of *Handlyng Synne,* a translation (1303) of William of Waddington's Anglo-French *Manuel des Péchiez.* The title suggests the idea of pondering one's sins and seeking means of correcting them. The work is purely didactic in intent, but Mannyng is no mere moralizer. His poem, while unoriginal, is adapted primarily to the purpose of telling *exempla;* it is therefore a noteworthy collection of tales. The Ten Commandments are each illustrated by from one to three tales; in similar fashion the Seven Deadly Sins, the Seven Sacraments, the Twelve Requisites of Shrift, and the Twelve Graces of Shrift are given pith and moment. The stories chosen are often pointed bits of social comment; they may attack matters of dress and behavior, the evils of tournaments and miracle plays, worldly priests, disobedient children, usurers, and misers. Most of the stories have the special merit of being short and simple, and the satire, while similarly direct, is neither malicious nor bitter. The tales of Pers the usurer, of Bishop Grosseteste and his love of music, of the miser who tried to devour his gold are all worth reading. As a fine example of a collection of *exempla, Handlyng Synne* is one of the best, and this is not said to detract from its values as moral doctrine. Neither the Anglo-French original nor the later *Manual of Sins* (c.1425) by a man named Englyssh is in any way so useful a work.

The other extreme, however, is amply illustrated by *The Ayenbite of Inwit,* or *The Remorse of Conscience.* This is a close translation of *Le Somme des Vices et des Vertues* of the thirteenth century, written by one Friar Lorens. The Middle English *Ayenbite* is inferentially by a certain Mich(a)el, a Kentishman connected with the cloister of St. Anselm in Canterbury, and is dated exactly in 1340. In a negative way it may be called a thoroughly medieval document, in that it contains all the limitations of the conventional medieval teacher without any of his special virtues. It is dull, depressing, without a semblance of humanity. Basically it stands as a treatise on the sins, purely expository, devoid of the saving grace of an illustrative tale. The passion of the medieval academician for division and subdivision glowers at the reader from every page. Much better is *The Mirror of St. Edmund* (c.1350), for here the injunction is not to die well— according to the *Ayenbite,* he has not learned to live who has not learned to die—but rather to live in perfection, honorably, meekly, lovingly. Both works are ascetic beyond the powers of present-day comprehension; but at least the author of the *Mirror* has a positive rather than a negative point of view.

There are many other such pieces, which can best be left to the specialist, and even the specialist has shown very little interest in the heavy religious verse and ponderous expression of John Gaytryge (c.1375) and William of Shoreham (c.1325). In such miscellaneous works the more technical aspects of the Christian ritual call for definition and explanation. So there is another large group of pieces dedicated to the services and the offices of the Church—Mass books, catechisms, a variety of prayer books or books containing prayers, meditations on climactic events in the life of the Saviour (especially, of course, on the Passion), and on the nature of ban and anathema; and back we come to the inevitable fact of death—seven questions to be asked of a dying man, an "excitation of comfort to them that be in peril of death," and actually a treatise of some 8,000 words of prose called *The Book of the Craft of Dying*. In all this slag there is some rich ore. One notable case in point is the readable and rewarding *Ancrene Riwle*, for by general consent it is the most effective piece of English vernacular prose between Wulfstan and Richard Rolle. It is a manual of devotional nature, intended for three young girls who are to become anchoresses. It was composed not long after 1200. Some fifty years later it was revised to apply to any sister who would withdraw herself from the world; in this form it is sometimes known as *The Ancrene Wisse*. Of its original author we know nothing. One manuscript specifies that the work was written by Simon of Ghent, Bishop of Salisbury; but this is taken to refer to the authorship of a Latin version, which may or may not have been the source. Another name often associated with the *Riwle* is that of Richard Poor (d.1237) of Tarente. Since the work has not been studied much until recently, there is still uncertainty about its beginnings; and yet it is clear that the *Riwle* itself, that version intended for the three girls, is the genesis. Whether the original was in French, Latin, or English is not yet established; the probabilities are that it was in English.

In its contents the *Riwle*, through eight separate chapters, gives full directions for services, prayers, devotions, and the spiritual life; for the complete worship of the Virgin; for the etiquette of meals, visiting hours, alms-giving, traffic, dress, and domestic activities; for the keeping of pets— the anchoress may have but one cat; and in general for all deportment within the nunnery. It proceeds to urge the requisite virtues, with special emphasis on patience and caution, modesty and self-effacement, diligence, and vigilance. It discusses at length the matter of Confession, its purpose and its efficacy. The conclusion explains that Love demands for its servants only the pure in heart; these pure in heart will alone be worthy of the Love that Christ has borne for mankind, that Love which is the supreme ruler of the world.

Unfortunately the idiom and tonality of the prose of *The Ancrene Riwle* render it impossible to translate the work in any manner worthy of the original. It is just near enough in flavor to modern prose so that it can be recognized as good prose; but its dialect is a difficult one for the uninitiated—it is one of the finest examples of the early Southern dialect—and its syntax is archaic. A literal translation will not do, and a free translation loses most of the original savor. It is simply a case of the untranslatable. For the rest, the author has a wide acquaintance with standard source works of his day: he knows the Church Fathers, the bestiaries, the popular homiletic materials, legends, and history. Nor is he averse to the use of homely incident and detail on the one hand or of allegorical devices on the other. Taken as a whole, the work offers an excellent compendium of Middle English taste, thought, and intellectual background; but it will not tolerate excerpts. For one thing, it is too comprehensive; for another, it is too closely integrated. Its total effect, however, is unmistakably one of dignity, liberality, sincerity, and vigor, to say nothing of essential piety and humanity. Its unusual willingness to assert the importance of women in Christian life is almost enough recommendation; its range and fundamental wisdom are a complete encomium.

After considering *The Ancrene Riwle,* the reader will be justified in feeling that other similar manuals, such as John Mirk's *Instructions for Parish Priests* (in verse of about 1400) or the Middle English versions of *The Rule of St. Benedict* (in both verse and prose of about the same date), are dreary items. Indeed, no further attention is due them. Instead, it would be better to examine the allegories of the Middle English vernacular, always keeping in mind that Bishop Grosseteste's Anglo-French *Le Chasteau d'Amour,* described on a preceding page, is the best work of this sort.

The Abbey of the Holy Ghost (*c.*1350), in prose, is relatively unimportant. This abbey is built upon Conscience; Righteousness and Purity cleared the ground for it; Meekness and Poverty laid the foundations; Obedience and Mercy built the walls, and so on—each part of the structure is the responsibility of some virtue or virtues. Four evil damsels, Envy, Pride, Hazard, and Evil Thoughts, sent by "a wicked ruler," visit the abbey and make trouble; but the Holy Ghost drives them out. Scarcely, we may conclude, an exciting story.

In the contemporaneous *Desert of Religion,* a fugitive from life finds himself in the wasteland of Hard Penance. A rather impressive opening is then buried under the driest kind of philosophical ramification of thought: in the desert are trees, and each tree has branches. In each case the branch represents a virtue or a vice, and it is traced to the main stock of virtue or vice whence it came.

However, *The Testament of Love* has a peculiar value, because it was for a long time attributed to Chaucer and was often printed among his works until it was finally rejected in the nineteenth century as non-Chaucerian for both linguistic and stylistic reasons. The author is Thomas Usk, who wrote it in prison while he was awaiting sentence (and, as it happened, execution) for having betrayed his master, John of Northampton. It was from the details given in this poem that there arose the Chaucer Legend, which had it that Chaucer spent some of his days in prison. At the outset Usk explains that he is awaiting a change of fortune and prays to Margaret, who, he tells us, is a woman betokening "grace, learning, or the wisdom of God, or else Holy Church." To escape some wild animals in a wood, the poet embarked on the ship Travail. He was driven to an island, where he found Margaret, "a pearl of price." Love, appealed to for comfort, reproached him for his faint heart and bade him persevere. The poet explains, not very convincingly, how he divulged a secret on compulsion. Love assures him that God and His Providence are great and good. The last two books of the three contained in the poem are rather weak reminiscences of Chaucer's *Hous of Fame* and Boethius's *Consolation of Philosophy,* of which we have already had a summary. The reference to Margaret, the pearl, associates the poem with a cult of French chivalric love poetry known as the Marguerite cult and brings *The Testament of Love* into immediate relation to Chaucer's *Parlement of Foules,* his *Legend of Good Women,* and the love poetry of the contemporaneous French poets Deschamps and Machaut. But back of all these poems in greater or less degree, as it lies back of nine tenths of all the medieval allegorical romances, is the famous French *Roman de la Rose*. For this, the most noted of European vision allegories of the age, there is room for only the barest outline. It falls into two sections: the first, by Guillaume de Lorris, was composed about 1227 and consists of 4,067 lines in short couplets; the second, a continuation by Jean de Meun(g), belongs to the years 1268-77 and contains the bulk of the poem, a solid effort of 22,047 lines.

The section by de Lorris is an *ars amandi,* and from the standpoint of subsequent medieval literature it is the more influential. The poet, a lover of love, beauty, and the joys of spring, is awakened on a May morning by the song of birds; he cannot resist the temptation to walk amid flowering meads and purling brooks. He comes into a beautiful garden enclosed by high walls, on which are delineated personifications: Hate, Felony, Avarice, Envy, Poverty, Old Age, and Hypocrisy. Idleness the portress, admits him. Within he finds the God of Love and his retinue. He is shown a rosebud, a symbol of his lady, and is wounded by an arrow from Cupid. His desire is to possess the rosebud; he is opposed by various allegorical personages—Chastity, Modesty, and Wicked Tongue, for example—and is assisted by others, such as Fair Welcome, Pity, and Frankness. Before the lover, after various millings around, is able to attain his objective, the portion of the poem by de Lorris breaks off.

Jean de Meun, who picks up the narrative, has sometimes been called the "Voltaire of the thirteenth century," and although he is scarcely the equal of his brilliant compatriot of the eighteenth century, still it is true that his lines are for the most part satirically discursive. The satire is directed at women and the clergy, the butts of the *fabliaux.* However, doctors, lawyers, merchants, and old people are also lampooned, with several illustrative *exempla.* The original story is well lost in the shuffle; but de Meun eventually allows the lover to attain his Rose.

It may be conceded that, in the history of French literature, de Meun's contribution is more important to the development of medieval thought than that of de Lorris. But in the story of English literature, it is the courtly allegory of de Lorris, with its idyllic framework, that is most frequently met with. While it is an exaggeration to maintain that every reference by an English medieval writer to babbling streams, singing birds, paintings on walls, and abstract characters in a garden represents an obligation to the *Roman de la Rose,* it is nearer the truth to say it than to deny it. Certainly every Middle English allegorical romance owes some kind of debt to de Lorris. As for the remainder of the poem, it is not particularly original; de Meun is more gifted as an organizer and compiler of well-tested material than he is as a blazer of new paths. Yet many of the details of story, of characterization, and of satirical attitude found in later works—in Chaucer's for instance—are traceable to de Meun. All in all, the *Roman de la Rose,* partly on its own merits as literature but even more because of its influence on subsequent European literature, deserves to stand as one of the major works of the Middle Ages.

4. Proverb, Precept, and Warning

Although the efforts of the medieval teacher were often expressed in the ingenious if occasionally tortuous manner of allegory, it is possible to find his moral preachment expressed in straightforward, even blunt, platitudes. Proverb and precept can be turned up among the sentences of almost any medieval writer of importance. In many cases, the Middle English cleric thought it worth while to collect them. Some of these collections, in fact, had their counterparts during the Old English period.

Thus, there are several versions in Middle English of *The Distichs of Cato,* as well as one in Anglo-Norman from early in the twelfth century. The *Distichs* had apparently as much popularity in the time of Chaucer as they had in the time of Alfred the Great; and there are allusions to them as late as 1500. Caxton printed the first of several early Modern English versions. Similarly, there was some miscellaneous didactic, gnomic stuff gathered together under the title *The ABC of*

*Aristotle (c.*1400). The appearance of the name of the great Stagirite is purely symbolic; Aristotle represented to the Middle Ages all human knowledge, although exactly how much the Middle Ages knew of the authentic works of Aristotle is a moot point. It is unnecessary to dwell upon either of these thoroughly commonplace collections, except to comment upon the fatuous though unquenchable thirst of mankind for the obvious and the trite. *The Proverbs of Alfred* and *The Proverbs of Hendyng,* in manuscripts of the thirteenth century, continue the tradition, but their wisdom is more secular and worldly-wise—"never tell thy foe that thy foot aches"; "greedy is the godless"; "when the cup is fullest, carry it most carefully"; "he is free with his horse who never had one."

The pedagogue and the child psychologist might be interested in the two works, *How the Wyse Man Taught Hys Sone* and *How the Good Wife Taught Her Daughter.* Both are late Middle English; but the second of them is much the later. It is as if the upbringing of women were a kind of afterthought. In view of the uphill struggle of women to get themselves educated, this afterthought has a sardonic historical confirmation. Taking them by and large, all these pieces of instruction tend to illustrate the somewhat disturbing fact that the standards of good conduct in life have changed very little from the time of the Old Testament to the present. But the literary accomplishment of the Biblical counterpart of these collections is far greater than that of the medieval versions; there is no possible comparison between the gripping power and beauty of Proverbs and Ecclesiastes and the pedestrianism of *The Proverbs of Alfred* and *The Proverbs of Hendyng,* to say nothing of the others.

If we now step aside from bare proverb and precept and look at the more ambitious general treatments of life on earth as the medieval teacher saw it, we are confronted with a number of individual works, nearly all in verse, whose net effect can best be described as depressing or tedious, or both. The best known of these is the *Poema Morale,* or *Moral Ode,* composed soon after 1200. It has a special importance because it is the first surviving vernacular poem written in the septenary line, or the fourteener. It appears to have been fairly popular; at least there are seven known manuscripts.

The poet observes that he is now older than he was and ought therefore to know more. He regrets his waste of opportunity, the imperfection of his accomplishments, and the barrenness of his old age. He begs the reader to profit by his own sad experience; God is ready to reward the virtuous and those who seek betterment. The piece turns next to the inevitable picture of Judgment Day, the Joys of Heaven, the Pains of Hell—let him who would attain Paradise keep away from the broad and easy road and follow the straight and narrow. On the whole, the poem is calm and temperate and, except for its sententiousness, capable of being swallowed with a minimum of distaste.

The same can scarcely be said of the others. There was the recurring motif of earth to earth, dust to dust (*Erthe upon Erthe,* in several versions, ranging in date from 1300 to 1625, and *Signs of Death, c.*1275). Man's life is brief; sickness, disaster, and old age come—these are the three messengers of death described in a poem of that name. (*c.*1350). The Devil lurks as the perpetual adversary (*The Enemies of Man, c.*1340). Where are all our joys and riches when we lie at the point of death? Here the vanity of human wishes, familiar to us in the *ubi sunt?* formula of the Old English elegiac poems, is once more a favorite theme. The Middle English pieces in this category, however, can never compete with the Old English elegies. St. Bernard and St. Bede both warn us of what is to come: Doomsday, the last trump, and the sifting of the corruptible and the incorruptible; therefore serve Christ and flee the Devil. These ideas are stated in a variety of poems, including *The Sayings of St. Bernard* (*c.*1275); *The Saws of St. Bede,* from the same date; *Doomsday* (*c.*1250); *On Serving Christ* (*c.*1275); *Memento Mori* (*A Song of Death, c.*1400); *Old Age* (*c.*1315); *Death* (*c.*1260); *Three Sorrowful Tidings,* and a group of fragmentary pieces dating from the fourteenth century. One notable little poem is *Maximian,* a paraphrase of the first six elegies of the Roman poet Cornelius Maximianus Gallus (*c.*500), which gives a pungent taste of decrepit old age—that dire human curse, which medieval writers like Jean de Meun and Chaucer paint in most repellent features. But the dreary imploring goes on: Spare us, O God! we live amid phantoms; all we have is dross of gold; long life is a vain illusion; well can we agree with St. Augustine that the world is contemptible; well can we be grateful to Isidore when he counseled fasting, prayer, and contrition. It all resolves itself to this: man is born to sorrow because of Adam's sin; even though he may be rich and happy, he is the thrall of death. The world is evil; let us keep watch and prepare ourselves. We could easily trade most of these lugubrious Middle English pieces, however, for the somber and unforgettable, though crotchety, verse of Bernard of Clairvaux's *Hora Novissima.*

5. Biblical Translation and Paraphrase

There is one thoroughgoing translation of the Bible in the Middle English period, that undertaken under the general supervision of John Wycliffe. For the rest, there are numerous isolated pieces that are translations or paraphrases of separate portions of the Scriptures, one of which, the *West Midland Prose Psalter* (*c.*1275), is not ineffective. The three parts of the Bible—the Old Testament, the Apocrypha, and the New Testament—all received an equal share of attention. *Genesis and Exodus,* for example, a poem of about 1250, summarizes the principal events of not only the two books named in the title but of portions of Numbers and Deuteronomy as well. Its source is in part the popular encyclopedic work by Petrus Comestor, a twelfth-century scholar from Troyes, France, entitled *Historia Scholastia.* Much of it, however, rests upon the *Lectiones* of the *Temporale* and reflects only those parts of Scripture that carry the "plan of salvation." We have seen how all works of this encyclopedic nature began with Creation and followed through to the bitter end of Doomsday. The narrative in the Middle English *Genesis and Exodus* is wry and spare; the poem as a whole compares unfavorably with the Caedmonian equivalents in Old English. In the Prologue, however, the author explains that the work is aimed at the unlearned, that they may know better how to love and serve God. In other words, it is more than likely that the poem, tallying with most of the works of its kind, was intended primarily for the instruction of the ignorant secular believer rather than for the setting straight of the ignorant churchman.

In like manner, the story of Joseph is the subject of a rather lively poem, *Joseph* (*c.*1300). A *Strophic Poem* of somewhat later date gives the gist of most of the historical books of the Old Testament as well as of Judith and The Maccabees from the Apocrypha. It is the crude raw material of great narrative —nothing more. A few grains of praise may be bestowed upon the so-called *Verse Version of the Old Testament* (*c.*1400) for its consideration of the Poetic Books of the Old Testament; but the failure of the Middle Ages to appreciate the grandeur of these pagan Poetic Books, while natural enough in view of the literalness of medieval dogma, is none the less regrettable from the standpoint of what is truly universal in literature.

One of the most sprightly paraphrases from the Apocrypha is *Susannah* (*Seemly Susan, The Pistill of Susan*), from about 1370 or a trifle later, a Scottish treatment of this hitherto neglected heroine of story. The tale of the thwarted lust of the Elders seems to have had some appeal in current popular literature; most of us are familiar with the references to a ballad on the subject put into the mouth of Sir Toby Belch in *Twelfth Night*. The Scottish chronicler, Wyntoun, ascribes the piece to a certain Huchown of the Awle Ryale, who is also, at one time or another, charged with the authorship of several romances and discursive works already mentioned, and has been a candidate for the position of the unknown Pearl Poet. The identity of Huchown, however, is so thoroughly obscure that there is little reason to accept any of these ascriptions as true.

There are, in addition, many separate works on the story of Adam and Eve (some aspects of which are related to the legend of the Holy Cross), on the Song of Solomon, and on the Psalms, including the *West Midland Prose Psalter* already mentioned, the *Surtees Psalter* (*c.*1325), and several individual poems on scattered Psalms. The New Testament was given precisely the same treatment as that applied to older portions of the Bible. Selections therefrom were arranged in a prose version (*c.*1400), at least some manuscripts of which were intended for the use of nuns. There are the usual sober and copious commentaries on the Gospels, the Pauline Epistles, and individual details of both. A few of these, such as the poem on the Woman of Samaria, come close to the saint's life. Needless to say, there is a vast amount of discussion of the Passion and of its sequel, which, of course, lies at the very heart of the Christian mystery. The Apocalypse does not seem to have challenged the imagination of these commentators, paraphrasers, or translators to the degree that might have been expected. To be sure, this Book of Revelation was invaluable to the medieval teacher because of its monitory quality; but only in *The Pearl* is there a distinctive example of a passage of Middle English poetry artistically influenced by the ardent poetic resources of the original.

Wycliffe and the translation of the Bible credited to him and his followers will be discussed later. Suffice to say for the present that, from the standpoint of the art of translation, the Wycliffe Bible is a prominent landmark, overshadowing completely the other Biblical translations accomplished during the Middle English period.

6. Dialogue, Debate, and Catechism

The use of dialogue for purposes of instruction is too well known to call for amplification. It has been a favorite device from the time of the sacred books of India to the present. In the Middle Ages, it is possible to recognize certain distinct kinds of dialogue: the question-and-answer, or catechistic, type; the argumentative interchange between two partisans, or debate; and the expository conversation designed to throw light upon a given topic. The line between one or another of these types is often barely distinguishable. It is convenient, however, to think in terms of simple dialogue, debate, and catechism. In the first two, the competitive aspect enters so naturally as to make a strict classification difficult. In the Old English period there were examples of dialogue in such pieces as *The Dialogue of the Body and the Soul* and *The Dialogues of Solomon and Saturn;* the debate, however, is associated chiefly with the medieval French and Franco-Latin writers, as it was popular in both northern France and Provence during the twelfth and thirteenth centuries.

The tradition of the dialogue between soul and body is given its finest English treatment in the Middle English *Debate between the Body and the Soul* (c.1300, with several versions from the fourteenth century). The original was probably a

Latin poem of the twelfth century. The Middle English versions, however, were given their initial impetus by some poet of more than ordinary ability, for the piece has a peculiar strength and is replete with personality.

A dead body is awaiting the approach of fiends to carry it off to Hell; beside it, inextricably bound to it, stand its soul. The two engage in mutual recriminations. Who was responsible for the present hopeless situation? The soul charges the body bitterly with crass self-indulgence, which led to sin; and as a result both are now damned. The body retorts that its actions were all dependent upon the soul; the soul has been the one that failed. There is a heated reply from the soul, and a rebuttal from the body. The question soon becomes academic, however, for hell-hounds burst upon the unfortunate victims; and from that point on, the the soul and body are united in a common fate; indeed, there is no distinction between them any longer; they are to experience only physical sensations. It is all bodily torture that the fiends inflict upon the corpse—glowing irons thrust into the body, obscene devils sporting about the victim and taunting it, a horrid hullabaloo until the demons drag away their quarry under a hill. The poet, who has seen all this in a dream, awakens in a fright and thinks on repentance.

In effect, then, the poem is another in the notable list of medieval vision poems; but the substance is so thoroughly unified, so carefully aimed at the awful prospect of eternal torture and impregnated with the sad reflection inevitable upon the thought, *memento mori,* that the reader can only applaud. Particularly noticeable is a lavish, eloquent use of the venerable *ubi sunt?* formula. The spectacle of the orgies of demons making holiday over their prize is too much for the dreamer; he awakens sweating from every pore. In this chastened mood it is easy to think of Christ and His infinite mercy and that "no sin is so great that Christ's grace is not greater still."

After such a vigorous and dramatic piece, *The Vices and Virtues,* a slightly older poem, while equally noble and dignified, seems tame and abstract. Here the soul and body appeal to reason as a referee; and reason pleads for harmony between the two; his manner is calm and judicial. But no discourse on as many as twenty-seven separate virtues can hope to have the same appeal as that of the hurt soul and desperate body in recriminative argument.

The remaining Middle English dialogues deal with the Virgin at the time of the Crucifixion, or with doctrinal matters, or with the disputes between Christians and Jews. We may pass them by and turn our attention to the debate—the poem in dialogue between two or more contestants, who present varying points of view or arguments concerning some general issue, and not devoid of the personal attack. Here we encounter one of the most attractive of Middle English poems, *The Owl and the Nightingale*. It is clearly of the early Middle English period; the consensus of scholars puts its date not far from 1225. One very dubious identification of the author places the poem a whole generation earlier.

The poet hears an owl and a nightingale disputing over the respective merits of their ways of life and attacking in most lively fashion each other's habits and activities and even personal appearance. The nightingale begins the contest. According to her, the owl has an ugly song, filthy habits, an ungainly personality; it is a creature of the dark, therefore evil. The owl replies first in terms of violence— if she had the nightingale in her claws, there would be a different song! An owl, she says, sings only when there is need for it; she does not induce her listeners to lust and sloth; she rids the barns and churches of mice; she is of use in the world. The nightingale insists that her song is of heavenly bliss; the owl reminds her that not song but repentance brings the listener to Heaven, and, furthermore, the nightingale's song never helped the poor and distressed, such as those in the waste places of Ireland. The nightingale accuses the owl of witchcraft. And so the battle goes, with little effect on either side, until the owl is so indiscreet as to observe that among her many uses to mankind, she serves as a good scarecrow when she is stuffed. "Thou criest aloud of thine own shame!" retorts the nightingale; and a chorus of birds takes up the cry. The owl is about to summon help from other birds of prey, but she remembers that the nightingale, early in the debate, had proposed the name of Master Nicholas of Guildford as arbitrator. The wren pleads for an amicable settlement; and all the birds fly off to the abode of Nicholas at Portisholm; the poet knows no more of the matter.

Here argument is met with argument, a true debate in the strict sense of the word. But what is the basic issue? Clearly the owl and the nightingale represent two *modi vivendi*. Shall we say that the owl, the practical one, is debating with the idealistic nightingale on the merits of their divergent points of view? Is it rational pragmatism against intuitive aestheticism? Is it a thirteenth-century version of the perennial debate between science and humanism? Is it the yeoman against the courtier? Or is it some much narrower interpretation that is intended; for example, does the owl represent an actual political faction in the realm, or perhaps the native Englishman inveighing against foreign favorites? There is in the poem an interesting slur on Irish priests. Perhaps such matters are unimportant. The poem obviously stands on its own feet; the author is a balanced and gifted observer, with a great deal of technical proficiency in his verse and some sharp insight into both human nature and the world in which human nature operates. There is no suggestion here of the ascetic or the ecclesiastical; in fact, the work is notable for its secular interest and its realistic grasp of life. The identity of its author, however, is still obscure. Whoever he was, and he was probably not Nicholas of Guildford, he stands out as a writer of unusual originality, force, and attainment in the handling of his craft.

Immediately influenced by *The Owl and the Nightingale* is *The Thrush and the Nightingale* (c.1300). This piece has something of the strength of its ancestor, but its subject is much more specific: it discusses *pro* and *con* the merits of women. The thrush is critical of the sex; the nightingale defends them—rather inconclusively, too—until the inspiration comes to her to remind the thrush that Christ was born of Mary, a woman. To this there can be no rebuttal; the thrush is baffled and willing to leave the country in contrition. *The Debate between the Heart and the Eye* (c.1350) raises the question whether the heart or the eye is the port of entry for sin. Reason, the judge, counsels both to repent; the eye with weeping, the heart with sorrow. An attractive poem is *The Book of Cupid*, or *The Cuckoo and the Nightingale* (c.1400), by Sir Thomas Clanvowe; in this the earthy cuckoo loses the decision to the amorous nightingale, and the nightingale, grateful to the poet for his award, calls for a parliament of birds to meet on St. Valentine's day.

Pure doctrinal dialogue, or catechism, between a learner and his master is not very inviting fare, unless it be something like Aelfric's diverting *Colloquy on the Occupations*. There is nothing in this sort of Middle English literature that surpasses the *Colloquy*. *Questions between a Master of Oxford and His Clerk* is a boring set of statements about God's ways, including His taste for certain flowers and birds. Some of the catechisms are in rhyming schemes. *Ypotis* introduces no less a pair of personages than Hadrian, Emperor of Rome, and the sage Epictetus; but these people are in reality shadowy prefigurations of St. John the Evangelist and Christ. As for the dialogue, *Inter Diabolus et Virgo*, disregarding the bad grammar of the title, we find it much more worth while to read the first three items in Child's great collection of ballads. The theme there is the same—the devil tries to gain possession of an innocent mortal by asking question and riddles; but he is confounded when the mortal answers them correctly. The more one delves about in these remote crannies of English literature, the more one admires the solid worth of *The Debate between the Body and the Soul* and of *The Owl and the Nightingale*.

The opportunity offered by this particular type of literature for the development of satire gives rise to the later tradition of attack on persons and institutions. From the spirited exchange between the owl and the nightingale we can see emerging the same genius and even some of the same technique that prompted the "flytings" of Dunbar and Kennedy in the fifteenth century. Thence the progress to such masterpieces of invective as Dryden's *Mac Flecknoe* and Pope's *Dunciad* is obvious.

7. Writings on Science and General Information

While it may be true that there was more real advancement of the cause of science in the works of Albertus Magnus and Roger Bacon than in all the rest of the English, Anglo-Latin, and Anglo-French works of the period put together, still the scattered writings of obscure pseudo-scientists are worth remembering. The kind of compilation and concretion of scientific lore that could be found in Old English literature remained fully as vital in the centuries immediately following the Norman Conquest. It is therefore safe to assume that the plant treatises, or *herbaria;* the animal lore; the leechdoms, such as the *Peri Didaxeon* and the *Medicina de Quadrupedibus;* the recipes and prescriptions; and even the therapeutic charms and incantations—these all continued to live throughout the Middle Ages. Before the slow encroachment of what we may call the findings of natural science, however, these assemblings of popular wisdom began to give ground in the halls of the medieval universities. The scholarly work of the Arab physicians and surgeons was well known; and the more educated writers were willing to make use of these new discoveries, or at least to recognize the presence of men like Avicenna, Lanfranc, Averroes, and John of Arderne in medicine and *chirurgerie.*

In the same way, the labors of astronomers and astrologers —for these two occupations linked together, as it were, a steed and a donkey of Apollo—continued the tradition represented in Old English literature by Bede and Byrhtferth. Arnoldus of Villanova (d.1314), author of *Rosarius Philosophorum,* held sway in the field of alchemy; and the dead hand of Ptolemy, working through his *Almagest,* influenced many disciples to turn their studies to the motions of the heavenly bodies and the effect of the heavens upon human destiny. We have still to wait for the great discoveries of Copernicus, Kepler, and Tycho Brahe on the very border between the Middle English period and the Renaissance. In the category of astronomy, however, aside from minor pieces it is not necessary to name, two works must be mentioned— Chaucer's *Astrolabe* and the *De Proprietatibus Rerum,* the latter written by the Franciscan Bartholomeus Anglicus and translated into the vernacular by John of Trevisa (1398). Chaucer's prose tract is a technical manual for the use of a particular astronomical instrument. The *De Proprietatibus Rerum* is in the nature of a general handbook, or *enchiridion*, of the natural sciences, as the fourteenth century understood them. Such general handbooks of encyclopedic quality will remind the reader of the collections of natural lore made by various Anglo-Latin and Anglo-French writers, such as John of Salisbury and Alanus de Lille, mentioned in the section on Anglo-Latin writers of the Middle English period. Another very popular compendium of information was Vincent de Beauvais's thirteenth-century *Speculum Maius*.

The special activities of sport, which included the art of hunting (or venery), archery, fishing, and falconry, can best be studied in *The Boke of St. Albans*, printed in 1485, though composed a generation or so earlier. This book was designed for the country gentleman; for his more lordly contemporary, *The Master of Game* was the great authority. The latter treatise was written at the beginning of the fifteenth century by Edward, Duke of York, grandson of Edward III. It is largely a translation of the Frenchman Gaston de Foix's *Déduits de la chasse*. In view of the enormous popularity of the chase as an aristocratic pastime, both works have the advantage of coming late in the age and thus of summing up the whole ancient and presumably honorable tradition. Earlier than either, however, was the *Treatise on Hunting* by the Norman Twici, chief huntsman of Edward II, and, according to the colophon of the manuscript, a certain Johan Gyfford, of whom nothing is known.

Further than these there are only some curious odds and ends of a general informative nature. The fragmentary quality of surviving Middle English literature is never so apparent as when one looks at the titles of some of these scattered works. We then begin to realize how much literature of and for the people has been irretrievably lost. Measures of weight, the distance between Heaven and earth, the significance of thunder in the different months of the year, the legal aspects and definition of robbery, recipes for making colors and for making iron as hard as steel—the reader may take his choice. One of the most interesting is a tract in verse (*c.*1375) on the constitutions of Masonry, which traces this famous society as far back as Euclid and enjoins strictly orthodox courtesy and right living as the practical basis of the fraternity, although the education suggested sounds more like a matter of expediency than of sheer idealism. There is the usual amount of miscellaneous legalistic prose—wills, charters, writs, and petitions—as well as a small number of letters of a business nature. Of these the fifteenth-century collection known as *The Paston Letters* (see page 269) is much the most celebrated representative. A good deal of the private and public correspondence of the Middle Ages is only just coming to light; it is likely to turn up in out-of-the-way libraries of church institutions and private manor houses. Thus the chapter-house records and library of a single institution, the Battle Abbey at Hastings, have alone yielded an amazing amount of material invaluable to the economic historian of the times. Unfortunately, this particular treasure-trove does little to illuminate the literature. Nevertheless, it is most likely that whatever additional information about the Middle Ages we shall get in the future will come from such a source.

What strikes the modern reader about most of these works of information, of course, is their uncritical nature, their failure to distinguish between fact and fancy. It is, indeed, as if the general reader of the time preferred to be entertained rather than informed. But, for that matter, much the same can be said of most of the works on "popular" science in the twentieth century; indeed, the romantic aspects of science will always have great appeal. The matter of dreams, for example, fascinated the Middle Ages, which knew virtually nothing of psychology; the very frequency of the dream device in the extensive vision literature is a sufficient illustration. In characteristic fashion, of course, the Middle Ages demanded an authority on dreams; and usually this authority was the commentary on the *Somnium Scipionis* by the obscure Macrobius of the fifth century. The *Somnium Scipionis*, it should be remarked, forms a portion of Cicero's *De Republica*. But John of Salisbury, Vincent de Beauvais, and minor authorities such as Bartholomeus Anglicus and Richard Holkot all had something to say about dreams, discussing the question whether they were a physiological phenomenon or a warning from on high. The reflections of Chaucer on this very point, particularly in his *Nun's Priest's Tale,* are both amusing and significant. Two works, *A Metrical Treatise on Dreams* (*c.*1300) and a prose *Dream-Book*, seem to be popular treatments of these authorities; but the works are irritatingly vague. The reader may well agree with Pertelote, the hen in Chaucer's tale, who advised her husband to purge himself if he wished to avoid unpleasant dreams.

There was another point, moreover, on which the medieval man, like the modern man, yielded to human nature, and that was the matter of the entertaining yarn about strange, far-off places. We are indebted to this weakness for one of the most renowned works of the era, *The Travels of Sir John Mandeville.* No less than 300 manuscripts of this prose narrative have survived. It had been printed in five different languages as early as 1500. It is still excellent reading; yet the author of this most successful book is one of the most elusive of any in the period and is likely to escape us forever. In the first place, this Sir John Mandeville of St. Albans, who, according to the story, began to travel in 1322 or 1332—it is hard to tell when —and then some years later wrote an account of his remarkable travels, is almost certainly not the author. The story told by the writer of how he came to compose the book is melodramatic, involving a strange invalid, a wise physician, and a death-bed statement: Sir John, falling ill in Liége, Flanders, in 1343, was persuaded by his physician, John ad Barbam, to tell in writing what he had seen on his travels in the world. Now a certain Jean d'Outremeuse of Liége, writing a *Myreur des Histors* later in the century, stated that in 1372 a Jehan de Bourgogne or John à la Barbe (*sic*), being on his death-bed, told d'Outremeuse that he was John de Mandeville, knight, who had fled England because he had killed a man. His testimony given, the sick man died and was buried in the Church of the Guillemins. Some who saw his tomb recognized the coat of arms as that of the Tyrrell family; but they were not positive on this point. The whole story smacks of fabrication; but a John de Mandeville does appear in the reign of Edward II of England—too early to fit well the Mandeville legend— and a Johan de Bourgoyne actually lived in England during the reign of the same king, fleeing from England in 1322.

D'Outremeuse further declared that he had inherited the library of "de Mandeville" and had written some additions to the *Travels*.

The general conclusion seems to be that d'Outremeuse made a tall tale out of the whole matter. It is altogether possible, however, that Jean à la Barbe, or John ad Barbam, the Liège physician, wrote the *Travels* under the name of John de Mandeville, which would be a not unusual name for the time. He would naturally write in French or Latin. It is likely that the work was originally in French; possibly d'Outremeuse wrote the Latin version that appeared soon after. The whole problem is notoriously complex. Two general theories, however, seem tenable. One is that "Sir John Mandeville," whoever he was, was not an Englishman and probably never lived in England. He shows too much ignorance of things English. The other is that his travels are faked; nearly every detail he gives can be found in the work of earlier writers; and the few that cannot be traced can be referred directly to the imagination of the author, who could not have been a mere automation. In any case, he had a tradition to work with, for there were other travelogues in the literature of Western Europe at this time, notably the genuine *Travels* of Marco Polo, from early in the fourteenth century.

This is not to say that *The Travels of Sir John Mandeville* is any the less interesting because the work is merely an English translation of a rather spurious original. If the author borrows from the Alexander legend, or from Vincent de Beauvais, or from the legend of Prester John, or from Marco Polo, it still is true that his book is a grand collection of the travel-lore of the time. One reads with enjoyment his arguments in favor of the world's being round (it should be remembered that his work was written a full century before Columbus), his accounts of the marvels of the East and of the wonders of Prester John's kingdom, his details of the wild life of the Tartars and of the luxurious appointments in the fabulous court of the Great Khan. What strikes the reader with special force is that all these stories, up to a certain point, sound completely credible. We need not worry because the book begins as a sober guide to the shrines of the Holy Land. This device is soon cast aside; we come almost at once to the kind of writing whose sole purpose is to entertain, and to entertain by transporting the readers to remote places where no tax collectors or bailiffs can pry into their affairs and where no brawling wives will shout at them over the kitchen fire.

8. Richard Rolle and His Cycle

Lest it be imagined that by the fourteenth century in England the minds of men were moving hopefully toward the dim horizons of unexplored lands and were considering the possibility that the earth might be round and were turning their backs upon the fleshless life of the spirit, it is important to consider Richard Rolle and his followers, for these individuals, contemporary with Marco Polo and the dubious Sir John Mandeville, represent the ultimate in English asceticism. The founder of this school, Richard Rolle, was born about 1300 at Thornton-le-Dale, Yorkshire. Under the patronage of Thomas de Neville, later archdeacon of Durham, he was sent to Oxford. Here the scholastic method and the rigorous exercises in logic were repugnant to him; he returned to Yorkshire and there plunged into what, from the purely spiritual point of view, was a romantic kind of adventure. Taking some articles of clothing from his father and his sister, he contrived a hermit's costume and left home. The first station in his indefinite pilgrimage was the estate of the Dalton family in Yorkshire. Sir John Dalton and his wife supported him until their deaths. Deprived of his local protectors, Rolle moved on from place to place, preaching among the people and spreading his concepts of the holy light that burned within him. He was viewed askance by many of the older clergy; but, on the other hand, he came to be accepted by some of the younger clerics. He was never ordained, however, and at no time was he more than a lay member of the Church. None the less, he was evidently a missionary of reputation. Even some miracles were attributed to him. Followers appeared and added to the writings that Rolle himself was disseminating. The female hermit, Margaret Kirkby, was a particularly strong influence upon Rolle's thought as well as his writing; and his best work is dedicated to her. Eventually he came to Hampole, in the south of Yorkshire, where he was a kind of spiritual advisor to a Cistercian monastery. Here he died in 1349, possibly from the

Black Death. For some reason, in spite of his holy life and his manifest impress upon many of the ascetics of his generation, he was never canonized, probably because in later years his ideas were too well received by the heretical Lollards, followers of Wycliffe.

The Richard Rolle cycle embraces a good many homilies and prose tracts and a considerable amount of religious verse. Much scholarship has been expended upon the knotty problem of the authorship of these various works—and, as so often happens, the tendency is now to take away from what was originally ascribed to Rolle and to assign it to his disciples. There is general agreement, however, on Rolle's authorship of about a dozen prose works, a few of which are extremely minor in scope, and about the same number of religious lyrics. But the qualities of this small number of pieces are unusual. In his prose style, Rolle is not far from the tradition first seen in Aelfric's homilies; he writes eloquently, with a goodly attention to rhetorical devices, including especially alliteration and antithesis. It is, however, a notably clear kind of prose; and the same is not true of most vernacular prose in the fourteenth century. As for the lyrics, they are very near to being distinguished poems. The secret of Rolle's success is that he was fundamentally a poet, and a romantic one at that, whether he was writing in prose or in verse. The mystical trinity of *dulcor, calor,* and *canor*—sweetness, warmth, and song—was something he developed through long contemplation of the inner light; and it served for effective composition pitched in an emotional key, in whatever medium the author chose to write.

To consider at once what Rolle conceived to be the ideal manner of life, it is best to take *The Form of Perfect Living,* a prose tract highly poetic in tone, addressed to Margaret Kirkby. According to this work, the evils of life result from spiritual flabbiness, sensuality, and the failure to distinguish between earthly evanescence and heavenly permanence. Instead, Man should devote himself entirely to Christ, despising all worldly presumption, filling the heart always with love of God and all His works, and holding ever before him the ideal of purity in perfection. Love in its divinest and fullest essences is the universal solvent; through it come the gifts of the Holy

Ghost and the cherishing of the name of Jesus. Truly, therefore, the contemplative life is the best.

Passing over one or two derivative versions of *The Form of Perfect Living,* of uncertain authorship, we come to another prose tract by Rolle, *Ego Dormio et Cor Meum Vigilat,* which develops the last portion of *The Form of Perfect Living.* As for the other pieces accepted as Rolle's, they do not differ much in tone from the two already mentioned. *A Commandment of Love to God* is obvious from its title; the shorter prose fragments, one of which is only fifty words in length, may be passed over. The *Meditatio de Passione Domini,* however, is unusual. It consists, in its two versions, of between five and seven thousand words of vivid devotional writing and deserves to be remembered in any account of Middle English literature dealing the the Passion. *On the Nature of the Bee (Moralia Richardi Hermite de Natura Apis),* in its tendency to link animal characteristics to traits of human nature, reminds the reader inevitably of the *Bestiary;* in its strict, logical outline, which follows a rigorously deductive method of development, it savors of the lecture hall or cloistered study.

The combination of lyric poet and mystic teacher and preacher, evident in these undisputed works by Rolle, sets the fashion for his followers, of whom at least three are known by name: Walter Hilton, William Nassyngton, and Juliana Lampit. There were probably many others. Hilton belongs to the next generation; he died at his retreat in the Augustinian house at Newark, Nottinghamshire, in 1396. Nassyngton was a contemporary of Hilton. Juliana Lampit, "a devout servant of our Lord, an anchoress at Norwich," attained the age of one hundred and died in 1443. Her *Fourteen Revelations of Divine Love,* a lengthy and pithless discourse, reveals nevertheless a beautiful religious spirit and a convincing otherworldliness. With Hilton and Nassyngton, however, the problems of authorship multiply themselves.

We are agreed that *The Scale of Perfection* is Hilton's. It is a long disquisition on the active versus the contemplative life: there are many kinds of contemplation, and they are all aided by the essential requisites of humility, faith, and hope. These are pre-eminent over prayer, a distant companion. Temptation, under such circumstances, can be overcome, and the Seven Deadly Sins as well; man's soul can be reshaped to true perfection, which is the proper end of all living. Probably by Hilton also is *An Epistle on Mixed Life,* which treats once more of the active and the contemplative. *Of Angels' Song* and the *Encomium Nominis Jesu* apply the ideals of Rolle and much of his fervor to the lyric admiration of virtue and joy in Jesus. Hilton, if he is the author, introduces in the *Encomium* a story of temptation that he himself once suffered. This autobiographical detail may be accepted for what it is worth. As for Nassyngton, he is much less distinguished, either as an identity or as a writer, than Hilton. Indeed, no single work can with any assurance be assigned to him, although he is given credit in some manuscripts for *A Treatise on Trinity and Unity,* which is a trite summary of Christian doctrine bound up in the form of a prayer in verse; for a paraphrase of Rolle's *Form of Perfect Living;* and, very questionably, for *The Mirror of Life,* a reworking of the *Speculum Vitae* by a certain John de Waldeby.

In a sense, the situation with respect to the Richard Rolle cycle is analogous to that of the Caedmonian or Cynewulfian cycles in Old English literature. We postulate the presence of a leader; and here, in the person of Richard Rolle, there can be no doubt. The tendency was at first to credit Rolle with most of the works written in his particular vein. Then it became apparent, from differences in the date and style of the various pieces, that he himself could not have written all of the many works attributed to him. Besides, we have the names of his most important disciples. There remain, nevertheless, many other works the authorship of which cannot be satisfactorily determined, at least for the present. There are so many of these, in fact, that it is impossible even to enumerate them here, but they cover most of the homiletic material or religious discussion already described. Some are almost purely expository on devotional matters; some are lyrics in verse; some are prose homilies. A few introduce some new metaphor—for example, we hear of the three arrows of Doomsday: the summons to resurrection, the arraignment, and the condemnation. We can find out also how we may know whether or not to love our enemies. We see an ingenious allegorization of the lives of Jacob and Benjamin. Several of the pieces meditate upon the Passion; several more upon the efficacy of prayer, particularly as a remedy against temptation.

Of all these miscellaneous unassigned pieces, however, the dismal *Pricke of Conscience* is the most famous; in fact, it is perhaps the best known work of the entire Rolle cycle. For a long time it was considered Rolle's own work, but the evidence for this is slim. The most that can be said is that this ambitious poem may be a reworking of some older poem by Rolle. Perhaps William Nassyngton is responsible. At any rate, the piece is a general manual of religious information and instruction. It survives under a variety of titles, which is confusing; but it may be summed up best under the descriptive subtitle, *Know Thyself*. As the poem testifies, man's earthly pride gets in the way of self-knowledge and also of the knowledge of God, who is omnipotent. Man has a foul beginning, a corrupt life, a disgusting old age, and is consumed by the insatiable worm. This earlier portion of the poem is drawn mainly from Pope Innocent III's *De Contemptu Mundi*. Earth is a battleground for Good and Evil; the planets and the stars look on; they observe that worldly success for men means their damnation. For these sentiments we are indebted to Bartholomeus Anglicus's *De Proprietatibus Rerum*. In successive books—there are seven in all—one hears of Death, its terrors and the causes thereof; of Purgatory and the functions thereof; of Doomsday and the signs thereof. The famous fourteen pains of Hell come forth to divert or alarm us, as we will; but there are also the joys of Heaven. Thomas Aquinas and others are the sources of the later parts of the poem. All in all, the entire work is characteristically derivative, in which respect alone it differs from the accepted work of Rolle, and it lacks the vividness and body of a work of similar import, Mannyng's *Handlyng Synne*. On the other hand, it is far more spirited and stimulating than *The Ayenbite of Inwit*.

It is a significant fact that in the fourteenth century, when the world was moving inevitably toward the Renaissance, there should have been an ascetic group as effective as that of Richard Rolle still to be found in England. The answer is in part that England was in the rear of the procession marching toward the Renaissance; it was almost the last important European country to feel the effects of that great human experience. At first glance Rolle and his followers seem throwbacks to the more austere thinkers of the monastic age, although they are at all times emotional and intuitive, where the disciplined monastic was intellectual and rational. But the Rolle school, from the very fact that it faced away from the prevailing tendencies, was protesting against the orders of the day. It was too conservative, even fundamentalist, to consider breaking a Church tenet, as did Wycliffe. Yet it rebelled, if only subconsciously, against the worldliness of the Church, with its Great Schism and elaborate though mundane organization and preference for brain over heart. At all events, in thus withdrawing themselves, the members of the Rolle school contributed a fresh intensity of feeling, a detachment from worldly considerations, and a profound idealism perceived for almost the last time in the Middle English period. And as a perpetuator of the prose tradition, especially in its more artistic forms, Richard Rolle himself is of truly valiant stature.

9. John Wycliffe and His Group

John Wycliffe was born near Richmond, Yorkshire, about 1320; he studied at Balliol College, Oxford, and became Master at Balliol in 1361. During the remaining twenty-three years of his life he occupied two or three benefices in the Church, ending with the benefice at Lutterworth in Leicestershire; he became a doctor of theology in 1372 and served in 1374 as an ambassador for the English Crown at the meeting of papal delegates at Bruges in Flanders. Some time during the late 1360's, at any rate before 1374, he wrote a tract, *Determinatio . . . de Dominio contra Unum Monachum,* which established him as a champion of the secular power of the State against the power of the Church. At no time in his life did he recede from this position; he was not by nature a compromiser. He soon gained the support of John of Gaunt, the powerful prince who was also Chaucer's patron, and of Lord Percy, one of the most influential of the many influential members of that illustrious northern family. Moreover, Wycliffe seems to have had the capacity to attract popular support as well. When, therefore, his trend toward heresy brought him into conflict with the established order in the Church, as was inevitable, he was able to fend off their prosecution. In spite of the serious differences between his beliefs and the doctrine of the orthodox churchman of his day, Wycliffe died in his bed in 1384, a generation before the Bohemian John Huss, whose heresies do not appear to be much more remarkable than Wycliffe's, was burned at the stake.

The technical details of the accusations brought against Wycliffe by the Church should doubtless be left to the students of ecclesiastical history. It is enough to observe that Wycliffe's attacks against the Church were made first on the solid front of its worldly organization—its endowment of the clergy and its defense of the right of the clergy to possess property; the excesses in the granting of indulgences; the corroding presence of simony and the abuse of tithing; the Church's aggressive, militant attitude. Wycliffe particularly objected to the exporting of English money to foreigners holding English benefices. The wealth of the Church, which it was inclined to flaunt, was another of his targets. He came to object to churchly display, to the elaborate prayers and intoning of the priests, to the snobbish preferences of Church officials for parishioners having money, and to their scorn for the poor.

Once these evils of what may be called the external aspects of the Church came under fire, it was not long before Wycliffe picked out vulnerable spots in its internal structure. Specifically he trained his sights on the theory of the Pope's infallibility and on the friars' doctrine of the Eucharist. In these matters he stepped over the line that separates dissent from outright heresy and in doing so became an early Protestant reformer. Indeed, it is extremely revealing to compare some of the changes called for in the Wycliffe reform with the changes later advocated by the sixteenth- and seventeenth-century English Puritans. For it is possible to see in Wycliffe and his movement at least the germs of the Puritan, especially if we consider his distrust of glamour in the ritual, his antagonism toward singing, and the fundamental objection to intermediacy between God and man. Nor was it all a matter of theory and doctrine with Wycliffe; he instituted an order of "povre prestes," whose only source of authority was to be the Bible, whose business was primarily the preparation of man for the life to come by preaching to rich and poor alike, not standing in the pulpits of fine churches but roaming about afoot through the land.

But Wycliffe's Lollards represented a premature movement toward reform. Their suppression by Henry V in 1414 showed that the fourteenth century was still a long way from successful Reformationist rebellion.

Fundamentally we are concerned here with a Wycliffe cycle rather than with the unquestioned canon of a single dominant literary figure. To Wycliffe himself, in addition to several expository tracts on various religious topics, one can assign some 300 existing sermons, which differ in several respects from the other homilies composed since the days of the tenth-century preachers. The Wycliffe sermons are fairly short, averaging about a thousand words. They rely heavily upon the paraphrase and interpretation of the Scriptures. A few indicate by their comments that they were intended primarily for the use of priests. Most unusual is the absence of *exempla*, for Wycliffe objected strongly to the inclusion of story. Nor are there any attacks in these sermons on social or political conditions; they are taken up entirely with matters of doctrine or ecclesiastical organization. Their points of assault have already been noted. It is remarkable how frequently Wycliffe attacks the papal office, the "abode of Antichrist," and the whole elaborate hierarchy of the Church's structure, false Christs, Pharisees, wolves within the sheepfold. Whatever their defects as literary compositions, these sermons are direct, lean, and spare; they express an utter conviction of the righteousness of their cause.

About 60 other sermons are to be referred to the Wycliffe cycle, though they are probably not by Wycliffe himself. The remaining writings in the cycle may be called generally didactic; they comprise (1) commentaries on the essential tenets of the Church, such as the *Credo;* (2) expositions of the *Paternoster* and the *Ave Maria,* of the Seven Deadly Sins and the Seven Works of Mercy; (3) discourses on marriage and the life of a servant of God; (4) statements of doctrine or personal belief; (5) polemics against simony, church temporalities, the intoning or chanting of prayers, the unjustified imprisonment of poor priests.

Among the many religious compositions of miscellaneous nature, the highly conservative element of the Wycliffite philosophy is especially noticeable. In addition to the broader objects of attack just mentioned, the group of writings assails miracle plays, games of chance, the exposing of relics for monetary gains (as we have it acknowledged in immortal fashion by Chaucer's Pardoner), paintings and images of sacred personages, and many other matters. In this group appears the name of John Gaytryge; he and the better known Nicholas of Hereford and John Purvey are the only Wycliffites whose names are to be found among the writers of the school.

It is not clear how large a part Wycliffe himself took in the celebrated translation of the Bible associated with his name. Aside from the supervisory role he probably assumed at the beginning, it is not possible that he did very much. This translation is in two parts. The first, covering the Old Testament and known as the Early Version, was completed somewhere between 1382 and 1384. In the meantime, Wycliffe had suffered a stroke in 1383; he died in the following year. Besides, the manuscripts agree in attributing the Early Version to Nicholas of Hereford. This first portion, which actually runs into the Book of Baruch in the Apocrypha, is a rough-and-ready kind of translation that suggests that Nicholas of Hereford was not a very good Latinist, nor did he have a good literary feeling for the possibilities of the vernacular. The second portion, or Later Version, was completed some time between 1388 and the end of the century. It is ascribed to John Purvey and collaborators; it is accurate and generally more effective than the Early Version, so much so as to be actually popular. More than 150 manuscripts of it survive.

This, the first complete translation of the Bible into the English language, has the absolute historical interest that any such work should command. It could never, however, be considered a rival of the King James Version or even of the Coverdale translations. On the other hand, it is far superior to the fragmentary translations of the Bible, such as the Old English interlinear glosses or the Old English translations of the Gospel, which imitate the Latin Vulgate so slavishly as to be little more than word-by-word translations, as are the Middle English psalters of about a century before Hereford and Purvey. It is revealing to place beside a passage from the Wycliffe Bible the corresponding passage from the King James Version. The superiority of the seventeenth-century translation is not merely owing to the fact that Modern English, even in its early stages, has command of a clearer and more flexible prose than Middle English, although that is indubitably true. It is rather that the translators of the King James Version had greater knowledge of the originals at hand and a much more sophisticated literary sense, fostered by the richness of early seventeenth-century literary traditions. Wycliffe and his group, however, were not thinking of producing a literary masterpiece so much as they were hoping to write something for the average Englishman of their time to use. The old fear that Aelfric voiced and to which the churchmen following him tacitly yielded—namely, that the holy Scriptures might get into the hands of the ignorant and so be misinterpreted or subverted—no longer preyed upon bold, independent, and comparatively advanced minds like Wycliffe's. In this fact alone the priest of Lutterworth towers above his coevals. That he was popular with the masses is evident, although he cannot be considered the prime instigator of the Peasants' Revolt, no matter how much a strict observance of his doctrines might logically lead to such a premature and pathetic social outburst. The spirit of intellectual freedom, however, of which Wycliffe was enamored and which he bravely represented, undoubtedly kindled a spark that the following century and a half might dim but could never quench.

10. The Middle English Lyric

Since man seems always to have been able to turn to a lyrical mood, it is no surprise to learn that the Middle English period contributed a generous share to the art of making songs. In dealing with the Middle English lyric, however, the problem is not unlike that which confronts one in dealing with medieval fiction. What has been reduced to writing is no true gauge of the actual facts of the situation. If we were to depend upon the chronology of the written remains of this Middle English lyric, we should consider the Anglo-Latin songs as coming first, the Anglo-French next, and the vernacu-

lar last of all. It is possible that this represents actual conditions, but it cannot be made an assumption. We know that
there was musical composition of some kind in the Old English period, although we can merely speculate on its true
nature. We know also that there were songs in the Old English period, such as Aldhelm's, which have been unfortunately
lost; these were in Latin. Were there any in English? It seems
incredible that there were none. The clerical influence in the
Old English period was not, however, sympathetic to secular
lyrics, except in isolated instances.

But with the appearance of the medieval troubadours, the
awakening of the Celtic genius from its long night's sleep, and
the shaping of student life in the medieval universities, the
repression suffered by the English lyric was shaken off, and we
come to the first of many notable periods in the history of
English song. Thousands of Middle English lyrics have now
been recovered, in part or as a whole, although thousands
more no doubt remain lost. With our increasing knowledge of
the Middle English language—its probable pronunciation, its
tonality, and its accentuation—there comes a slowly spreading
appreciation of the excellence of its lyrics as lyrics, for they
are often warm, lusty, graceful, passionate, devoted, and witty
by turns. Although the great majority of those recovered have
proved to be religious and exhibit, therefore, the typical
overcast of earthly emotion by the didactic and moralizing
tendencies of the period, still there is a great deal that is
human, animated, vital, and beautiful among these poems;
and those readers who look with proper amazement upon the
lavish offerings of the Renaissance lyric would do well to
ponder upon its honored ancestor in Middle English times.

The two great divisions that must be made in the Middle
English lyric comprise the religious and the secular. The line
between these two is not always discernible unless we adhere
faithfully to the test of subject matter or topic. Many a poem
of religious purpose and substance may be couched in the
amoristic language of the secular; and many a secular poem
skirts but partially the borderland of the mystic and devotional. For the greater part, however, the two divisions are
more than adequate. In both we must consider the Anglo-

Latin and Anglo-French as well as the English. It is not practicable to say anything here about the known or suggested musical settings of any of them.[6]

Because the religious lyric is much greater in number than the secular, it is advisable to consider it first. It must be subdivided into the Latin hymns, which belong to the kingdom of the Church and so are international in scope and circulation; the hymns to the Virgin; the sacred lullaby; the allegorical lyric; and the miscellaneous religious poem.

The Latin hymns go back to the missionary efforts of the great Church Fathers. Some of them, such as St. Nicetas's *Te Deum Laudamus,* have become an integral part of the ritual of the Church. In the Middle Ages these hymns were composed by devout clerics all over Europe; it is impossible to set up national boundaries for them. In form they are a development of Classical Latin prosody mixed with certain metrical forms peculiar to the classical Greek; and in addition they take on more modern refinements, such as alliteration and rhyme, both external and internal, masculine and feminine. The importance of these Latin hymns and their influence upon the vernacular poetry of the period can hardly be overestimated. In subject matter, as might be expected, the Latin hymns deal particularly with the imminence of Judgment, with the necessity for man to keep watch. They idolize Rome both as a city and as the abode of the Church; they speak in even more glowing terms of the wonders of the New Jerusalem that is in Heaven. The combination of almost impeccable metrical form and devotional warmth is amply illustrated by Hildebert's *Me receptet Sion illa* and, to a lesser extent, by Bernard of Clairvaux's *Hora Novissima,* both of

---

[6] The matter of church music in the Middle Ages is treated thoroughly in the *Oxford History of Music,* Vols. I and II. There is no comparable treatment of secular music, which has been rather a stepchild to the musicologists. But again the *Oxford History of Music* will be of help, since E. J. Dent has an excellent chapter, "Special Aspects of Music in the Middle Ages," in the introductory volume to this history. *The Columbia Gramophone's History of Music.* Nos. 1-5, has some valuable recordings of general European medieval music of ecclesiastical nature, which serves the purpose well, inasmuch as church music and poetry are international rather than national.

which form the basis for several noted English hymns of the nineteenth century, and the awe-inspiring *Dies Irae,* attributed to the thirteenth-century Thomas of Celano. Jacopone da Todi's *Stabat mater dolorosa* is almost as famous as the *Dies Irae* and assuredly more human. It is impossible to name all the well-known Latin hymns of the Middle Ages, but it cannot be said too often that they are the bedrock upon which much of Middle English religious poetry was built. They reached their peak, perhaps, before 1300; but no generation of the Middle Ages in Europe failed to contribute its share of them.

The hymns to the Virgin, which in themselves need no explanation, are to be found throughout the period in Latin, French, and English. The French poems of this sort were often inclined to elaborateness. Thus a part of Deguilleville's *Pèlerinage de la Vie Humaine,* translated by Chaucer as his *ABC* poem, is a series of stanzas glorifying the Virgin, with each stanza initiated by successive letters of the alphabet. Another type of hymn to the Virgin is illustrated by the Prologues to Chaucer's *Second Nun's Tale (Invocacio ad Mariam)* and *Prioress's Tale.* In both of these there is a demonstration of the mystic symbolism associated with these hymns to the Virgin—the reference to Mary as the unburnt bush, the Lily of Heaven, and other esoteric parallels. *In Worschip of that Mayden Swete; Of Alle Floures Feirest; Marie Mayden, Moder Mylde; Qween of Heuene, Moder and May*—these are revealing enough in their very titles. One famous Latin hymn of the eighth century, *Ave Maris Stella,* a favorite of mariners, was particularly popular in Middle English versions. Sometimes the lyrics were not general panegyrics so much as effusions about special incidents of Mary's life, such as the Annunciation, or about esoteric aspects, such as the Five Joys of the Virgin. A very affecting group considers Mary at the foot of the Cross (the *Stabat mater* theme).

The sacred lullaby, or song of the Virgin to the infant Christ, is an unusually tender and attractive type of medieval religious lyric, whose kinship to the hymn to the Virgin is self-evident. These lullabies are effective because they are eminently natural—they sound a human note any mother would be likely to express while she is singing her baby to sleep; they employ none of the rather precious artifices that mar some of the hymns to the Virgin. Allegorical lyrics are not so frequently met with as some of the other types of religious song, but Thomas de Hales's *A Love Rune,* praising the supreme ecstasy of the love of Christ, and the anonymous *The Falcon Hath Borne My Mate Away,* giving utterance to the sorrow engendered by the Crucifixion, would be notable in any literature.

The religious lyric of the Middle Ages, however, cannot fairly be represented by any one category. The comprehensive quality of these poems is revealed in a study of the miscellaneous group. Here there are no particular limitations of theme except that all the poems are pious, reflective, devotional, or didactic. Many of them contain at least some of the elements of the special kinds just described; they may be merely philosophical, or they may address themselves to the Virgin, or to Christ on the Cross, or to God the Father surrounded by all His saints. Whether we consider single collections, such as the *Thornton Lyrics,* the *Vernon-Simeon Lyrics,* or the *Cambridge Dd Lyrics,* or isolated poems, the depth and universality of feeling are for all to see. Yet while these are all tuned to the overtones of the world to come, very few of them are aridly theological or dogmatic. They are fond of the old themes that appealed to the Anglo-Saxon poet—the transitoriness of the world and its beauty and its riches. They reiterate the sinfulness of man and his ever-welling remorse. Some of these poems are little more than penitential songs. Others, particularly those of French origins, make use of formulas of love poetry, such as the anatomizing of the beloved, or details of dress and dwellings, which sound very like the secular, amoristic poetry of the troubadours. A few titles, chosen with some care, will suffice to illustrate: *Uncomly in Cloystre I Coure Ful of Care; Lutel Wot Hit Anymon* ("Man knows little of what is in store for him"); *Unkynde Man* ("Unnatural Man"); *When Adam Delf and Eve Span* ("It was all very simple then; but evil and sin have come into the world, and only the grave and Doomsday can right this wickedness"); *Now Bernes, Bolde and Blythe* ("My friends, I thank you; but now I must leave you all against my will, for Death, and beyond him Heaven or Hell, wait for my soul"); *The Mon*

That Luste to Liuen in Ese ("He must learn to feign and flatter, for the world is in perilous state"); *Hose Wolde Bethenke Him Weel* ("Whoso would consider well the evil of the world must rely wholly on God for his salvation"); *Crist Give Us Grace To Love Wel Holichurch; Man, To Refourme* ("Look well upon My wounds"); *He That Sith Him on the Rode* ("Whoever should see Christ on the cross would repent him well"); *Veni, Creator Spiritus; Jesu Crist, Heavene Kyng; An Orysoun to God the Sone; A Mourning Song for the Love of God; Iesu Dulcis Memoria* (a cycle of poems on the Passion); *When Y Se Blosmes Springe* ("I am reminded of His suffering"). An especially fine example of the religio-philosophical lyric is that most beautiful of medieval songs of winter, *Wynter Wakeneth Al My Care*—not for any physical description of a wintry scene, but because it catches exquisitely the elegiac mood that the dead of winter, particularly an English winter, can bring to even the most insensitive. Nor should *Timor Mortis* be overlooked, wherein the stark terror of death comes to even the Saviour on the Cross, to make Him cry out the haunting refrain, *Timor mortis conturbat me!*

Indeed, the universal mystery of death touches briefly even the Goliardic verse. Most of the secular lyric poetry of the Middle English period, however, is comparatively free of the dark shadow. For that matter, this Goliardic verse is not prone to look far beyond the delights of the moment. It is fundamentally the product of the medieval university, not in its more earnest moments, but in its moments of normal youthful espousal of the flesh. The spontaneous, unashamed tendency of the medieval man to shed his piety for a day or two and to create parodies of his religion is responsible for the creation of good St. Goliardus, whose ancestor in name is doubtless the catastrophic figure of Gula (Gluttony), most bestial of the Seven Deadly Sins. Witness *Piers Plowman,* if there should be any question about that bestiality.[7] The formation of the name Goliardus suggests a French origin, and it is

---

[7] The disastrous effect upon Gluttony of his swilling down at one time a gallon and a gill of ale is told in unforgettable if somewhat unprintable language in *Piers Plowman,* B text, Passus v, 344ff. The picture of Sloth in the same text, Passus v, 392ff., is almost as effective.

certain that French students contributed chiefly to the glorification of this saint of clay. For some time Walter Map, the mercurial Welshman, and Giraldus Cambrensis, his volatile contemporary and fellow countryman, were believed responsible for the appearance of Goliardic verse in England; but this kind of importation could not have been accomplished by these men alone. Not that Walter Map or Giraldus Cambrensis was not temperamentally capable of doing so; it is obvious that both had their Goliardic moments. But the tide of Goliardism was too powerful for any mere individual to control.

Much Goliardic verse was in Latin; some was in French or German or English; some alternated between the vernacular and Latin. It is not worth attempting to differentiate among these linguistic media at this point. They were lively songs, dedicated to the sublime trio of wine, women, and song. All the members of this trinity were put into the world to be enjoyed. It was drinking, girls (who were more often *puellae* than *virgines*), and singing that passed the time of day and of night as well. Vanity of vanities? Yes, to some extent; but these are golden vanities. The expression of this feeling for their fleeting joys constitutes the finest example in the Middle Ages of the time-honored theme of plucking the day and making the most of time. *Carpe diem*—not, however, in the world-weary attitude of a middle-aged sybarite, but with the reckless abandon of youth that cares little for consequences, knowing that Death will end all, but in no hurry to meet him. Why should not the most noble secular lyric of the Middle Ages spring from such soil?

> Gaudeamus igitur,
> Iuvenes dum sumus.
> Post iucundam iuventutem,
> Post molestam senectutem,
> Nos habebit humus.
>
> Ubi sunt qui ante nos
> In mundo fuere?
> Vadite ad superos,
> Transite ad inferos;
> Ubi iam? Fuere.

The thirteenth-century collection, *Carmina Burana*, contains most of the best Goliardic verse. There are other Latin poems of highly secular, amorous nature, and some of these veer into the courtly. On the other hand, the purely courtly lyric prospered chiefly in France. There is nothing of importance in England that is truly representative of this brittle, highly artificial, completely ingenious, and generally trite kind of lyric until we get to Geoffrey Chaucer and John Gower. The theme of nearly all of them is unrequited love leading to a wasting love-sickness attended by the usual insomnia and falling spirits.

With the secular love lyric the case is different. *Alysoun,* with its dainty refrain and sincere affection of the lover for his real and earthly love, would be a gem in the lyrical expression of any age. In the manner of the Old French *reverdie*, most of these lyrics speak in terms of spring—the season of lovers—and tell how all nature is influenced by the magic time of regeneration. *Lenten ys Come with Loue to Toune* and *The Cuckoo Song* (most famous of all Middle English lyrics) are the best of these. *The Cuckoo Song* has survived in a truly remarkable musical setting, a part song for several voices, which performs the double feat of demonstrating that the English have always possessed a beautiful folk music and that this music was well developed in the thirteenth century. In *The Cuckoo Song*, too, is the complete frankness of the early observer of nature, as well as his ingenuousness. The flowers spring, and the vernal air flows about the singers in wholesome draughts—not without the good manure of earth, however, for the bucks break wind. Few translators of this lyric into Modern English have had the courage to diverge at this point from Victorian reticence.

A few of these secular lyrics are in the mold of the medieval French *chanson d'aventure*. The poet is in the woods and fields; he meets a fair maid, and there is a love adventure in body or in soul, or in both. There is also the *estrif*, or dialogue between two lovers, as in *My Deth Y Loue, My Lyf Y Hate*, which tells in some 200 lines how a lover declared his distress and how he managed to melt the lady through successive stages of give and take. So also in the charming *When the Nyhtegale Singes*. But for the greater part the mirror is turned to the joys of love. *Love Is Soft, Love Is Swet, Love Is Good Sware* warns us that love brings sweetness but also pain and sorrow. Only occasionally do we get involved in the courtly catalogue of charms, as in *Ichot a Burde in Boure Bryght*. Instead, the lover is led by actual longing; weeping is his portion; but the spray swings on the bough and fowls in the frith are likewise smitten.

The reflective or philosophical lyric of the time, diffuse in nature, demands no particular attention. It merges indistinguishably with the religious lyric, when winter wakens the poet's care, or with longer pieces of expository nature, such as the *Poema Morale*. What one remembers more and more from the Middle English secular lyric is Alysoun's black eyes, her laughing face, her well-turned waist, her neck whiter than a swan's, and the "hendy hap," or gracious chance, that brought the lover into the sphere of her genuinely beloved influence.

11. Medieval Drama in England

Of all the many types of medieval literature, the drama has been the most difficult to trace with assurance. Many facts about it are indisputable, but there are many crucial questions that have never been answered and will probably never be settled to the satisfaction of all concerned.

It becomes increasingly clear, however, that English drama had an original growth. It is idle to attempt to see in its genesis any traces of the drama of classical Greece and Rome, or, for that matter, of the cognate European drama on the Continent. Its development coincided remarkably with the growth of English nationalism and reached its peak when the modern English nation was coming to full stature. It was, moreover, primarily the creation of the people as a whole, for while the Church gave it its initial impulse, it was the commoner of the Middle Ages who shaped it into the recognizable secular form it came to possess as the ancestor of the modern drama.

Ignoring the scattered residuum of the classical dramatic tradition, manifest in such general European imitations of the Roman theater as the tenth-century play on a Greek model, the *Christus Patiens,* or the plays of the German nun Hrotsvitha, of the same general date, we observe that the true begin-

nings of English drama are to be found in the elaborations
made in the ritual of the Church during the later Old English
period—elaborations based upon the fact that this ritual is
colorful, emotionally impressive, and essentially dramatic,
especially in the celebration of the two great festival seasons
of the Christian year, Christmas and Easter.

In his commentary on the Benedictine Rule, the *Regularis
Concordia . . . Monachorum,* Bishop Aethelwold of Winchester gives a full account of the so-called Easter trope, or
dramatic element interpolated in the reading of the Lesson
during the Easter Mass. Four of the clergy, representing the
Angel and the three Marys, dispose themselves near the altar;
the Angel asks the "women" whom they are seeking (*Quem
Quaeritis?*); they answer that they are seeking Jesus, and are
told, "He is not here, for He has risen!" The obvious purpose
of this and other tropes was to make more striking an already
striking text by catering to the instinctive human re-
action to dramatic representation. Among these other surviving tropes were some dealing with the Nativity and the
Ascension. But *Quem Quaeritis?* remains the most celebrated.
It was expanded and elaborated further to include events before and after the visit to the sepulcher of Christ. The physical
setting came to include not only the vicinity of the altar but
the entire church; and eventually it was considered necessary
to move out into the churchyard and thence from the confines
of holy ground to the market-place of the town. By this time
the representation of the spectacle had passed from the clergy
to the people; thenceforth, indeed, the clergy, as if embar-
rassed by the creature they had produced, inveighed against
plays as distracting and secular, if nothing more.

The trope, which developed into the liturgical drama, can
be called the first phase of the growth of the English theater.
The original Latin was gradually replaced by the vernacular,
although Latin phrases remained. The actual dating of these
various stages of progress is extremely difficult. If the tropes
began in the tenth century, however, the full-blown liturgical
drama would seem to have been a product of the twelfth century. A valuable specimen to illustrate the mixed nature of
the language is found in the *Shrewsbury Fragments,* which
are late versions of liturgical dramatic composition perhaps as

old as the twelfth century. These fragments also suggest that the liturgical play was given performances, presumably in churches and schools, long after the appearance of the next stage of medieval drama, the miracle play. *Adam,* a Norman play, which may perhaps be considered Anglo-Norman, shows the characteristic blend of Latin and vernacular. Evidently the thirteenth century was the period in which the miracle play as a separate type became discernible.

The term applied to this second phase of English drama was always the "miracle." The corresponding French play was known generally as the "mystery." Some scholars have insisted that the name "mystery" should be given to all plays treating of events mentioned in the Scriptures, and that "miracle plays" deal only with the lives of saints and their attendant miracles. The term "mystery play," however, has the double disadvantage of being both vague and foreign; it will not, therefore, be used again in the present work.

Granted the churchly elements in the origins of the miracle play, what secular elements can be found? The old entertainer, the English minstrel, of a lower social level than that enjoyed by the French troubadour, went about among the people with his songs and tricks, which no doubt included such staples of diversion as monologues, juggling, and acrobatics. In the later Middle Ages these entertainers emerged in bands, grouped together in the manner of the medieval guildsmen. The step from this to the troupe of professional actors was easy; and so there is little reason to doubt that the medieval minstrel contributed some ideas to the associations of willing amateurs who performed the miracle plays. Again, there is the question of folk drama. Festive gatherings of the people have always been likely to bring forth some sort of mimetics, associated particularly with folklore and the remains of folk religions. The folk dances were invariably symbolic of ancient rites attending spring or winter festivals. The rounds about the Maypole and the famous sword dances illustrate such celebrations; so, too, do the obscure plays of St. George, of Robin Hood and Maid Marian, in which singing as well as dancing took place. But what is the true relation of these to the medieval drama? It is a great misfortune that the survivals of this folk drama are all from a period later than that of the miracle plays.

It seems safe to assume, however, that the primary purpose of the medieval drama was entertainment, even when this drama was being enacted within the church. Moreover, it must always be remembered that the Church, having then no competitors, was tolerant of much that a present-day religionist might consider blasphemous. The medieval Church permitted the glorification of folly in the Feast of the Fools or the horse-play pointing fun at the Church in the homage paid to the Boy Bishop. These exhibitions were a type of safety valve comparable to the carnival preceding the coming of Lent. Therefore, while conservative churchmen could and did shake their heads in disapproval, and extreme reformers like the Lollards might rage, the medieval playwrights thought nothing of mixing sincere devotion with burlesque, of taking off the Nativity with a farcical childbirth in a shepherd's hut, or of giving the infant Jesus a ball with which to play, wishing by implication that He may grow up to be a good tennis-player.

The first miracle plays in England of which we have knowledge were in the Anglo-Norman period. Hilarius (*fl.*1125), a pupil of the great Scholastic Abélard and a notable singer of Goliardic songs, has left behind a play on the raising of Lazarus, one on Daniel, and one on St. Nicholas. There is some evidence that other similar plays were to be found at this time in England. Nothing is known about them, however, and to judge purely by the work of Hilarius, the plays of this date were still in Latin, were intended for a tolerably learned audience, and could be called miracle plays only because of their subject matter. At any rate, it was another two centuries before there were any plays or dramatic fragments in the vernacular. Possibly *The Harrowing of Hell*, from the thirteenth century, is the earliest English miracle play; but it has no clearly defined dramatic core. It is obvious, however, that this same century saw the definite molding of the miracle play.

One peculiarity of the English medieval drama, in contradistinction to the drama on the Continent, is that its secularization was assumed by the guilds. The reasons for this have never been explained, but it is obvious enough that the guilds, which played such a large part in the political, social, and religious life of the later Middle Ages, were a natural enough support for any kind of civic activity, as the production of miracle plays came to be.

In most cases, the miracle play was presented on a stage with wheels—the *pagina,* or pageant (a term applied to the spectacle as well as to the vehicle)—which was moved from one station to another in the town. The favorite feast day for performance was Corpus Christi Day, established officially in 1264. The feast day was, in fact, marked by a succession of plays from one station to another, so than an entire cycle could be presented to the townsfolk. This cycle usually embraced the progress of scriptural history from the Creation to the Day of Doom. So far as can be determined, the actors were local people, all men and all amateurs, at least before 1500. Many of the miracle plays possessed musical elements in the form of solos or part songs. Indeed, the fragment of a liturgical play, the *Caiphas* (which was apparently a role in a Palm Sunday play), contains the suggestion of several songs given by one actor in the same performance. The inference is clear; it seems altogether possible that we have hitherto underestimated the general importance of these musical elements. Moreover, in the miracle plays some simple stage properties were employed—a seat, representing the throne of God; some timber, standing for Noah's Ark; an opening in the floor of the pageant, with appropriate orifice, which indicated the entrance to Hell (the Hell Mouth). Later elaborations were made in the matter of properties: there is evidence of costuming and there is the pathetic mutton chop to represent Adam's lost rib. There is even later mention of wages paid the actors, although it is not at all clear when these wages became common practice.

The full details of the staging and presentation of these miracle plays are beyond the scope of the present volume.[8] Suffice it to say that the guilds put great effort into the production of the plays, and from time to time there appeared some playwrights of passable talent. Occasionally attempts were made to have a guild put on a play appropriate to that

[8] See the bibliography covering the present chapter.

guild's occupation—for example, the shipwrights might try a play about Noah's Ark; the goldsmiths would give The Adoration of the Magi; the bakers, The Last Supper. But such frequently humorous, ironic assignments were not the rule.

We are fortunate in having access to four great cycles of miracle plays and what seem to be fragments of some others. These four cycles are the plays of the Chester, York, Towneley (Wakefield), and Ludus Coventriae (Hegge) groups. There is little doubt that there were many others; probably every important town in England had something of the sort. Isolated performances are recorded at many places in the years between 1350 and 1475. The fragmentary cycles are those from Coventry (to be distinguished from the Ludus Coventriae or Hegge group just mentioned), from Newcastle, and from Norwich. A few plays, found in the possession of private families, are difficult to locate in their original setting. The Croxton Sacrament play, the Dublin Abraham play, the four Digby plays, and the Bodley Burial and Resurrection play complete the list. Obscure allusions to Paternoster plays are vexing. These were apparently plays relating the Paternoster to the Seven Deadly Sins and Four Cardinal Virtues, but we have no direct knowledge of them. Perhaps they illustrate some early stage of the morality play soon to be considered.

The Chester plays, 25 in number, are assigned a date as early as 1268-77. They certainly were being played in the early years of the fourteenth century. The York plays, 48 in number, including a superfluous fragment, probably originated about 1350. The Towneley plays, 32 in number, some of them incomplete, came into being not long after 1400. The Ludus Conventriae plays may have been late enough to have used a fixed stage, that is, near 1500. The individual plays are all interesting for one reason or another, but it is impossible to allow them much space. More effective than most are the three plays of the Digby Manuscript, from the fifteenth century: on the Conversion of Paul, on the life of Mary Magdalene, and on the Massacre of the Innocents. The Brome *Abraham and Isaac* is unusually good; it might even be called powerful, for its human qualities are far more compelling than in the average miracle play, and the characterization—the anguish of the father and the appealing trustfulness of the boy Isaac—are not easily forgotten.

All of the miracle plays surviving are anonymous. Here and there a play appears with enough individuality to claim our attention. In all such cases we see at work something of a more than ordinary talent; but there are no geniuses among the crowd. The one exceptional personality in all these play-wrights is that of the hypothetical "Wakefield Master," to whom is attributed a group of plays in the Towneley cycle. Included among these is *The Second Shepherds' Play*, which, while it is ostensibly a miracle play, is in reality given over largely to the escapade of the sheep stealer Mak. That Mak's wife Gill abets her husband by pretending that the stolen sheep is her newborn child is the ironic parallel to the Nativity already mentioned. The play has, in addition, a generous supply of slap-stick humor and more than a little satire.

In the fifteenth century, if not earlier, there grew up along-side the miracle plays another kind of play, which came to be known as the morality play. Here the characters, not Biblical or hagiographical figures but moral abstractions (virtues and vices), engaged in conflict over the prize of man's immortal soul, typifying in a small way the eternal battle between the Kingdom of God and the Kingdom of the Devil. The Macro plays (from the middle of the fifteenth century) give three of the best known morality plays: *Mankynde*, in which Man is attacked by Nought, New Gyse, and Now-a-Days and is rescued by Mercy; *Wisdom*, in which the human soul and its senses are put in plight by Lucifer, to be saved by Wisdom; and *The Castle of Perseverance*, the best of the group, in which the battle lines are drawn between Man's Good Angel and his forces against Man's Evil Angel and his troop. *Everyman*, regarded by some scholars as a translation of the Dutch morality play, *Elckerlijk*, is much the most celebrated of all medieval moralities. Man, dying, finds that none of his prized possessions or attributes can go with him on his melancholy journey save only Good Deeds.

As the type developed, the morality play became more and more realistic and historical, if not political, in its treatment of even the commonest spiritual situations. One can still remem-ber with pleasure the futile efforts of Idleness, the teacher, to get the inattentive Ignorance to spell his name—this, in fact, is about all that deserves to be remembered from *Wit and Science*. In the otherwise dull *Mundus et Infans* and *Hyckescorner*, suffering sinners are confined in the world until they can be released by Repentance. Indeed, the line between the later morality plays and the thoroughly realistic interludes of the sixteenth century is often extremely difficult to follow, and it is best to treat these later moralities as part of the rising Tudor drama of the Renaissance. Here would come the figures of Skelton, Medwall, and, somewhat later, John Heywood.

The general effect of these morality plays is to take one from the comparatively informal, even boisterous atmosphere of the miracle plays and introduce the schoolmaster, the preacher, the conscious literary artisan instead of the spontaneous and often gifted amateur. The great religious controversies of the Reformation brought about a new era in the literature, and the later morality plays reflect to a limited extent some of these controversies. They are inclined, beyond any other consideration, to seriousness. Often their message is devout and sincere; often, however, there is theological quibbling, if not outright cant.

At some time in the late fifteenth century, the morality play was extended to cover secular abstractions and allegory—an example of indeterminate date is *The Nice Wanton*, a lusty play setting forth the dreadful consequences that befall the badly brought-up child (Dalila), while her virtuous and very smug brother reaps the reward of impeccable good behavior.

This type of secular morality play became known as the interlude. Such a name would imply that the play was presented "between" the parts of something else—between the courses of a banquet or wedding feast? between the acts of other plays? as dialogue inserted among scenes and speeches? But the term *interludium* happens to be of long standing. As early as the thirteenth century it was applied to a piece, certainly of dramatic nature, which evidently enacts a scene from the same story as the *fabliau* already described, *Dame Sirith*. This fragment is the *Interludium de Clerico et Puella*. Slightly later is another fragment, the *Dux Moraud*, which represents the speeches of a character named Dux Moraud in a miracle play of secular nature that relates the miraculous redemption of an erring girl and parallels a lurid *exemplum* known as *The Tale of an Incestuous Daughter*.[9] Could such a secular play be considered a kind of moral interlude? And again, the burlesque "tragedy" presented by the peasants in Shakespeare's *A Midsummer Night's Dream*, the true and lamentable story of Pyramus and Thisbe, is explicitly called an interlude. Whatever the exact meaning, the interlude becomes, in the sixteenth century, the comic skit, an invaluable contribution to English comedy, for it transmits with zest the essential English love for the comic, the spirit that gave the country the name of Merrie England. Perhaps the true gift of medieval drama to the English theater is to be found in that comic spirit of the commoner.

Since the true story of the English interlude is properly a part of Renaissance literature, it is not appropriate to discuss it here. To return instead to the morality play, what about the stage presentation of these plays? Here we are left groping. They may well have been presented first by the people, under conditions similar to those attending the production of miracle plays. They may, on the other hand, have been given by the clergy on a fixed stage, on the church steps, or in the churchyard. And as to the actors, were they amateurs as were the players in the earlier miracle plays? There is some evidence that for the morality play *Mankynde* (*c.*1475) special players were chosen—the implication is that they were, so to speak, professionals; and this play has often been given a historical importance because of this possibility. On the other hand, *Mankynde* might have been written originally with amateur

[9] This is an *exemplum* on the efficacy of repentance, composed at some time in the fourteenth century, but its source must be at least a century older. It is echoed in the *Gesta Romanorum* and evidently had currency in northern Europe. A girl has a child by her father. She breaks the infant's neck, murders her mother, who has found out her secret, and then kills her father when he shows signs of repentance. She goes to the city, where she leads a life of dissipation, until one day when, casually going into a church, she is moved by the sermon to rise and publicly confess her sins. The bishop, with irritating calm, bids her wait until the sermon is over. She then drops dead, but an angel appears to announce that she has been granted mercy by Christ, and that her soul is now in Heaven. Let all who would repent do so in faith and hope.

actors in mind. The fact is that, so far as the production of morality plays before the Renaissance is concerned, we simply do not know enough to be able to assert anything with unshaken conviction. The great likelihood is, however, that by the middle of the sixteenth century there were groups of professional actors; there were fixed stages in inn courts, marketplaces, and the like. Perhaps the plays were produced also by church groups, university or school players. The conditions for the establishment of a professional theater were coming to ripeness. Besides, there was always the court chamberlain or Master of the Revels, who occupied a position analogous to that of the modern theatrical producer. The influence of both such men upon the development of the morality play and interlude, while problematical, must certainly be taken into account. Perhaps there were also men in the commoner's walk of life who were promoters of minstrel entertainment.

Such conditions, however, are all very dubious as far as the fifteenth century is concerned; this century in England should still be regarded as the Middle Ages. We are therefore obliged to confess ignorance of the exact nature of the stage production of the morality plays of the medieval period, just as we are obliged to confess ignorance of the precise origins of the morality play as a whole. The one mistake we must avoid is to assume that there was a direct succession of phases, represented by such a sequence as that of liturgical play to miracle play to morality play to interlude, because, while it is true that the domination of these successive types of play followed in this chronological order, it is not true that each type grew in biogenetic fashion out of its immediate predecessor. In fact, there seems to be good evidence to suggest that at one time miracle plays, morality plays, and interludes existed side by side and coeval.

There is salt and pith in *The Second Shepherds' Play* and the Towneley *Noah's Flood*. The pathos of the plea of trusting little Isaac in the Brome *Abraham and Isaac;* the somber brooding of doomed Everyman in the play of that name; the sprightliness, in varying kinds, of *The Nice Wanton* and *Fulgens and Lucres*—these are well worth reading and enjoying today. If we are gifted in the trick of putting ourselves in the place of a medieval commoner of Conventry or Norwich or York—and unfortunately very few of us are—we might be carried away by the spectacle of our friend and neighbor Hodge playing the part of the Virgin Mary. But in the great panorama of English literature in general and of the English drama in particular, too much time can easily be given to the medieval plays. For the specialist they are fascinating; but aside from their lusty yeoman's humor, which is the imperishable heritage of England, and their temporary influence upon certain types of abstract characters, they contribute little to English dramaturgy and are overrated as dramatic composition. So far as individual plays are concerned, the anthologist has probably been right all along. Those plays he commonly reprints are the only ones worthy of any special attention.

Chapter 4

Middle English Literature: Fourteenth and Fifteenth Centuries

1. The Pearl Poet and John Gower

IT HAS BECOME a convenience to assume that the four poems found in a single manuscript (Cotton Nero A X) are the work of a single author, known as the Pearl Poet, for in these four poems there are similarities in style, in poetic imagery, in language, and in total effect that give substance to the hypothetical existence of this poet. Various guesses have been made concerning his identity, some of them more than guesses, and a few individuals have been tentatively named. The Pearl Poet was probably not the Scotsman Huchown of the Awle Ryale or the "philosophical" Strode, to whom Chaucer speaks in the conclusion of his *Troilus and Criseyde*. He may or may not have been the John Prat or the John Donne on whom the authors of one of the most ingenious investigations of the subject have fixed.[1] The matter is at best something of a plaything for the academic mind. After all, the four poems are their own excuse for being. It is evident that the Pearl Poet—whoever he or they may be—possessed talent far beyond the ordinary. The poems are among the most attractive works of the entire Middle English period and certainly, as far as artistic achievement is concerned, on a par with the works of Chaucer and Gower and above the level of *Piers Plowman*.

These four poems were written in an isolated kind of Northwest Midland dialect, and their dates must lie between 1360 and 1400; the consensus puts them near 1370. Their author, then, was a contemporary of Chaucer, of the Piers Plowman Poet, and of Gower; and his work was a notable contribution to the first great flowering of English literature. He was perhaps a cleric or perhaps a layman with courtly

[1] See Oscar Cargill and Margaret Schlauch, *"The Pearl* and its Jeweler," in *PMLA*, XLIII, 1928, 79-104.

connections and a good education; his knowledge of theology and of aristocratic manners is authentic, and it can be shown that he was acquainted with Italian writers and with the French *Roman de la Rose,* as well as being thoroughly familiar with the Vulgate Bible. Moreover, he gives us four poems of remarkable literary range, moving from the tender and personal through the moral and didactic to the courtly and idealistic. He had an exceptional feeling for nature, which he uses most effectively as a descriptive background; and the rugged country of his West Midland home imparts to his poetry a grandeur and a massive quality most other works of the period lack entirely.

The first of the poems, *The Pearl,* is a work of some 1200 lines arranged in 101 12-line stanzas grouped, with one exception, in clusters of 5 stanzas. In each of these clusters, the 5 stanzas are held together by a quasi-refrain in the last line of each stanza; and some element of this quasi-refrain becomes an element of the first line in the next stanza cluster. This ingenious device of linkage is but one example of the Pearl Poet's technical ingenuity; it serves as a symbolic integrating instrument to represent the essential unity of the spiritual experience described in the poem. The author, furthermore, assumes the alliterative devices of the West Midland poetry of the fourteenth century and handles them with great skill.

The Pearl is in the main an elegy on the death of a little girl, possibly Margaret Hastings, daughter of the Countess of Pembroke and granddaughter of Edward III, possibly the poet's own daughter—but her identity is probably immaterial, since the poet expresses in his lines a generalized tender love for a child, with a tone of affection and pity that has seldom been equaled.

The poet on a fair August day (an interesting departure from the traditional May morning of the *Roman de la Rose* sequence) enters a pretty little arbor, where he looks in vain for the "precious pearl without a spot," which has slipped from his grasp into the grass. He is overcome, however, by a sleeping-stroke and has a wondrous vision. In his dream he finds himself in a marvelous land of fair fields, woodlands, and cliffs, with a broad river running by. He attempts to cross the stream, but he sees on the other side a radiant maiden all in white, her robes wrought with Orient pearls, on her head a coronet. It is his lost Pearl. He is amazed to find that she, who had been on earth less than three years and might perhaps be a countess [sic], is now a queen. How can it be? "We are all queens here," she answers, "and brides of the Lamb." She explains through the parable of the workers in the vineyard. The poet's puzzled questions are answered one by one. He sees revealed before him the New Jerusalem, the city flooded with radiance, and God upon His throne. A procession of the hundred and forty-four thousand who are spotless moves past him, led by the Lamb; among them is his little Pearl. Almost beside himself in ecstasy, the poet once more tries to cross the now mighty river that lies between him and the ineffable objects of his vision; but he awakens in the little arbor, sorrowful and yet happy, ultimately content in the thought that his Pearl is in God's care; all is well with him, thanks to the hope the blessed vision has given him.

In all important respects *The Pearl* is the most beautiful of Middle English vision poems. It appears to be a true threnody in a symbolistic style—the first example of its kind in English literature, for none of the Old English elegiac poems is thus directed toward an individual. To be sure, it has been described as an elaborate allegory on the blessedness of grace, but it may equally well be interpreted as the outpouring of a devoted man's personal grief. Although he knows many points of theological nicety, it is not necessary to assume that the poet was a clergyman. Rather his is the kind of knowledge any sensitive educated man of aristocratic environment in the fourteenth century might well have possessed. The combination of descriptive power, feeling for external nature, tenderness, and consolation in *The Pearl* is in itself enough to make its author one of the major writers of the age.

The other three poems fully sustain the reputation to which *The Pearl* entitles the Pearl Poet, although in all of these the possibly personal element of *The Pearl* has been laid aside. *Purity* (often called *Clannesse*) is the least important of the four, it is true; but it is scarcely negligible. A verse homily of some 1800 lines, it expatiates on the theme of purity, contrasting the sanctity of the Marriage Feast with the base conduct of man, shown from the Fall of the Angels through the Deluge and the destruction of Sodom and Gomorrah to the wickednesses of Nebuchadnezzar and Belshazzar. The work shows that the Pearl Poet was willing to draw upon sources as dissimilar as the Church Father Tertullian, on the one hand, and the *Travels of Sir John Mandeville* on the other. Especially effective is the vivid narration of the story of Sodom and Gomorrah; here the alliterative verse, joined with the unusually conservative, archaic-sounding dialect, gives something of the illusion that one is reading an exceptionally good example of the Old English Christian epic.

The third poem, *Patience*, like *Purity*, might well be classed simply as homiletic verse of the period, were it not for the excellence of the verse and its characteristic vigor of style. The subject of the homily is of course obvious; the illustrative *exemplum* is the story of Jonah, who typifies impatience, for he knew no security and contentment until he had submitted to the will of God. There is a great deal of enthusiasm on the part of the poet, a zest for the subject, and a certain amount of homely moralizing that is cogent—who tears his clothes in haste must sit in rags until they have been sewn up again.

It is *Sir Gawain and the Green Knight,* however, that has remained the best known of the Pearl Poet's poems. By most critics it is hailed as the best surviving Middle English romance, at least in the category of the moral romance. Some facts about this work have already been given. It runs to some 2500 lines in stanzas of varying length, averaging about 20 lines to the stanza. The body of the stanza is in alliterative long lines, but each ends in a quatrain preceded by a short "bob-line" monometer. There are four divisions, or "fyttes." As already pointed out, *Sir Gawain and the Green Knight* brings to life the ideal of chivalric knighthood—personal courage and personal chastity; perhaps we may call it a combination of physical and moral courage. Each of these two moral assets has a narrative element in the romance to serve as *exemplum*.

A marvelous knight, green in every feature of dress and physique, invades Arthur's court at Camelot during the Yuletide, insults the gathering, and demands a blow. The childish king is temporarily nonplussed, but Gawain volunteers and beheads the intruder. The decapitated knight, however, picks up his head and leaves, announcing rather casually, in view of the startling circumstances, that a meeting is now appointed between Gawain and himself a year and a day hence at the Green Chapel, where Gawain is to receive a blow in return. "So come, or be called recreant and coward!" In spite of the fearsome portent of the supernatural, Gawain sets out on the adventure to the veriest of "dark towers."

(This motif clearly tests the physical courage of the Arthurian knight. The central "beheading" incident is analogous to a story in the Irish Cuchlain Saga, *The Feast Of Bricriu*—another tribute to the cosmopolitan interests of the Pearl Poet.)

On his way, shortly before the time of the appointed rendezvous, Gawain stops for the Christmas season at a castle, where the lord and lady of the castle entertain him most hospitably. He is told to rest up for his expected ordeal. The lord departs each day to hunt; Gawain remains behind with the lady. Each evening Gawain and the lord, it has been agreed, are to exchange what they have won during the day. Gawain is tempted by the lady of the castle. On the first evening the lord gives Gawain his kill of deer; Gawain gives him a kiss. On the second evening the lord gives Gawain a boar's head; Gawain gives him two kisses. On the third evening the lord gives Gawain a fox skin; Gawain gives him three kisses, but he does not give him a green silk girdle of magic powers bestowed upon him by the lady—a girdle that gives Gawain the invulnerability he so sorely needs for his meeting with the Green Knight. Nevertheless, the relations of Gawain and the lady, though tense, have been on the whole innocent. When the time comes, Gawain goes forth to the Green Chapel and meets the Green Knight, who makes him submit to the formidable ax. The Green Knight tests Gawain with a blow that barely nicks the skin of his neck; and when Gawain, realizing that the bargain has been fulfilled, demands only a chance in a fair fight, he looks up to confront—the lord of the castle.

It seems that the whole affair has been arranged by Morgan le Fay, jealous sister of Arthur, to frighten Guenevere to death, if possible, and to discredit the knightly fellowship. But Gawain, though he has winced slightly under the blow and has not emerged unscathed from the ordeal of the bedchamber, has on the whole acquitted himself with honor. At the same time, he feels no particular elation; he thinks of himself rather as humiliated, especially because he withheld mention of the girdle. The only comfort he can find is that men have frequently been made fools of by women. He will therefore keep the girdle as a reminder against pride. And so when he returns to Camelot, it is agreed that each knight of the brotherhood should wear as baldric a bright green band, following Gawain's example.

The suggestion has often been put forth that this romance is an occasional work written to celebrate some knightly order, such as the Order of the Garter. Others have seen in the poem an allegory of spring, taking into account the verdant color of the Green Knight and his self-restoring neck, though this is truly forcing matters a bit. As far as symbolism goes, it has not been sufficiently remarked that green in Celtic folklore is connected not only with the supernatural but with the infernal, so that the Green Knight may well typify the evil against which all mankind must fight. None of these interpretations is impossible, particularly the first one; yet none is necessary to the enjoyment or comprehension of the poem, because *Sir Gawain and the Green Knight* is most significant as a magnificent specimen of the medieval romance. It has unity, coherence, and an artistic suspense. Its poetic insight cannot be minimized. The opening of the second "fytte," with its beautiful lyric description of the seasons; the colorful panoply of the hunting scenes; the picture of the forbidding English winter morning on which Gawain sets out to meet his grim adversary; the sinister environs of the Green Chapel; the humorous conversation between Gawain and the Green Knight at the close; the romantic, amoristic atmosphere of the bedroom scenes—these are what remain with the reader after he has read the poem; these and, if one chooses, the sincere idealism of the moral pattern that the medieval knight should trace in his goings and comings. We return constantly to an admiration of the Pearl Poet as a writer of beauty, power, and spiritual stability, which the age could ill afford to lose.

The case of John Gower is one of those innumerable examples of a poet who commanded a reputation in his own day but who has sunk into obscurity as time has passed him by. Very likely the fourteenth century read him as much as it read Chaucer; certainly he manifested nearly all the qualities of the average writer of his age. Indeed, we might call the second half of the fourteenth century the Age of Gower instead of the Age of Chaucer. But Gower, although he was a conscientious man and a learned man and a writer of better than ordinary technical proficiency, remains today a colorless figure, the weakest of the imposing quartet of Chaucer, Gower, the Pearl Poet, and the Piers Plowman Poet.

He seems to have been born in Kent about 1330. Much that has been advanced in theory about his life cannot be confirmed. At one time he was thought to have been a lawyer, or a physician, or a lay member of the clergy; but most of the records available today indicate that he was either a country gentleman or a merchant, more likely the latter. He was a friend of Chaucer, to whom Chaucer granted a power of attorney while he was out of the country in 1378. Possibly the two later became estranged; possibly they did not. Gower married late in life (1398), became blind (1401), and died presumably in 1408. No full chronicle of his life is possible, and such a chronicle would probably reveal little of significance. The epithet "moral," conferred upon him by Chaucer in the conclusion of *Troilus and Criseyde,* may apply to his life and certainly applies to his literary composition.

Of these compositions, some are in French, some in Latin; but his *magnum opus* is in English. Evidently the poet was skeptical about the future of the vernacular, but so was Francis Bacon two centuries later. We shall dismiss much of Gower's work summarily. Of the French works, there must be considered the *Mirour de l'Omme,* sometimes referred to as *Speculum Meditantis;* a collection of verse, *Cinkante*

Balades; and another set of balades known as the *Traitié* (*pour essampler les Amantz Marietz*). His Latin works comprise *Vox Clamantis* and three sets of political poems. His English masterpiece is, of course, the *Confessio Amantis,* but he wrote also a couple of "moral" balades in the vernacular.

The *Mirour de l'Omme* is an immense poem of about 30,000 lines, a manual of vices and virtues that reminds one of the many similar handbooks on sin and righteousness already mentioned; it is a kind of cross between *The Ayenbite of Inwit* and Robert Mannyng's *Handlyng Synne.* Gower offers little that is either fresh or new, although he is as usual consistent in his competence. Sin, according to him, is everywhere and has been everywhere since the birth of the Devil; all the trouble it makes, however, is due to the corruptibility of Man, not to God or to Nature. The only cure is repentance. This is scarcely a novel remedy, we may say; nor is the exposition of the cure at all original. As for the minor French poems, they are devoted entirely to the virtues of marriage; they are dignified and lofty in sentiment, though as balades they are surpassed by Chaucer's. And the cynical may well linger with relish over the fact that Gower, for all his praise of marriage, did not venture upon that blessed state until he had reached the virtually terminal age of three score and ten. He reminds us very much of old January in Chaucer's *Merchant's Tale;* in fact, it has been suspected by some that old January is a caricature of Gower—hence the supposed rift between Chaucer and his erstwhile friend. The date of Gower's marriage—and of his blindness—is just a trifle too late to make this piquant suggestion tenable.[2]

The *Vox Clamantis,* about one third the length of the *Mirour de l'Omme,* is a dream allegory on a subject otherwise

---

[2] Gower and Agnes Groundolf were married on or shortly after 25 January 1398. Chaucer's *Merchant's Tale* can hardly have been written much after 1396, although there still remains a possibility that it was composed as late as 1398. The chances favor the earlier date, however. At the same time, the identity of the name of the old husband in *The Merchant's Tale* with the name of the month in which Gower was married raises at least tempting speculation. Still, if Gower did not lose his eyesight until 1401, a year after Chaucer's death, then Chaucer was a grim prophet indeed, unless Gower's eyesight had been failing for some time.

rather neglected by the important writers of the day—the Peasants' Revolt of 1381. It is, to say the least, unflattering to the populace. As a matter of fact, the real purpose of *Vox Clamantis* is substantially that of the *Mirour de l'Omme:* to discuss the baseness of man, from the foulness of the clergy and other learned professions to the lewd conduct of the laborer. Here again is the old, familiar comment upon the inevitability of death and the necessity for repentance. The minor Latin poems, more restrained in tone, discuss the same subject as the political songs current in the vernacular— the growing confusion of the reign of Richard II and the hope for better days under Henry IV. The reader, however, will be more impressed by the vitality of the anonymous poems than by Gower's frozen utterances.

The two "moral" balades in English handle the matter of peace and "gode counseyle." The first was written after the accession of Henry IV and praises in anticipation the blessings to come after the cessation of civil strife; the second speaks of man in his customary medieval function as a world pilgrim. There is some doubt about the authenticity of the second.

To judge by the number of extant manuscripts, the *Confessio Amantis* was nearly as popular as *Piers Plowman* or *The Canterbury Tales*. There are three separate rescensions of the work between 1390 and 1393; the remarkable difference to be noted among these three versions is the changing attitude toward Richard II, owing to reasons obvious to any person with a moral sense. Between the first and second rescensions a passage laudatory of Chaucer was dropped out, whether by design or by accident is not clear. On this fact rests much of the belief that the two men quarreled; but the evidence here, as in the querulous lines of the head-link to Chaucer's *Man of Law's Tale*,[3] does not necessarily indicate a rift. For

[3] In the head-link in question, the Man of Law, having been called upon for a story, observes pontifically that he can hardly measure up to Chaucer's storytelling, mediocre as that may be. He then lists some of Chaucer's works, with special reference to *The Legend of Good Women,* and observes that he, Chaucer, never wrote such tales of abomination as the tale of Canacee, "that loved hir owene brother synfully;/ (Of swiche cursed stories I sey Fy!)." Gower, as it happens, wrote a version of the Canacee story in his

lack of further evidence, the whole question of hostility between the two poets must be waived.

The *Confessio Amantis* consists of eight books and a Prologue, the whole constituting nearly 34,000 lines. The Prologue is a dreary repetition of Gower's ideas as expressed in his earlier long poems—the times are bad, and he wishes everyone to realize the fact. Since nothing can be done about it, however, except to resort to prayer and to hope in repentance, the poet will speak of Love, a much more exhilarating topic. And so on a May morning he wanders in a wood and finds, as he had prayed to find, Venus and Cupid. Cupid would pass him by; but Venus, upon being told that the poet is her servant, skeptically refers him to her priest Genius for confession and absolution.

Genius submits the poet to a discourse on Vices, illustrated copiously by *exempla*—well over a hundred of them. Of these it need be said only that they are told with uniform neatness and dispatch; their author has narrative skill and economy, but very little vital juice. A few of the *exempla* have analogues in *The Canterbury Tales*. The treatment Gower gives the story of Apollonius of Tyre is probably the source of Shakespeare's *Pericles*. The framework of the whole work is, however, clumsy and often inappropriate; the grave application of heavy moral dictates to Love, which, Chaucer sardonically observed, "knoweth no lawe, by my panne!" is sometimes forced, sometimes amusing, sometimes absurd.

There is little doubt, nevertheless, that Gower pleased his age. For two hundred years after his death he was bracketed with Chaucer and Lydgate as a master of poesy. Both his and Lydgate's decline can probably be attributed to prolixity

---

Confessio Amantis. If this is an oblique reference to Gower's work, there still is no need to regard the reference as anything more than a passing criticism. The matter does not admit of final judgment.

In addition to the references to his own works which Chaucer makes in the head-link to *The Man of Law's Tale*, similar references occur in the Prologue to *The Legend of Good Women* and in the Retraction at the end of *The Canterbury Tales*. For other help in establishing the Chaucer canon we are indebted to the references in the works of John Lydgate and the statements of the fifteenth century scholar John Shirley.

and lack of essential originality. Gower composed more than 100,000 lines of verse, too often pedestrian, too often platitudinous, too deficient in humor and, more specifically, in the appropriate human touch. Assuredly Gower is one of the masters of the French octosyllable couplet; but his very excellence in this metrical form over a long stretch has a deadening effect not unlike that created by the faultless pentameter couplets in Pope's *Iliad*. The inescapable fact is that Gower was gifted, but he was not a man of genius; he was an altogether acceptable exemplar of the second-rate. Moreover, he was of his time and did not transcend it at any point.

2. Geoffrey Chaucer

To say that a man is the greatest writer of his time is to say that he brings into focus all the tendencies, characterisics, and ideals of the literature of the age. But it implies much more than that. It means that he can rise above the limitations of his generation and create that which any future generation can understand and appreciate—that he can, in other words, achieve what we must call, for lack of a better term, the universal. This is precisely what Geoffrey Chaucer accomplished. In his works are represented virtually all types of Middle English literature—romance, *fabliau*, vision, satire, homily, saint's life, sacred and secular lyric—written both singly and in various combinations. Moreover, in his amazing powers of observation, his human insight, his humor and pathos, his ribaldry and his dignity, he has appealed to all who have come to know him well.

If we can readily recognize what Chaucer is, we must recognize also what he is not. Although shrewd and wise—the kind of writer who can somehow be quoted in almost any human situation—he is not a thinker in the sense that he has a reasoned system of philosophy in life. Rather he is the complete man of the world, who knows that no system of philosophy can be made to apply to every human problem. Nor is he a poet of grandeur or of metaphysical depth. He is too close to the earth for that, too much of a pragmatist, too prone to dismiss a knotty question by referring it to the clerk or the divine. All in all, he is willing to take the world as he finds it, realizing that any other course will be merely asking for trouble. Consequently he is never a rebel or even a nonconformist; he is neither a Wycliffe nor a Roger Bacon, although he may agree that the Church contains abuses and although he may show an unusual interest in the science of his times.

The fact is that Chaucer was all his life a courtier, a man of general affairs who gave his professional life to the service of the Crown and did well enough to be considered a success. It would therefore be surprising if he had developed the point of view of the commoner. Furthermore, it is plain that his temperament was a leisurely one, that his personality was charming—a good companion at beer, "a popet in an arm t'enbrace for any womman"; but, although he was one of the most straightforward of all great writers, he was never surcharged with passionate haste. His writing was to him an avocation, tucked in here and there wherever the demands of a busy life might permit. Few of Chaucer's longer works were completed, either in design or in execution. The exceptions are, in fact, only *The Book of the Duchesse, The Parlement of Foules,* and *Troilus and Criseyde.*

The known facts about Chaucer's life pertain almost exclusively to his official career. They are of little use when it comes to an appraisal of his work. He was born somewhere between 1340 and 1343, more probably near the later date. He was the son of a prosperous wine merchant of London. He is first heard of as a page in the service of the Countess of Ulster. He served for a time in the Hundred Years War, was taken prisoner and ransomed. About 1366 he married into the family of the De Roets; a sister-in-law later became the wife of John of Gaunt, Duke of Lancaster. There is some evidence that Chaucer received legal training during the 1360's, but he was not a graduate of one of the universities. He was sent abroad on diplomatic missions as early as 1368; later he traveled on official business to Italy (in 1372 and again in 1378), to the Low Countries and France in 1377 and perhaps in 1378 as well. In 1373 he was made Comptroller of Customs and Subsidy of Wools, Skins, and Hides, with residence at Aldgate, London. He left this position in 1386, probably for political reasons. After a brief sojourn in Kent, he revived in fortune enough to win the office of Clerk of the King's

Works (1389); two years later he became Deputy Forester at North Petherton, Somersetshire. We tend to lose clear sight of him thereafter. Although he received various pensions, there is no record of further appointments. He died in October, 1400.

Chaucer's relations with John of Gaunt were close throughout the greater part of the lives of both men and especially during the 1360's and 1370's. The Duke's patronage and the obviously courtly nature of Chaucer's occupation were responsible for the casting of the poet's work in the mold of the aristocratic and chivalric. In his earlier poetry there is much imitation and practice of the traditions of contemporary French courtly verse, of the vision poem or allegory in the manner of the De Lorris portion of the *Roman de la Rose*. As Chaucer grew in stature, however, and developed into the mature artist, he revealed a remarkable grasp of the realistic and the satirical; and in *Troilus and Criseyde* and *The Canterbury Tales* he demonstrates an originality that stamps these works as something beyond the reach of any of the other writers of his age.

While it was once customary to divide Chaucer's literary career into (1) the French period (to 1372); (2) the Italian period (to 1385); and (3) the English period (to 1400), it is wiser to ignore such specious categorizing. Chaucer's first trip to Italy, however, was of inestimable value to him both as an intellectual and as an artistic revelation; although we are igonrant of the details of his visit, we are justified in likening it to the journey of Goethe to Italy four hundred years later. Moreover, it is undoubtedly true that Chaucer's work manifests influences from both the French and the Italian before it shows a full awakening to the possibilities of the English scene, an awakening the author experienced rather late in life.

Indeed, the courtly lyrics Chaucer wrote in the manner of contemporaneous French poets, such as Froissart, Machault, and his friend Deschamps, might well be mentioned first, if only to be dismissed almost at once. There is no possible way of dating most of these little poems. They present to us the familiar figure of the lover, "sighing like a furnace," complaining of the heartlessness of his beloved, and pining away in lovesickness. Many of them take the form of the balade—three 8-line stanzas with a refrain in the last line of each stanza, with or without an *envoy* dedicatory addressed to the patron. A few employ the ingenious form of the roundel—a short poem of 13 lines with a system of repetition, whereby line 1 becomes line 6 and line 11; line 2 becomes line 7 and line 12; line 3 becomes line 13. Since these pieces hardly represent the true Chaucer, although many of them are charming, and since they serve no critical purpose save to illustrate the poet's unusual technical proficiency and graceful lyric manner—assets all too often overlooked by most critics of Chaucer's poetry—they will be passed over.

Another type of contemporary French love poem, the *complainte,* turns up from time to time among Chaucer's minor works. For example, the *Compleynt unto Pite* is almost Elizabethan in the sustained "conceit" of the lover who addresses a bill of complaint to Pity, only to find that she is unfortunately lying on her bier. The *Compleynt of Mars* is an elaborate and difficult astrological allegory of illicit love, possibly based upon a scandal at the court of Edward III. The *Compleynt of Venus,* hypothetically a companion piece to the *Compleynt of Mars,* shows much experimentation in form and marks the first appearance in English literature of *terza rima.* It therefore illustrates well the essential difficulty of distinguishing between French and Italian influences in Chaucer's middle career. In general, the Chaucerian *complaintes* have each of them some point of interest, for one reason or another; but none of them amounts to more than a minor achievement.

Something of a curiosity is the *A.B.C. poem,* a hymn to the Virgin, which is a translation of a portion of Deguilleville's *Pèlerinage de la Vie Humaine.* Its sentiments are altogether typical of any poem composed on this subject during the Middle Ages. The device of beginning the successive stanzas with consecutive letters of the alphabet has given the poem its name.

The two works of Chaucer that show in fullest scope a French influence are his translation of the *Roman de la Rose* and *The Book of the Duchesse.* Concerning the first of these there is still dispute. Since Chaucer states, in his Prologue to

The Legend of Good Women, that he is responsible for a translation of the *Roman de la Rose,* we are willing to accept his part in the existing translation, but not without reservations. It is scarcely likely, to judge by the language and style of the surviving fragments, that he translated more than the first 1700 lines. As far as it goes, it is a competent translation, though a fragmentary one. It is obvious, however, that Chaucer knew the *Roman de la Rose* intimately and allowed the opening sections of the famous allegory to permeate the beginnings of several of his works. Nor is it unlikely that the pictures of abstract characters portrayed in the first part of the *Roman de la Rose* suggested to him some of the descriptive methods he employed later in his delineation of the immortal gallery of pilgrims in the Prologue to *The Canterbury Tales.*

The Book of the Duchesse is an elegy on the death of Blanche, the first wife of John of Gaunt. It may be presumed that the poem was written shortly after the event (1369) and is therefore the only important work by the poet that can be dated with some assurance. It is possible that *The Book of the Duchesse* takes precedence in time over *The Pearl* as the first personal elegy in English poetry, although fragments of older heroic poetry might be so construed. At any rate, the poem tells in octosyllabic couplets of the poet's dream: on a beautiful May morning he wandered in the woods, hearing the distant sounds of a hunt, until he came upon a man in black. He fell into conversation with this man and discovered that Fortune, playing chess with him, had taken his queen. The courtship of the lady and her surpassing beauty are both itemized in detail. When the poet learns that such beauty is really dead, he is struck with sympathetic grief. His vision, which in its inconsecutive quality catches admirably the characteristics of a dream, is preceded by a brief narrative of the separation of Ceyx and Alcyone and the bereavement of the wife. It is possible that this retelling of the Ceyx and Alcyone story, found originally in Ovid's *Metamorphoses,* was written earlier by Chaucer as a separate piece.

While *The Book of the Duchesse* has much grace and sincere feeling, it is much too long and contains one fault that Chaucer never entirely overcame, a tendency to parade knowledge in the form of intrusive learned allusions. Both of these weaknesses, however, are greatly improved in *The Parlement of Foules*. This charming work, although written in the 7-line Chaucerian stanza (rhyme royal) generally associated with the poet's more mature work, is an obvious example of Valentine poetry—a species of composition celebrating the festival of St. Valentine and the mating season, which originated at the French court during the second half of the fourteenth century.

In conformity with this Valentine tradition, *The Parlement of Foules* describes how all birdkind is assembled to choose mates under the benign eye of the goddess Nature. The center of interest is the female eagle and her choice among three likely candidates. The poem may therefore be a political allegory, representing the arrangement of the nuptials—we should scarcely call it a courtship—between young Richard II and Anne of Bohemia, or possibly the unsuccessful attempts to marry Richard to Princess Marie of France. In either case the poem must be dated between 1377 and 1382. It is not necessary, however, to assume this political allegory; at any rate it is hardly possible to prove its existence. But the charming roundel at the end of the work impresses the Valentine motif once and for all; and the delightful bickerings of the birds, who are arranged in classes suggestive of the divisions of the fourteenth-century English parliament, express a satirical spirit that cannot fail to appeal. Nor did Chaucer ever surpass in plain magnificence the opening lines:

> The lyf so short, the craft so long to lerne,
> Th' assay so hard, so sharp the conquerynge,
> The dredful joye, alwey that slit so yerne;
> Al this mene I by Love . . .

For that matter, he always had the happy gift of striking off memorable opening lines.

In deciding on the date and purpose of *The Hous of Fame*, we are confronted with a difficult, virtually unanswerable question. The poem is written in octosyllabic couplets, indicative of Chaucer's early works; but its author is obligated to Roman and Italian writers, notably to Virgil and Dante, and the tone of the poem is the tone of the mature Chaucer. By general consent it is placed before *Troilus and Criseyde,* and therefore somewhere between Chaucer's first Italian visit and 1382, although its chronological relationship to *The Parlement of Foules* sets up a further riddle. Moreover, *The Hous of Fame* is fragmentary, breaking off, indeed, before its ultimate purpose is clear to the reader. It seems more than likely that Chaucer himself modified his original plans for the poem as he progressed; the "little last" third book is as long as the other two books put together, and is incomplete at that.

At the beginning of *The Hous of Fame,* the poet has a vision in which he finds himself within a temple of Venus admiring a portrayal on the walls of the story of the *Aeneid.* Stepping outside, he discovers that he is on a great plain. An eagle swoops down from the sky to seize him. In the second book, the eagle and Chaucer are on a wild aerial journey, the poet clutched precariously in the eagle's claws; and the bird engages his unresponsive passenger in a pedantic talk about the nature of sound and the remarkable destination toward which they are headed—the House of Fame. And truly an amazing house this turns out to be —a temple-like structure built on ice, intricately carved and decorated, a building full of magic. Here the Lady Fame holds court, dispensing her favors and her disfavors with capricious whim. Leaving the house, the poet comes to a peculiar rumor factory, where all kinds of reports, great and small, true and false, are constantly emerging from the curious wicker edifice. A person of authority appears, but before we can be told who he is, the piece abruptly comes to an untimely end.

The Hous of Fame, particularly in its last book, bristles with erudite allusions. Obviously its satire is its most memorable component. There may have been some love design in the work as it was originally conceived—the opening sections hint strongly at this possibility—but if so, that design has been hopelessly blurred. Rather it is the stuffy pomposity of the guiding eagle, the arbitrary decisions handed down by Fame, the crowds of musicians, artificers, and sorcerers who throng about, and the rumors falling over themselves in their efforts to get out and be on their way which make this poem highly distinctive as well as original. Any meaning other than a satirical one has been lost to us, however; and as no primary source of the work is known to posterity, we must continue to speculate in indecisive fashion on what Chaucer's intentions actually were.

Little attention need be given to *Anelida and Arcite,* a strange fragment of uncertain age. It bears some faint relation to the legend of Thebes. The opening lines indicate that it is to be the romance of a faithless love between the "fals" Arcite and the shrinking Anelida. It continues as an elaborate *complainte* by the forsaken Anelida, and then suddenly breaks off. The *complainte* exhibits great metrical ingenuity but is otherwise wholly conventional. The possible relation of this fragment to either *The Knight's Tale* or *The Squire's Tale* is altogether obscure.

Similarly of importance only to the Chaucerian scholar is the prose translation of Boethius's *Consolation of Philosophy,* which is acknowledged by Chaucer and was probably completed some time near 1380. Since the gist of the *Consolation of Philosophy* has already been given, it need only be said here that Chaucer's translation demonstrates that he was not a major prose writer; and the dialectics of the work, never too convincing, cannot be considered well handled by the poet. The influence of Boethian *dicta* on Chaucer's work, however, is unmistakable. A set of eloquent balades—*Fortune, Truth, Gentilesse,* and *Lak of Stedfastnesse*—as well as a longer poem, *The Former Age,* actually reproduce better than the prose translation the spirit of individual passages in Boethius's work. The problem of Fortune's fickle gifts is, of course, fundamental in the *Consolation of Philosophy;* it serves also as a prime motif in both *Troilus and Criseyde* and *The Monk's Tale.* Fundamental also is the matter of "gentilesse"—essential virtue, which is innate and irrelevant to mere birth or rank. This theme is especially prominent in *The Wife of Bath's Tale. The Franklin's Tale,* and others in the Canterbury collection.

It is a temptation to linger over the sturdy and vigorous balades, *Lenvoy de Chaucer a Scogan* and *Lenvoy de Chaucer a Bukton,* because of their homely wit, their refreshing cynicism. Here emerges the typical Chaucer, keeping a delicate balance between the humorous and serious and never quite letting the reader know which is uppermost in the poet's mind. We may well take for granted that his friends Scogan, tutor to the sons of Henry IV, and Bukton, probably a London lawyer, were both amused and moved. The *Compleynt of Chaucer to his Empty Purse,* addressed to Henry IV and therefore probably Chaucer's last composition, is a piece of polite begging; but it seems to have been rather the conventional thing to write whenever a new patron swam into a medieval poet's ken, and too much should not be inferred from the mere existence of the poem. If it sheds light upon the tribulations of a poet who must depend upon a patron's favor, so do the lines of *Adam Scriveyn,* addressed to his amanuensis, illuminate the trials of a poet whose works are maltreated by careless scribes.

One troublesome poem is *The Legend of Good Women.* This is a collection of secular saints' lives, possibly in imitation of Boccaccio's *De Claris Mulieribus,* in which the protagonists are not, however, sainted ladies but rather martyrs to love. It seems a trifle remarkable that Cleopatra should be considered a "martyr" to love; but Thisbe, Dido, Hypsypile, Medea, Lucrece, Ariadne, Philomela, Phyllis, and Hypermnestra assuredly meet the requirements. The plan Chaucer originally conceived seems to have called for more than twice as many of these legends as are actually in existence; even so, the work is interrupted in the middle of a legend. The sources of the poet's versions of these classical tales are all obvious enough; many are from Ovid, but some are from scattered writers such as Virgil, Livy, Boccaccio, and others.

The legends themselves are far from inspired narratives as they appear in *The Legend of Good Women,* although in the *Legend of Cleopatra* there are some stirring lines describing the Battle of Actium. Indeed, the tales alone would form a negligible part of Chaucer's work. But they are introduced by a Prologue that is still a matter of much controversy. There are two versions of this Prologue: the first from about 1386; the second from probably as late as 1394, or after the death of Anne, first wife of Richard II. The two prologues differ somewhat in the arrangement of lines and in the insertion of material into the later prologue as well as in the dropping of lines from the first prologue. Both versions agree, however, that the poet in a vision meets the God of Love and a beautiful queen, Alceste. The God of Love reproaches him for his cynical treatment of love and of loving women—witness Criseyde and the translation of the *Roman de la Rose*. (This reference to the *Roman de la Rose* must apply to Jean de Meun's portion; and we have, unfortunately, no surviving evidence that Chaucer actually translated that part of the allegory, except, of course, the poet's own word.) The queen intercedes for the poet on condition that he write in penance a legendary of faithful women. In this Prologue there are two points of special interest. It contains a passage—the first of three—that lists Chaucer's acknowledged works and is therefore invaluable in checking a Chaucer canon, although both versions of the Prologue must be consulted, since some works mentioned in the later prologue do not appear in the earlier one. Moreover, the Prologue is the best example in English literature of a Marguerite poem, or poem in praise of the daisy, which was the flower sacred to a particular cult of French courtly love-poets. Above and beyond the mere matter of a literary cult, however, Chaucer's beautiful description of the daisy and the garden in which it grows—his own garden, where he comes to read and write after a day's work—offers the complete tribute to all gardens and stands as a true monument to what an Englishman has always loved.

The Legend of Good Women as a whole is generally assigned to the late 1380's. The earlier version of the Prologue was written after *Troilus and Criseyde,* possibly before Chaucer gave up his residence at Aldgate in 1386; there is, however, no way of telling when the various legends came into being. Because they were written in the iambic pentameter couplet associated with *The Canterbury Tales,* there is a feeling that they could hardly have been written much before the Prologue. It is certainly proper to assume, at any rate, that the Prologue is Chaucer's maturest achievement in the field of vision poetry, first made famous by the *Roman de la Rose.* Is Alceste a creation of the poet's own imagination, to whom he has given the name of a Greek heroine who was faithful to her husband even unto death? Is she Queen Anne of England? Is she the Queen Mother Joan? Again, we may take our choice, as we did among the allegorical possibilities of *The Parlement of Foules*. Aware as we are of Chaucer's courtly experiences, of course, we find it very likely that he made use of this kind of personal allegory; indeed, it is firmly believed by many that *The Legend of Good Women* was a kind of command performance ordered by Queen Anne—incomplete, perhaps, because Queen Anne died before the work was finished. This, however, is surmise, as are three fourths of the statements made about the genesis of Chaucer's works.

It remains to consider *Troilus and Criseyde* and *The Canterbury Tales*. Either work would have made Chaucer famous; taken together they assure him a position second to none in his time.

The origins of the legend of Troilus have been outlined on an earlier page. Chaucer's immediate source for *Troilus and Criseyde* was Boccaccio's *Filostrato* (*c.*1338), to which he was greatly indebted, for he took over all the major episodes of that work; but he added much of his own, not only in respect to incident but also, and particularly, in respect to characterization. His obligations to Benoît de St. Maure and to Guido delle Colonne were more general. It is believed that the actual writing of *Troilus and Criseyde* took place between 1381 and 1387; most experts think that the work was finished in 1385 or 1386.

Troilus and Criseyde might be considered only a chivalric romance, but its many virtues are so manifest that any such designation would be unworthy. In its five masterfully constructed parts it is a novel in verse—the first psychological novel in English literature, for the interplay of character and incident, as well as the epic sweep of the whole narrative, qualify it as a novel; and the remarkable probing of motive and insight into character render the term "psychological" highly appropriate. Moreover, so skillful is Chaucer's handling of dialogue, so fundamentally natural, that, when placed beside other works of the age, the text of *Troilus and Criseyde* seems as if it had been written in a later century. It is pleasant, incidentally, to speculate on what Chaucer's success would have been if he had lived in a time of the flourishing of the drama—in the Elizabethan Age, for example. On the basis of *Troilus and Criseyde* and many of *The Canterbury Tales,* we have every right to believe that he would have been a most effective dramatist, although his genius still remains epic rather than dramatic.

At the same time, the present-day reader must make certain concessions before he can judge *Troilus and Criseyde* fairly. For one thing, the poem is the tragedy of Troilus, not of Criseyde. In this respect, it is indeed a chivalric romance. Troilus is the hero; he wins prestige in combat inferior only to that of the peerless Hector of Troy; he attains his love; he loses her; he dies in epic combat. Therein lies his tragedy, as the medieval conception of tragedy would have it—an exalted personage brought to the vanity of vanities. The story, as is made clear in the first line, is the story of the "double sorwe" of Troilus. It matters not that Criseyde, the heroine, and Pandarus, the friend and go-between, are the two most striking characters in the work and the two most comprehensible to the reader of today. The poem is nevertheless, as Chaucer conceived it, the story of Troilus. Hence all the attention to Troilus's lovesickness, to his absurd fears and swoonings, to his almost morbid respect for Criseyde's and his own good name, to the clandestine nature of their love. Moreover, since Troilus is a prince and Criseyde is not a princess, marriage between the two is out of the question—no chivalric audience would have tolerated it.

As for Criseyde, she has been the topic of almost endless discussion, most of it purely subjective. The point to remember is that Chaucer almost leans over backward in his attempt to avoid any categorical judgment of her character. Perhaps it is enough to say that she is a thoroughly normal woman, both in her emotions themselves and the psychology thereof. She is feminine, vital, intelligent, and by nature affectionate. Her social status, thanks to the defection of her old reprobate father, Calchas, is rather shaky, although she is well liked by such influential people as Hector and Helen. She has primary concern for her good name, it is true; but what woman in her position would not? Perhaps she is too yielding, or, as Chaucer puts it, too "slydynge of corage," in the case of the "sodeyn" Diomede; but that is a matter about which no human being can afford to be dogmatic. Considering the fact that she is a commoner, her future is promising until Calchas ruins it by demanding that she be brought to live with him in the Greek camp. When the Trojan people, giddy and unstable as Chaucer considers any populace to be, demand Antenor in exchange for Criseyde, the love affair of Troilus and Criseyde is doomed. For Troilus is not willing to hazard visits to the Greek camp—he is one of the least venturesome heroes in all literature; Criseyde is not willing to elope with Troilus (there had been enough trouble in Troy over the abduction of women); and besides, Fortune will not have it so. There is throughout *Troilus and Criseyde* a powerful influence of determinism, and its author does not allow the reader to forget it. In other words, the tragedy of the love of Troilus and Criseyde appears to Chaucer as the consequence of an ineluctable marshaling of forces against which neither Troilus nor Criseyde can hope to prevail. And so when Criseyde leaves Troy and goes to live with her father, the impetuous and skillfully amorous Diomede replaces Troilus in her heart, although Chaucer indicates that he is not certain about this fact. He prefers to imply that she yields to opportunity and the promise of a future that is possibly more secure than her situation had been in Troy. When Criseyde abandons Troilus, she does it not without poignant regret on her part and that characteristic temporizing to which a person resorts when he or she is in a state of indecision in love. She postpones writing to Troilus; when she does write, she insists that the postponement of their planned reunion, unavoidable as she says, does not mean that she will never return. Yet we know full well that the time will come when Troilus will receive no more letters.

None the less, Chaucer refrains from harshness in his comments on Criseyde, for though she "falsed" Troilus and was at the very least "unkynde," the poet cannot bring himself to speak with contempt of one so fair and withal so lovable. In the Prologue to *The Legend of Good Women*, he allows the God of Love to speak disparagingly of Chaucer's works because the poet wrote of Criseyde, among others, and so committed heresy against the law of the God of Love. Actually,

however, Chaucer utters these occasionally unfavorable crit-
icisms of Criseyde only often enough to justify the theory that
Troilus has been treated badly and to give point to the
"tragedy" of Troilus's love. In his conception of Criseyde
there is nothing of the rigorous moralistic judgment bestowed
upon the heroine by Henryson, or the loose and licentious
kicking about of her reputation that characterized the later
popular ideas of "the lazarkite of Cressid's kind."

Little but admiration can be given Chaucer's delineation of
Pandarus, a smooth man of the world, not too successful in
his own love-making and probably not too energetic either,
but experiencing a vicarious satisfaction in bringing together
his best friend and his beloved niece to the consummation of
their love. Witty, shrewd, realistic, prone to homely wisdom
and proverb, and somehow sincere in his devotion to both
Troilus and Criseyde, Pandarus may strike the reader as effete
and brittle, the unwholesome product of an over-urbanized
society. Yet the story invariably picks up pace when Pandarus is
on the scene; and when he and Criseyde are together, Chaucer
is at his sophisticated best. The man he portrays in Pandarus impresses one as altogether recognizable, intelligent, and highly
civilized.

The wealth of proverbial wisdom in the poem, nearly always put into the mouth of Troilus or Pandarus, constitutes
a most appealing element in the work as a whole. Most of the
time such opportunities for commentary or reflection are presented with art; they do not clog the narrative. Only the long,
ill-advised soliloquy by Troilus on the nature of free will
versus necessity—taken over bodily from Boethius's *Consolation of Philosophy*—can be called intrusive; and even this is
logical enough in reference to the fundamentally fatalistic
philosophy of the poem. For Chaucer, not without violence to
the doctrine of Boethius, leaves necessity the winner in the
controversy.

The intellectual colors in *Troilus and Criseyde* are rich
enough; the glimpses of a feudal, chivalric society are no less
attractive for the poet's sublime disregard of anachronism.
The story, however, is never permitted to slow down as a
concession to these ornaments; it is, indeed, admirably built
up. Chaucer does not trouble himself unduly with full details

of the entire affair between Troilus and Criseyde. He concentrates upon the sudden attack by Love on the cocksure Troilus and how it laid low that Trojan prince; on the revelation of this love to Pandarus and Pandarus's often elaborate stratagems to unite Troilus with his beloved; on the consummation of the passion of the lovers and their temporary happiness; on the unfortunate events that separate the two; on the feverish and ultimately vain anticipation by Troilus of the return of his lady; on the all too successful wooing of Criseyde by Diomede; on the sardonic laughter of Troilus when he leaves this world and looks down upon out "litel spot of erthe." Chaucer ends the poem with thoroughly medieval reflections upon the vanity of human wishes and the felicity that is in Heaven above. This concession to the taste of the times, however, does not wipe away the manifest fact that the poet has exhibited here even better than in most of his works that astonishing knowledge of humanity that makes even the stereotyped courtly hero Troilus real and that shapes Criseyde and Pandarus into remarkable characterizations.

There is some possibility that *The Canterbury Tales* was conceived as a series of *exampla* on virtues and vices—something, perhaps, like Robert Mannyng of Brunne's *Handlyng Synne* or Gower's *Confessio Amantis*. If so, the design was not completed and is therefore not demonstrable. It is simpler and withal more accurate to assume that Chaucer was out to regale the reader with a series of tales, now amusing, now edifying, and chiefly entertaining. It is difficult to visualize Chaucer as a preacher (whereas it is not difficult so to visualize either Mannyng or Gower), although in *The Parson's Tale* he projected himself well enough into the character of the Parson to show that he was fully capable of a well-developed medieval sermon. But he was ever at heart the born storyteller, a supreme reporter of humanity, with the power to portray most boldly the social and human types of his age. At the same time, he was willing to discuss different aspects of such an important secular institution as marriage. Still, the thoughtful reader will always feel that with Chaucer the story is the thing—the story and the characters that go with it. The message can take care of itself. In the various tales the poet gives us plenty of moral consideration; but it is in the minds and on the lips of the Canterbury pilgrims and does not necessarily represent Chaucer himself. Indeed, it would be as difficult to define Chaucer's philosophy of life on the basis of *The Canterbury Tales* as it would be to define Shakespeare's philosophy of life on the basis of his plays, and for the same reasons. Both poets took life as they found it; and when one is surrounded by teeming, brawling, dynamic humanity, there is little time for philosophy.

The circumstances underlying the framework of *The Canterbury Tales,* the assembling of pilgrims at the Tabard Inn for the trip to Canterbury, are too familiar to call for discussion. They would obviously be even more familiar to Chaucer, who must have seen a great number of such pilgrimages start out from Southwark. That the pilgrims agree to tell two stories each way, which would call for a full program of nearly a hundred and twenty stories, where as there are only twenty-four accepted tales in the collection, four of these unfinished —this is sufficient comment upon the avocational nature of Chaucer's writing. Only two methods of grouping these stories are clear: the method of pairing tales in a "quarrel group," in which one pilgrim tells a story directed at another pilgrim (or his profession) and receives tit for tat; and a "discussion group," illustrated by the half-dozen stories dealing with the problem of marriage. Otherwise Chaucer depends upon the inspiration suggested by the incidents of his framework—incidents spontaneously conceived and most artfully arranged. For this framework is no mere series of convenient pegs on which to hang a given tale; it is an integral part of the whole, because it serves not only to impart life and movement and a wholesome realism to the entire collection—truly a story in itself—but also as an admirable vehicle for individual characterization. We should have none of the brilliant pictures of the Host, for example, were it not for this framework. And although some have seen in the frameworks used by Boccaccio in his *Decameron* and especially by Sercambi in his *Novelle* (where an actual pilgrimage is the setting) possible influences on Chaucer's design, still there is no denying that Chaucer has taken a device familiar even in the Middle Ages and bent it magnificently to his purposes, an imperishable monument to his creative powers.

There is no complete agreement on the exact order of all *The Canterbury Tales;* but, in view of the fact that there are no less than 90 manuscripts extant, in varying stages of completeness, it would be remarkable if there were any close agreement. For our purposes the order is immaterial. Suffice it to say that virtually every type of Middle English literature is represented here, except the medieval drama, and this is at least referred to. Likewise, every class of Middle English society stands before us, except the nobility, who would be out of place anyhow in a pilgrimage of this sort. The Knight, a soldier of fortune perhaps, but a knight all the same, is accorded the greatest respect and serves as a kind of arbiter in situations in which the brash Host, master of ceremonies, might not venture to interfere. Even the members of the Church present do not command the full deference that the Knight commands. It is his lot to begin the telling of stories, but it is inconceivable that any other pilgrim could have begun the game.

Each member of the pilgrimage who gives us a tale tells one appropriate to his occupation, his station in life, and his personality. One may draw certain conclusions about Chaucer's attitude toward some of these people, although such conclusions are risky. But it is obvious that Chaucer respected the honest members of the Church, such as the Parson and the Prioress (and possibly the Monk), and was bitter toward the parasitic members, such as the Friar, the Pardoner, and the Summoner. His remarks about the guildsmen, who belonged to "a solempne and greet fraternitee," are brief and deferential. Toward the artisans he shows sometimes brutal frankness, yet he is amused by them and sympathetic, although he is condescending toward their churlishness, which, he assures us, he must reproduce even if it offend. To those members of society whom he likes and admires he may be gently satirical, in complete good humor; but he admits these as equals, whereas he does not so admit the commoners. If this be snobbishness on Chaucer's part, the snobbishness natural to a courtier in an age that still bore the heavy hand of feudalism, we must accept it as such. One thing, at least, is obvious enough. Chaucer hates sham and pretense, and he can be bitter. It is a great mistake to think of him as essentially a man of pure good nature. No more sustained irony and sarcasm can be found in English literature than he exhibits in *The Merchant's Tale* and in long stretches of the Prologue to *The Wife of Bath's Tale*. In reading these pieces and the short *Lenvoy de Chaucer a Bukton*, we may be justified in thinking of Chaucer as disillusioned about marriage and certainly contemptuous of old age. His remarks are given with too much relish to be credited merely to the Merchant or to the Wife of Bath.

There is no room here to discuss the many sides of this fascinating personality. Returning to *The Canterbury Tales* as a whole, we find *The Knight's Tale*, a polished medieval romance on the loves of Palamon and Arcite for Emily, heading the list. Palamon, who first saw Emily from his prison window, wins her from Arcite, but not before Arcite, winner of her hand in a tournament, has been destroyed through the intervention of the gods. This story, derived from Boccaccio's *Teseide*, is revived in the Elizabethan play *The Two Noble Kinsmen. The Knight's Tale* is the longest of *The Canterbury Tales*, the most elaborate and aristocratic in its ideals and courtly tone but, in spite of some excellent passages, hardly the most memorable, because Chaucer allows one of his greatest gifts, that of characterization, to languish. The tale is received, as might be expected, with polite approbation; but the drunken Miller breaks in with his magnificent *fabliau* which tells how a carpenter was beguiled—one of the most brilliant and scandalous narratives in English literature. The Reeve, once a carpenter, retaliates with a tale of two Cambridge students who avenged themselves upon an arrogant, thieving miller. Here, in passing, we meet for the first time an authentic use of dialect for purposes of local color and realism. The first group of *The Canterbury Tales* is then completed by the unfinished tale of the Cook, who is even more of a chronic alcoholic than the Miller. Although this tale does not proceed far enough for us to be able to judge it fairly, it was obviously to be a *fabliau* with promising potentialities for indecency.

At this point in the collection some of the manuscripts carry *The Tale of Gamelyn,* already described.

A long prologue and "head-link," in which there may be some fuel for the argument that Chaucer and Gower became estranged, leads on to a tale by the pompous Man of Law; it is a Constance romance of distinction.[4] Following this comes a dullish *fabliau* by the Shipman, a tender though essentially bigoted little miracle tale (almost a saint's life) by the Prioress concerning a little Christian boy martyred by the "cursed Jewes," and then *Sir Thopas,* the delightful parody of the decadent romances, recounted by Chaucer himself. In one short "fytte" and a few lines of a second, the poet achieves a masterpiece of getting nowhere. The Host, however, cannot abide Chaucer's effort and rudely interrupts. The poet, slightly nonplussed, then plunges into the ineffably dreary prose *Tale of Melibeus,* an endless harangue upon the virtue of Prudence. He is allowed to proceed to the bitter end. If this is a satire on the literary taste of the time that a clever trifle like *Sir Thopas* fails to please, while a portentous fallen cake like *The Tale of Melibeus* is tolerated, then it is excellent satire. Perhaps, however, we are giving Chaucer credit for too much subtlety; perhaps he really thought that *The Tale of Melibeus* was a superior performance, incredible as it may seem to us. At any rate, the Monk follows the *Melibeus* with a dismal series of short "tragedyes," instructive stories of great folk brought by

[4] The Constance theme involves a heroine married happily to a king or potentate but afflicted with a wicked mother-in-law, step-mother, or even a lustful, treacherous servant. Hers is the theme of the Calumniated Queen. Her enemy accuses her of monstrous birth, and she is cast adrift with her offspring in an open boat. But she is always a model of fortitude, and God sees that she drifts eventually to a place of refuge. In Chaucer's *Man of Law's Tale,* Constance is first affianced to the young Emperor of Syria; he is killed by his mother at the wedding feast because he has accepted Christianity; Constance is set adrift and finally arrives in Northumbria, where she marries King Alla. Her child is reported by the jealous mother-in-law to be a monster. Once more she is set adrift, this time with her child, and ends up at her home in Rome, whence she had departed originally for Syria. Alla, on a pilgrimage to Rome to gain pardon for the crime of putting his mother to death, is reunited with wife and child.

Fortune to death or disgrace. This depressing progress is halted by the Knight, and the Monk retires into the sulks. The narrative group concludes with the remarkable and light-hearted satire of *The Nun's Priest's Tale,* a beast story of Chauntecleer and the Fox, designed as an *exemplum* on the evils of flattery but making its effect today largely through the domestic bumblings of the stuffy husband, Chauntecleer, and the sauciness of his sprightly favorite wife, the hen Pertelote.

Following the order given by Skeat, which has been modified recently by the Robinson and the Manly-Rickert Chicago editions, we come next to *The Physician's Tale,* the old story of Appius and Virginia, with some comment on the bringing up of children. Then the Pardoner, having wet his whistle, embarks upon his remarkable self-exposé and tale. As an exhibition of shameless hypocrisy, the Pardoner's Prologue would be difficult to match anywhere. *The Pardoner's Tale* itself is a powerful homily on self-indulgence in general, with an *exemplum* that by common consent is one of Chaucer's masterpieces, for its melodrama of the three rioters who sought and found Death all too easily is told with a brevity and a bitter irony that are alike unforgettable.

The so-called "marriage group" is opened without preliminaries by the Wife of Bath. Her Prologue is even more revealing than the Pardoner's—an astonishingly poignant human document; but the Wife of Bath, *mulier calida,* is nevertheless normal and likeable, at least to men, though unscrupulous in a thoroughly feminine way. In her life with her five husbands she has always believed in the theory that the best defense is a good offense; and by using all her female tricks, including scolding, falsehood, deceit, tears, and general ruthlessness, she has clawed her way to a position of complete dominance, or "sovereinetee," over her husbands. This, she submits, is the secret of a successful marriage. Her tale, a vigorous story based on the motif of the Loathly Lady, parallels the romance of *The Weddyng of Syr Gawayne and Dame Ragnell* already referred to, and drives the nails into the thesis laid down in her Prologue—except for the marring effect of a discourse on "gentilesse," [5] which, on the lips of the Wife of Bath, sounds rather incongruous.

Interrupted by an exchange of uncomplimentary *fabliaux* between the Friar and the Summoner, the first of which is weak and the second highly unsavory—neither of them calls for further comment—the marriage group is resumed by the Clerk, whose tale of Griselda, a type of moral romance already described, asserts the complete mastery of the husband. The Clerk, however, is only a theorist; and besides, even he admits that Griselda is of a type scarcer than the proverbial teeth of a hen. The Merchant soon sets him right with his grim tale of the unfortunate marriage of doting old January and fresh, winsome May. No more searing picture of the follies of old age or of the essential deceitfulness of certain women has ever been painted. For although his wife cuckolds him in the most flagrant manner, and he catches her in the very act, she is able to persuade the besotted January that everything is as it should be. *The Squire's Tale,* a fantastic romance, resembling in some features the content of *Anelida and Arcite,* is only a fragment; but we may put it into the marriage group as a sop to women, who, according to the female falcon in the story, are in their basic virtue and loyalty much abused by men. But since the Squire is unmarried, he may also be classified as a theorist like the Clerk. The kindly, gentlemanly Franklin, a sort of ancestor of the landed gentry of future centuries, tells a Breton *lai,* the upshot of which is that marriage can succeed only with mutual co-operation and trust as well as a fidelity to one's word, even though it may mean personal dishonor in the eyes of a knowing world.

---

[5] "Gentilesse"—good breeding, personal integrity, Christian charity ("pitee"), innate virtue. It is a subject discussed in Boethius's *Consolation of Philosophy,* whence its appearance in Chaucer. It is not a matter of birth, rank, position, or riches. In fairness to the Wife of Bath, it should be remarked that the lecture the bride delivers to her husband on this topic is logically sound enough, though it is rather ill-timed. She is showing that the knight, having promised the hag to marry her, must keep his word as a knight, regardless of personal inclinations—the basic theme, incidentally, of *The Franklin's Tale.* Unfortunately, this lecture dulls the dramatic impact of the story.

Dorigen has rashly vowed to her importunate lover that she will yield to him only when the rocks have been removed from the coast of Brittany, because she loves her husband, Arveragus, and fears peril to him while he is at sea. When the young lover Aurelius, through the help of a magician, succeeds in this impossible-seeming task, Dorigen, on the advice of her husband, prepares to keep her promise. Such nobility of soul, however, is too much for the young lover, who has become infected with this same "gentilesse," and the story ends in a wallow of altruism. No doubt Chaucer intended the Franklin's moral to settle the whole discussion of marriage, for his counsel is as the world would have it. As effective achievements, however, The Merchant's Tale and the Prologue to The Wife of Bath's Tale remain in the mind of the modern reader; and the more discerning will have difficulty in avoiding the inference that the Wife of Bath wins the debate. For only the callow Squire and the idealistic Franklin give marriage much of a chance, since the Clerk's hero, Walter, is an impossible creature. The woman is triumphant in all the other stories, even in The Merchant's Tale. In the war between the sexes she will always win, in practice if not in theory.

The remaining stories in The Canterbury Tales are somewhat in the nature of an anticlimax. The Second Nun's Tale is a conventional saint's life of St. Cecilia, very likely written rather early in Chaucer's career. When a Canon and his Yeoman join the pilgrimage shortly before it reaches Canterbury, the resentful Yeoman first frightens away his master by hinting ominously that he will expose him and then actually regales the group with a revelation of the crookedness of alchemists. The Canon's Yeoman's Tale is valuable for its demonstration that Chaucer, who all through his poetry shows he was an accomplished astronomer—his Astrolabe is a manual for the use of a particular astronomical instrument—evidently was familiar also with many aspects of alchemy. One sometimes meets with the current theory that he was once gulled by an unscrupulous alchemist. The Manciple contributes a brief, pithy, although sententious tale of fabliau-like tone, which explains how crows first became black; his purpose, however, is to warn against the danger of too much talk. Finally the Parson is persuaded to deliver an exhaustive and exhausting sermon on the Seven Deadly Sins, which, like *The Tale of Melibeus,* grinds on ponderously and remorselessly to its conclusion. It serves its purpose, at least; it ends *The Canterbury Tales* on a moral note and gives Chaucer an appropriate opportunity to write a "retraction" at the finish, which begs forgiveness for any tales which might "sownen into synne." This retraction, being something of a convention, need not be accepted too literally as indicating Chaucer's actual feelings on the subject of his earthier stories.

Such is the catalogue of *The Canterbury Tales.* No simple outlines can do them justice; to appreciate their richness and universality of human experience they must be read firsthand, not in summaries or translations. Little has been said here of the sources of the stories themselves. *The Knight's Tale,* as has been remarked, is an adaptation of Boccaccio's *Teseide,* very much as *Troilus and Criseyde* derives from Boccaccio's *Filostrato;* the various *fabliaux,* while analogous to specimens in French and other continental literature, seem to be basically Chaucer's own; *The Clerk's Tale* draws upon a work by Petrarch; *The Monk's Tale,* an example of the "mirror for magistrates" or *speculum principum* type of instruction piece, is suggested by Boccaccio's *De Casibus Virorum et Feminarum Illustrium.* Many of the other tales have analogues found elsewhere in medieval literature; they may have direct sources that have thus far eluded us, or they may be mainly original. *The Merchant's Tale* and the Prologue to *The Wife of Bath's Tale* borrow much from such dissimilar people as Jean de Meun, Eustace Deschamps, Walter Map, and St. Jerome. The influence here and there of Ovid, Vincent de Beauvais, Guillaume de Lorris, Alanus de Insulis, Pope Innocent III, Livy, and Virgil must be assumed for *The Canterbury Tales* as well as for other works by Chaucer; the details are for the specialist to point out. Lucan, Marco Polo and Mandeville, Suetonius, Claudian, Theophrastus, Valerius, and others bob up occasionally in the swirling mass of authors whom Chaucer knew first- or second-hand and whom he does not hesitate to invoke. He was familiar also with certain chroniclers, such as the Anglo-Norman Nicholas Trivet; and through *florilegia* (or anthologies of "thoughts and sayings" of classical authors) he knew of Juvenal and perhaps of some other late Roman writers. By and large, then, he was an unusually well-read man for his time; the "twenty bookes, clad in blak or reed," which his Clerk of Oxford preferred above fiddles and psalteries, Chaucer himself possessed with many left over. And if, in his earlier career, he relied heavily upon some of these books, he came nevertheless to depend more and more upon himself. His last works are highly original, with an originality that is one of Chaucer's most priceless assets, although, to repeat, he never quite overcame the innocent habit of showing off his reading and his learning. If, as a prying critic has observed, his perusal of a book was likely to be confined to the first rather than to the latter portion of that book —well, the poet was a busy man and evidently an easy-going one; and many of the books were doubtless formidable reading.

Chaucer's reputation, as time went on, suffered the usual fluctuations and vicissitudes, made more extreme by the difficulties his language raised for ignorant posterity. In the generation after his death, his fame was high and his influence great. As the English language, however, proceeded through its rather remarkable changes from Middle English to Modern English, Chaucer's texts became more and more of a mystery; and the poet's reputation in consequence sank to that of a rude, uncultured pioneer, to be rescued only (with the perennial exceptions of The Canterbury Tales and Troilus and Criseyde) when a proper knowledge of medieval England, its tastes, philosophy, and language, brought the world to a full appreciation of Chaucer's essential greatness.

The Canterbury Tales, as a unit, was first printed by Caxton in 1485; yet it was not until 1532 that an edition of his complete works was published by William Thynne. This edition, which contained some Chauceriana now rejected, is the basis for the Tudor estimate of Chaucer, which is not very high. Speght's edition of 1598 was something of a minor landmark. Some editions appeared in the early eighteenth century, notably the very bad one by Urry. It was not until 1775, however, when Tyrwhitt published his excellent edition, that modern Chaucerian scholarship can be said to have begun,

and with it a just consideration of the poet's virtues as well
as his defects.

No longer is it sufficient to say with Pope:

> Our sons their fathers' failing language see,
> And such as Chaucer is, shall Dryden be.

For Chaucer is not of the past. He is more "modern" than
nine tenths of the authors studied in traditional courses in
English literature. Nor is it any proper service to his memory
that he should be considered a native wood-bird wild or the
morning star of song. His strong, bracing reality of touch; his
pungent humor and graceful personality; his essential worldly
wisdom; and his consummate craft—these are what will
recommend him to generations still to come as one of the
half-dozen greatest English writers. It is foolish to think of
him as a mere dilettante in letters; his garden is too rich in
soil. Perhaps it was all said by John Dryden two and a half
centuries ago when he observed that Chaucer "must have been
a man of a most wonderful comprehensive nature." To this it
may be added that, in a sane and normal way, he knew all the
hopes, desires, aspirations, and stumbling blocks that intrude
upon the path of feeble man; he was acquainted with the night
and he was also acquainted with the day.

3. The Last Century of Middle English Literature

No century in the history of English literature since the
Norman Conquest has been more often reproached for its
barrenness than the fifteenth; and certainly its accomplishment
is by any standard comparatively insignificant. Perhaps the
unsettling effects of the Hundred Years War were too strong
in the first half of the century; and perhaps the Wars of the
Roses bore down too heavily during its third quarter. Such
explanations, however, are not convincing. The best answer
that can be found to the question why more good literature
was not written in the fifteenth century is that there were not
enough good writers. To be sure, there was plenty of literary
activity. The drama, as we have seen, was producing both
miracle plays and morality plays; the interludes were in the

offing. There was much composing of romances; the popular tales flourished. The lyric, secular as well as religious, was not only plentiful but at times distinguished. Balladry was evidently common enough;[6] so was the writing of chronicles. Of towering individuals skilled in the art of writing, however, there were none at all.

As it happens, the figure of Chaucer dominated the literature of the entire century. But there was no one able to rival in importance the prominent writers of the fourteenth century. Not only were there no Chaucers; there were no Gowers, no Pearl Poets, no Piers Plowman Poets. Such comparatively sterile periods can be expected from time to time; their sterility, however, is always more apparent than real. The very dearth of gifted writers is usually a sign that a blood transfusion is required and that new styles and new interests are needed. The whole fifteenth century is therefore significant as an age of transition. Decaying medievalism was still covering the promise of the Renaissance, for which England was not yet prepared. The rate of literary advance had in consequence been slowed down, still to await the accelerating force of a new spirit.

Since all of the literary types that flourished in fifteenth-century English literature have now been mentioned, we need consider here only the individual figures who managed to push themselves above the crowd. In the field of fifteenth-century poetry, there were the devoted disciples of Chaucer, writing both in England and in Scotland. These half-dozen poets wrote most of the fifteenth-century poetry that is worth noticing, unless we make exceptions of the sometimes exquisite anonymous lyrics of the age. In prose the most conspicuous writer was Sir Thomas Malory, himself a last scion of the aristocratic line of medieval romance writers. The historiography of the century would be represented best by Lord

[6] Probably the Robin Hood cycle was building up during this century, as well as a great many other ballad cycles. One charming piece of pastoral nature that can be assigned pretty certainly to the fifteenth century is *The Nutbrown Maid,* which is a dialogue between a man and woman on the subject of inconstancy in woman. The lady makes a spirited defense of woman's constancy. In general, however, this poem should be regarded as a dramatic lyric rather than as a ballad in the strict sense of the word.

Berners's translation of Froissart's *Chronicle* (not published, however, until 1523-5). This is the first of a magnificent succession of Renaissance translations. The chronicles of Capgrave and Wyntoun have already been named. In theology there was the sturdy and courageous reformer Reginald Pecock (1395?-1460?).

The literature of the post-Chaucerian era, however, when viewed as a whole, is most important as poetry; English prose was still very much of a fledgling. This poetry has a strong predilection for allegory and an almost inevitable tendency to gravitate toward the didactic. Both of these trends have been previously noted as characteristic of medieval literature in general. We may say, then, that the fifteenth century kept as well as it could the qualities and ideals of medieval literature, and in addition most of the forms, without contributing anything especially new or vital. It is, therefore, by way of becoming decadent and symptomatic of the terminal stages of medievalism.

We must pass over the various bits of Chauceriana that were at one time or another actually attributed to Chaucer. To the bibliophile and antiquarian John Shirley (d.1456) we we are obliged for much information about Chaucer's works; but some errors have evidently crept into some of Shirley's statements. On the basis of these errors Chaucer has been saddled with the authorship of typical love allegories such as *The Cuckoo and the Nightingale, The Letter of Cupid, The Testament of Love,* and *The Court of Love.* Of these, *The Cuckoo and the Nightingale* is by Sir Thomas Clanvowe (d.1404); *The Letter of Cupid* is by Thomas Occleve, of whom more in a moment; and *The Testament of Love* is by Thomas Usk (d.1388). *The Court of Love,* which was not composed until the beginning of the sixteenth century, can be discussed most conveniently, because of its date and general nature, along with the work of Stephen Hawes. Another piece of about 1400, *The Plowman's Tale,* has already taken its place in the tradition of the Piers Plowman Poet.

More sprightly, though far too long, is *The Tale of Beryn,* an anonymous story in verse (1425?), which purports to be the second tale told by the Merchant on the Canterbury pilgrimage. Its Prologue, which gives an account of the pilgrims after they have arrived at their Canterbury inn, is particularly amusing in the manner of a *fabliau*, but it lacks the art of Chaucer.

The first of the English Chaucerians in point of time was probably Thomas Occleve (Hoccleve) (1370?–*c*.1450), a Londoner who left a rather interesting picture of his city in *La Male Regle*. In fact, he was one of the few Chaucerians of the period who continued in any appreciable way the tradition of English city life as it was sketched in *The Canterbury Tales*. For the greater part, the fifteenth-century "sons of Geoffrey" preferred to follow their master in his capacity as allegorist, author of *The Book of the Duchesse, The Parlement of Foules,* or *The Hous of Fame*. This fact alone is enough to confirm these English Chaucerians in their medievalism. Occleve himself, in *The Letter to Cupid,* derives his work from Chaucer's *Legend of Good Women* and combines in thoroughly medieval style the amoristic with the religious in his defense of women's chastity. He reveals himself, however, as a not very vigorous writer given to moralistic hairsplitting. His *Regement of Princes,* adapted from the thirteenth-century Roman Aegidius's *De Regimine Principum,* is better; it is a handbook for the edification of the sons of Henry IV, garnished with many rather plain tales, from which it is clear that the author was no Lollard and had, indeed, a very conservative religious outlook. All in all, the work is a typical example of the "mirror for magistrates" school of composition. Although the *Regement of Princes* is usually considered Occleve's best work, the average reader, if he had to read Occleve at all, would prefer *La Male Regle,* which is a kind of autobiographical "testament," telling us more of Occleve himself and of his London, about which we would fain know more, and less about how princes should conduct themselves, concerning which we already know more than enough.

With John Lydgate our tale must be unceremoniously shortened, for although in actual volume of output he was one of the most copious writers in English literature, he was also one of the most mediocre of poets. His birth is obscure; it probably took place near 1373. For most of his life he was a monk at Bury—in other words, at the Benedictine abbey at

Bury St. Edmunds. He indicates in his *Testament* (1445?) that he underwent a difficult youth in the Church; perhaps he was, like Browning's Fra Lippo Lippi, taken at too young an age. Be that as it may, he dedicated himself to the writing of poetry in the manner, as he saw it, of his "maister Chaucer," whose works he knew authoritatively. In fact, he joins John Shirley and Chaucer himself as the most important witnesses as to the authentic list of the master's writings.

It is utterly impractical to discuss thoroughly in a short compass the long list of works in the Lydgate canon. Considering the generally third-rate quality of most of them, the impracticality is welcome. Between twenty and thirty pieces have been definitely assigned to Lydgate; they run to a total of more than 130,000 lines. It is only fair to Lydgate, however, while observing that he was in no respect the consummate artist that Chaucer was, to insist that he was no illiterate in poetry either. His works all suffer from the, to us, fatal flaw of overwordiness, a fault he himself and, it is to be feared, his whole literary generation seem to have regarded as an artistic virtue. Parenthetically it is to be observed that one of the symptoms of the Renaissance first detected in fifteenth-century England is its word-consciousness, its desire to increase the potentialities of the English vocabulary—a desire that led at one extreme to the ridiculous coinages and borrowings of classical words and word formations (the "aureate" terms) and at the other extreme to the misuse and abuse of stale synonyms ranged in apposition.

At the same time, Lydgate has a narrative sense that all this wordiness cannot forever dull. He can hardly be said to have any special powers of characterization. He renders a service, however, by giving full accounts of what English literature might otherwise have lacked—for instance, a version in the vernacular of the legend of Thebes (*The Story of Thebes*, c.1420), and a detailed recounting of the legend of Troy (unless the metrical romances, such as *The Geste Historial* or *The Seege of Troy*, already referred to, precede Lydgate's *Tory Book* of 1412-20, which is virtually impossible to determine). These two enormous poems alone comprise nearly half the lines Lydgate wrote.

But "the monk of Bury" was no worldling like his master.

He was by instinct a cleric and a teacher. Therefore occasional, philosophical, fabulistic works came off his pen—*The Churl and the Bird* (1398?); *Horse, Goose, and Sheep* (1400?); the saints' lives of St. Edmund (1444), St. Alban and St. Amphabel (1439), St. Margaret (1430), St. Austen (1440), Our Lady (1410), and possibly St. George (1425?); a reworking of the old romance of *Guy of Warwick* (1423?); verses for Queen Margaret's entry into London (1445). His forte, however, was allegory and instructive pieces in the "mirror for magistrates" manner. *The Serpent of Division* (1400) was prompted by the dynastic schism attending the accession of Henry IV. *The Flower of Courtesie* (c.1401), *The Court of Sapience* (c.1403), *Reason and Sensuality* (1407), and *Complaint of the Black Knight* (c.1402) carry their own commentaries in their titles. If any one of Lydgate's allegorical poems needs to be illustrated further, it would be *The Temple of Glass* (c.1403), for this is probably the most readable of the lot, the most typical of its author, and the best suited to illustrate the nature of his indebtedness to Chaucer.

The poet in a vision finds himself in a temple of glass; on its walls are sundry images from classical legend as well as the figures of some classical deities. There follows a lamentation about Love, which is both beautiful and cruel. A particularly dazzling lady dedicates herself to Venus, since she cannot be with her beloved. Venus promises her comfort, provided she be constant. A knight is in similar sad case. Venus promises him his reward, provided he be chaste and dedicate himself to his lady. Soon the goddess brings together the two suppliants amid a complete series of moral purgations, attended by joyous chorus and festive progress.

A prominent detail of the poem is a sequence of long lyric prayers to Venus and complaints from her suffering devotees. Palamon and Arcite, old January and youthful May, Dorigen, and Grisilde appear in the lines of the work, as does Chaucer's name. The resemblances to *The Hous of Fame* are notable. The knight reminds one somewhat of the man in black in *The Book of the Duchess*. Aside from the weakness of all this obviously derivative matter, the chief faults of the poem are its length and its static action.

The fact that many other minor pieces of allegorical or hagiographical nature have been attributed to Lydgate is some indication of the popularity of such pieces at this particular time. It seems incredible that the living tissue of *The Canterbury Tales* could have failed thus signally to promote further growth. Possibly the most energetic work that Lydgate wrote —if he wrote it—is *London Lickpenny* (1435); yet it has always been relegated by commentators on the period to the category of the minor. Here is a passable picture of London as a kind of fifteenth-century Vanity Fair, which from its very nature is obliged to pay attention to some of the sights and smells of the city. Lydgate, however, prefers to base his fame on such warmed-over pies as *The Falls of Princes* (1430-38), his longest work, an adaptation of Boccaccio's *De Casibus* with some recollection of Chaucer's *The Monk's Tale;* or on the *Pilgrimage de Mounde* (*c.*1428), a "prolix Pilgrim's Progress," based on Deguilleville's *Pèlerinage de la Vie Humaine* or, worst of all, on the *Secreta Secretorum* (*c.* 1446), which is a mélange of pseudo-science, philosophy, and theology made even more confusing by the muddy continuation of the poem offered by Lydgate's admirer, Bennet Burgh. Two prose works, *The Damage and Destruction in Realms* (1400), a review of the situation engendered in England by the initial breach between Yorkist and Lancastrian, and another version of the *Pilgrimage* (1413), have been credited to Lydgate; the first is probably authentic, the second probably not. The autobiographical *Testament* has been tentatively dated 1445; it must be one of the last works by the poet.

Almost a full generation was to pass before the third English Chaucerian, Stephen Hawes (1475-*c.*1525), was born; and the turn of the century was passed before either of Hawes's surviving works came into existence. The poet was a groom of the chamber for Henry VII, first of the Tudors; but nothing in his poetry suggests the rising materialism of the Tudor dynasty. Hawes's intellectual and literary father was Lydgate; his intellectual and literary grandfather was Chaucer. Thus his *Example of Virtue,* written about 1503 and printed by de Worde in 1512, is a poem in Chaucerian stanzas on the pursuit of purity in life, allegorical in frame and content. His much better known *Pastime of Pleasure,* composed in 1505 and published by de Worde in 1509, is one of the last gasps of its *genre:*

> Graunde Amoure, the hero of the poem, relates that after falling asleep in a flowery vale he sees the Lady Fame appear to him. She says that La Belle Pucel dwells in the magic tower of Music, but that giants bar the way thither. After serving a long apprenticeship to the Ladies Grammar, Logic, and Rhetoric, who constitute the Trivium, and Arithmetic, Music, Geometry, and Astronomy, who constitute the Quadrivium, and after having slain the giants with his sword, Clara Prudence, Graunde Amoure finally wins La Belle Pucel, marries her, grows old, and dies.

Yet in fairness to Hawes it must be noted that his personifications are personifications of learning rather than of abstract virtue. Even he could hardly avoid all the implications of humanism that were in the air.

Contemporary with the poems of Hawes and written in much the same spirit as *The Pastime of Pleasure* is *The Court of Love,* long regarded as Chaucer's.

> Here Philogenet of Cambridge loses his way in the palace of Cytherea, where Admetus and Alcestis are co-rulers. Philabone, a lady of the court, informs him of the rules of the place, and shows him the persons who have obeyed or broken the laws of love. Among these are those individuals who have deliberately refused to love and are now tormented by regrets. The poet enters the service of the fair lady, Rosial, who at first treats him harshly but becomes gracious at the entreaty of Pity. The poem is concluded by a choir of birds, of whom each one intones a hymn to the Church.

Even the casual reader of Chaucer's works will be reminded of the anonymous author's many obvious obligations to the master.

It is a great relief to turn from the tired lines of Hawes and the mechanical passages of *The Court of Love* to consider the Scottish Chaucerians. As it happens, Scottish literature in the fifteenth century had not much more than a hundred years of positive achievement behind it; but this fact was advantageous in that it meant a certain enthusiasm and freshness, which was sorely needed among courtly and clerical writers of the age. The solid virtues of Barbour's *Bruce* and the feebler fragmentary efforts of John Major ("Blind Harry") in a poem on the subject of the Scottish patriot William Wallace (composed about 1460) laid a foundation for Scottish narrative poetry. The Scottish Chaucerians nevertheless chose the allegorical path as their English brothers did; and only the unusual personalities of men like Henryson and Dunbar prevented these Scottish Chaucerians and their tradition from sinking into the doldrums into which the English Chaucerians had managed to fall.

The first in line among the Scottish Chaucerians is appropriately King James I of Scotland (1394-1437). His romantic life, nineteen years of which were spent in captivity in England, included a love-marriage to Jane Beaufort, granddaughter of John of Gaunt, and an untimely death by assassination. The admiration of King James for Chaucer is manifest; we may say literally, moreover, that he married into Chaucer's literary sphere. The result is *The Kingis Quair* (1423), a vision allegory of now familiar mold, which has, however, the virtue of sincerity, since it was written to celebrate his wooing of Jane Beaufort. It is graceful, delicate in feeling, thoroughly idealistic in tone, but not very impressive. The social prestige of its author and his apparently attractive personality undoubtedly helped the fame of the poem; and when it is placed beside Lydgate's allegorical poems, its virtues are enhanced. It should be remembered in passing that the use of Chaucer's seven-line stanza by a writer of royal blood gave the verse form its better known name, "rhyme royal." Two other pieces, which reveal glimpses of contemporary Scottish peasant life, *Christ's Kirk on the Green* and *Peblis to the Play*, may or may not be by King James. They belong at any rate to Scottish popular traditions later made famous by Burns and Scott.

To leave aside the inept imitation of *The Parlement of*

Foules called *The Book of the Howlat* ("Owlet") by Sir Richard Holland (*c.*1450) is no difficult task. The miscellaneous pieces of Middle Scottish prose and the ephemeral popular scraps of verse can also be ignored.

The next Scottish Chaucerian to appear was Robert Henryson, who was born about 1430 and died in 1506. The name was common in Scotland at this time; the poet was master of the Grammar School in the Benedictine Abbey at Dunfermline, and was possibly connected at one period with the University of Glasgow. Nothing of importance is otherwise known about his life; it seems to have been spent in the career of a placid teacher and pedagogue, with the conservative *mores* that habitually go therewith. Although he may have been a strict moralist, as his poems often indicate, he had nevertheless a sense of fun, which his burlesque *Sum Practysis of Medecyne* demonstrates, as well as his sprightly fables,— *The Cok and the Iasp, The Uponlandis Mous and the Burges Mous, Schir Chantecleir and the Fox, The Lyoun and the Mous,* and *The Wolf and the Lamb.* Furthermore, the long and popular *Robene* and *Makyne,* a pastoral comedy in verse, bucolic and satirical, depicting the lost opportunities of a panting swain, is humorous and deft beyond the average.

Among his other poems, *Orpheus and Eurydice* is not important in any way; but *The Abbay Walk* is a rather beautiful expression of resignation to the will of God. *The Bludy Serk,* allegorical in nature, has the virtue of compression, a virtue most of the poet's colleagues scorned. *In Praise of Age* is in marked contrast to the Chaucerian dislike of advancing years. But with all the directness and simplicity of Henryson, as evinced in *The Garmont of Gud Ladies,* he reveals sometimes a grim underlying motif, a rather savage tone of *memento mori,* apparent not only in a trifle like *Thre Deid Pollis* but also in his best work, *The Testament of Cresseid.*

This, the most distinguished treatment of the story of Troilus and Cressida to be written between Chaucer and Shakespeare, was printed originally in the 1532 edition by Thynne of Chaucer's works as an extra book to Chaucer's *Troilus and Criseyde.* Henryson, after acknowledging the debt he owes to "worthie Chaucer," raises the question whether Chaucer judged the matter aright. To the Scotsman's schoolmaster mind, ruled by morality in logic absolute, Cressida is deserving of some kind of retribution, not of leniency.

Diomed tires of Cresseid and casts her out; she takes refuge with her father Calchas, who is as "old and unwholesome" in Henryson's poem as he was in Chaucer's. Saturn strips her of joy and beauty; the Moon strikes her with leprosy. As she sits by the road, in leper's habit, with cup and clapper, the proud and lusty Troilus, cured in the main of his love-sorrow, comes riding past. Their eyes meet; it seems to the prince that he has seen the leper's face somewhere before, but so dreadful is the woman's condition that he cannot recognize her. Nor does her failing eyesight recognize him; but, having received alms from him, she is told who it was that gave her charity. She dies after sending him a ring he had once given her.

This harsh and, to the modern reader, unmerited chastisement of Cressida is tempered by the essential pathos and drama of the whole scene, which has been justly regarded by many as the most gripping passage in all fifteenth-century poetry. The question how much Henryson put a blight upon Cressida or how much this blight was already recognized as her proper punishment remains unanswered; the net effect, however, is the same in either case. Cressida is thenceforth a wanton—depraved, unhealthy, evil to the very core of her being. When Shakespeare has Ulysses observe:

> Fie, fie upon her!
> There's language in her eye, her cheeks, her lip,
> Nay, her foot speaks: her wanton spirits look out
> At every joint and motive of her body . . .

he is but following the current conception of Cressida, although he spares her the visitation of leprosy. Yet, while Henryson brings her to infamy and death, Shakespeare does not punish her. Instead, he allows her to disappear from the scene while the action of his play busies itself with other matters. Perhaps this is the greater insult.

William Dunbar (1465?-1530?) is an even more arresting

figure than Henryson; in many ways he is the most proficient poet of the entire fifteenth century. For a time he was in the Church; later he was an occasional ambassador for the Scottish king James IV. We are reminded at this point of Chaucer's career. Dunbar's work falls naturally into three categories —formal allegory, satirical and comic verse, and religious poetry. The formal allegories are *The Thrissil and the Rois*, celebrating the marriage in 1503 of James IV and Margaret Tudor, sister of King Henry VII of England (a union whereby the Stuarts later came to the throne of England); *Bewty and the Prisoner*, of negligible quality; and his best known work of this kind, *The Golden Targe*, wherein the poet in a vision is wounded by the arrows of Beauty in spite of his targe, or shield, of Reason.

In all these allegories there is a lean and spare force that is most praiseworthy; it can fairly be said that Dunbar in this respect approaches his master Chaucer more nearly than any of his contemporaries. The same qualities of wiriness and vigor are apparent in his satirical and comic poems. Here he may resort to personal satire, as in the attack upon his contemporary fellow-Scotsman and fellow-poet, William Kennedy (1450?-1508?), known as *The Flyting of Dunbar and Kennedie*. Such attacks, however, were in the nature of sport; and for all the coarseness and heavy hitting, they are scarcely comparable to the malice of Dryden's *Mac Flecknoe* or Pope's *Dunciad*. The testament of Mr. Kennedy continues the game in less sure-fisted fashion. On the other hand, Dunbar is capable of realistic characterizations of the broadest sort, as in *The Twa Mariit Wemen and the Wedo*, which is as unabashed as the Prologue to Chaucer's *Wife of Bath's Tale*. Court poet though he may have been, Dunbar has, like Chaucer, an exceptional eye for the commoner; *The Devil's Inquest* and *The Tailyeouris and Soutaris* prove that, of all the fifteenth-century Chaucerians, Dunbar comes closest to the spirit of *The Canterbury Tales*. Perhaps it is this awareness of the commonalty of man that could endear Dunbar to the twentieth-century reader, if only the difficulty of the Anglo-Scottish dialect of his poems did not operate to his disadvantage, as it handicaps all the Scottish Chaucerians far more than their master Chaucer.

On the other hand, Dunbar's elegiac poems of miscellaneous moral preachment, headed by the beautiful *Lament for the Makaris* (1508), smell more strongly of the medieval lamp. *The Merle and the Nychtingall* is virtually a medieval debate on the respective merits of earthly and heavenly love; *The Worldis Instabilitie* is actually another example, with Boethian overtones (see Chaucer's *Lak of Stedfastnesse*), of the "mirror" literature designed for the admonition of princes; *All Eardly Joy Returnis in Pane* writes its own critique. *The Dance of the Sevin Deidlie Synnis*, however, is a weird extravaganza, completely in the modern manner, depicting the sinful outcasts hopping about under the surly goading of Mahoun (Mahomet). To compare this piece with Lydgate's kindred *Dance of Macabre* is sufficient to show at once the difference between the talented Scotsman and the pedestrian Englishman.

Sometimes Dunbar steps into the field of pure hymnology, as in *The Ballet of Our Lady*. To criticize him justly is not too easy; he seems at one moment to be of the Middle Ages; in the next he appears suddenly shaking hands with a typically Tudor figure like Skelton. There can be no doubt whatsoever of Dunbar's virility as an artist and observer; nor is his craftsmanship anything but excellent.

Another poet of interest, though of a lesser talent than Dunbar's, is Gavin Douglas. His dates are as uncertain as those of all his prominent contemporaries in literature. He was born some time around 1475 and died, according to most authorities, in 1522. He is the most completely transitional figure of all the Scottish Chaucerians. His *Palice of Honour* (1501) reminds one very much of Chaucer's *Hous of Fame*. *King Hart* (c.1510) comes rather close to Bishop Grosseteste's *Chasteau d'Amour*:

King Hart (Heart) is made captive by Dame Plesance, and is rescued by Dame Pietie; then he marries the charming enemy who overcame him in the first place. But, after seven years, Age knocks at the gate of the palace of Plesance; and all the young and flighty courtiers who once had surrounded her flee and are finally followed by the lady herself. Reason and Wit then warn King Hart to return to his own castle, where he is soon attacked by the hideous army of Decrepitude. Before Hart dies he makes an ironic testament.

Douglas's chief fame, however, is based upon his translation of the *Aeneid* (1513), an important offering on the altar of the English Renaissance humanists, a work in which he exhibits his best powers—a good control of a free iambic pentameter couplet and considerable descriptive vividness. It is not especially smooth verse, and yet its roughness lends to the translation an effectiveness it might otherwise not have attained.

Finally there is Sir David Lindsay, youngest of the Scottish Chaucerians (1490?-1555?). He is the most thoroughly professional courtier of the group. A particular office, that of guardian to young King James V, set his literary activity on the track of precept and instruction. *The Dreme* and *Ane Satyre of the Thre Estaitis* express a pithy, rather droll wisdom in a man not at all blind to the abuses of Church and State and willing enough to speak his mind about them. In the fuller sense, Lindsay is a Chaucerian only in style and perhaps in personality, because his thrusts at contemporary conditions seem more closely identifiable with the reforms of the sixteenth century and hence with the Renaissance. On the other hand, a glance at his works demonstrates that he has not shaken off medieval habits. *The Monarche* is a long poem in the form of a dialogue "betwix Experience and the Courteour, off the Miserabyll Estait of the World"—typical enough in manner and substance to please the most confirmed medievalist and suggestive as well of the most conservative of material for a medieval morality play. Lindsay's *Tragedie of the late Cardinal Beaton* is patterned after Lydgate's *The Falls of Princes* and Chaucer's *The Monk's Tale*. But again, *The Testament of the Papingo* is very like Skelton's *Speke Parrot* as a satire on the court. *Squire Meldrum*, a narrative poem about a friend, and *The Complaint of Bagsche*, a poem about the king's hound, deal in agreeable fashion with personalities either human or canine and show a sympathetic side to Lindsay's writing not too obvious in his other works.

A discussion of fifteenth-century prose must necessarily be

limited mainly to Malory's *Morte Darthur*. But *The Repressor of Over Much Blaming of the Clergy* (1455) by the anti-Lollard cleric and reformer Reginald Pecock, already mentioned, must stand as the leading controversial prose piece of the times. Unfortunately, Pecock was suppressed by his superiors, and whatever influence his work might have exerted was therefore thwarted.

It is manifestly impossible, moreover, to overlook two collections of letters that bring the fifteenth century to life better than almost anything else written in the age. The letters of the Paston family of Norfolk and of the merchant house of Cely are remarkable. The *Paston Letters* are particularly interesting. They cover the years from 1440 to 1486—the colorful days of the Wars of the Roses and the coming of the Tudors. Here are violence and anarchy, domestic love and courtship, and the meals and minutiae of daily usages in a fascinating mixture, artless and informal.

The most fitting writer, however, with whom to close an account of Middle English literature is Sir Thomas Malory (Maleore). It is a pity that we know so little about his life. He was probably a knight of Warwickshire and a follower of the famous Earl of Warwick, the King-maker. His dates run from somewhere near 1408 to about 1471; but the obscurity that hangs over the path of any fifteenth-century literary investigator is ever-present in Malory's case. It is believed that in 1451 Sir Thomas became the victim of fortuitous political circumstances growing out of the intrigues that preceded the outbreak of the Wars of the Roses, and that he spent the remaining twenty years or so of his life in prison. There he compiled his *Morte Darthur,* a full account in prose of the career of Arthur and his Knights of the Round Table, which was obviously based for the greater part upon the important French collections of the thirteenth and fourteenth centuries, such as the prose *Lancelot,* for example (see pp. 70-71). Caxton's edition of this work (1485),[7] one of the glories of

---

[7] Something should be said here about William Caxton, for although he is not to be considered a writer (except for some rather sprightly prefaces), he was of inestimable value to the cause of English literature as the first great printer in England, a true herald of the Renaissance. Perhaps he should be given more credit

his press, is prefaced by a brief essay by the printer that tells worlds about the attitude of the fifteenth century toward Arthur and his saga. Caxton here expresses respectful skepticism about Arthur as a historical figure, and by implication reveals the same skepticism concerning the Arthurian knights; he prefers that the reader take them as he will. But, says Caxton in effect, the prestige of Arthur, one of the Nine Worthies of the World, is so great that the publication of Sir Thomas Malory's book is essential.

There, in fact, is the whole point of the matter. Malory is writing, even as late as 1470, of battles long ago and of far-off things that, if not forgotten, are at least remote enough to appeal as distant scenes of glory will always appeal. It would be difficult to find a better account of the break-up of a great human order than Malory gives in the last book of *Morte Darthur*. The story is already familiar from our consideration of the medieval romances. Malory's naïve style moves along in leisurely fashion. There is more than enough of tournaments and fighting, of minor knights traversing the

---

as a biographer than has been hitherto accorded him. *The Lives of the Fathers* (1495) was printed after his death. He was born about 1422 and died in 1491. He was apprenticed to Robert Large, a wealthy mercer of London; later he went to Flanders to finish his apprenticeship. For a time he was a merchant in Bruges, but he retired in 1471 and gave all his efforts to the business of printing. He translated Raoul de Fevre's *Recuyel of the Histories of Troye,* which he printed in 1474, the first book published in English. In the following year, he moved to London and set up his press there; the first book printed in England was *Dictes and Sayings of the Philosophers* (1477). From that time until his death he was busy with printing and editing. Ninety-two works from his press have survived, representing seventy-four different books. In these publications he showed a fine range of interest, for the list includes books of morality, religious books, service books, books of social teaching, fables, histories, books of statutes, political works, scientific works, romances, and *The Canterbury Tales,* as well as *Morte Darthur.*

Following Caxton as famous printers in the early English Renaissance were the Alsatian Wynkyn de Worde (d.1534), Richard Pynson (d.1530), and the Frenchman Julian Notary (d.1520?). With the death of Pynson the uttermost frontiers of the Middle Ages have been attained; he and his contemporaries are strictly subjects of the next period.

scene in bewildering number. On the other hand, it is unfortunate that Malory did not finish the tale of Tristan. The multitudinous details concerning the Holy Grail are perplexing until we realize that this is one of the most complex legends in all literature. But at least it is presented here in something approaching full form; and there is also more of Galahad and of Lancelot than anywhere else in Middle English literature. If Malory had been able to give depth and characterization to the Knights of the Round Table, he would have been the true forerunner of the English novel that some of his special admirers have thought him to be. As it is, he gives us excellent narrative, but no more true delineation of character than could be found in most of the dozens of Middle English romances that preceded *Morte Darthur*. There is pathos in the parting of Lancelot and his son Galahad—the son to attain the Holy Grail, the father forever denied it. There is equal pathos in the departure of Arthur to Avalon. The final chapters of the story, particularly those reporting the outcome of the ultimately unhappy affair of Lancelot and Guenevere, give us all the romantic wistfulness of Malory, who is looking back through rose-colored spectacles at an age that has gone forever. The comment by Sir Ector, brother of Lancelot, is, in its quaint way, the final statement:

And when he waked it were hard any tongue to tell the doleful complaints that he made for his brother. "Ah, Lancelot," he said, "thou were head of all Christian knights, and now I dare say," said Sir Ector, "thou Sir Launcelot, there thou liest, that thou were never matched of earthly knight's hand. And thou were the courteoust knight that ever bare shield. And thou were the truest friend to thy lover that ever bestrad horse. And thou were the truest lover of a sinful man that ever loved woman. And thou were the kindest man that ever struck with sword. And thou were the goodliest person that ever came among press of knights. And thou were the meekest man and the gentlest that ever ate in hall among ladies. And thou were the sternest knight to thy mortal foe that ever put spear in the rest." Then there was weeping and dolor out of measure.

The year Caxton published Malory's *Morte Darthur* was also the year Henry Tudor came to the throne—the mercantile ruler rather than the chivalric sovereign. Columbus was soon to land on an island in the Bahamas. Meanwhile Caxton's press was operating away with the promise of a new dissemination of learning and all that this portends. The modern era was coming to push Malory and the other writers of the fifteenth century back into a moribund age. And as Malory left the scene, the City of God, which the Middle Ages had been preaching so fervently even while the City of Man was being built under the very feet of the preachers, was withdrawing farther and farther away into that empyrean region where it most appropriately belonged; and the City of Man, in which all modern humanity still lives and struggles, was responsible for this withdrawal. The Renaissance, reaching England at long last, had come to stay.

Table of Abbreviations

Revised Bibliographies of English Literature*

General

1. BIBLIOGRAPHIES, REFERENCE BOOKS

Allibone, S. A., *A Critical Dictionary of English Literature and British and American Authors*, 3 v., Philadelphia, 1899; Supplement J. F. Kirk, 2 v., 1902.

Annual Bibliography of English Language and Literature, Mod. Humanities Research Assn., 1920, *Cambridge*, 1921 — (in progress).

Bibliographical Society, London, *Transactions*, Publications, 1893 —

* The place of publication is not given unless it is other than London or New York.

The Cambridge Bibliography of English Literature, ed. F. W. Bateson, 4 v., Cambridge, 1940; Supplement, ed. G. Watson, 1955.

Courtney, W. P., *Register of National Bibliography*, 3 v., 1905–12.

Cross, T. P., *A List of Books and Articles designed as an Introduction to the Bibliography and Methods of English Literary History*, 9th edn., Chicago, 1941.

Esdaile, A. J. K., *The Sources of English Literature, a Bibliographical Guide for Students*, Cambridge, 1928; *A Student's Manual of Bibliography*, 1931.

Gayley, C. M., and F. N. Scott, *An Introduction to the Methods and Materials of Literary Criticism*, Boston, 1899.

Halkett, S., and J. Laing, *A Dictionary of Anonymous and Pseudonymous Literature of Great Britain*, rev. edn., 7 v., Edinburgh, 1926–34.

Harbage, A., *Annals of the English Drama, 975–1700*, Philadelphia, 1940.

Harvey, Sir P., *The Oxford Companion to English Literature*, Oxford, 1911.

Hazlitt, W. C., *Handbook to the Popular, Poetical, and Dramatic Literature of Great Britain*, 1867; continued as *Collections and Notes*, 6 v., various dates; G. J. Gray, *A General Index to Hazlitt's Handbook and his Bibliographical Collections*, 1891.

Kennedy, A. G., *A Concise Bibliography for Students of English*, Stanford University, 1945.

Koerting, G., *Grundriss der Geschichte der englischen Literatur*, 5th edn., Münster, 1910.

Lowndes, W. P., *The Bibliographer's Manual of English Literature*, rev. edn., H. G. Bohn, 11 v., 1858-64.

McKerrow, R. B., *An Introduction to Bibliography for Literary Students*, Oxford, 1927.

Northup, C. S., *A Register of the Bibliographies of English Language and Literature*, New Haven, 1925.

Schücking, L. L., and W. Ebisch, *Grundlinien einer Bibliographie zum Studium der englischen Philologie*, Leipzig, 1931.

Sears, M. E., and M. Shaw, *Essay and General Literature Index*, 1934; supplements.

Spargo, J. W., *A Bibliographical Manual for Students of the Language and Literature of England and the United States*, 2nd edn., Chicago, 1941.

Thrall, W. F., and A. Hibbard, *A Handbook to Literature*, 1936.

The Year's Work in English Studies, English Assn., 1919 — (in progress).

2. HISTORY OF ENGLISH LITERATURE. CRITICISM

Baker, E. A., *The History of the English Novel*, 10 v., 1924-39.

Baugh, A. C., et al. *A Literary History of England*, 1948.

Bradner, L., *Musae anglicnae: A History of Anglo-Latin Poetry*, 1500-1925, 1940.

Bush, D., *Mythology and the Renaissance Tradition in English Poetry*, Minneapolis, 1932: *Mythology and the Romantic Tradition in English Poetry*, Cambridge, Mass., 1937.

The Cambridge History of English Literature, ed. Sir A. W. Ward and A. R. Waller, 14 v., Cambridge, 1907-16.

Chambers, R., *Cyclopaedia of English Literature*, rev. edn., D. Patrick, 3 v., Philadelphia, 1902-04.

The Channels of English Literature, ed. O. Smeaton, 8 v., 1912-25.

Courthope, W. J., *A History of English Poetry*, 6 v., 1895-1910.

Creizenach, W., *Geschichte des neueren Dramas*, 5 v., Halle, 1893-1926.

Dixon, W. M., *English Epic and Heroic Poetry*, 1912.

Dunlop, J., *The History of Fiction*, rev. edn., H. Wilson, 2 v., 1888.

Elton, O., *The English Muse*, 1933.

Garnett, R., and Sir E. Gosse, *English Literature: an Illustrated Record*, 4 v., 1903.

Greg, W. W., *Pastoral Poetry and Pastoral Drama*, 1906.

Hallam, H., *Introduction to the Literature of Europe*, 4 v., 1837-9.

Handbooks of English Literature, ed. J. Hales, 10 pts., 1895-1903.

Henderson, T. F., *Scottish Vernacular Literature*, 1898.

Johnson, S., *The Lives of the Most Eminent English Poets*, 4 v., 1781, ed, G. B. Hill, 3 v., Oxford, 1905.

Legouis, É., and L. Cazamian, *Histoire de la littérature anglaise*, Paris, 1924, Engl. tr., 2 v., 1926-7.

Magnus, L., *English Literature in its Foreign Relations*, 1300-1800, 1927.

Millar, J. H., *A Literary History of Scotland*, 1903.

Nicoll, A., *British Drama*, 1925.

Periods of English Literature, ed. G. Saintsbury, 12 v., Edinburgh, 1897-1908.

Raleigh, Sir W. A., *The English Novel*, 1894.

Saintsbury, G., *A History of Criticism and Literary Taste in Europe*, 3 v., 1900-1904; *A Short History of English Literature*, 1898.

Seccombe, T., and Sir W. R. Nicoll, *History of English Literature*, 2 v., 1906.

Smith, G. G., *Scottish Literature*, 1919.

Taine, H., *Histoire de la littérature anglaise*, 4 v., Paris, 1863-4, Engl. tr., 2 v., Edinburgh, 1872.

ten Brink, B., *Geschichte der englischen Literatur*, 2 v., 1877-93, Eng. tr., 3 v., 1883-96.

Types of English Literature, ed. W. A. Neilson, 5 v., Boston, 1907-16.

Ward, Sir A. W., *A History of English Dramatic Literature to the Death of Queen Anne*, rev. edn., 3 v., 1899.

Warton, T., *The History of English Poetry*, 3 v., 1774-81, ed. W. C. Hazlitt, 4 v., 1871.

Wellek, R., and A. Warren, *The Theory of Literature*, 1949.

3. COLLECTIONS

Abbotsford Club, Publications, Edinburgh, 1837-1865.

Bannatyne Club, Publications, Edinburgh, 1825-58.

Camden Society (founded 1838, incorporated with Royal Hist. Soc., 1897), Publications (in progress).

Early English Text Society, Publications, Orig, ser., 1865 —; Extra Ser., 1867 — (in progress).

Hunterian Club, Publications, Glasgow 1873-80.

Maitland Club, Publications, Glasgow, 1828-59.

Malone Society, *Collections, Reprints, Studies*, Oxford, 1907 — (in progress).

Materialen zur Kunde der älteren englischen Dramas, ed. W. Bang, Louvain, 1902 —; continued as *Materials for the Study of the Old English Drama*, ed. H. de Vocht, 1925 —

Roxburghe Club, Publications, 1818-73.

Royal Society of Literature, Publications, 1823 —

Scottish Text Society, Publications, Edinburgh, 1884 — (in progress).

Spalding Club, Publications, Aberdeen, 1841-71; 1897-1910 (New Spalding Club).

Surtees Society, Publications, 1835 —

. . . . . .

Chalmers, A., *The British Essayists*, 45 v., 1817; *The Works of the English Poets*, 21 v., 1810.

Craik, H., *English Prose*, 5 v., 1893-6.

Dodsley, R., *A Select Collection of Old Plays*, ed. W. C. Hazlitt, 15 v., 1874-6.

The English Poets, ed. T. H. Ward, 5 v., 1880-1919.

Representative English Comedies, ed. C. M. Gayley, 3 v., Boston, 1903.

The Oxford Book of English Prose, Oxford, 1925; *The Oxford Book of English Verse*, ed. Sir A. T. Quiller-Couch, new edn., Oxford, 1919.

4. ENGLISH LANGUAGE

Arntz, H., *Handbuch der Runenkunde*, Halle, 1935.

Baugh, A. C., *History of the English Language*, 1935, rev. edn., 1957.

Bradley, H., *The Making of English*, 1904.

Brook, G. L., *A History of the English Language*, Fair Lawn, N. J., 1958.

Brunner, K., *Die englische Sprache: ihre geschichtliche Entwicklung*, Halle, 1950-51.

Curme, G. O., *College English Grammar*, Richmond, Va., 1925; *Syntax*, 1931; *Parts of Speech and Accidence*, Boston, 1935.

Elliott, R. W. V., *Runes: an Introduction*, Manchester, 1959.

Emerson, O. F., *The History of the English Language*, 1894, rev. edn., 1915.

Greenough, J. B., and G. L. Kittredge, *Words and their Ways in English Speech*, 1901.

Jespersen, O., *Growth and Structure of the English Language*, Leipzig, 1919, rev. edn., 1955.

Jones, D., *An Outline of English Phonetics*, 1932.

Kaluza, M., *Historische Grammatik der englischen Sprache*, 2 v., Berlin, 1900-07.

Kennedy, A. G., *A Bibliography of Writings on the English Language*, Cambridge, Mass. and New Haven, 1927; *Current English*, 1935.

Kruisinga, E., *An Introduction to the Study of English Sounds*, Groningen, 1957.

Lindelöf, U., *Grundzüge der Geschichte der englischen Sprache*, Leipzig, 1928.

Luick, K., *Historische Grammatik der englischen Sprache*, Berlin, 1930.

Marckwardt, A. H., *Introduction to the English Language*, 1942.

McKnight, G. H., *English Words and their Background*, 1923; with B. Emsley, *Modern English in the Making*, 1928.

Mossé, F., *Esquisse d'une histoire de la langue anglaise*, Paris, 1947.

Onions, C. T., *Advanced English Syntax*, 4th edn., 1927.

Pons, E., *Cours de philologie anglaise*, Paris, 1953.

Robertson, S., *The Development of Modern English*, 1936, rev. edn., 1954.

Smith, L. P., *Words and Idioms: Studies in the English Language*, 4th edn., 1933.

Sweet, H., *History of English Sounds*, 1888; *A New English Grammar, Logical and Historical*, 2 pts., Oxford, 1892-9.

Wrenn, C. L., *The English Language*, 1949.

Wyld, H. C., *Historical Study of the Mother Tongue*, 1906.

5. PROSODY AND PROSE RHYTHM

Abercrombie, L., *Principles of English Prosody*, pt. 1, *The Elements*, 1923; *Poetry: Its Music and Meaning*, Oxford, 1932.

Alden, R. M., *English Verse*, 1903.

Guest, E., *History of English Rhythms*, ed. W. W. Skeat, 2 v., 1882.

Ormond, T. S., *English Metrists*, Oxford, 1921.

Patterson, W. M., *The Rhythm of Prose*, 1916.

Saintsbury, G., *A History of English Prosody*, 3 v., 1909-10; *A History of English Prose Rhythm*, 1912.

Schipper, J. M., *Englische Metrik*, 3 v., Bonn, 1881-8.

Verrier, P., *Essai sur les principes de la metrique anglaise*, 3 v., Paris, 1909-10.

The Anglo-Saxon Period

1. BIBLIOGRAPHY, LITERATURE, AND LANGUAGE OF THE ANGLO-SAXON PERIOD

Anderson, G. K., *The Literature of the Anglo-Saxons*, Princeton, 1949.

Anderson, L. F., *The Anglo-Saxon Scop*, Toronto, 1903.

Andrew, S. O., *The Old English Alliterative Measure*, 1931.

The Anglo-Saxon Poetic Records, ed. G. P. Krapp and E. Van K. Dobbie: I. *The Junius Manuscript*; II. *The Vercelli Book*; III. *The Exeter Book*; IV. *Beowulf and Judith*; V. *The Paris Psalter and the Meters of Boethius*; VI. *The Anglo-Saxon Minor Poems*, 1931-53.

Anglo-Saxon Poetry, comp. and tr. R. K. Gordon, 1927.

Bartlett, A. C., *The Larger Rhetorical Patterns in Anglo-Saxon Poetry*, 1935.

Baxter, J. B., C. Johnson and J. F. Willard, *An Index of British and Irish Writers, A. D. 400-1520*, Paris, 1933.

Bliss, A. J., *The Metre of 'Beowulf'*, Oxford, 1958.

Bonjour, A., "Poésie héroique du moyen age et critique littéraire," *Romania*, LXXVIII, 243-255.

Bonser, W., *An Anglo-Saxon and Celtic Bibliography*, 2 v., Oxford, 1957.

Brandl, A., *Geschichte der altenglischen Literatur*, Strasburg, 1908.

Bright, J. W., *Anglo-Saxon Reader*, rev. edn. by J. R. Hulbert, 1935.

Brooke, S. A., *History of Early English Literature to the Accession of King Alfred*, 2 v., 1892.

Chambers, R. W., *On the Continuity of Old English Prose from Alfred to More and his School*, Oxford, 1932.

Clark, J. W., *Early English: a Study of Old and Middle English*, 1957.

Enkvist, N. E., *The Seasons of the Year: chapters on a motif from 'Beowulf' to 'The Shepheardes Calendar'*, Copenhagen, 1957.

Ericson, E. E., *The Anglo-Saxon Speech*, Lund, 1927.

Feist, S., "The Origins of the Germanic Languages and the Indo-Europeanizing of North Europe," *Language*, VIII, 245-254.

Flom, G. T., *Introductory Old English Grammar and Reader*, 1930.

Girvan, R., "The Medieval Poet and his Audience," in C. L.

Wrenn and G. Bullough, edd., *English Studies Today*, Oxford, 1951, pp. 85-97.

Greenfield, S. B., "The Formulaic Expression of the Theme of 'Exile' in Anglo-Saxon Poetry," *Speculum*, XXX, 200-06.

Gummere, F. B., *The Beginnings of Poetry*, 1901.

Hart, W. M., *Ballad and Epic*, Boston, 1907.

Hecht, H., and L. L. Schücking, *Die englische Literatur im Mittelalter:* Vol. I: L. L. Schücking, *Die angelsächsische und frühmittelenglische Dichtung*, Potsdam, 1927.

Heusinkveld, A. H. and E. J. Bashe, *A Bibliographical Guide to Old English*, Iowa City, 1931.

Heusler, A., "Deutche Versgeschichte, mit Einschluss des altenglischen und altnordischen Stabreimes," *Paul's Grundriss der germanischen Philologie*, #8, Vol. I, 1925; Vol. II, 1929.

Huchon, R., *Historie de la langue anglaise: I, des origines à la conquête normande*, Paris, 1924-30.

Huppé, B. F., *Doctrine and Poetry: Augustine's influence on Old English poetry*, Albany, 1959.

Irving, E. B., Jr., "Latin Prose Sources for Old English Verse," *JEGP*, LVI, 588-95.

Jackson, W. T. H., *The Literature of the Middle Ages*, 1960.

Kennedy, C. W., *The Earliest English Poetry*, 1943; *An Anthology of Old English Poetry*, 1960.

Ker, N. R., *A Catalogue of Manuscripts Containing Anglo-Saxon*, Oxford, 1957; *English Manuscripts in the Century after the Norman Conquest*, 1960.

Magoun, F. P., Jr., "Oral-Formulaic Character of Anglo-Saxon Narrative Poetry," *Speculum*, XXVIII, 446-67; with J. B. Bessinger, "The Sutton Hoo Ship-Burial: a chronological bibliography, *Speculum*, XXIX, 116-24 and XXXIII, 515-22.

Meritt, H. D., *Fact and Lore about Old English Words*, Palo Alto, 1954.

Old English Poems, tr. C. F. Newton and S. Thompson, Chicago, 1918.

Old English Poetry, tr. J. D. Spaeth, Princeton, 1922.

Philpotts, B. S., "Wyrd and Providence in Anglo-Saxon Thought," *E&S*, XIII, 7-24.

Pons, E., *La thème et la sentiment de la nature dans la poésie anglo-saxonne*, Strasburg, 1925.

Pope, J. C., *The Rhythm of 'Beowulf'*, New Haven, 1942.

Quirk, R. and C. L. Wrenn, *An Old English Grammar*, 1955.

Renwick, W. L. and H. Orton, *The Beginnings of English Literature to Skelton*, 1939.

Ricci, A., "The Chronology of Anglo-Saxon Poetry," *RES*, V, 257-66.

Select Translations from Old English Poetry, ed. and tr. A. S. Cook and C. B. Tinker, Boston, 1902.

Select Translations from Old English Prose, ed. and tr. A. S. Cook and C. B. Tinker, Boston, 1908.

Sisam, K., *Studies in the History of Old English Literature*, 1953.

Specimens of Anglo-Saxon Poetry, ed. W. A. Craigie, 3 v., Edinburgh, 1923-31.

Thompson, S., *Motif-Index of Folk Literature*, Bloomington, Ind., 1933 —.

Timmer, B. J., "The Elegiac Mood in Old English Poetry," ES, XXIV, 33-44; "Heathen and Christian Elements in Old English Poetry," *Neophil.*, XXIX, 180-85; "Wyrd in Anglo-Saxon Prose and Poetry," *Neophil.*, XXVI, 24-33 and 213-28.

Wardale, E. E., *Chapters on Old English Literature*, 1935.

Whitelock, D., "Anglo-Saxon Poetry and the Historian," *Transactions of the Royal Historical Society* (1949), 75-94.

Wilson, R. M., *The Lost Literature of Mediaeval England*, 1952.

Wrenn, C. L., "On the Continuity of English Poetry," *Anglia*, LXXVI, 41-59.

Wright, C. E., *The Cultivation of Saga in Anglo-Saxon England*, Edinburgh, 1939.

Wülker, R., *Grundriss zur Geschichte der angelsächsichen Literatur*, Leipzig, 1885.

Wyld, H. C., "Diction and Imagery in Anglo-Saxon Poetry," *E & S*, XI, 49-91.

2. HISTORY, MANNERS, AND CUSTOMS OF ANGLO-SAXON ENGLAND

Aberg, N., *The Anglo-Saxons in England*, Uppsala, 1927.

Allison, T., *English Religious Life in the Eighth Century*, 1929.

Andrews, C. H., *The Old English Manor*, Baltimore, 1892.

Ault, N., *Life in Ancient Britain*, 1920.

Blair, P. H., *An Introduction to Anglo-Saxon England*, Cambridge, 1956.

Bonser, W., "Survivals of Paganism in Anglo-Saxon England," *Transactions of the Birmingham Archaeological Society*, LVI, 37-70.

Brown, G. B., *The Arts in Early England*, 7 v., 1903-1937.

Capper, D. P., *The Vikings of Britain*, 1937.

Carpenter, S. C., *The Church in England, 597-1688*, 1954.

Chadwick, H. M., *The Origin of the English Nation*, Cambridge, 1907.

Chambers, R. W., *England before the Norman Conquest*, 1926.

Christiansen, R. T., *The Vikings and the Viking Wars in Irish and Gaelic Tradition*, Oslo, 1931.

Clapham, A. W., *English Romanesque Architecture before the Conquest*, Oxford, 1930.

Clemen, C., *Altgermanische Religionsgeschichte*, Bonn, 1934.

Collingwood, R. G., and J. N. L. Myres, *Roman Britain and the English Settlements*, Oxford, 1936.

Crawford, S. J., *Anglo-Saxon Influence on Western Christendom, 590-1500*, Oxford, 1933.

Deanesley, M., *A History of the Mediaeval Church, 590-1500,* 1925; rev. edn., 1950.

DeVries, J., *Die Welt der Germanen,* Leipzig, 1935.

Douglas, D. C., and G. W. Greenaway, ed., *English Historical Documents, vol. II, 1042-1189,* 1953.

Ekwall, E., ed., *A Concise Dictionary of Old English Place-Names,* Oxford, 1936; rev. edn., 1960; *Studies in English Place- and Personal-Names,* Lund, 1931.

Forsberg, R., *A Contribution to a Dictionary of Old English Place-Names,* Uppsala, 1950.

Fox, C., and B. Dickins, ed., *The Early Cultures of North-West Europe,* 1950.

Freeman, E. A., *A Short History of the Norman Conquest of England, Vol. I,* 1867.

Grönbech, V., tr. W. Worster, *The Culture of the Teutons,* Oxford, 1931.

Gross, C., *Sources and Literature of English History from the Earliest Times to about 1485,* 1910.

Gummere, F. B., *Founders of England,* 1930.

Gunsell, L. V., *The Archaeology of Wessex,* 1958.

Harder, H., *Die Religion der Germanen,* Leipzig, 1937.

Haverfield, F. J., *The Roman Occupation of Britain,* Oxford, 1924.

Hodgkin, R. H., *A History of the Anglo-Saxons,* Oxford, 1935; rev. edn., 1952.

Jerrold, D., *An Introduction to the History of England from the Earliest Times to 1204,* 1949.

Jessup, R., *Anglo-Saxon Jewellery,* 1950.

Jolliffe, J. E. A., *Pre-Feudal England: the Jutes,* Oxford, 1933.

Kendrick, T. D., *Anglo-Saxon Art to A. D. 900,* 1938; *British Antiquity,* 1950; *A History of the Vikings,* 1930.

Laistner, M. L. W., *The Intellectual Heritage of the Early Middle Ages,* Ithaca, 1957; *Thought and Letters in Western Europe, A. D. 500 to 900,* 1931.

Leeds, E. T., *Celtic Ornament in the British Isles down to A. D. 700,* Cambridge, 1933; *Early Anglo-Saxon Art and Archaeology,* Oxford, 1936.

Levison, W., *England and the Continent in the Eighth Century,* Oxford, 1946.

Maitland, F. W., *Domesday Book and Beyond,* 1897.

Martin-Clarke, Mrs. D. W., *Culture in Early Anglo-Saxon England,* Baltimore, 1947.

Moorman, J. R. H., *A History of the Church in England,* 1953.

Myres, J. N. L., "The Preesnt State of the Archaeological Evidence for the Anglo-Saxon Conquest," *History,* XXI, 317-30.

Oman, C. W. C., *England before the Norman Conquest,* 1910.

Philippson, E. A., *Germanisches Heidentum bei den Angelsachsen,* Leipzig, 1929.

Poole, A. L., ed., *Mediaeval England,* Oxford, 1958.

Ramsay, J. H., *The Foundations of England,* 1898.

Rand, E. K., "A Romantic Approach to the Middle Ages," MS, III, 1-14.

Reed, T. D., *The Rise of Wessex*, 1947.

Rosteutscher, J. H. W., "Germanische Schickselsglaube und angelsächsische Elegiendichtung," *Eng. Stud.*, LXXIII, 1-31.

Ryan, A. M., "A Map of Old English Monasteries and Related Ecclesiastical Foundations, A. D. 400-1066," *Cornell Studies in English*, #28, Ithaca, 1939.

Schuette, G., *Our Forefathers: the Gothonic peoples*, 2 v., Cambridge, 1929-33.

Seebohm, F., *The English Village Community*, 1883; *Tribal Custom in Anglo-Saxon Law*, 1902.

Snell, F. J., *The Age of Alfred*, 1912.

Stenton, F. M., *The Danes in England*, 1927; *Anglo-Saxon England*, 1943: "The Historical Bearing of Place-Name Studies: the Danish Settlement of Eastern England," *Transactions of the Royal Historical Society*, XXIV, 1-24; "The Historical Bearing of Place-Name Studies: the English Occupation of Southern Britain," *Transactions of the Royal Historical Society*, XXII, 1-22; "The Historical Bearing of Place-Name Studies: Anglo-Saxon Heathenism," *Transaction of the Royal Historical Society*, XXIII, 1-24; "The Historical Bearing of Place-Name Studies: the Place of Women in Anglo-Saxon History," *Transactions of the Royal Historical Society*, XXIV, 1-13.

Stephenson, C., Mediæval History: *Europe from the fourth to the sixteenth century*, 1935.

Storms, G., *Anglo-Saxon Magic*, 1948.

Thompson, J. W., *An Economic and Social History of the Middle Ages, 300-1500*, 1928; *An Introduction to Mediaeval Europe, 300-1500*, 1931.

Wadstein, E., *On the Origin of the English*, Uppsala, 1927.

Whitelock, D., *The Beginnings of English Society*, Harmondsworth, 1952; *English Historical Documents, Vol. I, c. 500-1042*, 1955.

Young, G. M., *The Origin of the West Saxon Kingdom*, 1934.

Zachrisson, R. E., *Romans, Kelts, and Saxons in Ancient Britain*, Uppsala, 1927.

3. OLD ENGLISH POETRY

A. The Heroic Epic and Elegiac Poems

Adams, J. F., *"Wulf and Eadwacer: an interpretation,"* MLN, LXXIII, 1-5.

Andersson-Arngart, O. S., *The Seafarer: an interpretation*, Lund, 1937.

Angus, W. S., "The Battlefield of Brunanburh," *Antiquity*, XI, XI, 283-93.

Anglo-Saxon and Norse Poems, ed. and tr. N. Kershaw, Cambridge, 1922.

Aurner, N. S., *Hengest: a study in Early English hero legend,* Iowa City, 1921.

Batchelor, C. C., "The Style of the *Beowulf,*" *Speculum,* XII, 330-42.

The Battle of Brunanburh, ed. A. Campbell, 1938.

The Battle of Maldon and Short Poems from the Saxon Chronicle, ed. W. J. Sedgefield, Boston, 1904.

Beowulf, ed. F. Klaeber, 1922-50; ed. A. J. Wyatt and R. W. Chambers, Cambridge, 1914; ed. C. L. Wrenn, 1953-58; tr. C. W. Kennedy, 1940; tr. C. B. Tinker, rev. edn., 1910; tr. F. B. Gummere, 1909; tr. W. E. Leonard, 1932; tr. G. Bone, 1945; tr. A. Strong, 1925; tr. M. Waterhouse, Cambridge, 1950; tr. E. Morgan, Addington, 1952; tr. J. C. Hall, rev. ed. by C. L. Wrenn and J. R. R. Tolkien, 1940 and 1950.

Blomfield, J., "The Style and Structure of 'Beowulf,'" RES, XIV, 396-403.

Bond, G., "Links between 'Beowulf' and Mercian History," SP, XL, 481-93.

Bonjour, A., "*Beowulf* and the Snares of Literary Criticism," *Etudes Anglaises* X, 30-36; "*Beowulf* et l'épopée anglo-saxonne," *La table ronde,* #132, pp. 140-51; *The Digressions in 'Beowulf',* Oxford, 1950; "Monsters Crouching and Critics Rampant: or the Beowulf Dragon Debated," PMLA, LXVIII, 304-12; "On the Sea-Images in *Beowulf,*" JEGP, LIV, 111-15; "The Technique of Parallel Descriptions in *Beowulf,*" RES, n.s., II, 1-10; "The Use of Anticipation in *Beowulf,*" RES, XVI, 290-99.

Bouman, A. C., "'Leodum is minum': Beadohild's Complaint," *Neophil.,* XXXIII, 103-13.

Bowra, C. M., *Heroic Poetry,* 1952.

Bracher, F., "Understatement in Old English Poetry," PMLA, LII, 915-34.

Brandl, A., "Beowulf-Epos und Aeneis in systematischer Vergleichung," *Archiv,* CLXXI, 161-73.

Brodeur, A. G., *The Art of Beowulf,* Berkeley, 1959; "The Climax of the Finn Episode," *University of California Publications in English,* III, #8, Berkeley, 1943; "Design and Motive in the Finn Episode," *University of California Publications in English,* XIV, Berkeley, 1943; "Design for Terror in the Purging of Heorot," JEGP, LIII, 503-13; "The Structure and Unity of *Beowulf,*" PMLA, LXVIII, 1193-95.

Brown, C., "*Beowulf* and the *Blickling Homilies* and Some Textual Notes," PMLA, LIII, 905-16.

Cabanis, A., "*Beowulf* and the Liturgy," JEGP, LIV, 195-201.

Campbell, J. J., "Oral Poetry in *The Seafarer,*" *Speculum,* XXXV, 87-96.

Carpenter, R., *Folk Tale, Fiction, and Saga in the Homeric Epics,* Berkeley, 1946.

Carroll, B. H., Jr., "An Essay on the Walther Legend," *Florida State University Studies*, V, 123-79; "On the Lineage of the Walther Legend," GR, XXVIII, 34-41.

Chadwick, H. M., *The Heroic Age*, 1912; with N. K. Chadwick, *The Growth of Literature*, Cambridge, 1932.

Chadwick, N. K., "The Monsters and Beowulf," *The Anglo-Saxons*, ed. P. Clemoes, 1959.

Chambers, R. W., *Beowulf: an introduction to the study of the poem*, 1932; rev. edn., 1959; *Man's Unconquerable Mind: studies of English writers from Bede to W. P. Ker*, 1938.

Cook, A. S., "Beowulfian and Odyssean Voyages," *Transactions of the Connecticut Academy of Arts and Sciences*, XXVIII, New Haven, 1926; "Greek Parallels to Certain Features of the *Beowulf*," PQ, V, 226-34.

Creed, R. P., "The Making of an Anglo-Saxon Poem," ELH, XXVI, 445-54.

Cress, J. E., " 'Ubi Sunt' Passages in Old English: sources and relationships," *Vetenskaps-Societetens i Lund Arsbok* (1956), pp. 25-41.

Dehmer, H., "Die Grendelkämpfe Beowulfs im Lichte moderner Mährenforschung," GRM, XVI, 202-18.

Deor, ed. K. Malone, 1933.

Dickins, B., *Runic and Heroic Poems of the Teutonic Peoples*, Cambridge, 1915.

Du Bois, A. E., "The Dragon in *Beowulf*," PMLA, LXXII, 819-22; "The Unity of *Beowulf*", PMLA, XLIX, 374-405.

Dunleavy, G. W., "A 'De Excidio' Tradition in the Old English *Ruin*?" PQ, XXVIII, 112-18.

Elliott, R. W. V., "The Runes in *The Husband's Message*," JEGP, LIV, 1-8; "The Wanderer's Conscience," ES, XXXIX, 193-200.

Engelhardt, G. J., "*Beowulf*, a study in dilatation," PMLA, LXX, 825-52.

Fanger, D., "Three Aspects of Beowulf and his God," NM, LIX, 172-79.

Fisher, P. F., "The Trials of the Epic Hero in *Beowulf*," PMLA, LXXIII, 171-83.

Forster, L., "Die Assoziation in Deors Klage," *Anglia*, LXI, 117-21.

Four Icelandic Sagas, ed. and tr. G. Jones, Princeton, 1935.

French, W. H., "*Widsith* and the Scop," PMLA, LX, 623-30.

Gang, T. M., "Approaches to *Beowulf*," RES, n.s., III, 1-12.

Girvan, R., *Beowulf and the Seventh Century*, 1935; "Finnsburuh," *Proceedings of the British Academy*, XXVI, Oxford, 1941.

Goldsmith, M. E., "The Christian Theme of *Beowulf*," MAE, XXIX, 81-101.

Gordon, I. L., "Traditional Themes in *The Wanderer* and *The Seafarer*," RES, n.s., V, 1-13.

Greenfield, S. B., "Attitudes and Values in *The Seafarer*," SP,

LI, 15-20; "*The Wife's Lament* Reconsidered," PMLA, LXVIII, 907-12.

Haber, T. B., *A Comparative Study of the Beowulf and the Aeneid*, Princeton, 1931.

Hamilton, M. P., "The Religious Principle in *Beowulf*," PMLA, LXI, 309-30.

Herben, S. J., "Beowulf, Hrothgar, and Grendel," *Archiv*, CLXXIII, 24-30; "The Ruin," MLN, LIV, 37-39.

Hoops, J., *Kommentar zum Beowulf*, Heidelberg, 1932.

Hotchner, C. A., *Wessex and Old English Poetry, with Special Consideration of 'The Ruin'*, Lancaster, Pa., 1939.

Hübener, G., "*Beowulf* and Germanic Exorcism," RES, XI, 163-81.

Hulbert, J. R., "*Beowulf* and the Classical Epic," MP, XLIV, 65-75; "The Genesis of *Beowulf*: a caveat," PMLA, LXIV, 1168-76; "Surmises Concerning the Beowulf Poet's Source," JEGP, L, 11-18.

Kaske, R. E., "*Sapientia et Fortitudo* as the Controlling Theme of *Beowulf*," SP, LV, 423-56.

Klaeber, F., "Die christlichen Elemente im *Beowulf*," *Anglia*, XXXV, 111-36; 249-70; 453-82, and XXXVI, 169-99.

Krappé, A. H., "Les dieux jumeaux dans la réligion germanique," APS, VI, 1-25.

Laborde, E. D., *Byrhtnoth and Maldon*, 1936.

Lawrence, W. W., *Beowulf and the Epic Tradition*, Cambridge, Mass., 1928.

Lumiansky, R. M., "The Dramatic Audience in *Beowulf*," JEGP, LI, 545-50; "The Dramatic Structure of the Old English *Wanderer*," Neophil., XXXIV, 104-12.

Mackenzie, D. A., *Teutonic Myth and Legend*, 1934.

Magoun, F. P., Jr., "The Theme of the Beasts of Battle in Anglo-Saxon Poetry," NM, LVI, 81-90.

Malone, K., "Beowulf," ES, XXIX, 161-72; ed. *Early English Manuscripts in Facsimile: the Thorkelin Transcripts of 'Beowulf'*, Copenhagen, 1951; "The Finn Episode in *Beowulf*," JEGP, XXV, 157-72; "Time and Place in the Ingeld Episodes of *Beowulf*", JEGP, XXXIX, 76-92.

Mossé, F., *La Saga de Grettir*, Paris, 1933.

Nist, J. A., *The Structure and Texture of 'Beowulf'*, Sao Paolo, 1959.

The Old English Elegies. tr. C. W. Kennedy, Princeton, 1936.

O'Loughlin, J. L. N., "*Beowulf*: its Unity and Purpose," MAE, XXI, 1-13.

Philpotts, B. A., *Edda and Saga*, 1932.

Pirkhofer, A., *Figurengestaltung im Beowulf-Epos*, Heidelberg, 1940.

The Poetic Edda, tr. H. A. Bellows, Princeton, 1936.

Raglan, F-R. S., *The Hero: a study in tradition, myth, and drama*, 1936.

Robertson, D. W., Jr., "The Doctrine of Charity in Medieval Literary Gardens: a topical approach through symbolism and allegory," *Speculum*, XXVI, 24-49; "Historical Criticism," *English Institute Essays*, 1950-1951, pp. 3-31.

Rogers, H. L., "Beowulf's Three Great Fights," RES, n.s., VI, 339-55.

Routh, H. V., *God, Man and Epic Poetry: a study in comparative literature*, Cambridge, 1927.

Rumble, T. C., "From *Eardstapa* to *Snottor on Mode:* the structural principle of *The Wanderer*," MLQ, XIX, 225-30.

The Saga of Hrolf Kraki, tr. S. M. Mills, introd. by E. V. Gordon, Oxford, 1933.

The Saga of the Volsungs, tr. M. Schlauch, 1949.

Salmon, V., "*The Wanderer* and *The Seafarer*, and the Old English Conception of the Soul," MLR, LV, 1-10.

Schneider, *Englische und nordgermanische Heldensage*, Berlin, 1933.

Schröbler, I., "Beowulf und Homer," *Beiträge zur Geschichte der deutschen Sprache und Literatur*, LXIII, 305-46.

Schücking, L. L., "Das Königsideal im *Beowulf*," *Bulletin of the Modern Humanities Research Association*, III, 143-54.

The Seafarer, ed. I. L. Gordon, 1960.

Sisam, K., "Beowulf's Fight with the Dragon," RES, n.s., IX, 129-40.

Smithers, G. V., "The Meaning of *The Seafarer* and *The Wanderer*," MAE, XXVI, 137-53; XXVIII, 1-22 and 99-104.

Stanley, E. G., "Old English Poetic Diction and the Interpretation of *The Wanderer, The Seafarer, and The Penitent's Prayer*," *Anglia*, LXXIII, 413-66.

Stjerna, K., *Essays on Questions Connected with the Old English Poem of Beowulf*, tr. J. H. Clark Hall, Coventry, 1912.

Storms, G., "The Figure of Beowulf in the Old English Epic," ES, XL, 3-13.

The Story of Grettir the Strong, tr. E. Magnusson and W. Morris, *Collected Works of William Morris*, 24 v., 1910-15; see v. 7.

Timmer, B. J., "Beowulf: the Poem and the Poet," *Neophil.*, XXXI, 122-26.

Tolkien, J. R. R., *Beowulf: the Monsters and the Critics*, Oxford, 1937.

Treneer, A., *The Sea in English Literature from Beowulf to Donne*, Liverpool, 1926.

Tucker, S. I., "Return to *The Wanderer*," EIC, VII, 229-37.

Van Meurs, J. C., "*Beowulf* and Literary Criticism," *Neophil.*, XXXIX, 114-30.

Wadstein, E., "The Beowulf Poem as an English National Epos," APS, VIII, 273-91.

Waldere, ed. F. Norman, 1934.

Ward, J. A., "*The Wife's Lament: an interpretation*," JEGP, LIX, 26-33.

Whitelock, D., *The Audience of 'Beowulf'*, 1951.

Widsith, ed. K. Malone, 1935.

Woolf, H. B., "On the Characterization of *Beowulf*," ELH, XV, 85-92.

Wright, H. G., "Good and Evil; Light and Darkness; Joy and Sorrow in *Beowulf*," RES, n.s., VIII, 1-11.

B. THE CHRISTIAN EPIC AND SHORTER POEMS

Burrow, J. A., "An Approach to *The Dream of the Rood*," *Neophil.*, XLIII, 123-33.

Bütow, H., "Das altenglische Traumgesicht vom Kreuz," AF, #78, Heidelberg, 1935.

Campbell, J. J., ed., *The Advent Lyrics of "The Exeter Book*," Princeton, 1959; "Structural Patterns in the Old English Advent Lyrics," ELH, XXIII, 239-55.

Chambers, R. W., M. Förster, and R. Flower, edd., *The Exeter Book of Old English Poetry*, 1933.

Clubb, M. D., ed., *Christ and Satan, an Old English Poem*, New Haven, 1925.

Cook, A. S., ed., *Christ*, Boston, 1900; ed., *The Old English 'Elene', 'Phoenix', and 'Physiologus'*, New Haven, 1919; "Cynewulf's Part in our *Beowulf*," *Transactions of the Connecticut Academy of Arts and Sciences*, XXVII, 385-406.

Cordasco, F., "The Old English *Physiologus*: its problems," MLQ, X, 351-55.

Das, S. K., *Cynewulf and the Cynewulf Canon*, Calcutta, 1942.

Dickins, B. and A. S. C. Ross, edd., *The Dream of the Rood*, 1934.

Elliott, R. W. V., "Cynewulf's Runes in *Christ II* and *Elene*, ES, XXXIV, 49-57; "Cynewulf's Runes in *Juliana* and *The Fates of the Apostles*," ES, XXXIV, 193-204.

Emerson, O. F., "Originality in Old English Poetry," RES, II, 19-31.

Erhardt-Siebold, E. von, "Die lateinische Rätsel der Angelsachsen," AF, #61, Heidelberg, 1925.

Frampton, M. G., " 'Caedmon's Hymn'," MP, XXII, 1-15.

Gerould, G. H., "Studies in the *Christ*," *Eng. Stud.*, XLI, 1-19.

Gollancz, I., *The Caedmon Manuscript of Anglo-Saxon Biblical Poetry*, Oxford, 1927.

Gradon, P. O. E., ed., *Cynewulf's 'Elene'*, 1958.

Greenfield, S. B., "The Theme of Spiritual Exile in *Christ I*," PQ, XXXII, 321-28.

Grendon, F., *The Anglo-Saxon Charms*, 1930.

Holthausen, F., ed., *Cynewulfs Elene*, Heidelberg, 1937.

Irving, E. B., Jr., *The Old English 'Exodus'*, New Haven, 1953; "Latin Prose Sources for Old English Verse," JEGP, LVI, 588-95.

Keller, W., "Zum altenglischen Runengedicht," *Anglia*, LX, 141-49.

Kennedy, C. W., tr., *Early English Christian Poetry*, 1952.

Klaeber, F., ed., *The Later 'Genesis,' and Other Old English and Old Saxon Texts Relating to the Fall of Man,* Heidelberg, 1931.

Kurtz, B. P., "Gifer the Worm: an essay toward the history of an idea," *University of California Publications in English,* II, #1, Berkeley, 1929, pp. 235-61.

Lever, J. W., "*Paradise Lost* and the Anglo-Saxon Tradition," RES, XXIII, 97-106.

Menner, R. J., ed., *The Poetical Dialogue of Solomon and Saturn,* 1941.

Mildenberger, K., "The Unity of Cynewulf's *Christ* in the Light of Iconography," *Speculum,* XXIII, 420-32.

Peters, L. J., "The Relationship of the Old English *Andreas* to *Beowulf*," PMLA, LXVI, 844-63.

Philip, Brother A., "The Exeter Scribe and the Unity of the 'Christ,'" PMLA, LV, 903-09.

Sarrazin, G., *Von Kädmon bis Kynewulf,* Berlin, 1913.

Schlauch, M., "'The Dream of the Rood' as Prosopopoeia," *Essays and Studies in Honor of Carleton Brown,* 1940, pp. 23-24.

Schaar, C., *Critical Studies in the Cynewulf Group,* Lund, 1949.

Sisam, K., *Cynewulf and his Poetry,* Oxford, 1933.

Smith, A. H., ed., *Three Northumbrian Poems,* Oxford, 1933.

Taylor, A., *The Literary Riddle before 1600,* Berkeley, 1948.

Timmer, B. J., ed., *Judith,* 1952; *The Later Genesis,* Oxford, 1948, rev. edn., Oxford, 1954.

Tupper, F., *The Riddles of The Exeter Book,* Boston, 1910.

Williams, B. C., ed., *Gnomic Poetry in Anglo-Saxon,* 1937.

Woolf, R., ed., *Juliana,* 1955; "The Devil in Old English Poetry," RES, n.s., IV, 1-12; "Doctrinal Influences on *The Dream of the Rood*," MAE, XXVII, 137-53.

Wrenn, C. L., *The Poetry of Caedmon,* 1948.

4. ANGLO-LATIN LITERATURE OF THE OLD ENGLISH PERIOD

Arngart, O. A., *Early English Manuscripts in Facsimile: the Leningrad Bede,* Copenhagen, 1952.

Asser, *Life of King Alfred,* ed. W. H. Stevenson, Oxford, 1904.

Bede, *Historia Ecclesiastica Gentis Anglorum,* ed. C. Plummer, 2 v., Oxford, 1896; *History of the Church of England,* tr. T. Stapleton, 2 v., Oxford, 1929; *Opera Historica,* ed. and tr. J. E. King, 2 v., 1920; *Works,* ed. J. A. Giles, 12 v., 1843-4; *History of the English Church and People,* tr. L. Sherley-Price, Harmondsworth, 1954; *Bede's Ecclesiastical History,* tr. J. Stevenson and L. C. Jane, 1956.

Blair, P. H., *Bede's "Ecclesiastical History of the English Nation" and its Importance Today,* Jarrow, 1959.

Boniface, St., *The English Correspondence of Saint Boniface,* ed.

and tr. E. Kylie, 1924; *The Letters of Saint Boniface*, tr. E. Emerton, 1940.

Chambers, R. W., *Bede*, Oxford, 1936.

Dobiache-Rojdestvensky, O., "Un manuscrit de Bède à Leningrad," *Speculum*, III, 314-21.

Duckett, E. S., *Alcuin, Friend of Charlemagne: his World and his Work*, 1951; *Anglo-Saxon Saints and Scholars*, 1947; *Saint Dunstan of Canterbury: a study of monastic reform in the tenth century*, 1955.

Garmonsway, G. N., "The Development of the Colloquy," *The Anglo-Saxons*, ed. P. Camoes, 1959, pp. 248-61.

Gaskoin, C. J. B., *Alcuin, his Life and his Work*, 1904.

Giles, J. A., *Six Old English Chronicles*, 1848; *The Works of Gildas and Nennius*, 1841.

Gillett, H. M., *Saint Bede the Venerable*, 1935.

Hook, W. F., *Lives of the Archbishops of Canterbury*, 12 v., 1860-64.

Jackson, K., "Nennius and the Twenty-Eight Cities of Britain," *Antiquity*, XII, 44-55.

James, M. R., *Two Ancient English Scholars: St. Aldhelm and William of Malmesbury*, Glasgow, 1931.

Jones, C. W., "Bede as Early Medieval Historian," M & H, IV, 26-36.

Jones, P. F., *A Concordance of the "Historia Ecclesiastica" of Bede*, Cambridge, Mass., 1929.

Laistner, M. L. W., "Bede as a Classical and a Patristic Scholar," *Royal Historical Society Transactions*, XV, 69-94.

Menzies, L., *St. Columba of Iona*, 1920.

Millar, E. G., *English Illuminated Manuscripts from the Tenth to the Thirteenth Century*, Paris-Brussels, 1926.

Ogilvy, J. D. A., *Books Known to Anglo-Latin Writers from Aldhelm to Alcuin*, Cambridge, Mass., 1936; "A Noteworthy Contribution to the Study of Bede," *University of Colorado Studies, Series B: Studies in the Humanities*, Boulder, 1941, pp. 261-64.

Pitman, J. H., ed. and tr., *The Riddles of Aldheim*, New Haven, 1925.

Raby, F. J. E., *A History of Christian-Latin Poetry from the Beginnings to the Close of the Middle Ages*, Oxford, 1927, rev. edn., 1957.

Simpson, W. D., *The Celtic Church in Scotland*, Aberdeen, 1935.

Stephens, G. R., *The Knowledge of Greek in England in the Middle Ages*, Philadelphia, 1933.

Stevens, C. E., "Gildas Sapiens," EHR, LVI, 353-73.

Thompson, A. H., ed., *Bede: his Life, Times, and Writings*, Oxford, 1935.

Thompson, E. M., "The History of English Handwriting, A.D. 700-1400," *Transactions of the Bibliographical Society*, 1901.

Wallach, L., *Alcuin and Charlemagne*, Ithaca, 1959.

Wells, B. E., "Alcuin the Teacher," *Constructive Quarterly*, VII, 531-32.
West, A. F., *Alcuin and the Rise of the Christian Schools*, 1892.

5. ALFRED THE GREAT AND HIS TIMES

Alfred, *King Alfred's Old English Version of the Consolation of Boethius*, ed. and tr. W. J. Sedgefield, Oxford, 1900; *King Alfred's Old English Version of St. Augustine's Soliloquies*, ed. H. L. Hargrove, New Haven, 1902; *King Alfred's West Saxon Version of Gregory's "Pastoral Care,"* ed. H. Sweet, EETS, 1871-72; *The Old English Version of Bede's "Ecclesiastical History,"* ed. and tr. T. Miller, 2 v., 1890-98; *The Proverbs of Alfred,* ed. W. W. Skeat, Oxford, 1907; *The Whole Works of King Alfred the Great,* ed. J. A. Giles, 2 v., 1858.
The Anglo-Saxon Chronicle, ed. G. N. Garmonsway, 1953; tr. E. E. C. Gomme, 1909; tr. J. Ingram, 1912.
Barrett, H. M., *Boethius: some aspects of his times and work,* Cambridge, 1940.
Borniski, L., *Der Stil Königs Alfreds,* Leipzig, 1931-34.
Bruce, J. D., *The Anglo-Saxon Version of the Book of Psalms,* Baltimore, 1894.
Campbell, A., ed., *The Tollemache Orosius,* 1954.
Clarke, C., ed., *The Peterborough Chronicle, 1070-1145,* 1958.
Classen, E., and F. E. Harmer, edd., *An Anglo-Saxon Chronicle from British Museum Cotton Ms. Tiberius B IV,* Manchester, 1926.
Dickins, B., *The Genealogical Preface to the Anglo-Saxon Chronicle,* Cambridge, 1952.
Duckett, E. S., *Alfred the Great,* Chicago, 1956.
Hayward, F. H., *Alfred the Great,* 1936.
Ker, N., ed., *Early English Manuscripts in Facsimile: The Pastoral Care and King Alfred's Translation of St. Gregory's "Regula Pastoralis"* Copenhagen, 1956.
Kuhn, S. M., "Synonyms in the Old English Bede," JEGP, XLVI, 168-76.
Larson, L. M., *Canute the Great . . . and the Rise of Danish Imperialism during the Viking Age,* 1912.
The Laws of the Earliest English Kings, ed. and tr. F. L. Attenborough, Cambridge, 1922.
The Laws of the Kings of England from Edmund to Henry I, ed. and tr. A. J. Robertson, Cambridge, 1925.
Lees, B. A., *Alfred the Great, the Truth-Teller, Maker of England,* 1915.
The Parker Chronicle, 832-900, ed. A. H. Smith, 1935.
Patch, H. R., *The Tradition of Boethius,* 1935.
Plummer, C., *The Life and Times of Alfred the Great,* Oxford, 1902.

Potter, S., "Commentary on King Alfred's "Orosius,'" *Anglia*, LXVI, 385-437.

Rositzke, H. A., ed., *The C-Text of the Old English Chronicles*, Bochum, 1940.

Timmer, B. J., *Studies in Bishop Waerferth's Translation of the Dialogues of Gregory the Great*, Groningen, 1934.

Whitelock, D., ed., *Early English Manuscripts in Facsimile: Peterborough Chronicle*, Copenhagen, 1954.

6. AELFRIC AND HIS WORKS: WULFSTAN AND HOMILETIC PROSE

Aelfric, *Aelfric's Colloquium on the Occupations*, ed. G. M. Garmonsway, 1939; *The Homilies of the Anglo-Saxon Church*, ed. and tr. B. Thorpe, 2 v., 1844-46; *Aelfric's Lives of the Saints*, ed. W. W. Skeat, 2 v., EETS, 1881-1900; *The Old English Version of the Heptateuch*, ed. S. J. Crawford, EETS, 1922.

Anderson, G. K., "Notes on the Language of Aelfric's English Pastoral Letters in Corpus Christi College 190 and Bodleian Junius 121," *JEGP*, XI, 5-13.

Assmann, B., "Angelsächsische Homilien und Heiligenleben," *Grein und Wülker's Bibliothek der angelsächsischen Prosa*, V, iii, Cassel-Göttingen, 1889.

Benedict, St., *The Rule of St. Benet*, ed. H. Logeman, EETS, 1888.

Bethurum, D., "The Form of Aelfric's 'Lives of the Saints,'" *SP*, XXIX, 515-33; *The Homilies of Wulfstan*, Oxford, 1957.

The Blickling Homilies of the Tenth Century, ed. R. Morris, EETS, 1874-80.

Clemoes, P. A. M., "The Chronology of Aelfric's Works," *The Anglo-Saxons*, ed. P. Clemoes, 1959, pp. 212-47.

Colgrave, B., *The Earliest Saints' Lives Written in England*, Cambridge, 1958.

Darlington, R. R., ed., *The Vita Wulfstani of William of Malmesbury*, 1929.

Gem, S. H., *An Anglo-Saxon Abbot, Aelfric of Eynsham*, Edinburgh, 1912.

Gerould, G. H., "Abbot Aelfric's Rhythmic Prose," *MP*, XXII, 206-10.

Glunz, H. H., *History of the Vulgate in England from Alouin to Roger Bacon*, Cambridge, 1933.

The Gospel of Nicodemus, ed. S. J. Crawford, Edinburgh, 1927.

Henel, H., ed., *Aelfric's De Temporibus Anni*, 1942.

The History of the Holy Rood-Tree, ed. A. S. Napier, 1894.

The Holy Gospels in Anglo-Saxon, Northumbrian, and Old Mercian Versions, ed. W. W. Skeat, 4 v., Cambridge, 1871-77.

Jones, C. W., *Saints' Lives and Chronicles in Early England, together with The First English Translations of "The Oldest Life* of Pope St. Gregory the Great" by a Monk of Whitby and "The Life of St. Guthlac of Crowland" by Felix, Ithaca, 1947.

Jost, K., *Wulfstandstudien*, Bern, 1950.

Kurtz, B. P., *From St. Anthony to St. Guthlac: a study in biography*, Berkeley, 1926.

Lamb, J. W., *Saint Wulfstan, Prelate and Patriot*, 1935.

Loomis, G., "Saint Edmund and the Lodbrok (Lothbroc) Legend," *Harvard Studies and Notes in Philology and Literature*, XV, 1-23.

McIntosh, A., *Wulfstan's Prose*, 1950.

Millar, E. G., ed., *The Lindisfarne Gospels*, 1924.

Robinson, J. A., *The Times of St. Dunstan*, Oxford, 1923.

Sisam, K., "Mss. Bodley 340 and 342. Aelfric's *Catholic Homilies*," RES, VII, 7-22.

Stauffer, D. W., *English Biography before 1700*, Cambridge, Mass., 1930.

Warner, R. D. N., *Early English Homilies from Vespasian D. XIV*, 1917.

White, C. L., *Aelfric: a new study of his life and writings*, Boston, 1897.

Whitelock, D. ed., *Sermo Lupi ad Anglos*, 1939.

Willard, R., "The Address of the Soul to the Body," *PMLA*, L, 957-83; "Vercelli Homily VIII and the *Christ*," *PMLA*, XLII, 314-30; "Vercelli Homily XI and its Sources," *Speculum*, XXIV, 76-87.

Wilson, R. M., "Some Lost Saints' Lives in Old and Middle English," *MLR*, XXXVI, 161-72.

7. OTHER OLD ENGLISH PROSE WRITINGS

The Anglo-Saxon Version of the Story of Apollonius of Tyre, tr. B. Thorpe, 1834.

Cockayne, T. O., *Leechdoms, Wort-Cunning, and Starcraft of Early England*, 3 v., 1864-66.

Crawford, S. J., ed., *Byrhtferth's Manual* (*A.D. 1011*), 1929.

Evans, J., *Magical Jewels of the Middle Ages and the Renaissance, Particularly in England*, Oxford, 1922.

Goepp, P. H., "The Narrative Material of *Apollonius of Tyre*," ELH, V, 150-72.

Goolden, P., ed., *The Old English "Apollonius of Tyre,"* Oxford, 1958.

Grattan, J. H. G. and C. Singer, *Anglo-Saxon Magic and Medicine*, 1952.

Haskins, C. H., *Studies in the History of Medieval Science*, 1924.

Herrtage, S. J. H., ed., *Gesta Romanorum*, 1879.

Henel, H., "Studien zum altenglischen Computus," *Beiträge zur englischen Philologie*, #26, Leipzig, 1934.

Lindsay, W. M., *The Corpus, Epinal, Erfurt, and Leyden Glossaries*, 1921.

Meritt, H. D., *Old English Glosses,* 1946.

Nehab, J., *Der altenglische Cato,* Berlin, 1879.

Payne, J. F., *English Medicine in the Anglo-Saxon Times,* 1904.

Raith, J., ed., *Die alt- und mittelenglischen Apolloniusbruchstücke, mit dem Text der "Historia Apollonii" nach der englischen Handscriftengruppe,* Munich, 1956.

Riesman, D., *The Story of Medicine in the Middle Ages,* 1935.

Robertson, A. J., ed., *Anglo-Saxon Charters,* Cambridge, 1939.

Singer, C., *From Magic to Science: Essays on the Scientific Twilight,* 1928.

Storms, G., Anglo-Saxon Magic, 1948.

Thorndike, L., *A History of Magic and Experimental Science during the First Thirteen Centuries of our Era,* v. 1, 1923.

Wright, C. E., ed., *Early English Manuscripts in Facsimile: Bald's Leechbook,* Copenhagen, 1956.

Wright, T., *Biographia Britannica Litteraria,* 2 v., 1942-46.

The Middle English Period

1. BIBLIOGRAPHY, LITERATURE, AND LANGUAGE OF THE MIDDLE ENGLISH PERIOD

Atkins, J. W. H., *English Literary Criticism: the Mediaeval Phase,* Cambridge, 1943.

Baldwin, C. S., *Three Medieval Centuries of Literature in England, 1100-1400,* Boston, 1932.

Behrens, D., "Französische Elemente im Englischen," *Paul's Grundriss der germanischen Philologie,* Vol. I, part 2, Strasburg, 1901.

Benham, A. R., *English Literature from Widsith to the Death of Chaucer: a source book,* New Haven, 1916.

Bethurum, D., ed., *Critical Approaches to Medieval Literature,* 1960.

Bloomfield, M. W., *The Seven Deadly Sins,* East Lansing, 1952; "Symbolism in Medieval Literature," MP, LVI, 73-81.

Brown, C. F. and R. H. Robbins, *An Index of Middle English Verse,* 1943.

Caplain, H., "The Four Senses of Scriptural Interpretation and the Medieval Theory of Preaching," *Speculum,* IV, 282-90.

Chambers, R. W., *English Literature at the Close of the Middle Ages,* Oxford, 1945; "The Lost Literature of Medieval England," *Library,* VI, 293-321.

The Chief British Poets of the Fourteenth and Fifteenth Centuries, ed. W. A. Neilson and K. G. T. Webster, 1916.

The Chief Middle English Poets, ed. and tr. J. L. Weston, Boston, 1914.

Cross, T. P., *Motif-Index of Early Irish Literature*, Bloomington, Ind., 1952.

Dunbar, H., *Symbolism in Medieval Thought and its Consummation in the "Divine Comedy,"* New Haven, 1929.

Emerson, O. F., *A Middle English Reader*, 1915.

Fourteenth Century Verse and Prose, ed. K. Sisam, Oxford, 1921.

Green, R. H., "Dante's Allegory of Poets and the Medieval Theory of Poetic Fiction," CL, IX, 118-28.

Haskins, C. H., *Studies in Mediaeval Culture*, Oxford, 1929.

Kane, G., *Middle English Literature: a critical study of the romances, the religious lyrics, and "Piers Plowman,"* 1951.

Ker, W. P., *English Literature: Mediaeval*, 1912.

MacCulloch, J. A., *The Harrowing of Hell: a comparative study of early Christian doctrine*, Edinburgh, 1930.

MacDonald, A. J. M., *Authority and Reason in the Early Middle Ages*, 1933.

A Medieval Anthology, Being Lyrics and Other Short Poems Chiefly Religious, Collected and Modernized, ed. and tr. M. G. Segar, 1915.

Menger, L. E., *The Anglo-Norman Dialect: a manual of its phonology and morphology*, 1904.

Moore, S., *Historical Outlines of English Phonology, and Morphology*, Ann Arbor, 1925.

Oakden, J. P., *Alliterative Poetry in Middle English: the Dialectal and Metrical Survey*, Manchester, 1930; *A Survey of the Traditions*, 1935.

Old English and Medieval Literature, ed. G. H. Gerould, 1929, rev. and enl., 1933.

Patch, H. R., *The Goddess Fortuna in Medieval Literature*, Cambridge, Mass., 1927; *The Tradition of Boethius*, 1935; *The Other World According to Descriptions in Medieval Literature*, Cambridge, Mass., 1950.

Peters, J. D., *Complaint and Satire in Early English Literature*, Oxford, 1956.

Political Poems and Songs . . . Edward III . . . to Richard II, ed. and tr. T. Wright, 2 v., 1859-61.

The Political Songs of England from the Reign of John to that of Edward II, ed. and tr. T. Wright, 1839.

Renwick, W. L. and H. Orton, *The Beginnings of English Literature to Skelton*, 1939.

Schofield, W. H., *English Literature from the Norman Conquest to Chaucer*, 1906.

Scottish Poetry from Barbour to James IV, ed. M. M. Gray, 1935.

Serjeantson, M. S., *A History of Foreign Words in English*, 1935.

Singleton, C. S., "The Irreducible Dove," CL, IX, 129-35.

Smalley, B., *The Study of the Bible in the Middle Ages*, Oxford, 1941, 1952.

Some Minor Poems of the Middle Ages, ed. M. G. Segar, 1917.

Specimens of Early English, ed. R. Morris and W. W. Skeat, 3 v., Oxford, 1882.

Spicq, P. C., *Esquisse d'une histoire de l'exegèse latine au Moyen Age*, Paris, 1944.

Stenton, F. M., *The First Century of English Feudalism*, Oxford, 1932.

Thomas, P. G., *English Literature before Chaucer*, 1924.

Thompson, S., *Motif-Index of Folk Literature*, Bloomington, Ind., 1932-58.

Tout, T. F., *The Political History of England, 1216-1377*, 1905.

A Treasury of Middle English Verse, Selected and Rendered into Modern English, comp. M. R. Adamson, 1930.

Vickers, K. H., *England in the Later Middle Ages, 1272-1485*, 1938.

Vising, J., *Anglo-Norman Language and Literature*, 1923.

Wardale, E. E., *An Introduction to Middle English*, 1937.

Wells, J. E., *A Manual of the Writings in Middle English, 1050-1400*, New Haven, 1916; supplements, New Haven, 8 v., 1919-41.

Wilson, R. M., *Early Middle English Literature*, 1939.

Wright, J. and E. M., *An Elementary Middle English Grammar*, 1923.

2. HISTORY, MANNERS, AND CUSTOMS OF ENGLAND, 1066-1485

Abram, A., *English Life and Manners in the Later Middle Ages*, 1913.

Balfour-Melville, E.W.M., *James I, King of Scots, 1406-1437*, 1936.

Bateson, M., *Medieval England: English feudal society from the Norman Conquest to the Middle of the Fourteenth Century*, 1904.

Bennett, H. S., "The Author and his Public in the Fourteenth and Fifteenth Century," E & S, XXIII, 7-24; *Life in the English Manor, 1150-1400*, Cambridge, 1938; *Chaucer and the Fifteenth Century*, 1947; *English Books and Readers, 1475-1557*, 1952.

Bond, F., *Gothic Architecture in England*, 1905.

Carlyle, R. W. and A. J., *A History of Medieval Political Theory in the West*, 6 v. Edinburgh, 1909-36.

Chaytor, H. J., *From Script to Print*, Cambridge, 1945, rev. edn., 1950.

Cheyney, E. F., *The Dawn of a New Era, 1250-1453*, 1936.

Coulton, G. G., *Medieval Panorama*, 1938.

Crosby, R., "Oral Delivery in the Middle Ages," *Speculum*, XI, 88-110; "Chaucer and the Custom of Oral Delivery," *Speculum*, XIII, 413-32.

Crossley, F. H., *The English Abbey, its Life and Work in the Middle Ages*, 1935.

Davis, H. W. C., *England under the Normans and Angevins, 1066-1272*, 1935.

Deanesley, M., *A History of the Medieval Church, 590-1500*, 1925, rev. edns., 1950.

Fairholt, F. W., *Costume in England: a history of dress to the end of the eighteenth century*, 4th edn., enl. and rev. by H. A. Dillon, 1896.

Gasquet, F. A., *English Monastic Life*, 1904.

Gross, C., *The Sources and Literature of English History from the Earliest Times to about 1485*, 2nd ed., rev. and enl. 1915.

Hadley, W., *The Fifteenth Century*, 1926.

Haskins, C. H., *The Normans in European History*, 1915.

Hepple, R. B., *Medieval Education in England*, 1932.

Holmes, M. R., *Medieval England*, 1924.

Homans, G. C., *English Villagers of the Thirteenth Century*, Cambridge, Mass., 1941.

Home, G. C. and E. Foord, *Mediaeval London*, 1927.

Hulme, E. M., *The Middle Ages*, 1929, rev. edn., 1938.

Jenks, E., *Law and Politics in the Middle Ages*, 1898; *A Short History of English Law from the Earliest Times to . . . 1938*, 5th edn., enl., 1938.

Jessopp, A., *The Coming of the Friars*, 1889.

Kelly, A. R., *Eleanor of Aquitaine and the Four Kings*, Cambridge, Mass., 1950.

Little, A. G. and F. Pelster, *Oxford Theology and Theologians, ca. 1282-1302*, Oxford, 1934.

Loomis, L. H., "The Auchinleck Manuscript and a Possible London Bookshop of 1330-40," PMLA, XLVII, 595-627.

MacKinney, L. C., *The Medieval World*, 1938.

Mallet, C. E., *A History of the University of Oxford*, 3 v., 1924.

Maxwell, H. E., *The Early Chronicles Relating to Scotland*, Glasgow, 1912.

McMahon, C. P., *Education in Fifteenth-Century England*, Baltimore, 1947.

Mediaeval England, ed H. W. C. Davis and F. P. Barnard, Oxford, 1935.

Moss, H. S. B., *The Birth of the Middle Ages*, Oxford, 1935.

Olson, C. C., "The Minstrels at the Court of Edward III," PMLA, LVI, 610-12.

Oman, C. W. C., *The History of England . . . 1377-1485*, 1906.

Owst, G. R., *Literature and Pulpit in Medieval England*, Cambridge, 1933.

Pirenne, H., *A History of Europe from the Invasions to the Sixteenth Century*, tr. B. Miall, 1939.

Poole, R. L., *Chronicles and Annals: a brief outline of their origin and growth*, Oxford, 1926.

Rosenberg, M. V., *Eleanor of Aquitaine*, Boston, 1937.

Russell, J. C., *British Medieval Population*, Albuquerque, 1948; "The Clerical Population of Medieval England," *Traditio*, II, 177-212.

Russell, P., *William the Conquerer*, 1933.

Salzman, L. F., *English Life in the Middle Ages*, 1926; *English Trade in the Middle Ages*, Oxford, 1931.

Saunders, O. E., *A History of English Art in the Middle Ages*, Oxford, 1932.

Sellery, G. C. and A. C. Krey, *The Founding of Western Civilization*, 1929.

Siedschlag, B. N., *English Participation in the Crusades*, Bryn Mawr, 1939.

Singer, C. J., *From Magic to Science: essays on the scientific twilight*, 1928.

Stephenson, C., *Medieval History: Europe from the Fourth to the Sixteenth Century*, 1935.

Taylor, H. O., *The Medieval Mind*, 2 v., 1911.

Thompson, J. W., *An Economic and Social History of the Middle Ages, 300-1500*, 1928; *A History of the Middle Ages, 300-1500*, 1931; *The Literacy of the Laity*, Berkeley, 1939.

Thorndike, L., "Elementary and Secondary Education in the Middle Ages," *Speculum*, XV, 400-08.

Trevelyan, G. M., *England in the Age of Wycliffe*, 1899.

Tuker, M. A. R., *Cambridge*, 1907.

Tupper, F., *Types of Society in Medieval Literature*, 1926.

Waddell, H. J., *The Wandering Scholars*, 1927.

Walker, C. H., *Eleanor of Aquitaine*, 1950.

Wulf, M. C. J. de, *History of Medieval Philosophy*, tr. E. C. Messenger, 2 v., 1926.

3. ANGLO-FRENCH AND ANGLO-LATIN WRITERS OF THE MEDIEVAL PERIOD

The Anglo-Latin Satirical Poets and Epigrammatists of the Twelfth Century, ed. T. Wright, 2 v., Rolls Ser., 1872.

Baldwin, C. S., *Medieval Rhetoric and Poetic*, 1928.

Fox, J. C., "Marie de France," EHR, XXV, 303ff. and XXVI, 317ff.

Map, Walter, *De Nugis Curialium*, ed. and tr. M. R. James, 1914.

Sertillanges, A., *Les grandes thèses de la philosophie thomiste*, Paris, 1929.

The Oxford Book of Medieval Latin Verse, comp. S. Gaselee, Oxford, 1928.

Stevenson, W. H., *Early Scholastic Colloquies*, Oxford, 1929.

Warnke, K., *Die Lais der Marie de France*, Halle, 1925.

4. MEDIEVAL ROMANCES, TALES, BALLADS, AND CHRONICLES

Ackerman, R. W., *Index of the Arthurian Names in Middle English*, Palo Alto, 1952; "Henry Lovelich's 'Merlin'", PMLA, LXVII, 473-84.

Annual Bibliography of Arthuriana, ed. by J. J. Perry, M. Schlauch, and P. A. Brown, pub. MLQ, 1940 —.

Baugh, A. C., "The Authorship of the Middle English Romances," *Modern Humanities Research Bulletin*, XX, 13-28 (1950); "Improvisation in the Middle English Romances," *Proceedings of the American Philosophical Society*, CIII, 418-54.

Brown, A. C. L., " 'Iwain': a study in the origins of Arthurian Romance," *Harvard Studies and Notes in Philology and Literature*, Boston, 1900.

Billings, A. H., *A Guide to the Middle English Metrical Romances*, 1901.

Bruce, J. D., *The Evolution of Arthurian Romance from the Beginnings down to the Year 1300*, Baltimore, 1923.

Capellanus, A., *The Art of Courtly Love*, tr. J. J. Parry, 1941.

Cary, G., *The Medieval Alexander*, Cambridge, 1956.

Chambers, E. K., *Arthur of Britain*, 1927.

Cross, T. P. and W. A. Nitze, *Launcelot and Guenevere: a study on the origins of courtly love*, Chicago, 1930.

The English and Scottish Popular Ballads, ed. F. J. Child, 5 v., Boston, 1883-98.

English and Scottish Popular Ballads, ed. G. L. Kittredge and H. C. Sargent, Boston, 1904.

Everett, D., "A Characterization of the English Medieval Romances," E&S, XV, 98-121; *Essays on Middle English Literature*, Oxford, 1955.

French, W. H., *Essays on King Horn*, Ithaca, 1940; with C. B. Hale, *Middle English Romances*, 1930.

Gautier, L., *Les épopées françaises*, Paris, 1878-92.

Gerould, G. H., *The Grateful Dead: the history of a folk story*, 1908; *The Ballad of Tradition*, 1932.

The Gests of King Alexander of Macedon, ed. F. P. Magoun, Jr., Cambridge, Mass., 1929.

Gist, M., *Love and War in the Middle English Romances*, Philadelphia, 1947.

Gough, A. B., *The Constance Saga*, Berlin, 1902.

Graves, R., *The English Ballad: a Critical Survey*, 1927.

Griffin, N. E., *Dares and Dictys: an introduction to the study of medieval versions of the story of Troy*, Baltimore, 1907.

Heather, P., "Precious Stones in the Middle English Verse of the Fourteenth Century," *Folk-Lore*, XLII, 217-64.

Hibbard (Loomis), L. A., *Medieval Romance in England: a study of the sources and analogues of the non-cyclic metrical romances,* 1924.

Hoops, J., "Der Begriff 'Romance' in der mittelenglischen und frühneuenglischen," AF, #68 (1929).

Jaffray, R., *King Arthur and the Holy Grail,* 1928.

Jubainville, H. d'A. de, *The Irish Mythological Cycle and Celtic Mythology,* tr. R. I. Best, Dublin, 1903.

Ker, W. P., *Epic and Romance: essays on medieval literature,* 1897; rev. edns, 1908, 1958.

Lewis, C. B., *Classical Mythology and Arthurian Romance,* 1932.

Lewis, C. S., *The Allegory of Love: a study in medieval literature,* Oxford, 1936.

Lippmann, K., *Das ritterliche Persönlichkeitideal in der mittelenglischen Literatur des 13. und 14. Jahrhunderts,* Leipzig, 1934.

Loomis, R. S., *Celtic Myth and Arthurian Romance,* 1927; *Arthurian Tradition and Chrétien de Troyes,* 1949; *Wales and the Arthurian Legend,* Cardiff, 1956; with L. H. Loomis, *Arthurian Legends in Medieval Art,* 1938.

Marie de France, *Seven Lais,* ed. and tr. E. Rickert, 1901.

Matthews, W., *The Tragedy of Arthur: a study of the Alliterative 'Morte Arthure',* Berkeley, 1960.

Maynadier, G. H., *The Arthur of the English Poets,* Boston, 1907.

Medieval Narrative, comp. and tr. M. Schlauch, 1929.

Middle English Humorous Tales in Verse, ed. G. H. McKnight, Boston, 1913.

Mosher, J. A., *The Exemplum in the Early Religious and Didactic Literature of England,* 1911.

Nutt, A. T., *The Influence of Celtic upon Medieval Romance,* 2nd ed., 1904; *The Legends of the Holy Grail,* 1902.

Old English Ballads, ed. F. B. Gummere, Boston, 1894.

Owings, M. A., *The Arts in the Middle English Romances,* 1952.

Owst, G. R., *Preaching in Medieval England,* Cambridge, 1926.

The Oxford Book of Ballads, ed. A. T. Quiller-Couch, Oxford, 1910.

Painter, S., *French Chivalry: chivalric ideas and practices in medieval France,* Baltimore, 1940.

Patch, H. R., "The Adaptation of Otherworld Motifs to Medieval Romance," *Philologica: the Malone Anniversary Studies,* Baltimore, 1949, pp. 115-23.

Pope, M., "The Romance of Horn and 'King Horn'," MAE, XXV, 164-67.

Pound, L., *Poetic Origins and the Ballad,* 1921.

Reinhard, J. R., *The Survival of 'Geis' in Medieval Romance,* Halle, 1933.

Rhys, J., *Studies in the Arthurian Legend,* Oxford, 1891.

A Selection of Latin Stories, from Manuscripts of the Thirteenth and Fourteenth Centuries, ed. T. Wright, 1842.

Specimens of Early English Metrical Romances, ed. G. Ellis, rev. edn. by J. O. Halliwell, 1848.

Spence, L., *A Dictionary of Medieval Romance and Romance Writers,* 1913.

Tatlock, J. S. P., *The Legendary History of Britain: Geoffrey of Monmouth's 'Historia Regum Britanniae' and its Early Vernacular Version,* Berkeley, 1950.

Three Middle English Romances: King Horn, Havelock, Beves of Hampton, tr. L. Hibbard (Loomis), 1911.

Trounce, A. McI., "English Tail-Rhyme Romances," MAE, I, 87-108, 168-82 and II, 30-50.

Vinaver, E., *The Works of Sir Thomas Malory,* 3 v., Oxford, 1947.

Weston, J. L., *From Ritual to Romance,* Cambridge, 1920; *King Arthur and his Knights: a survey of Arthurian romance,* 1899; *The Legend of Sir Gawain: studies upon its original scope and significance,* 1897; *The Romance Cycle of Charlemagne and his Peers,* 1901.

5. RELIGIOUS AND MORAL WRITINGS OF THE MEDIEVAL PERIOD

Ancren Riwle: the Nun's Rule . . . Modernized by James Morton, introd. by F. A. Gasquet, Oxford, 1924; *The Recluse,* ed. J. Pohlsson, 2 parts, Lund, 1911-18.

Becker, E. J., *A Contribution to the Comparative Study of the Medieval Visions of Heaven and Hell,* Baltimore, 1899.

Bennett, J. W., *The Rediscovery of Sir John Mandeville,* 1954.

The Book of Vices and Virtues, ed. W. N. Francis, 1942.

Bright, A. H., *New Light on 'Piers Plowman',* pref. by R. W. Chambers, 1928.

Carnegy, F. A. R., *The Relations between the Social and Divine Order in William Langland's Vision,* Breslau, 1934.

Chambers, R. W., "Recent Research upon 'The Ancren Riwle'," RES, I, 4-23.

Chew, S., *The Virtues Reconciled: an iconographic study,* Toronto, 1947.

Cook, G. H., *The English Mediaeval Parish Church,* 1954.

Cornelius, R., *The Figurative Castle,* Bryn Mawr, 1930.

Crosby, R., "Robert Mannyng of Brunne: a new biography," PMLA, LVII, 15-28.

Darwin, F. D. S., *The English Mediaeval Recluse,* 1944.

Donaldson, E. T., *Piers Plowman: the C-Text and its Poet,* New Haven, 1949.

Dunning, T. P., *Piers Plowman: an interpretation of the A-Text,* 1937.

Erzgräber, W., *William Langland, eine Interpretation des C-Texts,* Heidelberg, 1957.

Fisher, J. H., "The French Versions of the *Ancrene Riwle*", *Festschrift for John G. Kunstmann* (Middle Ages-Reformation-Volkskunde, Chapel Hill, 1959, pp. 65-74.

Fowler, D. C., "John Trevisa and the English Bible," MP, LVIII, 81-98.

Frank, R. W., *Piers Plowman and the Scheme of Salvation*, New Haven, 1957.

Gerould, G. H., *The Northern English Homily Collections*, Lancaster, Pa., 1902; *Saints' Legends*, Boston, 1916.

Huganir, K., *The Owl and the Nightingale: sources, date, author*, Philadelphia, 1931.

Hulbert, J. R., "*Piers Plowman* after Forty Years," MP, XLV, 215-25.

Huppé, B. F., "*Piers Plowman*: the Date of the B-Text Reconsidered," SP, XLVI, 6-13.

Hussey, M., "The Petitions of the Paternoster in Medieval English Literature," MAE, XXVII, 8-16.

Kaske, R. W., "The Use of Simple Figures of Speech in *Piers Plowman*: a study of the figurative expression of ideas and opinions," SP, XLVIII, 571-600.

Knott, T. A. and D. C. Fowler, *Piers Plowman: a Critical Edition of the A-Text*, Baltimore, 1952.

Knowles, D., *The Religious Orders in England*, 1948-50; 1955-57.

Krapp, G. P., *The Legend of St. Patrick's Purgatory: its later literary history*, Baltimore, 1900.

Langland, W., *The Vision of Piers Plowman*, tr. W. W. Skeat, 1905.

Lumiansky, R. M., "Concerning *The Owl and the Nightingale*," PQ, XXXII, 411-17.

Magoun, F. P., Jr., "*Ancrene Wisse vs. Ancrene Riwle*," ELH, IV, 112-14.

Metcalfe, W. M., *Legends of Saints in Scottish of the Fourteenth Century*, Edinburgh, 1888-96.

The Owl and the Nightingale, ed. J. W. H. Atkins, Cambridge, 1922; ed. J. E. Wells, Boston, 1907; ed. J. H. G. Grattan and G. F. H. Sykes, 1935.

Pantin, W. A., *The English Church in the Fourteenth Century*, Cambridge, 1955.

Peterson, D. L., "*The Owl and the Nightingale* and Christian Dialectic," JEGP, LV, 13-26.

Robertson, D. W. and B. Huppé, *Piers Plowman and the Scriptural Tradition*, Princeton, 1951.

South English Legendary, ed. C. D'Evelyn and A. Mill, 1956.

St. Patrick's Purgatory, comp. S. Leslie, 1932.

Skeat, W. W., *Early English Proverbs, Chiefly of the Thirteenth and Fourteenth Centuries*, Oxford, 1910.

Suddaby, E., "The Poem, *Piers Plowman*," JEGP, LIV, 91-103.

Taylor, A., *The Proverb*, Cambridge, Mass., 1931.

The Travels of Sir John Mandeville, ed. M. Letts, 1953.

Troyer, H. W., "Who is Piers Plowman?" PMLA, XLVII, 368-84.

Utley, F. L., *The Crooked Rib*, Columbus, 1944.

Wells, H. W., "The Construction of 'Piers Plowman,'" PMLA, XLIV, 123-40.

Whiting, B. J., "The Origin of the Proverb," *Harvard Studies and Notes in Philology and Literature*, XIII, Boston, 1931.

Zeeman, E., "Piers Plowman and the Pilgrimage to Truth," E&S, XI, 1-16.

6. RICHARD ROLLE AND OTHER MYSTICS

Allen, H. E., *Writings Ascribed to Richard Rolle, Hermit of Hampole, and Materials for his Biography*, 1927; *The English Writings of Richard Rolle*, 1931.

Comper, F. M. M., *The Life of Richard Rolle, together with an Edition of his English Lyrics*, 1928; *The Fire of Love and the Mending of Life*, 1920.

Gardner, H., "Walter Hilton and the Mystical Tradition in England," E&S, XXII, 103-27.

Hodgson, G. E., *The Sanity of Mysticism: a study of Richard Rolle*, 1926.

Hort, G., *Sense and Thought: a study in mysticism*, 1936.

Knowles, D., *The English Mystical Tradition*, 1961.

Molinari, P., *Julian of Norwich: the teachings of a fourteenth century mystic*, 1958.

Selected Works of Richard Rolle, Hermit, ed. G. C. Haseltine, 1930.

Yorkshire Writers: Richard Rolle of Hampole, an English Father of the Church, and his Followers, ed. C. Horstmann, 2 v., 1895-6.

7. WYCLIFFE

Deanesley, M., *The Lollard Bible and Other Medieval Biblical Versions*, Cambridge, 1920.

Gray, M. M., "The Prose of Wyclif's Bible," *London Quarterly*, CLIX, 354-62.

Lechler, G. V., *John Wycliffe and his English Precursors*, tr. P. Lorimer, 2 v., 1878.

Loserth, J., *Wyclif and Huss*, tr. M. J. Evans, 1884.

Poole, R. L., *Wycliffe and Movements for Reform*, 1899.

Select English Works of John Wyclif, ed. T. Arnold, 3 v., Oxford, 1869-71.

Select English Writings by John Wyclif, ed. H. E. Winn, 1929.

Summa de Ente, by Johannes Wyclif, Libri primi tractatus primus et secundus, comp. and ed. S. H. Thompson, Oxford, 1930.

Workman, H. B., *John Wyclif, a Study of the English Medieval Church*, Oxford, 1926.

8. THE MIDDLE ENGLISH LYRIC

Ancient Songs and Ballads, comp. J. Ritson, 3rd edn., rev. by W. C. Hazlitt, 1877.

Brittain, F., *The Medieval Latin and Romance Lyric to A. D. 1300,* Cambridge, 1937.

Brook, G. D., *The Harley Lyrics,* Manchester, 1948.

Brown, C. F., *English Lyrics of the XIIIth Century,* Oxford, 1932; *Religious Lyrics of the XIVth Century,* Oxford, 1924 (rev. edn. by G. Smithers, 1952); *Religious Lyrics of the XVth Century,* Oxford, 1939.

Chaytor, H. J., *The Troubadours,* Cambridge, 1912.

Comper, F., *Spiritual Songs from English Manuscripts of the Fourteenth to Sixteenth Centuries,* 1936.

The Early English Carols, ed. R. L. Greene, Oxford, 1935.

Early English Lyrics, Amorous, Divine, Moral, and Trivial, comp. E. K. Chambers and F. Sidgwick, 1907.

Gaselee, S., *The Transition from the Late Latin Lyric to the Medieval Love Poem,* Cambridge, 1931.

Hanford, J. H., "The Progenitors of Golias," *Speculum,* I, 38-58.

The Index of Middle English Verse, comp. and ed. C. F. Brown and R. H. Robbins, 1943.

Moore, A. K., *The Secular Lyric in Middle English,* Lexington, Ky., 1951.

Person, H., *The Cambridge Middle English Lyrics,* Seattle, 1953.

Raby, F. J. E., *A History of Secular Latin Poetry in the Middle Ages,* 2 v., Oxford, 1934.

Robbins, R. H., *Secular Lyrics of the XIVth and XVth Centuries,* Oxford, 1952; "The Authors of the Middle English Religious Lyrics," *JEGP,* XXXIX, 230-38; "The Earliest Carols and the Franciscans," *MLN,* LIII, 239-45.

Sisam, K., *Fourteenth Century Prose and Verse,* 1921.

Wehrle, W., *The Macaronic Hymn Tradition in Medieval English Literature,* Washington, 1933.

9. MIDDLE ENGLISH DRAMA

Brooks, N .C., "The *Sepulchrum Christi* and its Ceremonies in Late Medieval and Modern Times," *JEGP,* XXVII, 147-61.

Cawley, A. C., *The Wakefield Pageants in the Towneley Cycle,* Manchester, 1958.

Chambers, E. K., *The English Folk-Play,* Oxford, 1933; *The Mediaeval Stage,* 2 v., Oxford, 1903.

Cosbey, R. C., "The Mak Story and its Folklore Analogues," *Speculum,* XX, 310-17.

Craig, H., *English Religious Drama of the Middle Ages,* Oxford, 1955.

Farnham, W., *The Medieval Heritage of Elizabethan Tragedy*, Berkeley, 1936.

Frank, G., *Medieval French Drama*, Oxford, 1954.

Fry, T. B., "The Unity of the 'Ludus Coventriae,'" SP, XLVIII, 527-70.

Gardiner, H. C., *Mystery's End: an investigation of the last days of the medieval religious stage*, New Haven, 1946.

Gayley, C. M., *Plays of our Forefathers and Some of the Traditions upon Which They Were Founded*, 1907.

Harbage, A., *Annals of English Drama, 975-1700*, 1940.

Henshaw, M., "A Survey of Studes in Medieval Drama, 1933-1950," *Progress of Medieval and Renaissance Studies*, XXI, 7-35; "The Attitude of the Church toward the Stage to the End of the Middle Ages," *Mediaevalia et Humanistica*, VII, 3-17.

Lewis, C. S., *The Allegory of Love*, 1936.

Manly, J. M., "The Miracle Play in Mediaeval England," *Essays by Divers Hands*, new series, V-VII, 133-153, 1927.

McNeir, W. F., "The Corpus Christi Passion Plays as Dramatic Art," SP, XLVIII, 601-28.

Pollard, A. W., *English Miracle Plays, Moralities, and Interludes*, 8th edn., rev., 1927.

Prosser, E., *Drama and Religion*, Palo Alto, 1961.

Purvis, J. S., *The York Cycle of Mystery Plays*, 1951.

Salter, F. M., *Medieval Drama in Chester*, Toronto, 1955.

Specimens of the Pre-Shakespearean Drama, ed. J. M. Manly, 2 v., Boston, 1897.

Stratman, C. J., *A Bibliography of Medieval Drama*, Berkeley, 1954.

Tiddy, R. J. E., *The Mummers' Play*, Oxford, 1923.

Williams, A., *The Characterization of Pilate in the Towneley Plays*, East Lansing, 1955.

Young, K., *The Drama of the Medieval Church*, 2 v., Oxford, 1933.

10. THE PEARL (OR GAWAIN) POET AND GOWER

Ackerman, R. W., "Gawain's Shield: Penitential Doctrine in *Gawain and the Green Knight*," *Anglia*, LXXVI, 254-65.

Cargill, O. and M. Schlauch, "The Pearl and its Jeweler," PMLA, XLIII, 105-23.

Chapman, C. O., "The Musical Training of the Pearl Poet," PMLA, XLVI, 177-81; "The Authorship of *The Pearl*," PMLA, XLVII, 346-53.

Clark, J. W., "Observations on Certain Differences in Vocabulary between 'Cleanness' and 'Sir Gawain and the Green Knight,'" PQ, XXVIII, 261-73; "The Gawain Poet and the Substantival Adjective," JEGP, LXIX, 60-64; "On Certain 'Alliterative' and 'Poetic' Words in the Poems Attributed to the 'Gawain-Poet,'"

MLQ, XII, 387-98; "Paraphrases for 'God' in the Poems Attributed to the 'Gawain-Poet,'" MLN, LXV, 232-36.

Cleanness, in *Selections from Early English Poems,* ed. I. Gollancz and L. Day, 1913.

Coffman, G. R., "John Gower, Mentor for Royalty," PMLA, LXIX, 953-64.

Conley, J., *"Pearl* and a Lost Tradition," JEGP, LXX, 805-24.

Dodd, W. G., *Courtly Love in Chaucer and Gower,* Boston, 1913.

Fisher, J., "A Calendar of Documents Relating to the Life of John Gower the Poet," JEGP, LVIII, 1-23.

Fison, P., "The Poet in Gower," *Essays in Criticism,* VIII, 16-26.

Gower, J., *The Complete Works of John Gower,* ed. G. C. Macaulay, 4 v., Oxford, 1899-1902.

Greene, W. K., *"The Pearl:* a new interpretation," PMLA, XL, 814-27.

Madaleva, Sister M., *Pearl: a Study in Spiritual Dryness,* 1925.

Manly, J. M., "On the Question of the Portuguese Translation of Gower's 'Confessio Amantis,'" MP, XXVII, 467-72.

Markman, A. M., "The Meaning of 'Sir Gawain and the Green Knight,'" PMLA, LXXII, 574-86.

Moorman, C. W., "'Sir Gawain and the Green Knight,'" MS, XVIII, 158-72; "The Role of the Narrator in 'The Pearl,'" MP, LIII, 73-81.

Patience, a West Midland Poem of the Fourteenth Century, ed. H. Bateson, 2nd edn., rev., 1918.

The Pearl, the Bowdoin edn., Boston, 1932; ed. with modern rendering by I. Gollancz, rev. edn., 1907; ed. C. G. Osgood, Boston, 1906; ed. with prose rendering by C. G. Osgood, Cambridge, Mass., 1907; ed. E. V. Gordon, Oxford, 1953.

Purity, a Middle English poem, ed. R. J. Menner, New Haven, 1920.

Robertson, D. W., Jr., "The Heresy of 'The Pearl,'" MLN, LXV, 152-54; "The Pearl as a Symbol," MLN, LXV, 155-60.

Schofield, W. H., *Symbolism, Allegory, and Autobiography in 'The Pearl',* Baltimore, 1909.

Sir Gawain and the Green Knight, tr. S. O. Andrew, 1929; tr. T. H. Banks, 1929; ed. J. R. R. Tolkien and E. V. Gordon, 1925.

11. CHAUCER

A. BIBLIOGRAPHY

Five Hundred Years of Chaucer Criticism and Allusion, ed. C. F. E. Spurgeon, 3 v., Cambridge, 1925.

Griffith, D. D., *A Bibliography of Chaucer, 1908-1953,* Seattle, 1955.

Hammond, E. P., *Chaucer: a bibliographical manual,* 1908.

Purdy, R. R., "Chaucer Scholarship in England and America: a review of recent trends," *Anglia,* LXX, 245.

Tatlock, J. S. P and A. G. Kennedy, *A Concordance to the Complete Works of Geoffrey Chaucer and to the Romaunt of the Rose,* Washington, 1927.

B. EDITIONS

Chaucer, G., *The Book of Troilus and Criseyde,* ed. R. K. Root, Princeton, 1926; *The Canterbury Tales,* ed. J. M. Manly and E. Rickert, 8 v., Chicago, 1940; *The Complete Works of Geoffrey Chaucer,* ed. W. W. Skeat, 7 v., Oxford, 1894-97; *The Complete Works of Geoffrey Chaucer,* Students' Cambridge Ed., ed. F. N. Robinson, Boston, 1935 (rev. edn., Boston, 1957); *The Student's Chaucer,* ed. W. W. Skeat, Oxford, 1895; *Chaucer's Poetry: an anthology for the modern reader,* ed. E. T. Donaldson, 1958; *The Portable Chaucer,* tr. T. Morrison, 1949; *Geoffrey Chaucer, The Canterbury Tales,* tr. N. Coghill, 1952.

C. STUDIES

Baldwin, R., "The Unity of *The Canterbury Tales,*" *Anglistica* #5, Copenhagen, 1955.

Baum, P. F., *Chaucer: a critical appreciation,* Durham, N. C., 1958.

Bennett, H. S., *Chaucer and the Fifteenth Century,* Oxford, 1947.

Bennett, J. A. W., *'The Parlement of Foules': an interpretation,* Oxford, 1957.

Bonner, F. W., "The Genesis of the Chaucer Apocrypha," SP, XLVIII, 461-81.

Bowden, M., *Commentary on the General Prologue to 'The Canterbury Tales,'* rev. edn., 1960.

Brusendorff, A., *The Chaucer Tradition,* Copenhagen, 1925.

Chaucer, G., *Life Records,* Chaucer Soc., Ser. 2, 1871-1900.

Chesterton, G. K., *Chaucer,* 1932.

Chute, M., *Geoffrey Chaucer of England,* 1946.

Coghill, N., *The Poet Chaucer,* 1949; *Geoffrey Chaucer,* 1956.

Cowling, G. H., *Chaucer,* 1927.

Crow, M. M., "Materials for a New Edition of the Chaucer Life-Records," *University of Texas Studies in English,* XXXI, 1-12.

Cummings, H. M., *The Indebtedness of Chaucer's Works to the Italian Works of Boccaccio,* Cincinnati, 1916.

Curry, W. C., *Chaucer and the Medieval Sciences,* 1926, rev. edn., 1960; "Destiny in Chaucer's *Troilus,*" PMLA, XLV, 129-68.

Dempster, G., "Dramatic Irony in Chaucer," *Stanford University Publications in Language and Literature,* IV, #3, Palo Alto, 1932.

Donaldson, E. T., "Chaucer the Pilgrim," PMLA, LXIX, 928-36.

Fansler, D. S., *Chaucer and the Roman de la Rose,* 1914.

French, R. D., *A Chaucer Handbook*, 1927.

Gerould, G. H., *Chaucerian Essays*, Princeton, 1952.

Giffin, M., *Studies of Chaucer and his Audience*, Hull, Que., 1956.

Hadow, G. E., *Chaucer and his Time*, 1914.

Héraucourt, W., *Die Wertwelt Chaucers*, Heidelberg, 1939.

Hulbert, J. R., *Chaucer's Official Life*, Chicago, 1912.

Jefferson, B. L., *Chaucer and the 'Consolation of Philosophy' of Boethius*, Princeton, 1917.

Kirby, T. A., *Chaucer's Troilus: a study of courtly love*, Baton Rouge, 1940.

Kittredge, G. L., *Chaucer and his Poetry*, Cambridge, Mass., 1915.

Kleinstück, J. W., *Chaucer's Stellung in der mittelalterlichen Literatur*, Hamburg, 1956.

Lawrence, W. W., *Chaucer and the Canterbury Tales*, 1950.

Legouis, E. A., *Geoffrey Chaucer*, tr. L. Lailavoix, 1913, 1960.

Lounsbury, T. H., *Studies in Chaucer, his Life and Writings*, 3 v., 1892.

Lowes, J. L., *Geoffrey Chaucer and the Development of his Genius*, Boston, 1934.

Lumiansky, R. M., *Of Sondry Folk: the dramatic principle in the 'Canterbury Tales'*, Austin, 1955.

Malone, K., *Chapters on Chaucer*, Baltimore, 1951.

Manly, J. M., *Some New Light on Chaucer*, 1926; *Chaucer and the Rhetoricians*, 1926.

Masefield, J., *Chaucer*, Cambridge, 1931.

McDonald, C. O., "An Interpretation of Chaucer's *Parlement of Foules*," *Speculum*, XXX, 444-57.

Morsbach, L., *Chaucer's Canterbury Tales und das Decameron*, Berlin, 1934.

Muscatine, C., *Chaucer and the French Tradition*, Berkeley, 1957.

Olson, C. C., "The Emerging Biography of a Poet," Third College of the Pacific Lecture, Stockton, 1953.

Owen, C. A., "The Canterbury Tales: Early Mss. and Relative Popularity," *JEGP*, LIV, 104-10; "The Plan of the Canterbury Pilgrimage," *PMLA*, LXVI, 820-26; "The Development of *The Canterbury Tales*," *JEGP*, LVII, 449-76.

Patch, H. R., *On Rereading Chaucer*, Cambridge, Mass., 1939.

Plimpton, G. A., *The Education of Chaucer*, Oxford, 1936.

Pratt, R. A., "The Order of *The Canterbury Tales*," *PMLA*, LXVI, 1141-67.

Preston, R., *Chaucer*, 1952.

Price, D. J. and R. M. Wilson, *The Equatorie of the Planetis*, Cambridge, 1955.

Rickert, E., comp., *Chaucer's World*, ed. C. C. Olson and M. W. Crow, 1948.

Root, R. K., *The Poetry of Chaucer*, 1906, rev. edn., 1922.

Ruggiers, P. G., "The Form of *The Canterbury Tales*," *College English*, XVII, 439-44.

Schaar, C., *The Golden Mirror: studies in Chaucer's descriptive technique and its literary background*, Lund, 1955.

Schlauch, M., "Chaucer's Doctrine of Kings and Tyrants," *Speculum*, XX, 133-56.

Shannon, E. F., *Chaucer and the Roman Poets*, Cambridge, Mass., 1929.

Shelley, P. van D., *The Living Chaucer*, Philadelphia, 1940.

Slaughter, E. E., *Virtue According to Love in Chaucer*, 1957.

Sources and Analogues of Chaucer's 'Canterbury Tales', ed. W. F. Bryan and G. Dempster, Chicago, 1941.

Speirs, J., *Chaucer the Maker*, 1951.

Spielman, M. H., *The Portraits of Chaucer*, Chaucer Soc., 1900.

Stavrou, C. M., "Some Implications of Chaucer's Irony," *South Atlantic Quarterly*, LVI, 454-61.

Tatlock, J. S. P., *The Mind and Art of Chaucer*, Syracuse, 1950.

Three Chaucer Studies, contrib. R. Krauss, H. Braddy, and C. R. Kase, ed. C. F. Brown, 1932.

12. THE FIFTEENTH CENTURY

Atkinson, G., *Les nouveaux horizons de la Renaissance*, Paris, 1934.

Aurner, N. S., *Caxton: Mirrour of Fifteenth Century Letters*, Boston, 1926.

Bennett, H. S., *The Pastons and their England: studies in an age of transition*, Cambridge, 1922; "The Author and his Public in the Fourteenth and Fifteenth Centuries," *E&S*, XXIII, 7-24; *Chaucer and the Fifteenth Century*, Oxford, 1947.

Berdan, J. M., *Early Tudor Poetry, 1485-1557*, 1920.

A Book of London English, 1384-1425, ed. R. W. Chambers and M. Daunt, Oxford, 1931.

Chambers, E. K., *English Literature at the Close of the Middle Ages*, Oxford, 1945.

Everett, D., *Essays in Middle English Literature*, ed. P. Kean, Oxford, 1955.

Fifteenth Century Prose and Verse, ed. A. W. Pollard, 1903.

Hammond, E. P., *English Verse between Chaucer and Surrey*, Durham, 1927.

Kingsford, C. L., *English Historical Literature in the Fifteenth Century*, Oxford, 1913.

Murison, W., *Sir David Lyndsay, Poet and Satirist of the Old Church in Scotland*, Cambridge, 1938.

Scudder, V. D., *Le Morte Darthur of Sir Thomas Malory and its Sources*, 1917.

Smith, G. G., *Scottish Literature: Character and Influence*, 1919.

Smith, H. M., *Pre-Reformation England*, 1938.

Stearns, M. W., *Robert Henryson*, 1949.

Taylor, R. A., *Dunbar, the Poet and his Period*, 1931.

Tucker, L. L. and A. R. Benham, *A Bibliography of Fifteenth-Century Literature*, Seattle, 1928.

Vinaver, E., *Malory*, Oxford, 1929; *The Works of Thomas Malory*, 3 v., Oxford, 1947.

Index

This index does not include references to periods and aspects of English literature. For these the reader should consult the table of contents. Titles are included in their alphabetical places, not under the author.